NEW TESTAMENT COMMENTARY

NEW
TESTAMENT
COMMENTARY

By

WILLIAM HENDRIKSEN

Exposition

of

Paul's Epistle

to the Romans

VOLUME I

Chapters 1—8

BAKER BOOK HOUSE

GRAND RAPIDS, MICHIGAN

FOREWORD

A heart-warming book is Romans. It is filled with instruction touching both life and doctrine. It imparts comfort in life and, as every faithful pastor knows, and ever so many other people have testified, also in the hour of death.

However, this book is very controversial. On many passages high-ranking interpreters differ. In connection with issues in dispute I have not tried to avoid taking a position. Among them, as concern chapters 1–8, are the following:

1. Paul writes, "to all in Rome who are beloved of God" (1:7). Were those addressed predominantly Jews or Gentiles? See pp. 20–23.

2. When the apostle uses the verb *to justify* or the noun *justification* in such passages as 3:24; 4:25; 5:1, 16, 18, is he using these words in (a) a causative sense, or (b) a declarative (forensic) sense? See pp. 130, 245.

3. In 5:1 did Paul say: (a) "We have peace," (b) "Let us have (or: continue to have) peace," or (c) "Let us enjoy the peace we have"? See pp. 168, footnote 140.

4. Who is the person described in Rom. 7:14–25? Is he: (a) an unbeliever, (b) an immature believer, or (c) Paul himself, the believer, and by extension, the believer generally? See pp. 225–230.

5. When, in 8:26b, the apostle states that "the Spirit himself (αὐτὸ τὸ πνεῦμα) intercedes for us with unspoken groanings," does he mean that it is indeed *the Spirit* who groans, or does he mean that *we* groan, repeating the thought of verse 23? See pp. 273–277.

It will become clear that here and there I differ with those for whom I have the highest respect, and whose writings I warmly recommend. May the cause of the gospel prosper even through differences in interpretation!

William Hendriksen

TABLE OF CONTENTS

LIST OF ABBREVIATIONS

A. *Book Abbreviations*

A.R.V.	American Standard Revised Version
A.V.	Authorized Version (King James)
Gram. N.T.	A. T. Robertson, *Grammar of the Greek New Testament in the Light of Historical Research*
Gram. N.T. (Bl.-Debr.)	F. Blass and A. DeBrunner, *A Greek Grammar of the New Testament and Other Early Christian Literature*
Grk. N.T. (A-B-M-W)	*The Greek New Testament,* edited by Kurt Aland, Matthew Black, Bruce M. Metzger, and Allen Wikgren
I.S.B.E.	*International Standard Bible Encyclopedia*
L.N.T. (Th.)	Thayer's *Greek-English Lexicon of the New Testament*
L.N.T. (A. and G.)	W. F. Arndt and F. W. Gingrich, *A Greek-English Lexicon of the New Testament and Other Early Christian Literature*
M.M.	*The Vocabulary of the Greek New Testament Illustrated from the Papyri and Other Non-Literary sources,* by James Hope Moulton and George Milligan
N.A.S. (N.T.)	New American Standard Bible (New Testament)
N.E.B.	New English Bible
N.I.V.	New International Version
N.T.C.	W. Hendriksen, *New Testament Commentary*
R.S.V.	Revised Standard Version
S.BK.	Strack and Billerbeck, *Kommentar zum Neuen Testament aus Talmud und Midrasch*
S.H.E.R.K.	*The New Schaff-Herzog Encyclopedia of Religious Knowledge*
Th.D.N.T.	*Theological Dictionary of the New Testament,* edited by G. Kittel and G. Friedrich, and translated from the German by G. W. Bromiley

LIST OF ABBREVIATIONS

B. *Periodical Abbreviations*

EQ	*Evangelical Quarterly*
ET	*Expository Times*
GTT	*Gereformeerd theologisch tijdschrift*
JBL	*Journal of Biblical Literature*
ThG	*Theologie und Glaube*
ThZ	*Theologische Zeitschrift*

Please Note

In order to differentiate between the second person plural (see Rom. 1:11: "I am yearning to see y o u") and the second person singular (see Rom. 2:1: "Therefore you have no excuse"), the letters in "y o u pl." are spaced, those in "you sing." are not.

Introduction

to

The Epistle to the Romans

I. Its Applicability Always and Everywhere

The church of Rome consisted of Jews and Gentiles. Which group predominated? See Section IV of this Introduction; also see on the following passages: 1:5, 6, 13; 2:17ff.; 7:1–6; 11:13; 15:15f. There was the danger that one group would look down with *disdain* on the other: the Jews on the Gentiles (2:1f.), the Gentiles on the Jews (11:18). Paul therefore emphasizes that "there is no distinction between Jew and Greek, for the same Lord is Lord of all" (10:12).

Today, too, this truth needs to be stressed, for the fact that, in a certain sense, "before God all men are equal" is by no means universally acknowledged. Even the church, sad to say, has not always taken to heart the full implications of this principle.

The people addressed in this epistle were also being exposed to another evil, namely, the heresy of concluding that since salvation is not dependent upon works, but rests entirely on grace, therefore the performance of good deeds is unnecessary; in fact, might even become an obstacle to full spiritual development. If salvation is the product of grace, why not, by means of living in sin, offer grace ample scope to operate? Why not "continue in sin that grace may bound"? See 6:1.

Most decisively does Paul refute this line of reasoning. He argues that for those who "have become united with Christ" (6:5) such a course is simply impossible, and that those who think otherwise are laboring under a pernicious *delusion*, "For the wages of sin is death, but the free gift of God is life in Christ Jesus our Lord" (6:23).

Today, too, especially in certain fundamentalistic circles, a kind of antinomianism is being propagated. We are being told that the believer is not under the law in any sense whatever. Therefore, as long as he trusts in Christ as his personal Savior he can more or less do whatever he pleases. Works are of no account. Did not Paul say, "For by grace y o u have been saved through faith; and this not of yourselves; (it is) the gift of God; not of works, lest anyone should boast"?

The answer is: Shortquoting Paul is unjustified. Paul continues, "For his handiwork are we, created in Christ Jesus *for good works,* which God prepared beforehand that we should walk in them." He who quotes Eph. 2:8, 9 should also quote verse 10. He who appeals to Titus 3:5a must accord equal weight to verses 5b, 14.

Here in Romans Paul's denunciation of antinomianism is scorching, withering, "We who died to sin, how can we any longer live in it?" (6:2),

3

And as to not being in any sense under the law, Rom. 13:8, 9 teaches the opposite. So do I Cor. 9:21; Gal. 5:14.

The Greek and Roman world of Paul's day was indeed a hopeless world. It was a realm filled with *despair*. According to the Greek (and afterward also the Roman) conception, at the moment of death there is no hope for the body, nor even for the soul. Reluctantly the latter departs from the body either with the dying breath or through open wounds. It enters the very dismal realm of the shades. Or else it simply ceases to exist. The Stoics mostly thought that it is the rational universe that persists; individuals do not. The Iliad ends with funeral rites.

Today among many people a somewhat similar attitude prevails. With respect to any life after this life, uncertainty reigns supreme. And with respect to mankind's future here on earth, pessimism is more and more gaining the upper hand. There is little talk now of "making the world safe for democracy" or of "waging a war to end all wars." Even in certain religious circles concerted Christian action in order to promote the glory of God in every sphere is frowned upon.

Also in this respect the study of the book of Romans is rewarding. This book offers hope. In fact, the subject of hope—for which see also the books of Psalms, Acts, Hebrews, and especially I Peter—is mentioned more often in Romans than in any other New Testament book. The apostle even tells us, "It was in hope that we were saved" (8:24), a hope well-founded (8:26–39). He calls the Divine Being "the God of hope" (15:13). From start to finish this book proclaims good tidings (3:24; 4:16–25; 7:24, 25; chapter 8 in its entirety; 11:33–36; 13:8–14; 16:25–27). And it encourages Christian action (12:9–21; 13:7; 14:19; 15:30; 16:1, 2).

At the root of every question is the question of man's guilt. "How can a man be righteous before God" (Job 9:2; 25:4). Paul, too, asked this question. So did Luther, and so does everybody, consciously or unconsciously. Romans answers it.

It is, accordingly, a book for every age, including our own.

II. Its Author

With few exceptions scholars agree that it was indeed the apostle Paul who wrote Romans. The evidence favoring this conclusion may, without exaggeration, be called overwhelming. The arguments that have been advanced against it—for example, "Luke, in the book of Acts, never mentions the establishment of a church in Rome; so Paul could not have written a letter to the Romans"—are so absurd that they merit no further comment.

For the sake of climactic effect the evidence in favor of Pauline authorship will be traced in reverse chronological order (from later to earlier).

4

Eusebius, the great church historian, writing at the beginning of the fourth century, refers to "the fourteen [sic!] letters of Paul," and in the same context (*Ecclesiastical History* III.iii.4, 5) makes mention of Romans as being one of them. Origen (fl.210–250), Tertullian (fl.193–216), and Clement of Alexandria (fl.190–200) are in full agreement.

The Muratorian Fragment (about 180–200), so named because it was published by Cardinal Ludovico A. Muratori (1672–1750), who had discovered it in the Ambrosian Library at Milan, contains the oldest extant list of New Testament writings. It is incomplete, is written in poor Latin and includes titles of books that were read in the church of Rome during the early days. In connection with Romans this Fragment reads:

"Now the epistles of Paul, what they are, whence and for what reason they were sent, they themselves make clear to him who is willing to understand. First of all he wrote at length to the Corinthians . . . then to the Galatians . . . and to the Romans on the order of the Scriptures, intimating also that Christ is the chief matter in them."

Irenaeus (fl. about 182–188) states, "Paul, speaking to the Romans, declares, 'Much more they who receive abundance of grace and righteousness will reign in life by the one, Christ Jesus'" (*Against Heresies* III.xvi), freely quoting Rom. 5:17. In this and several other statements Irenaeus clearly ascribes the authorship of Romans to Paul.

Going back even farther we reach the days of Marcion, who came to Rome shortly before the year 144. His canon of sacred writings consists of ten Pauline epistles plus Luke, all edited to suit the heretic's personal theology. He recognizes Romans as one of Paul's chief works.

The early apostolic fathers were not in the habit of mentioning the names of the holy men of God whom they quoted. Nevertheless, the fact that they are quoting, whether literally or (as often) freely, is frequently very clear, as is also the identity of the one whom they are quoting.

This is true, for example, with respect to Polycarp, bishop of Smyrna. This valiant Christian hero, "a disciple of John," suffered martyrdom in the year 155. In his letter *To The Philippians* VI.ii he shows that he is well acquainted with Paul's epistles, including Romans. In a sentence which reflects both Rom. 14:10, 12 and II Cor. 5:10 he writes, "If, then, we beseech the Lord to forgive us, we ourselves ought also to forgive, for we stand before the eyes of the Lord God, and we must all appear before the judgment seat of Christ, and each must give an account of himself." The following quotation from this same letter shows that the mind and heart of this devout early martyr were immersed in the writings of Paul:

"These things, brothers, I write to y o u concerning righteousness. I do so not on my own initiative, but because y o u first invited me. For neither am I, nor is any other like me, able to rival the wisdom of the blessed and glorious Paul, who, when he was living among y o u, in the presence of his contemporaries taught accurately and steadfastly the word of truth, and who also, when he was absent, wrote letters to y o u. By means of the study of these letters y o u will be able to build yourselves up in the faith given to y o u . . ." III.i, ii.

Ignatius, bishop of Antioch, while on his way to Rome and martyrdom, in the beginning of the second century A.D., wrote a number of letters, mostly to churches. These letters again clearly show that he was acquainted with, and highly regarded, Paul's epistles, including the one to the Romans. Note, for example, the following resemblances:

Romans		Cf. Ignatius *To The Ephesians*
1:3	of the seed of David	XVIII.ii
4:20	was strengthened in faith	X.ii
8:5, 8	carnal versus spiritual people	VIII.ii
6:4	newness of life	XIX.iii

A great admirer of Paul was Clement, bishop of Rome during the final decades of the first century. In his letter *To The Corinthians* he writes, "Take the epistle of the blessed Paul the apostle . . . With true inspiration he charged y o u concerning himself and Cephas and Apollos, because even then y o u were given to partisan discord." Cf. I Cor. 3:1–9. That he was also thoroughly acquainted with another epistle written by the same apostle, namely Romans, is clear from XXXV.v, vi. Cf. Rom. 1:29–32. In this case not only does he use many of Paul's words, but he even arranges some of them in the same order: "unrighteousness, wickedness, greed (or covetousness)." And at the close of this little paragraph compare Clement's "Not only those who do them are hateful to God but also those who approve of them," with Paul's "They not only continue to do these very things but also approve of those who practice them."

This brings us, finally, to the apostles and their own writings. II Peter 3:15, 16 reads as follows:

"Bear in mind that the patience of our Lord means salvation, just as our beloved brother Paul, according to the wisdom given him, wrote y o u, as also (he writes) in all his letters, speaking in them of these matters. . . ."

It is not surprising, therefore, that there is a close resemblance between Peter's letters and Paul's, as is evident especially when Romans and I Peter are placed side by side:

Romans		Cf. I Peter
12:1	a sacrifice acceptable to God	2:5
12:2	be not fashioned	1:14
12:3	as God has allotted to each	4:10
12:9	love without hypocrisy (see the original)	1:22 (see the original)
12:10	love of the brothers	2:17

In conclusion, whoever rejects the Pauline authorship of Romans must also reject the Pauline authorship of I and II Corinthians, Galatians, Ephesians, Colossians, etc. The writer who in Rom. 3:20–24; 4:3 proclaims the deeply satisfying doctrine of "justification not by human merit but by faith" does so also in Gal. 2:16; 3:6, 11; Titus 3:5–7. The inspired artist who in Rom. 12:5 pictures the church as Christ's body with its many members has not changed his identity in I Cor. 10:17; 12:12–14, 27; Eph. 1:22, 23; Col. 2:19. The exhorter who in Rom. 12:6–8 insists that these members shall use their respective talents for the benefit of the entire body emphasizes the same duty in I Cor. 12:15–26, 28–31; Eph. 4:11–16. And the warm-hearted enthusiastic philanthropist of Rom. 15:15–28 is also the gift collector and benefactor of II Cor. 8 and 9. He calls himself "Paul, servant of Jesus Christ, apostle" (Rom. 1:1). We have every reason to believe him.

Saul, whose Roman name was *Paul*[1] was born at Tarsus, a center of Greek culture, a university city located in Cilicia, near the northeastern corner of the Mediterranean Sea. He received his early training in Jerusalem under that most distinguished doctor of the Law, Gamaliel, grandson of the famous Hillel. The witnesses who stoned Stephen laid their garments at the feet of Paul (Acts 7:58). Immediately after Stephen's death Paul took a leading part in the persecution of Christians. He put his whole soul into this task. He "breathed threatening and slaughter against the disciples of the Lord" (Acts 9:1). Not satisfied with waging the persecution in Jerusalem, he even asked of the high priest letters to the synagogues in Damascus that he might bring bound to Jerusalem "any that were of the Way, whether men or women" (Acts 9:2).

Then something happened that would bring about a radical change not only in the life of Saul of Tarsus but in the course of all future history.

It was the hour of noon and the sun was shining in all its strength. Paul was approaching Damascus to destroy the Christian community in that city. Suddenly, a light from heaven, brighter than the sun, shone around him. "And he fell upon the earth, and heard a voice saying to him, Saul, Saul, why do you persecute me? And he said, Who art thou, Lord?" The voice answered, "I am Jesus whom you are persecuting; but rise and enter into the city, and you will be told what you must do" (Acts 9:3–6).

The men who accompanied Paul saw the light but could not distinguish the Person. They heard the voice or sound, but could not understand the words. Paul, on the other hand, saw the Lord and heard his words. Arriving in Damascus, he received his sight through the ministry of Ananias, who also baptized him. He began his evangelistic work in Damascus:

> *And at once in the synagogues he proclaimed Jesus, that he is the Son of God. And all who heard him were amazed and asked, "Is not he the man who in Jerusalem raised havoc among those who call on this name? And has he not come here for the purpose of bringing them bound before the chief priests?" But Saul increased the more in strength, and confounded the Jews who dwelt in Damascus, proving that this is the Christ* (Acts 9: 20–22).

---

1. For more information on these names see N.T.C. on I and II Thessalonians, p. 38.

Paul spent some time in Arabia, but Scripture does not tell us what he did there. When he returned to Damascus, his preaching aroused such opposition that he had to flee for his life, for the Jews were plotting to kill him. They had the co-operation of the civil authorities. Paul's report is as follows:

> In Damascus the governor under Aretas the king guarded the city of the Damascenes in order to take me: and through a window was I let down in a basket by the wall, and escaped his hands (II Cor. 11:32, 33).

Fully three years after his conversion Paul arrived in Jerusalem (Gal. 1:18). He tried to join the disciples but they were all afraid of him, for they did not believe that he was really a disciple. But Barnabas, a big-hearted Levite of Cyprus who had been converted earlier (Acts 4:36, 37), removed their apprehension and introduced Paul to Peter and to James, the Lord's brother. "To visit Cephas [Peter]" had been Paul's purpose when he started out from Damascus (Gal. 1:18). While in Jerusalem, the former persecutor preached fearlessly to the Greek-speaking Jews (Acts 9:28, 29). They immediately plotted to kill him. Hence, the brothers decided to send Paul away. In a vision the Lord himself confirmed this decision.

Paul had spent only fifteen days with Peter, as he himself states in Galatians 1:18. This is in complete harmony with the account which we find in Acts 22:17–21:

> And it happened that, when I had returned to Jerusalem and was praying in the temple, I fell into a trance, and saw him [the Lord] saying to me, Make haste and quickly get out of Jerusalem; because they will not accept your testimony concerning me . . . Depart: for I will send you far away to the Gentiles.

Accordingly, the apostle left Jerusalem before he had seen the rest of the apostles and before he had become known by sight to the churches in Judea. Nevertheless, believers everywhere had heard the good news. "The man who once persecuted us is now preaching the faith he formerly tried to destroy." They glorified God (Gal. 1:23).

Paul's friends brought him to Caesarea and sent him off to Tarsus.

It is probable that the apostle labored in Tarsus and the surrounding territory for several years, founding the churches that are mentioned in Acts 15:41. When Barnabas, who had been sent to Antioch in Syria, saw the progress of the gospel in that great city and the need of an additional worker, he went to Tarsus to seek Paul and brought him to Antioch. Together they labored here for a year. The church grew rapidly and became the starting point for Paul's mission to the pagan world (Acts 9:30; 11:20–26).

About this time a great famine occurred "over all the world," just as had been predicted by the prophet Agabus. Luke tells us that this famine took place in the days of Claudius (Acts 11:28). He was emperor during the years 41–54. At Antioch contributions for the relief of the Christians in

Judea were made. By the hands of Barnabas and Paul these were sent to Jerusalem. This trip probably occurred about the year 44, shortly before the death of Herod Agrippa I (Acts 12:1). The two men, having accomplished their mission, returned to Antioch.

The extension of the church from Antioch by means of *three great missionary journeys* began at this time. The Holy Spirit directed the church to set apart Barnabas and Paul for the work to which God had called them. So, "when they had fasted and prayed and laid their hands on them, they sent them away" (Acts 13:1-3). We do not know how long a time this first missionary journey occupied. All we can say is that it must be assigned, in general, to the period 44-50. For the details of this journey, followed by the Jerusalem Conference, see Acts 13:1—15:35. It is clear that on this trip Paul and his companions did not travel very far to the west. The journey was confined to the island of Cyprus and the southern part of the Roman province of Galatia.

The second journey is described in Acts 15:36—18:22. Its probable date is 50/51-53/54. It covered far more territory than did the first trip. In fact, this time the missionaries did not stay in Asia but actually entered Europe. Evangelistic work was carried on in Macedonia (Northern Greece) and Achaia (Southern Greece). The cities visited were respectively (a) Philippi, Thessalonica, Berea; and (b) Athens and Corinth. In the latter city Paul remained a long time (Acts 18:11, 18), preaching and supporting himself by working at his trade of making tents. It was also from this city that the apostle sent his epistle to the Galatians, and, perhaps a little later, the two epistles to the Thessalonians. On the homeward stretch of this tour Paul stopped at Ephesus but did not remain there very long. He promised, however, to return (Acts 18:20, 21). By way of Caesarea he came back to Antioch.

On his third journey (53/54-57/58; Acts 18:23—21:16) Paul, "having passed through the upper country," came to Ephesus, thus fulfilling his promise (Acts 19:1). He remained here a long time (Acts 19:8, 10; 20:31) and was very successful. It is probable that all or most of "the seven churches of Asia" (Rev. 1:4) were founded during this period. Also, it would seem that before writing I Corinthians the apostle made a second visit to Corinth (II Cor. 12:14; 13:1), returning shortly afterward to Ephesus. A little later he wrote a letter to the Corinthians, the one we call I Corinthians.

When he finally left Ephesus Paul went to Macedonia. It was here (in Philippi perhaps?) that he wrote II Corinthians. And so the apostle came at last to Corinth, his third visit to that city. It was when he was about to depart from Corinth that he wrote Romans (Rom. 15:22-25; cf. Acts 20:3).

The triumph of the gospel during the period of Paul's three missionary journeys was truly amazing. It has been estimated that by the close of the apostolic period the total number of Christians in the world had reached half a million. Ever so many missionaries and lay witnesses contributed to bring about this result. Undoubtedly the most effective worker of them all was "God's chosen vessel," the apostle Paul. He was "a *Hebrew* of the Hebrews," a *Roman* citizen by birth, and versed in the "wisdom" of the *Greeks.*

There were certain external factors which favored Paul and his message, such as

1. a world government
2. world peace
3. a world language (Greek)
4. famous Roman roads linking the various parts of the world
5. world skepticism with respect to pagan deities
6. the dispersion of the Jews and of their monotheistic religion among the nations of the world
7. the translation of the Old Testament into Greek, in a sense the world language.

Nevertheless, there were also formidable obstacles. Journeying up and down the Roman Empire in order to blaze a trail for the gospel was a task beset with great dangers (II Cor. 11:23–28). Moreover, the enemies were many and relentless. Therefore, although we do not wish to detract in the least from the significance of the aforementioned favorable circumstances, *more* than this was needed if the gospel were to triumph. *More* was also divinely provided.

God, in his wonderful providence, prepared not only external conditions which favored the spread of Christianity, but also *the man* who was going to make use of these conditions. Paul had been "separated from his mother's womb" in order to proclaim the gospel to the Gentiles (Gal. 1:15–17).

What kind of person, then, was Paul?

He was a man with a *brilliant intellect,* an *iron will,* and a *compassionate heart.*

1. *brilliant intellect*

Paul was a thinker of the first order, a man with a penetrating mind, well-versed in the Old Testament, and able to grasp the connection between its precious passages and the doctrine of salvation in Christ. Far from being the creator of a brand-new theological system, as some seem to think, he discovered the doctrine of justification by faith in such Old Testament passages as Gen. 15:6; Ps. 32:1f.; Hab. 2:4. See Rom. 1:17; 3:21f.; 4:3. He also understood that what made this marvelously gracious solution of man's guilt-problem possible was Messiah's vicarious sacrifice, as Isaiah's fifty-third chapter teaches. That Paul was indeed well acquainted with the contents of that chapter is clear from Rom. 10:16 (cf. Isa. 53:1), and is probably also indicated in I Cor. 15:3 (cf. Isa. 53:5–12). And may not the following references point in the same direction: Rom. 4:25 (cf. Isa. 53:4, 5); Rom. 5:19 (cf. Isa. 53:11); Rom. 8:34 (cf. Isa. 53:12); and I Cor. 5:7 (cf. Isa. 53:7)?

This plan of salvation is in harmony with the words of Jesus recorded in Matt. 20:28; Mark 10:45; John 6:51; 10:11, 14, 16, 28; and also with those spoken by the Lord in connection with the institution of the Lord's Supper, and recorded by both Paul (I Cor. 11:23–26) and his close friend and frequent travel companion Luke (22:19, 20, on which see N.T.C. on Luke, pp. 961–964).

Several passages in Paul's epistles reveal consummate literary skill. In this connection reference is generally made to Rom. 8, I Cor. 13, and I Cor. 15. But are not the language and the style of the following passages equally superb: Rom. 2:17–29; 5:1–11; chapter 12; I Cor. 4:11–13; II Cor. 5:1–10; 11:22–33; Gal. 2:19–21; Eph. 2:8–10; 2:14–21; 6:10–20; Phil. 3:7–21; 4:4–9; I Tim. 3:16?

A combination of astuteness and wisdom is evident in what may be called Paul's *Mission Strategy,* embracing such points as the following:

a. Work in the great urban centers, so that from there the message may spread to the surrounding towns and villages.

b. Make use of the synagogue, in order to reach not only Jews but also Gentile proselytes.

c. Show that new-dispensation events are the fulfilment of old-dispensation prophecies.

d. Adapt the gospel message to the culture and the needs of the hearers.

e. Do follow-up work by means of return visits, letters, and special envoys.

f. Promote unity between rich and poor, Gentile and Jew, by asking the more prosperous churches to help the poorer ones.

2. *iron will*

Coupled with his penetrating mind was Paul's invincible determination to be a channel of blessing for men. His slogan was: "Woe to me if I do not preach the gospel . . . I have become all things to all men that by all possible means I may save some" (I Cor. 9:22), to the glory of God (I Cor. 10:31).

This indomitable purpose and resolution must certainly be considered an element in the explanation of the apostle's willingness to endure persecution for the sake of the cause to which he was so ardently devoted. How tremendous his sacrifice! How unlimited his willingness to suffer for the sake of Christ and his kingdom! Here are Paul's own words, II Cor. 11:23–28:

> In labors far greater,
> In prisons more often,
> In scourgings above measure,
> In exposure to death often.
> Of the Jews five times I received forty lashes minus one.
> Three times I was beaten with rods,
> Once I was stoned,
> Three times I suffered shipwreck,

11

A night and a day have I been in the deep;
In journeyings often,
In perils of rivers,
In perils of robbers,
In perils from my countrymen,
In perils from the Gentiles,
In perils in the city,
In perils in the wilderness,
In perils at sea;
In perils among false brothers,
In labor and toil,
In watchings often,
In hunger and thirst,
In fastings often,
In cold and nakedness.
Besides everything else
There is that which presses upon me daily,
Anxiety for all the churches.

Even when we limit ourselves to the story concerning Paul as recorded in the book of Acts we stand amazed at the amount of suffering which this hero of faith, *in order to accomplish his unwavering and consuming purpose,* was willing to endure. But when we add to the record of Acts what Paul himself tells us here in II Cor. 11, words fail to express our admiration for this great gift of God to the church! Cf. J. D. Quin, "Seven Times he wore chains," *JBL,* Dec. 1978, pp. 574, 575.

Moreover, it should be borne in mind that II Cor. 11 was written *before* the apostle's imprisonment in Jerusalem, Caesarea, and Rome (Acts 20:22, 23; 21:11, 27–28:31). This also means, of course, that *Paul had already experienced all the trials mentioned in II Cor. 11 before he composed his epistle to the Romans!* Keeping this in mind will make the study of Romans even more interesting and profitable.

In speaking about the apostle's iron will, his hewing to the line no matter what the cost, this resoluteness must not be misconstrued. It did not amount to bullheadedness. The beauty of Paul's philosophy was exactly this, that when principle was at stake—for example, that of Christ's all-sufficiency for salvation—he was unbending, but in matters not involving principle he could be very accommodating, flexible, conciliatory. Therefore, instead of charging the apostle with inconsistency, we should credit him with kindness. When the Judaistic party in Jerusalem demanded that *Titus* be circumcised, Paul did not yield to its clamor (Gal. 2:3). Yet, he circumcised *Timothy* (Acts 16:3). It was one thing to circumcise a person of mixed parentage, as was Timothy, and to do this in order to make him a more effective witness among the Jews; it was an entirely different matter to force circumcision on Titus (both of whose parents were Gentiles) and, in general, on all the Gentiles, *with the implication that unless they received this sacrament they could not be saved* (Acts 15:1).

Paul's flexibility probably also explains his willingness, after his arrival in Jerusalem from his third missionary journey, to yield to the suggestion that he join four men who had taken a temporary Nazirite vow and pay for their offerings (Acts 21:17-26). The question whether this concession on his part was wise does not concern us at this point. The fact that must be emphasized is this: Paul, while taking a firm position on matters of principle, was always willing to yield on matters neither forbidden or enjoined. He followed this course purposely and consistently, as I Cor. 9:20, 21 shows.

Of the American poet John Greenleaf Whittier it has been said that he "yielded in smaller matters, that he might win in the greater."[2] The same could be said of Paul.

3. *compassionate heart*

The apostle's "drive" would not have been so keen had it not been activated by this third factor. Various phases of the apostle's intensely emotional personality are exhibited in the book of Acts and in the epistles. Here was a *marvelously loving heart,* a truly great soul!

Having formerly persecuted the followers of Jesus, after his conversion Sorrow, hearty and profound, walked with Paul (I Cor. 15:9; I Tim. 1:15). That to such a bitter persecutor Christ had revealed himself as a loving Savior baffled him. He just could not get over it (Eph. 3:8; I Tim. 1:16). It caused his heart to overflow with lasting, humble gratitude! For this and for other reasons his epistles are full of magnificent doxologies (Rom. 9:5; 11:36; 16:25-27; Eph. 1:3f.; 3:20f.; Phil. 4:20; I Tim. 1:17; 6:15; II Tim. 4:18), which are the spontaneous utterances of the man who wrote, "*For the love of Christ constrains us*" (II Cor. 5:14). Having been "laid hold on" by Christ, the apostle in turn was eager to burn himself out for the salvation of others (I Cor. 9:22; 10:33; II Cor. 12:15).

His heart ached intensely because so many of his own people (Israelites) were not saved (Rom. 9:1-3; 10:1). Anxiety for all his churches pressed upon him daily (II Cor. 11:28). How fervent and touching were his prayers for them (Eph. 3:14-19; I Thess. 3:9-13). *How he loved them,* so that he could write, "We were gentle in the midst of y o u as a nurse cherishes her own children. So, being affectionately desirous of y o u, we gladly shared with y o u not only the gospel of God but also our own souls . . . For now we really live if y o u stand fast in the Lord" (I Thess. 2:7, 8; 3:8). How earnest were his pleadings (II Cor. 5:20; Gal. 4:19, 20; Eph. 4:1), and how tactful! Though for their own good he was able to rebuke the wayward very sharply (Gal. 1:6-9; 3:1-4), even this was a manifestation of the love of his great, throbbing heart. Is it any wonder that, when occasion demanded it, out of the eyes of a man with an ebullient spirit and loving heart there welled forth fountains of tears (Acts 20:19, 31), so that both in II Cor. 2:4 and in Phil. 3:18 these are mentioned? And is it at all surprising that, on the

---

2. A. H. Strong, *American Poets and Their Theology,* Philadelphia, etc., 1916, p. 124.

other hand, on one occasion the tears of his friends, because of his imminent departure and the afflictions in store for him, well-nigh broke his heart (Acts 21:13)? Truly Paul's *weeping* when he writes about the enemies of the cross of Christ is as glorious as is the *joy, joy, joy* that sings its way through his epistle to the Philippians!

III.   Its Place and Date of Composition

The following facts point to Corinth as *the place* where the apostle composed the epistle to the Romans:

1. He commends to the church Phoebe whom he calls "a servant of the church of Cenchrea." Now Cenchrea was the eastern port of Corinth. It is generally, and probably correctly, assumed that Phoebe carried Paul's letter to its destination.

2. He calls Gaius his "host." This person may well have been the one of that name mentioned in I Cor. 1:14, where the apostle informs the Corinthians that he had baptized this member of their congregation. In Rom. 16:23 Gaius is sending greetings.

3. Also extending a salutation is Erastus. Cf. II Tim. 4:20, "Erastus remained *at Corinth.*" An inscription discovered on a paving-block *at Corinth* reads, "Erastus laid this pavement at his own expense." *If* these references are to the Erastus of Rom. 16:23, they confirm the theory that Romans was composed in Corinth.

Determination of *the time* of composition is perhaps somewhat more difficult. At least opinions differ rather widely. The question must be answered, "When was Paul in Corinth under circumstances that harmonized with the situation as pictured in his letter to the Romans?"

His *first* stop in that place was during the second missionary journey (Acts 15:36—18:22). According to Acts 15 this journey began soon after the close of the Jerusalem Conference, though exactly how soon afterward has not been revealed. See Acts 15:30, 36. If the date A.D. 50 is assigned to that gathering, as is generally done, the somewhat flexible date 50/51–53/54 for the entire second missionary journey may well be correct. Nevertheless, it cannot have been during *this* stay at Corinth that the apostle wrote Romans. That letter clearly belongs to a considerably later time period, when Paul's missionary labors in the eastern part of the empire were nearing their completion. Note the following: "From Jerusalem and round about, as far as Illyricum, I have fully preached the gospel of Christ" (Rom. 15:19); "I no longer have any room for work in these regions" (15:23). Cf. 1:10: ". . . now *at last.*"

Shall we then link Romans with Paul's *second* journey to Corinth, the painful visit implied in II Cor. 12:14; 13:1? But this trip must have been of short duration and made under circumstances unfavorable for the composition of this great epistle. As indicated earlier, it was probably made during Paul's very lengthy stay at Ephesus, and *before* he wrote I Corinthians.

Everything points to the probability that Paul wrote Romans toward the close of his three-month ministry in Achaia (Greece), mentioned in Acts 20:3; hence during his *third* recorded visit to Corinth on his *third* missionary journey (Acts 18:23—21:16).

On his subsequent *departure* from Corinth Paul's original plan had been to sail directly from Greece to Syria, in order from there to travel to Jerusalem with gifts for its poor saints, charitable contributions made by their fellow-Christians in Macedonia and Achaia. But the timely discovery of a plot against the apostle's life changed this plan, so that, instead, he returned to Jerusalem by way of Macedonia (Philippi) and Mysia (Troas). See Acts 20:3-6; Rom. 15:25.

The third missionary journey had already lasted a long time before Paul left Corinth. This is clear from the fact that even before reaching Corinth on this trip the apostle had spent "two months" and "two years" at Ephesus (Acts 19:8, 10). In fact, all in all he seems to have worked there for a period of "three years" (Acts 20:31). The date for his entire third missionary journey was therefore probably 53/54-57/58, and the date for the composition of the epistle to the Romans, just before his departure from Corinth, was probably 57 or 58. Since it was Paul's intention to reach Jerusalem by Pentecost (Acts 20:16), we can perhaps be even more specific and say that the letter was probably written *toward the close* of the winter and/or *during the beginning* of the spring.

A considerably earlier date for the third missionary journey and for Romans brings the story into conflict with the date for Paul's accusation before Gallio (Acts 18:12-17) during the apostle's second missionary journey. It has been established that Gallio's consulship fell within the period 51-53.[3] Also, such an early date would result in the necessity of moving back the dates of Paul's arrival in Jerusalem, his arrest, and his imprisonment in Caesarea during the administration of Felix (and later on, of Festus). And since Felix probably did not become governor until the year 52,[4] it would then be difficult to explain how Paul, in his defense before this governor, could say, "Knowing that *for many years* you have been a judge over this nation, I cheerfully make my defense."

IV. Its Addressees

Under this heading an attempt will be made to answer two questions: How did the church of Rome originate? Which group predominated numerically: Jews or Gentiles?

During Christ's earthly ministry (A.D. 26-30) people were brought out of the darkness into the light (John 3:26; 12:19). However, not all "followers"

---

3. See J. J. Foakes Jackson and Kirsopp Lake, *The Beginnings of Christianity*, Grand Rapids, 1966, Vol. V, pp. 460-464.

4. See Josephus, *Antiquities* XX.137; *Jewish War* II.247.

possessed "saving faith" (Matt. 13:1–7, 18–22; John 6:66), though some did (Matt. 13:8, 23; Luke 12:32; John 17:6–8). Included in the group of those who were genuine believers were not only Jews (Matt. 19:28) but also Gentiles (Matt. 8:10, 11; cf. 21:41) and Samaritans (John 4). Moreover, on and after Pentecost the number of disciples increased by leaps and bounds (Acts 2:41; 4:4). Gospel activity was resumed in Samaria. Philistia and probably even Ethiopia heard the message (Acts 8).

What was taking place in all these regions did not go unnoticed elsewhere, for, although modern methods of communication—radio, television, telephone, etc.—were nonexistent, people traveled extensively, thereby keeping each other informed about happenings in all parts of the Roman Empire. Soon, too, Damascus and Syria counted believers among their inhabitants. One of them was Ananias (Acts 9; for an even earlier reference to Syria see Matt. 4:24).

Travel was heavy in those days and, notwithstanding dangers, was relatively safe because of the still prevailing Pax Romana (reign of peace enforced by the Roman Empire).

There were ships. Admittedly they were not as luxurious as those of today. In fact, they were not even primarily intended for passenger service or tourism. Many of them were cargo vessels that brought grain to various places, especially to Rome; that is, to its ports or harbors. Rome's huge population—estimated variously at 1,000,000 to 1,500,000—needed to be fed.

In addition to these freighters there were also many smaller vessels. However, ships and boats were not always available. Navigation generally took place between the beginning of March and the middle of November. But when these vessels were plying the waters, their owners and/or captains were willing, for a consideration, to take aboard passengers. As the book of Acts indicates, Paul made frequent use of this mode of travel.

There were also those famous Roman roads: Via Appia, Via Cornelia, Via Aurelia, Via Valeria, etc. They were of sturdy and durable construction and were furnished with distance markers. Twenty main highways issued from Rome's "Golden Milestone," each diverging into numerous branches, so that the various parts of the empire were bound together by a huge network of arteries.[5] To go from one city to another, people would often make use of both means of travel: they would get to their destinations by sea and land. Thus, in order to reach Rome a Philippian might take the Egnatian Way from Philippi to Dyrrachium. Then by ship he would cross the Adriatic to Brundisium. From there the Appian Way would take him to Rome.

From the New Testament and from other sources one gains the impression that there were many great travelers. So, for example, Aquila and Priscilla (or Prisca) at different intervals in their lives must have traveled

---

5. See W. V. Von Hagen, *The Roads That Led to Rome,* Cleveland and New York, 1967.

from Pontus to Rome and from there to Corinth (Acts 18:2); later to Ephesus (Acts 18:18, 19; I Cor. 16:19), then to Rome (Rom. 16:3), and subsequently back to Ephesus (II Tim. 4:19). Luke too traveled extensively. So did Timothy, Titus, and especially Paul! See II Cor. 11:25, 26.

Why did people go to Rome? For any one of the following reasons, or for a combination of two or more of them: to settle there, to conduct business, to ply a trade, to pursue a profession, to study, to escape arrest (it was easy to "get lost" in this big city), to satisfy their curiosity concerning the metropolis on the Tiber about which so many rumors had been circulating, to visit friends and relatives, and best of all, to bring the gospel to the Romans. There must have been other incentives that led people to this city. Also, thousands of individuals had actually been *deported* to Rome. Others were involved in the movements of military forces.

Why do I mention all this? To emphasize the fact, often overlooked, that there is every reason to believe that the gospel must have reached Rome at an early date. In their fear of indulging in "wild speculation" some forget that "realistic historical imagination" is not only justifiable but necessary. This is sometimes overlooked. So, for example, there are those who minimize the importance of Pentecost (Acts 2) for the establishment of the church in Rome. Because they can find no record of any connection between Pentecost and conversions taking place in Rome at such an early date, they reject the idea that there was such a relationship. Or they will say that the visitors from Rome who attended the Feast in Jerusalem and later on returned to their homes were not in a position to start a church.

But the evangelist Luke has definitely reported that among those who witnessed the astounding miracles attending the outpouring of the Holy Spirit there were "visitors from Rome, both Jews and proselytes" (Gentile converts to Judaism). See Acts 2:10. Is it not reasonable to believe that at least some of these visitors from Rome were among the three thousand converts (Acts 2:41)? Having returned to their homes, would they have failed to tell their friends and relatives in Rome what they had seen and heard in Jerusalem? And must we indeed believe that from that moment on they would have ignored the opportunity to pelt newly arrived or returning travelers with questions about the "Jesus is the Christ" movement and the outpouring of the Holy Spirit as proof of Christ's exaltation to the position at the Father's right hand?

Not many years after the great Pentecost described in Acts 2 friends may also have come to Rome from mission-minded Antioch in Syria. Even before A.D. 44 the gospel had been proclaimed in that city, where "the disciples were first called *Christians*" (Acts 11:26). The church at Antioch contained several men who were qualified to spread the good tidings (Acts 13:1). So, since all roads led to Rome and travel back and forth was heavy, it is at least conceivable that some of these mission-minded Antiochians at an early date proclaimed the gospel in Rome, adding strength to the very young church. Soon members of other churches—for example, those in

Philippi, Corinth, and Ephesus—may well have co-operated, for between each of them and Rome communication was constant.

It will have become evident that in its earliest beginnings the Roman church was probably started not (except indirectly) by any apostle but by the rank and file of those Jews and proselytes who had witnessed the miracles of Pentecost and had afterward returned to their homes in Rome. It should be stressed that these "lay" people were *Jews* or, in some cases had at one time been converted to the *Jewish* religion. It should not cause surprise therefore if we discover that in its very beginnings the church in Rome revealed this Jewish character.

Are there any records that lend further support to this theory? A fourth century A.D. Latin father, known as "Ambrosiaster," in the Introduction to his *Commentary on Romans,* informs us that the Roman church was founded not by the apostles but by certain Jewish Christians who imposed a "Judaic form" on it. Does not this Judaic form remind us of what is recorded in Acts 15:1; 21:17–24 with reference to the church at *Jerusalem?*

In its subsequent history did the establishment or further growth of the church in Rome leave any traces in historical records? There is nothing of a very clear and substantial nature. But Suetonius (*Life of Claudius* XXV.ii), has handed down this statement: "Claudius expelled the Jews from Rome because they were constantly making disturbances at the instigation of Chrestus." The spelling *Chrestus* to indicate *Christus* (= Christ) was not unusual. So interpreted, this bit of information could shed light on Acts 18:2, which similarly reports a banishment of the Jews from Rome during the reign of emperor Claudius (date of his reign A.D. 41–54). Suetonius, then, might be saying that with the introduction of Christianity into Rome quarrels broke out between those Jews who had accepted the Christian religion and the others of their race who remained hostile to the new faith. Erroneously (if Chrestus = Christus), yet understandably, Suetonius regarded Christ as the instigator. But though this interpretation—Chrestus=Christus—is possible, it is not necessarily correct, and has not been accepted by all expositors.[6]

Aside from his sermon on the day of Pentecost did the apostle *Peter* contribute anything to the establishment of the Roman church? Two extremes must be avoided. On the one hand that of the Roman Catholic Church, which, on the basis of an early tradition, ascribed to Peter a twenty-five year episcopacy (A.D. 42–67) over the church in Rome; on the other, the position of those who deny or at least cast doubt on *any* connection between Peter and that church.

As to the first extreme, if it were factual, Peter would have occupied the position of supreme authority in the Roman church during a period includ-

---

6. Lenski is among those who reject the identification. See his *Interpretation of The Acts of the Apostles,* Columbus, 1944, p. 745. See, however, also F. J. Foakes Jackson and Kirsopp Lake, *op. cit.,* Vol. V, p. 295.

ing the very year when Paul sent his epistle to that body of believers. Yet in his list of greetings, addressed to individual believers in Rome, Paul never even mentions Peter. See Rom. 16:3–15. Is it at all possible that Paul would have been guilty of such neglect and breach of etiquette?

And as to the second extreme, an appeal is often made to Rom. 15:20, which is then interpreted to imply that, before Paul wrote Romans, Christ had not yet been named in Rome; at least no apostle as yet had entered that city. However, that interpretation of Rom. 15:20 is not necessarily correct.

It would seem that when Paul was released from his first Roman imprisonment and was traveling to various congregations of his far-flung spiritual domain (see N.T.C. on I and II Timothy and Titus, pp. 39, 40), Peter was in Rome. He wrote the letter that came to be known as "the First Epistle of Peter." It was addressed to "the elect who are sojourners in Pontus, Galatia, etc." Note its closing salutation: "The church [literally *she*] that is in Babylon, elect together with y o u, greets y o u" (I Peter 5:13). In all probability this "Babylon" is Rome. Is not this identification the starting point from which one should proceed in the explanation of the same designation in Rev. 17:5? However, these events—Paul's release, Peter's writing— occurred *after* Paul wrote Romans.

We know therefore that, at least toward the close of his life, Peter labored in the church of Rome. Had he perhaps been there before? Did his Pentecost sermon, heard and transmitted by the visitors from Rome, indirectly qualify him for the title "founder" of the Roman church?

These questions cannot be answered with any degree of certainty. The book of Acts leaves many gaps. It makes allowance for many years, from A.D. 33 on, during which Peter *may* have been strengthening the church of Rome. Clement of Alexandria writes that Peter "had publicly preached the word in Rome" (*Hypotuposeis,* as quoted by Eusebius VI.xiv.6). And even somewhat earlier Irenaeus made the statement, "Peter and Paul went westward and founded the church in Rome" (*Against Heresies* III.i.1; cf. Eusebius V.viii.3). But of these statements of Clement and of Irenaeus there are various interpretations and evaluations. We probably do well to reserve our judgment. We should add, however, that according to tradition Mark's Gospel was composed to satisfy the urgent request of the people of Rome for a written summary of Peter's preaching in that city.

As to *Paul's* part in the establishment of this church, it is clear from Rom. 1:10; cf. 15:28, that at the time of the writing of this letter the apostle, though being himself a Roman citizen by birth (Acts 22:28), had not yet set foot in Rome. It is also clear, however, that he had met, at least had become acquainted (whether directly or indirectly) with several of the people belonging to Rome's church (16:3–15). He was eager to see Rome, and even more, to meet his friends there. He was actually going to reach the capital of the Roman Empire, but in a manner that had not been included in *his* plan but in *God's* (Acts 25:11, chapters 27, 28). In Rome Paul, *the prisoner,* was going to be very effective in proclaiming the gospel (Phil. 1:12–14). But at the time when this epistle was being written these future developments had not been revealed to him.

In the church of Rome which group predominated numerically: Jews or Gentiles? In the main there are three views:

1. The Roman church consisted mainly of Jews.[7]

Arguments used in support of this theory:

a. Paul was a Jew. In Rom. 3:9 he writes, "Are *we* better than they?" Moreover, note the preceding context: "the Jew" (verse 1) and "the Jews" (verse 2). Accordingly some of the modern translations have even inserted the word "Jews" into the text of Rom. 3:9; hence "we Jews."

Answer. In its continuation verse 9 shows that the author is now no longer thinking exclusively of Jews. He now proceeds from the fact that "all men," both Jews and Greeks, are by nature "under sin." That this is true with respect to the Greeks or Gentiles he has demonstrated in 1:18–32. That it holds also in the case of the Jews he has made clear in 2:1–3:8. So he now specifically turns his attention to himself and the church he is addressing, as a pastor who is facing his "congregation," and he asks, "What then? Are we—*y o u and I*—any better?" He means, "better than humanity (Jews and Greeks) in general?" His answer amounts to, "Not at all, for we too belong to this entity (the entire human race) on which God's judgment rests. No one is righteous, not even one."[8] Or somewhat wider: "we" = *I and all other true believers.* See also on 3:9.

b. In 7:1 Paul says, "I am speaking to men who know *the law* [or simply *law*]." He must be addressing especially the Jews, for they alone had been trained in the knowledge of God's holy law.

Answer. He is addressing the Jewish contingent of the church to be sure, but not necessarily *especially* the Jews. If Paul is thinking of the law of God, found in the Old Testament and summarized in the ten commandments, the answer might be as follows: Many a believer from among the Gentiles had entered the church by way of the synagogue. Even as a proselyte to the Jewish faith he had become acquainted with the law of God. And as a Christian he had come to understand that law far better. Conclusion: what Paul says here in Rom. 7:1 does not prove that most of the members of the Roman church were Jews by race.

Also, room must be left for the possibility that *law* here in Rom. 7:1 means "law in general." See on that passage. If so, then too, Rom. 7:1 fails to prove that most of the addressees were Jews by race.

---

7. T. Zahn, *Introduction to the New Testament,* English tr. Edinburgh, 1909, Vol. I, p. 422; and before him F. C. Bauer, *Paul, the Apostle of Jesus Christ,* English tr. 1873, Vol. I, pp. 321 ff. Other defenders of this view: W. Manson, N. Krieger, J. A. C. Van Leeuwen and D. Jacobs, etc.

8. In this connection see especially A. F. N. Lekkerkerker, *De Prediking van het Nieuwe Testament, De Brief van Paulus aan de Romeinen,* Nijkerk, 1971, p. 129.

c. Rom. 9–11 pertains especially to the Jews. It concerns *Israel.*

Answer. To a considerable extent this must be granted. But this does not mean that most of the addressed were Jews. In fact, it is exactly this section which shows that most of the addressees were converts from the Gentile world, for Paul regards the Jews as being, by and large, distinct from the people to whom he is directing his remarks. The apostle is thinking of two groups: Gentiles and Jews. When he is describing the condition and destiny of the Jews, he deliberately employs the pronouns *they, their, them.* Examples: "*Theirs* is the adoption" (9:4); "My heart's desire for *them* is that *they* may be saved" (10:1). Note especially the distinction the apostle makes between the third person, referring to the Jews, and the second, referring to the addressed: "*They* were broken off because of *their* unbelief, and *you* are established through faith" (11:20). Similarly in 11:24 Paul makes a distinction between "you" and "these natural branches" (obviously the Jews). This use of the third person to indicate Israel continues through verse 31.

d. The dialectical method of argumentation employed here shows that the writer is addressing Jews, for that was the method they appreciated. Their former teachers, the rabbis, were in the habit of resorting to this form of lecturing.

Answer. Greeks—for example, Socrates—were not unfamiliar with this stylistic device. Besides, Paul was conscious of the objections his opponents might advance against his doctrines. So, very effectively, he anticipates their objections, and by means of the question-and-answer method clinches his argument. See 9:14; 9:19; 10:18, 19; 11:1; 11:11; 11:19f. More on this under heading V of this Introduction.

2. The Roman church consisted mainly of Gentiles.[9]
Proof:

a. In Rom. 1:5, 6 the apostle states ". . . we received grace and apostleship (to call) people from among all the Gentiles to the obedience that springs from faith, among whom y o u are also . . ."

b. 1:13 ends with the words, "in order that I might obtain some fruit among y o u also, as I have among the rest of the Gentiles."

c. In 11:13 Paul says, "I am talking to y o u Gentiles. Inasmuch as I am the apostle to the Gentiles, I magnify my ministry."

d. 15:15 reads, "I have written to y o u rather boldly on some points, so as to remind y o u of them again, because of the grace God gave me to be a

---

9. Among those who favor this view are the following: W. Sanday and A. C. Headlam, *A Critical and Exegetical Commentary on the Epistle to the Romans (International Critical Commentary),* Edinburgh, 1902, p. xxxii f.; M.-J. Lagrange, *Saint Paul, Épître aux Romains,* Paris, 1950, pp. xxi–xxiv; H. Ridderbos, *Aan De Romeinen, (Commentaar Op Het Nieuwe Testament),* Kampen, 1959, pp. 6–10; and John Murray, *The Epistle to the Romans,* Grand Rapids, 1959, Vol. I, pp. xxi, xxii.

minister of Christ Jesus to the Gentiles . . . that the Gentiles might become an offering acceptable to God." Note also how very frequently the word "Gentiles" occurs in 15:9–18.

e. The fact that in the list of greetings Paul singles out certain individuals (see verses 7, 11, and 21) as being his fellow-countrymen also confirms the conclusion that not the Jews but the Gentiles constituted the majority of the church in Rome.

3. These arguments would seem to be unanswerable. Nevertheless, an attempt has been made to refute them. In what in many respects is a splendid commentary—I would urge the readers by all means to study it—C. E. B. Cranfield[10] attempts to prove that it is not possible to establish whether most of the members of the church at Rome were Jews or were Romans. In my opinion his *refutation* of the position that *Jewish* Christians formed the majority is adequate, and his view that at the time of Paul there must, nevertheless, have been a considerable number of Jews in the Roman church is well argued. But when he states that the expression "among whom y o u are also" may mean no more than that the Roman church was situated in the midst of the Gentile world, and that in 1:13 the expression "as among the rest of the Gentiles" may be considered slightly inexact, I must dissent.

My conclusion, therefore, is that theory No. 2, namely, that most of the members of the Roman Church were Christians from the Gentiles, is correct, though the exact proportion of Jews to Gentiles is unknown.

A few facts should be added, however. First of all, since in the first and second centuries church buildings in the sense in which we think of them today were not yet in existence, families would hold services in their own homes. Such services would be attended by the members of the household: perhaps father, mother, children, sometimes other close relatives (cf. Luke 12:53), servants. If the house was large enough to accommodate others, they too were invited. The early church numbered many hospitable members, ready and eager to offer their facilities for religious use: meetings, services, etc. Thus, in Jerusalem "many were gathered together and were praying" in the house of Mary, the mother of John Mark (Acts 12:12). Lydia graciously invited Paul, Silas, Timothy, and Luke to use her home as their headquarters (Acts 16:15, 40). WhereverAquila and Prisca went they would if at all possible welcome the worshipers to their home. Hence, both at Ephesus (I Cor. 16:19) and at Rome (Rom. 16:3–5) there was "a church at their house." Laodicea too had a house-church (Col. 4:15). Corinth may have had a house-church at the home of Gaius. In Laodicea Nympha performed the duty of hostess to the members of the church of which she was a member.

---

10. *The Epistle To The Romans (International Critical Commentary)*, Edinburgh, 1975, Vol. I, pp. 18–21.

How many of these house-churches there were in Rome we do not know. The house-church mentioned in Rom. 16:5 may not have been the only one; 16:14 ("the brothers with them") and 16:15 ("all the saints with them") may indicate others. And there may have been more, especially in such a large city.

In connection with the present subject—whether the Jews or the Gentiles predominated in the Roman church, while fully maintaining that most of the members had been gathered into the church from the Gentiles (whether directly or indirectly), can we not leave open the possibility that, among the various units composing this church, there may have been at least one, a house-church, in which not the Gentiles but the Jews predominated numerically?

Far more important, however, is the fact that the author of Romans is not mainly interested in the question whether there were more Jews or more Gentiles among those whom he was addressing. *His* emphasis is on the fact that both Jew and Gentile are by nature "under sin" (Rom. 3:9); in other words, that "all have sinned and fall short of the glory of God" (3:23); that the way of salvation through faith in Christ is open to all (3:24); that Abraham is the father of all that believe (4:11, 12); and that for all who are in Christ Jesus there is no condemnation (8:1f.). *We* may talk about Jew versus Gentile. *Romans stresses the idea of unity.* One of its most precious passages is 10:12, 13:

"For there is no distinction between Jew and Greek; for the same Lord is Lord of all, and abounds in riches for all who call on him. For whoever calls on the name of the Lord will be saved."

V. Its Occasion and Purpose

On this subject there is considerable difference of opinion. Much has been written about it, especially in recent years.[11]

As was pointed out earlier, Paul had reached the end of his mission work in the *eastern* part of the Roman Empire. He had "planted" (I Cor. 3:6) the gospel in the large centers (and in some of the smaller towns besides). From

---

11. From the almost endless number of books and articles on this subject I wish to call attention merely to the following:

K. P. Donfried (editor and contributor), *The Romans Debate,* Minneapolis, 1977. In this book the question, "Why did Paul write Romans?" is explored by nine American and European scholars.

John Knox and C. R. Cragg, *The Epistle to the Romans* (Vol. IX in *The Interpreter's Bible*), New York and Nashville, 1954, pp. 358-363.

E. F. Harrison, *Romans* (Vol. X. in *The Expositor's Bible Commentary*), Grand Rapids, 1976, pp. 5, 6. An excellent summary!

G. W. Barker, W. L. Lane, J. R. Michaels, *The New Testament Speaks,* New York, Evanston, and London, 1969, pp. 192, 193. Excellent mission emphasis!

H. Ridderbos, *Aan De Romeinen,* pp. 10-14.

these centers—such as Syrian Antioch, Philippi, Corinth, Ephesus—the word of the Lord was spreading widely (cf. Acts 19:20, 26; Rev. 1:4, 11). In fact Paul himself had proclaimed the good tidings of salvation from Jerusalem all the way to present-day Yugoslavia and Albania (Rom. 15:19). The gospel had even reached Rome, though Paul himself had never visited this city. He did, however, have many friends there, intimate acquaintances whom he loved dearly.

So now he hopes that the yearning he has cherished for many years, namely, to go to Rome (Rom. 15:23; cf. 1:10, 11; Acts 19:21) may at last be satisfied.

He realizes, however, that he cannot immediately sail to Rome by way of the Corinthan Gulf and Ionian Sea, for he has been conducting a campaign for the benefit of the poor saints in Jerusalem. Since this drive has been successful Paul, according to a previous promise (I Cor. 16:4), intends, the Lord willing, to go to Jerusalem, so that, in person, he, accompanied by others, may present the gifts that have been collected for the poor (Acts 24:17). And then he will wend his way to Rome! That was the plan.

But why does Paul want to visit Rome's church? What, exactly, is his purpose?

The initial answer must be that Paul, being an intensely warm and loving person, desires to go to Rome in order to be a blessing to his friends (Rom. 1:10, 11) and to be refreshed by them (15:32). Moreover, it is for this same reason that he, now that it is impossible for him to go to Rome *immediately,* communicates with the Roman church by means of this letter. He writes to the Romans because he loves them. They are his friends "in Christ," and by means of this letter he imparts his love to them, praises them (1:8), informs them about his constant prayers for them (1:9), asks them to pray for him (15:30), and informs them about his traveling plans (1:10–12; 15:24 f.).

It is strange that this deeply personal reason (desire for fellowship, etc.), a reason clearly brought out by the apostle himself, is often overlooked. At times the emphasis is placed entirely on theological motivation or on mission incentive: Paul wants to correct the errors of the antinomians and/or wants to make Rome the headquarters for the evangelization of Spain. To be sure, these matters are important, but we should *begin* with the reason first stated by Paul himself in this very epistle.

All the more does Paul feel the necessity of writing this letter and by means of it asking the Roman church to remember him in prayer, because he is not at all sure that he will ever reach Rome. Rom. 1:10 introduces this fear, and 15:31 clarifies what the apostle has in mind. There are two things he fears: (a) that the Jews may kill him; (b) that the Jerusalem "saints" may not even be willing to accept the bounteous gift coming to them from the *Gentiles.*

As to the first misgiving, that it was not groundless is clear from such a passage as Acts 20:3 (because of a plot by the Jews Paul had to change his traveling plan), and from Acts 14:19; 17:5, 13; 18:6, 12 f.; 23:12–21; II

Cor. 11:24, 32, 33. Moreover, Paul's misgiving was not entirely subjective. He was constantly receiving intimations from the Holy Spirit, hints of impending hardships (Acts 20:22, 23). See also 21:10, 11, 27f.

As to the second fear, though the brothers welcomed Paul and his companions warmly (Acts 21:17), to what extent this warm welcome also included appreciation for the "collection" on which Paul had spent so much time and effort is not made clear.

The fact here mentioned, namely, that to the mind of Paul the possibility was real, the prospect formidable, that he might never get to see his dear friends in Rome, explains why he had to write *this* type of letter, one which, in its first seven chapters is characterized by argumentative style. Note, for example, the series of expressions such as, "What then shall we say?" See 4:1; 6:1; 7:7; 8:31; 9:14, 30. Not only is this kind of style reminiscent of the manner in which Paul, *the missionary,* had during his many travels been arguing with his bitter opponents, the unbelieving Jews, but it also shows that he is conscious of the fact that Rome's little church is surrounded by a huge army of such unbelievers. Paul, therefore, in this letter to the Romans, is showing the Roman church how it should defend itself against the constant onslaught of these opponents; yes, how it might even win some of them for Christ! If the addressees can no longer contact Paul himself, they will at least be able to read and reread this precious letter.

This also indicates that the epistle to the Romans is not really "a complete compendium of Christian Doctrine." If it had been Paul's intention to draw up such a document, he would surely have included far more material. *Paul is a very practical man. He knows exactly what the Roman church needs. Guided by the Holy Spirit, he fulfils that need. Moreover, since the doctrine at stake, namely, that concerning the manner in which sinners are saved, is basic, what is presented in 1:16–8:39 is urgently needed not only by the church in Rome but by every church, every believer, every sinner, down through the ages.*

By and large the condition of the Roman church must have been very encouraging (1:8; 15:14; 16:19). But that cannot mean that the intellectual maturity of its membership was complete and/or that its moral and spiritual development left nothing to be desired. On the contrary, this church too had its weaknesses. It was in need of instruction with respect to God's promises to Israel. So one of the purposes of this epistle was to supply that instruction (chapters 9–11). More light was also needed on the question of clean versus unclean foods. That light too is richly supplied (14:13–18).

Not only *information* but also *exhortation* or *admonition* was needed, and this especially with respect to such matters as obedience to civil authority (chapter 13) and the proper attitude of "the strong" toward "the weak" (14:1–12; 15:1–4). And in connection with the need—then, now, always—of such virtues as unity, humility, and above all love, who will wish to deny that Rom. 12 is one of the finest not only in Scripture but in all of literature?

What has been said so far clearly indicates that the ardent desire to be a blessing to the church in Rome was definitely included in Paul's purpose in writing this letter. The view according to which the apostle intended *merely* to pass through Rome in order to make it a base of operations for mission activity in Spain is incorrect. Rom. 15:24 ("I hope to visit y o u while passing through") is balanced by 1:15 ("I am eager to preach the gospel also to y o u who are in Rome").

For the rest, it remains true that one of the items included in Paul's aim was securing the co-operation of the Roman church in connection with his contemplated journey to Spain, as 15:24 clearly shows.

In conclusion, to arrive at a complete answer to the question, "Why did Paul write Romans?" the following two Pauline passages should not be ignored:

"I have become all things to all men, in order that, by any and all means, I might save some" (I Cor. 9:22).

"Whether therefore y o u eat or drink, or whatever y o u do, do all to the glory of God" (I Cor. 10:31).

A great missionary indeed was Paul. His heart burned with love for people, and even more with love for God, the One who had rescued him, even him, formerly a bitter persecutor of God's precious children! He just "could not get over it!" It seems as if across the span of the centuries we can still hear him say, "I have been crucified with Christ; and it is no longer I who lives, but Christ who lives in me, and that (life) which I now live in flesh I live in faith, (the faith) which is in the Son of God, who loved me and gave himself up for me" (Gal. 2:20).

But one does not need to be a famous missionary like Paul to render service in God's kingdom, a service recognized by God himself. There was, for example, sister Phoebe of Cenchrea, a harbor of Corinth, located a little to the east of that great cosmopolitan center. Always she was ready to render service to the Lord and his cause. When she heard that the great missionary was composing a letter addressed to his dear friends in Rome, did she volunteer her willingness to deliver it? Or did Paul himself take the initiative in asking her to render this service? However this may have been, it is clear that she was standing ready, *always* ready to do whatever she could do out of love for her Lord and Savior.

I believe that the purpose and the occasion of Paul's epistle to the Romans have now been made clear.

VI.   Its Text

A few words should be written about the integrity of the text of Romans. Does the Greek text on which our translations are based faithfully represent what Paul actually wrote *to the church in Rome?*

There are those who doubt it, and this for the following reasons:

1. Not every manuscript contains the reading "in Rome" in 1:7 and 1:15. In 1:7 a variant substitutes "all who are in the love of God" for "all who are in Rome, beloved of God." Also in verse 15 "in Rome" is then omitted.

2. The strikingly beautiful doxology, "Now to him who is able to establish y o u . . . be glory forever through Jesus Christ. Amen," which in our Bibles is found at the close of chapter 16, is in some sources found at the close of chapter 14; in others, at the close of chapters 14 and 16; and in one very early papyrus (Chester Beatty) at the close of chapter 15.

3. As to the greetings (16:3-15), there are those who maintain that they point to the church of Ephesus rather than to that of Rome, as the group for which they were intended; for

a. How could Paul have known so many persons in Rome? He himself had never been there. But he had spent a long time in Ephesus.

b. Prisca (or Priscilla) and Aquila were living in Ephesus shortly before this (Acts 18:18, 19; I Cor. 16:19), and Epaenetus is called "the first-fruits" (= first convert to Christ) in *Asia*. This again reminds us of Ephesus, not of Rome.

c. The sharp reprimand of 16:17, 18 is out of line with the words of praise the apostle addresses to those whom he has in mind in 1:8; 15:14. Sharp condemnation and warm commendation do not go together. Therefore chapter 16 must have been addressed to another audience than those to whom Paul is speaking in the preceding chapters.

Though it must be admitted that not every problem can be solved, the following answers to these doubts about the integrity of the text deserve consideration:

As to 1: The omission of "in Rome" is a rare exception. The phrase "in Rome" has decisive manuscript support. Besides, the context favors reference to a definite place. Note especially verse 10, "I keep pleading that somehow by God's will now at last the way may be opened for me to come to y o u." Could it be that the heretic Marcion, who was rejected by the Roman church, had something to do with the omission of this phrase in 1:7, 15?

As to 2: The *best* manuscripts favor 16:25-27 as the proper place for this doxology. According to the testimony of Origen it was Marcion who deleted everything in Romans following 14:23. His negative attitude toward the Old Testament and its "god" or "demi-urge" is well-known. So there were too many statements in chapter 15 he did not like. See especially verse 4. Nevertheless, Romans must have a proper conclusion. It is therefore not surprising that the doxology at the close of chapter 16 was transferred to chapter 14. Once the process of moving a passage from one place to another begins, where will it end? It must be admitted, however, that the exact reason why the Chester Beatty manuscript has placed the doxology at the close of chapter 15 is not known. But this does not in any way cancel the fact that its place at the close of chapter 16 is favored by the strongest manuscript evidence.

As to 3:

a. Because of the heavy and constant traffic between Rome and other cities, it is reasonable to suppose that the apostle had met these people on his journeys. In a few cases he may have received ample information about them from friends. Moreover, the very reason that he had not been in Rome himself makes it all the more probable that by warmly greeting those he did know he desired to gain an entrance into the hearts of the entire Roman church.

b. As has been indicated previously, Prisca and Aquila were great travelers. Besides, what is so unreasonable about supposing that they went back to the place where they had lived before, namely, Rome? Together with ever so many others they returned when the edict of expulsion was no longer in effect. And as to Epaenetus, the fact that he was "the first-fruits of Asia" surely does not mean that he had to remain in Asia for the rest of his life.

c. The warning of 16:17, 18 concerns certain definite individuals, "false teachers" perhaps, who are always and everywhere trying to destroy God's kingdom. That Paul is not withdrawing his favorable estimate of Rome's church is very clear from the context. See verse 19.

It has become clear, therefore, that the arguments against the integrity of the text of Paul's epistle to the Romans are very weak indeed!

For more on the arrangement of the text of Romans 16, in connection with Harry Gamble's study, see Vol. II of the present commentary.

VII.   Its Theme and Summary

Does Romans have a theme? If by "theme" is meant a subject from which the author never digresses, the answer is *No.* This letter touches on a variety of subjects: Paul's desire to visit Rome (1:10), God's wrath (1:18), Adam versus Christ (5:12–21), antinomianism (6:1), soul struggle (7:15–24), present suffering contrasted with future glory (8:18), Israel (chapters 9–11), love (12:9), taxes (13:6), vegetarianism (14:2), the strong and the weak (14:1; 15:1), philanthropy (15:25–27), Spain (15:28), Phoebe (16:1), Satan (16:20).

On the other hand, if by "theme" is meant a central topic, which, having been announced, is subsequently taken up again and again, either as a whole or in part, the answer is *Yes.*

This theme was the product not of human excogitation but of divine implantation in the heart and mind of struggling Saul of Tarsus.

Applicable to him are these poetic lines:

> O long and dark the stairs I trod
> With trembling feet to find my God,
> Gaining a foothold bit by bit,

Then slipping back and losing it.
Never progressing; striving still
With weakening grasp and faltering will,
Bleeding to climb to God, while he
Serenely smiled, unnoting me.
Then came a certain time when I
Loosened my hold and fell thereby;
Down to the lowest step my fall,
As if I had not climbed at all.
Now when I lay despairing there,
Listen . . . a footfall on the stair,
On that same stair where I afraid,
Faltered and fell and lay dismayed.
And lo, when hope had ceased to be,
My God came down the stairs to me.

Anonymous

". . . justified freely by his grace, through the redemption which is in Christ Jesus" (Rom. 3:24).

The theme of Romans, introduced in 1:16, 17 . . . "The righteous shall live by faith . . .", expressed more fully in 3:21–24, 28, reflected in such passages as 5:1; 8:30–34; 9:30–32; 11:23–26; 16:26, is never absent from the writer's mind.

Justification by faith (Rom. 5:1), spread out into "justification by grace through faith" (see 3:22–24; cf. Eph. 2:8), is clearly the theme of Romans. It is also the theme of Galatians. There is a close resemblance between the larger and the smaller epistle. Gen. 15:6, "Abraham believed God, and it was credited to him as righteousness," is quoted in both letters (Rom. 4:3, 9, 22; Gal. 3:6). Cf. James 2:23. Among other verbal resemblances are:

Rom. 1:17 and Gal. 2:16; 3:11	Rom. 13:8 and Gal. 5:14
Rom. 6:6–8 and Gal. 2:20	Rom. 13:13, 14 and Gal. 5:16, 17
Rom. 8:14–17 and Gal. 4:5–7	Rom. 14:12 and Gal. 6:5

Nevertheless, there is also a striking difference between the two. Not only does this difference refer to size and subject matter—the larger epistle containing much material that is not found in the smaller—it pertains also and especially to the manner in which the apostle speaks to the addressees.

Romans sets forth calmly that for every sinner, whether Jew or Gentile, there is salvation full and free through faith in Christ, apart from law works. Galatians, in a tone that is not nearly as calm and at times becomes fiery, defends this glorious gospel against its detractors. Its denunciations are withering.

Chapter
1:1–15   Here in Romans, after a *Prologue,* in which Paul *greets* the Christians in Rome (1:1–7), and informs them that he is *thanking* God

for the fact that their faith is being proclaimed everywhere, and that he is *asking* God to grant him the opportunity to visit and preach the gospel among them (verses 8–15), he announces and develops *the theme* of that gospel as follows:

JUSTIFICATION BY FAITH

1:16—3:31 Justification by faith, apart from the works of the law, is:

1—3   A. Real and Necessary
1. Theme: "The gospel is the power of God for salvation to everyone who exercises faith, . . . as it is written, But the righteous shall live by faith" (1:16, 17).
2. The *Gentiles* need this justification (1:18–32).
3. The *Jews* also need it (2:1—3:8).
4. Accordingly, "there is none righteous, not even one" (3:9–20).
5. "But now, apart from law, a righteousness from God has been revealed, a righteousness through *faith* in Jesus Christ . . ." (3:21–31).

4   B. Scriptural
1. The Example of Abraham (4:1–12).
2. This Example Shows that God's Promise is Realized Through Faith, not Works (4:13–25).

5—8   C. Effective; that is, Producing the Desired Results; Such As:
1a. *Peace and its Concomitants,* including Assurance of Complete Salvation (5:1–11).
1b. The Certainty and Copiousness of Salvation Confirmed by the Parallel Adam—Christ (5:12–21).
2a. *Holiness* (6:1–14).
2b. Who is Y o u r Master? Sin or God? (6:15–23).
3a. *Liberty:* Freedom from the Law (7:1–6).
3b. The Sinner's Relation to God's Law, in the Light of Paul's Own Experience and That of Others Like Him (7:7–13).
3c. Paul's Own Experience and That of Others Like Him (continued): The Wretched Man's Struggle and Victory (7:14–25).
4a. "No Condemnation" for Those in Christ Jesus (8:1–30).
4b. *Super-invincibility,* that is, Being More Than Conquerors (8:31–39).

Having shown that the doctrine of justification—hence salvation—by faith is Real and Necessary (chapters 1–3), Scriptural (chapter 4), and Effective, i.e., fruit-producing (chapters 5–8), Paul proceeds to prove, in chapters 9–11, that it is also Historical, in the sense that in the course of history God's most precious promises were ever intended for, and realized in, the *believing* remnant, that this is true today (while Paul was writing), and will so continue.

Chapters 12–16 contain the *Practical Application* of all this. In other words, these concluding chapters show how those who have been justified (and therefore saved) by God-given faith, should reveal their gratitude in lives of love toward their fellowmen and devotion to their gracious Triune God.

Further details with respect to chapters 9—16—Outline and Explanation of the text—is reserved for N.T.C. on Paul's Epistle to the Romans, Volume II, which is now being prepared.

Commentary

on

The Epistle to the Romans

Chapter 1:1–15

Prologue

Outline

Salutation.
1:1–7

Paul's thanksgiving and desire to visit Rome.
1:8–15

CHAPTER 1:1-15

1 1 Paul, a servant of Christ Jesus, a called apostle, one set apart for the gospel of God, 2 which he promised beforehand through his prophets in (the) sacred Scriptures, 3 concerning his Son, who, according to the flesh was born of the seed of David, 4 but by virtue of[12] the Spirit of holiness, was, by means of the resurrection from the dead, appointed to be the Son of God *invested with power*, namely, Jesus Christ our Lord, 5 through whom and for whose sake we received the gift of apostleship, in order to bring about obedience of faith,[13] among all the Gentiles, 6 including also y o u, the called of Jesus Christ;

7 to all in Rome who are beloved of God, saints by virtue of having been called: Grace to y o u and peace from God our Father and the Lord Jesus Christ.

Salutation
1:1-7

1. Paul, a servant of Christ Jesus, a called apostle, one set apart for the gospel of God...

This is the beginning of Paul's lengthiest opening salutation. For a comparison note the following list which, in an ascending series, indicates the number of words *in the original* for each salutation:

I Thessalonians	19	II Corinthians	41
II Thessalonians	27	Philemon	41
Colossians	28	I Corinthians	55
Ephesians	28 (or 30)	Titus	65
II Timothy	29	Galatians	75
Philippians	32	Romans	93
I Timothy	32		

As in his epistle to Titus so here in Romans Paul introduces himself as a *doulos* (pl. *douloi* in Phil. 1:1) of Christ Jesus. As the English equivalent of *doulos* some prefer—some even insist on—*slave*. It must be granted that such traits as the slave's required absolute submission to his master and thorough dependence on him, as also the master's ownership of and unrestricted authority over his slave, can be applied, though in a far more exalted sense, to the relation between Christ and believers. See, for exam-

---

12. Or: in accordance with
13. Or: based on faith; or: springing from faith

37

ple, I Cor. 3:23; 6:19b, 20. Nevertheless, since with the concept *slave* we generally associate such ideas as involuntary service, forced subjection, and (frequently) harsh treatment, many have, probably correctly, concluded that "slave" is not the best English equivalent in *this* context.

Besides, it should be borne in mind that Paul was "a Hebrew of Hebrews" (Phil. 3:5), thoroughly at home in the Old Testament. Therefore when he calls himself "a *doulos* of Christ Jesus," he is probably reflecting on passages in which Abraham (Gen. 26:24), Moses (Num. 12:7), Joshua (Josh. 24:29), David (II Sam. 7:5), Isaiah (Isa. 20:3), etc., are called Jehovah's *servants*. Is it not even possible that the figure of the wholeheartedly committed Servant described in Isa. 49:1–7; 52:13; 53:11 contributed to the meaning of the word *doulos* here in Rom. 1:1?

Paul presents himself as a servant *of Christ Jesus*.[14] The personal name *Jesus,* meaning either "he will certainly save" (cf. Matt. 1:21), or "Jehovah is salvation," which ultimately amount to the same thing, is preceded by the official designation *Christ* (Anointed). Of this Christ Jesus, Paul is a servant, completely surrendered to his Master.

This servant is at the same time "a called apostle."

Now in the broadest sense an *apostle* (Greek *apostolos,* a term derived from a verb which means *to send, to send away on a commission, to dispatch)* is anyone who is sent or by whom a message is sent; hence, an ambassador, envoy, messenger. In classical Greek the term could refer to a naval expedition, and "an apostolic boat" was a cargo vessel. In later Judaism "apostles" were envoys sent out by the Jerusalem patriarchate to collect tribute from the Jews of the Dispersion. In the New Testament the term takes on a distinctly religious sense. In its widest meaning it refers to any gospel-messenger, anyone who is sent on a spiritual mission, anyone who in that capacity represents his Sender and brings the message of salvation. Thus used, Barnabas, Epaphroditus, Apollos, Silvanus, and Timothy are all called "apostles" (Acts 14:14; I Cor. 4:6, 9; Phil. 2:25; I Thess. 2:6; cf. 1:1; and see also I Cor. 15:7). They all represent God's cause, though in doing so they may also represent certain definite churches whose "apostles" they are called (cf. II Cor. 8:23). Thus Paul and Barnabas represent the church of Antioch (Acts 13:1, 2), and Epaphroditus is Philippi's "apostle" (Phil. 2:25).

But in determining the meaning of the term *apostle* here in Rom. 1:1 it will be far better to study those passages in which it is used in its more usual sense. Occurring ten times in the Gospels, almost thirty times in Acts, more than thirty times in the Pauline epistles (including the five occurrences in the Pastorals), and eight times in the rest of the New Testament, it generally (but note important exception in Heb. 3:1 and the exceptions already indicated) refers to the Twelve and Paul.

14. Why "Christ Jesus" instead of "Jesus Christ"? For a possible answer to this question see N.T.C. on I Tim. 1:1, p. 51.

In that fullest, deepest sense a man is an apostle *for life* and *wherever he goes.* He is clothed with *the authority of* the One who sent him, and that authority concerns both *doctrine and life.* The idea, found in much present-day religious literature, according to which an apostle has no real office, no authority, lacks scriptural support. Anyone can see this for himself by studying such passages as Matt. 16:19; 18:18; 28:18, 19 (note the connection); John 20:23; I Cor. 5:3–5; II Cor. 10:8; I Thess. 2:6.

Paul, then, was an apostle in the richest sense of the term. His apostleship was the same as that of the Twelve. Hence, we speak of "the Twelve and Paul." Paul even stresses the fact that the risen Savior had appeared to *him* just as truly as he had appeared to Cephas (I Cor. 15:5, 8). That same Savior had assigned to him a task so broad and universal that his entire life was henceforth to be occupied with it (Acts 26:16–18).

Yet Paul was definitely *not* one of the Twelve. The idea that the disciples had made a mistake when they had chosen Matthias to take the place of Judas, and that the Holy Spirit later designated Paul as the real substitute, hardly merits consideration (see Acts 1:24). *But if he was not one of the Twelve yet was invested with the same office, what was the relation between him and the Twelve?* The answer is probably suggested by Acts 1:8 and Gal. 2:7–9. On the basis of these passages this answer can be formulated thus: The Twelve, by recognizing Paul as having been specially called to minister to the Gentiles, were in effect carrying out through him their calling to the Gentiles.

The characteristics of full apostleship—the apostleship of the Twelve and Paul—were as follows:

In the first place, the apostles have been chosen, called, and sent forth by Christ himself. They have received their commission directly from him (John 6:70; 13:18; 15:16, 19; Gal. 1:6).

Secondly, they are qualified for their tasks by Jesus, and have been ear-and-eye witnesses of his words and deeds; specifically, they are the witnesses of his resurrection (Acts 1:8, 21, 22; I Cor. 9:1; 15:8; Gal. 1:12; Eph. 3:2–8; I John 1:1–3). Note: though Acts 1:21, 22 does not apply to Paul, the other passages do apply to him. Paul too had seen the Lord!

Thirdly, they have been endowed in a special measure with the Holy Spirit, and it is this Holy Spirit who leads them into all the truth (Matt. 10:20; John 14:26; 15:26; 16:7–14; 20:22; I Cor. 2:10–13; 7:40; I Thess. 4:8).

Fourthly, God blesses their work, confirming its value by means of signs and miracles, and giving them much fruit upon their labors (Matt. 10:1, 8; Acts 2:43; 3:2; 5:12–16; Rom. 15:18, 19; I Cor. 9:2; II Cor. 12:12; Gal. 2:8).

Fifthly, their office is not restricted to a local church, neither does it extend over a short period of time; on the contrary, it is for the entire church and for life (Acts 26:16–18; II Tim. 4:7, 8).

Note "a *called* apostle." This surely is much better than either "called an apostle" or "called to be or to become an apostle." What the original means is that Paul was an apostle by virtue of having been effectively called by God to this office. Similarly the people he addresses were *saints* by virtue of having been called, "saints by (divine) vocation." See on verse 7.

As a called apostle, Paul had been "set apart for the gospel of God." From the beginning he had been designed by God for the proclamation of the gospel. Note especially Gal. 1:15, where the apostle expresses himself as follows, ". . . it pleased him who separated me from my mother's womb and called me through his grace, to reveal his Son in me, in order that I might preach his gospel among the Gentiles. . . ."

Paul speaks of "the gospel *of God*" or "*God's* gospel." And it is indeed the God-spell, the *spell* or *story* that tells us what *God* has done to save sinners. For that very reason it is an *evangel* or *message of good tidings*. It is the glad news of salvation which God addresses to a world lost in sin. Not what *we* must do but what *God* in Christ has done for us is the most prominent part of that good news. This is clear from the manner in which the noun *evangel* and the related verb, *to proclaim an evangel, to bring good news,* are used in the Old Testament. See LXX on Ps. 40:9; 96:2; Isa. 40:9; 52:7; 61:1; and Nah. 1:15.

Here in Rom. 1 the term "gospel of God" (verse 1) has two modifiers, one in verse 2, the other in verse 3 f.

2. ... which he promised beforehand through his prophets in (the) sacred Scriptures ...

This passage is indeed very important. It shows us how Paul, inspired by the Holy Spirit, wants us to regard the Old Testament. He clearly views the old and the new dispensation as belonging together. He regards (a) the Old Testament and (b) the good news of salvation as proclaimed by Jesus and his messengers, as being a unit. Speaking by and large we can say that the Old Testament contains the promises; the New Testament shows how these promises had been, were being, and were going to be fulfilled.

When Paul says "his prophets" he has reference, of course, not only to such holy men of God as Isaiah, Jeremiah, etc., but also to Moses, Samuel, David, etc. To speak in language which even children can understand:

> The Old is by the New explained,
> The New is in the Old contained.

or similarly:

> The New is in the Old concealed,
> The Old is by the New revealed.

What Paul writes here is exactly what Jesus also proclaimed; and this not only in those well-known passages: Luke 24:25–32, 44–48, to which reference is often made in this connection, but certainly also in Luke 4:21 (in the context 4:16–30), "Today, in y o u r very hearing, this passage of Scripture is being fulfilled," and in Luke 22:37, "For I tell y o u, what has been written must be fulfilled in me: 'And he was numbered with the transgressors.' Yes, that passage about me is reaching its fulfillment." For more on this subject see N.T.C. on Luke, p. 977, and on Philippians, pp. 81–85.

The point to be emphasized here is that both Jesus (see John 10:35; 17:17) and Paul esteemed the Old Testament very highly. They deemed it to be *sacred*. When a person rejects the Old Testament, he is therefore also rejecting Jesus and Paul!

We now proceed to the second modifier of the term "the gospel of God." It is this:

3, 4. ... concerning his Son, who, according to the flesh was born of the seed of David, but by virtue of [or: in accordance with] the Spirit of holiness, was, by means of the resurrection from the dead, appointed to be the Son of God *invested with power*, **namely, Jesus Christ our Lord ...**

Interpreters differ rather sharply in their explanation of these lines. My own interpretation is based, to a large extent, on my conclusions with respect to the meaning of the original. So, I invite students of the Greek to study the footnote.[15]

---

15. The following questions should be asked and answered:

a. What is the meaning of the acc. of σάρξ as here used?

b. Does the verb ὁρίζω (of which the gen. s. m. aor. pass. participle appears here) have the meaning *to declare* (as in certain translations) or *to appoint*?

c. Does the phrase ἐν δυνάμει modify υἱοῦ θεοῦ or ὁρισθέντος?

d. What is the meaning of πνεῦμα ἁγιωσύνης?

e. What is the meaning of κατά before πνεῦμα ἁγιωσύνης?

f. Do κατὰ σάρκα and κατὰ ἁγιωσύνης form a contrast between two elements within Christ's human nature? Do they refer to Christ's human versus his divine nature?

g. What is the meaning of ἐξ in verse 4?

Answers:

a. This word has a variety of meanings in Paul's epistles. For the list see footnote 187, p. 217. Meaning f. seems to be intended here, for it was according to his human nature (not his divine nature) that Jesus was a descendant of David.

b. Elsewhere in the New Testament this verb uniformly has the sense *to determine, decree, appoint*. See also NT.C. on Luke 22:22, p. 969. There is no good reason to weaken this meaning to "to declare." Nevertheless, *to declare, make known,* may well be included in *to appoint,* as here used.

c. This phrase probably modifies the immediately preceding words; hence, "Son of God invested with power." But even if it is construed with the verb, the resultant meaning would be almost the same.

d. The term "the Spirit of holiness" is derived from Isa. 63:10 f. Cf. Ps. 51:11. The reference here in Rom. 1:4 is to the Holy (divine, exalted) Spirit.

e. As one of the meanings of κατά, followed by the acc., L.N.T.(Th.), p. 328 gives *through, by virtue of*. This connotation of *agency* became especially widespread in later Koine Greek. Perhaps there is a combination here of agency and standard of measurement. The rendering "by virtue of" may be as good as any.

f. Definitely not. There is indeed a contrast, but that contrast is between (a) what Christ *was* as to his human nature, and (b) what he *became* by virtue of the Spirit of holiness. In other words, the contrast is between Christ's state of humiliation and his state of exaltation. One cannot very well place an *element* of Christ's human nature over against the third *Person* of the Holy Trinity.

g. We must be very careful here. The meaning "since" (hence, "since the resurrection from the dead") cannot be entirely ruled out. It may be correct. See Mark 10:20 "since (or from) my youth." However, the meaning "because of," for which see Rev. 16:10 ("They gnawed their tongues because of pain") would seem to be somewhat more natural here.

41

Paul confesses Jesus to be God's Son. He means that the Savior was God's Son entirely apart from and antecedently to his assumption of the human nature. *He is the Son of God from all eternity; hence, he is God.*

This confession harmonizes with what the apostle says elsewhere. Thus, in Rom. 9:5, according to what is probably the best reading and interpretation, Paul calls Jesus "over all God blest forever." In Titus 2:13 he describes him as "our great God and Savior." He is, in fact, "the One in whom all the fulness of the godhead is concentrated" (Col. 2:9). Cf. Phil. 2:6.

Now it is this Son who, without laying aside his divine nature, assumed the human nature. Though he was rich, yet for our sake he became poor, in order that we through his poverty might become rich (II Cor. 8:9). In the fulness of time he was born of a woman (Gal. 4:4). Throughout his earthly sojourn he was indeed "a man of sorrows and acquainted with grief" (Isa. 53:3). Exactly how it was possible for the completely intact and glorious divine nature of the Savior to dwell in intimate union with his human nature, the latter burdened with the load of our guilt and all the unspeakable agonies this condition implied, surpasses human comprehension.

Our passage also informs us that with respect to this human nature Jesus "was born of the seed of David." This was in fulfilment of the oft repeated promise. See II Sam. 7:12, 13, 16; Ps. 89:3, 4, 19, 24; 132:17; Isa. 11:1–5, 10; Jer. 23:5, 6; 30:9; 33:14–16; Ezek. 34:23, 24; 37:24; Matt. 1:1; Luke 1:27, 32, 33, 69; 3:23–31; John 7:42; Acts 2:30; II Tim. 2:8; Rev. 5:5; 22:16. Had he not been a descendant of David he could not have been the Messiah, for prophecy concerning him must be fulfilled.

His state of humiliation, however, could not last forever. As a reward for his willingness to endure it, he was, by virtue of the Spirit of holiness, appointed to be the Son of God "in power" or "invested with power."

With respect to Christ's "appointment" from eternity, effectuated in time, see Ps. 2:7, 8; Acts 13:33; Heb. 1:5; 5:5. The implied exaltation took place by means of his resurrection from the dead; that is, his glorious resurrection was the first important step in his journey to glory. It was followed by Christ's ascension, coronation, and act of pouring out the Holy Spirit.

In the expression "he was appointed to be the Son of God *invested with power,*" all emphasis falls on the words in italics. As has already been pointed out, from all eternity he was the Son of God, but during his period of humiliation his power, in its fullest degree, was, as it were, hidden from view. By means of his glorious resurrection his investiture with power not only was enhanced but also began to shine forth in all its glory. The expression here used reminds us of Peter's statement, made in a very similar context, namely, "Without a shadow of doubt, therefore, let all the house of Israel be assured that God has made him both Lord and Christ, this Jesus whom y o u crucified" (Acts 2:36). That statement did not imply that before his resurrection Jesus was not Lord and Christ. It meant that the power, majesty, and glory of his exalted office was now beginning to shine forth in all its augmented brilliance.

Now Rom. 1:4 informs us that this manifestation of Christ's investiture with power was brought about by "the Spirit of holiness." This "Spirit of holiness" must not be identified with the *spiritual* over against the *physical* element in Christ's human nature, or with his *divine* as contrasted with his *human* nature, but with the Holy Spirit, the third person in the divine Trinity.

But though the third person is distinct from the second, the two, the Holy Spirit and Christ, are most intimately related. Says Dr. H. Bavinck (my translation from the Dutch):

"To be sure, the Spirit of holiness was already dwelling in Christ before his resurrection; in fact, from the moment of his conception, for he was conceived by the Holy Spirit (Luke 1:35), was filled with the Holy Spirit (Luke 4:1), received him without measure (John 3:34) . . . But this glory which Christ possessed inwardly, was not able to reveal itself outwardly. He was flesh, and because of the weakness of the flesh he was put to death on the cross (II Cor. 13:4). But in death he laid aside this weakness, and severed every connection with sin and death. God, who, for our sake, delivered up to death his own Son, also raised him from death, through his Spirit, who, as Spirit of holiness, dwells in Christ and in all believers (Rom. 8:11). He raised him in order that from that moment on he would no longer live in the weakness of the flesh but in the power of the Spirit."[16]

It was because of this great power that the exalted divine-and-human Savior from his heavenly throne poured out the Spirit upon his church, imparting strength, conviction, courage, and illumination to those who previously had been very weak. Also it was this energy that enabled him to bring about conversions by the thousands, so that even according to the testimony of enemies "the world was being turned upside down" (Acts 17:6). Moreover, it was as a result of the exertion of this mighty influence that the barrier between Jew and Gentile, a wall so formidable that its removal must have seemed impossible, was actually broken down. And it was on account of this force that the glorious gospel of the risen and exalted Savior began to penetrate every sphere of life and is still doing this today.

The impartation of *life* is generally ascribed to the Holy Spirit:

> Thy Spirit, O Lord, makes life to abound,
> The earth is renewed, and fruitful the ground;
> To God ascribe glory and wisdom and might,
> Let God in his creatures forever delight.

> See Ps. 104:30, 31

---

16. *Gereformeerde Dogmatiek*, Kampen, 1918, third edition, Vol. III, pp. 488, 489.

If, then, the *impartation* of life is ascribed to the Holy Spirit, is it not logical that here in Rom. 1:4 the *renewal* of life—Christ's resurrection—is also ascribed to him?

Paul concludes this summary of names of the One who is the heart and center of "the gospel of God" (verse 1) by adding, "Jesus Christ our Lord." This meaningful title shows what the One who is being described means to the apostle; in fact, to the church in general, and to that of Rome in particular. Note "*God's* Son" (verses 3, 4a) ". . . *our* Lord" (verse 4b). Observe also the combination of the personal name Jesus=Savior with the official name Christ=Anointed One. Adoration: *Lord* (Owner, Ruler, Provider) is placed side by side with Appropriation: *our* Lord. It is by means of "Jesus Christ our Lord" that the true gospel reaches its climax. Apart from him salvation is impossible. With him as our joyfully recognized Sovereign, the object of our trust and love, damnation is unthinkable. See Rom. 8:1.

Having already introduced himself in verse 1, Paul now adds some more information about himself; that is, about himself in relation to "Jesus Christ our Lord" from whom he had received his important commission:

5. ... through whom and for whose sake we received the gift of apostleship, in order to bring about obedience of faith, among all the Gentiles ...

Literally the passage reads, "through whom and for whose sake we received *grace and apostleship.*" Many translators have retained these words, in that order, in their versions. So interpreted, Paul would be saying that he had received two things: (a) grace; that is, God's unmerited favor, imparting salvation, plus (b) apostleship.[17] This interpretation may be correct.

Personally I favor the other view, namely, that what we have here in verse 5 is an instance of *hendiadys* (the "*one* by means of *two*" figure of speech; that is: *one* concept is expressed by *two* nouns connected by *and*), and that the meaning is, accordingly, "the gift (or grace) of apostleship." I favor this interpretation and translation for the following reasons:

1. In the present context it is hard to see why Paul would have to emphasize that he is a man saved by grace.

2. Also in Rom. 15:15, 16 the "grace" mentioned is Paul's ministry, his apostolic office.[18] And cf. 12:6.

When Paul says, "*We* received," he is in all probability using the literary or writer's plural.[19] If so, he is referring to himself, not also to others.

When did Paul receive from "Jesus Christ our Lord" the gift of apostle-

---

17. This view is defended by J. Murray, *op. cit.*, Vol. I, p. 13; also by S. Greijdanus, in another precious work, *De Brief van den Apostle Paulus aan de Gemeente te Rome (Kommentaar op het Nieuwe Testament)*, Amsterdam, 1933, Vol. I, p. 67. It is favored by many other commentators and by most translators.

18. This view (heniadys) is also favored by the following commentators, among others: Bruce, Cranfield, Ridderbos, Van Leeuwen and Jacobs; and by such translations as: Berkeley Version, Good News for Modern Man, Knox, Moffat, N.E.B., etc.

19. See Gram. N.T., pp. 406, 407.

ship, with the implied mandate to exercise it? Many passages occur to the mind; for example: Acts 9:1-19 (note especially verse 15); 18:9, 10; 22:6-21; 26:12-18; Rom. 15:15, 16. Among all of them there are two that deserve more than passing notice:

In the first, Jesus is represented as addressing Paul in connection with the unforgettable vision the latter received while as a relentless persecutor he was on his way to Damascus. In answer to Paul's question, "Who art thou, Lord?" the Lord answered, "I am Jesus, whom you are persecuting. But arise and stand on your feet, for I have appeared to you for this purpose, to appoint you (to be) a servant and a witness of what you have seen of me and what I will show you. I will rescue you from your own people and from the Gentiles, to whom I am sending you, to open their eyes in order that they may turn from darkness to light and from the dominion of Satan to God, so as to receive forgiveness of sins and a place among those who are sanctified by faith in me" (Acts 26:15b-18).

In the second, which reports what happened shortly afterward, while Paul was praying in the temple, it is stated that he fell into a trance and heard the Lord saying to him, "Depart, for I will send you far away to the Gentiles" (Acts 22:21).

In both of these passages the apostle is described as a man who received his apostolic mission from Jesus Christ. See also N.T.C. on Gal. 1:1.

Note "through whom and for whose sake." This means that not only is it true that Paul received his apostleship from or through Christ, but it is also a fact that he received it in order that by means of it he might proclaim the name of Christ and promote his cause.

The purpose for which Paul was appointed was to bring about *obedience of faith.* Such obedience is based on faith and springs from faith. In fact, so very closely are faith and obedience connected that they may be compared to inseparable identical twins. When you see the one you see the other. A person cannot have genuine faith without having obedience, nor vice versa.[20]

A striking illustration of this fact is offered by the apostle himself in two synonymous passages, the one concerning *faith;* the other, concerning *obedience:*

Rom. 1:8, ". . . I thank my God through Jesus Christ for y o u all, because y o u r faith is being proclaimed throughout the entire world."

Rom. 16:19, "For the fame of y o u r obedience has reached everyone." It is by means of obedience of faith that a person embraces Christ.

After Paul has written ". . . in order to bring about obedience of faith among all the Gentiles," he continues:

6. . . . including also y o u, the called of Jesus Christ . . .

It is clear that Paul, who in verses 1-5 has been speaking not only about

---

20. In the Dutch language the two are sometimes combined into one word: *geloofsgehoorzaamheid.*

himself and his apostolic office but also about the Christ-centered gospel, now turns specifically to those whom he is addressing. To be sure, they had never been absent from his mind. But he now mentions them as those who were definitely included in the number of people for whom the gospel was intended.

Speaking by and large, the apostle rejoices in being able to state that Rome's membership had not only been *invited* to embrace Jesus Christ as Lord and Savior, but had also, by God's sovereign grace, *responded favorably* to the invitation. Paul is speaking therefore about what is often termed "the effectual call" (Rom. 8:28, 30; 9:24 I Cor. 1:9, 24, 26, etc.).

Implied in these words is also the fact that Paul is deeply conscious of the fact that he has a definite, a very special, right to address these people. Is he not "the apostle (par excellence) to the Gentiles"? In addition to the immediately preceding verse (verse 5) see also Rom. 11:13; 15:16; Gal. 2:8, 9; Eph. 3:8; I Tim. 2:7. And is not the most natural implication of the words "among all the Gentiles, including also y o u" (or "among whom y o u are also") this, that those whom Paul here addresses were mostly Gentiles by race, and had at one time been Gentiles also by religion? See *Introduction,* Section IV.

When Paul names those he is addressing "the called of Jesus Christ," he means "those who by virtue of having been effectively called belong to Jesus Christ, are his people." They are even now his very own, having been given to him by the Father. See John 10:27, 28. Cf. John 17:6, 9, 24; Titus 2:14; I Peter 2:9. See also I Cor. 6:19, 20. This inclusion in God's family is also implied in the words:

7. . . . to all in Rome who are beloved of God, saints by virtue of having been called: . . .

By means of the phrase "to all in Rome who are beloved of God" Paul continues what he had begun in verse 6, namely, to describe those whom he addresses. This time he includes in his description the name of the place where they are living, *Rome.* For the reason why we believe that the words "in Rome" are a genuine part of the text see *Introduction VI,* under *As to 1,* p. 27.

As to the expression "beloved of God" (or "loved by God"), a study of the book of Romans in its entirety reveals that for Paul these words indicate not only that God *now* loves the believers in Rome but also that he had loved them from all eternity (cf. Jer. 31:3), and would never stop loving them (Rom. 8:31–39). We know that this is the apostle's view, for, as he sees it, God's concern for his children is an unbreakable chain (Rom. 8:29, 30). It reaches from one eternity to the next. It is a love that *precedes, accompanies, and follows* their love for God. And, of course, even men's love for God must not be viewed as an independent entity. Rather, "We love because he first loved us" (I *John* 4:19). The same idea is certainly implied in *Paul's* teaching on this subject. See Rom. 5:5–11; 8:28.

Paul adds, "saints by virtue of having been called."

46

Though *interpreters* have spared no efforts in calling attention to *this* meaning of the original,[21] *translators* continue to offer: "called to be saints." But that is not what Paul says. He is telling the Roman Christians what, by grace, they *are* even now. He is stating that something has happened to them: they have been effectively called. *By this inner or effective call is meant that operation of the Holy Spirit whereby he so applies the gospel to the minds and hearts of sinners that they become aware of their guilt, begin to understand their need of Jesus Christ, and embrace him as their Lord and Savior.* Thus these people become *saints,* that is, people who have been "set apart" in order to live lives to the glory of the Triune God as revealed in Christ Jesus.

As mentioned earlier, Paul had been thoroughly drilled in the contents of what we today call the Old Testament. He knew that during the old dispensation there were certain places, objects, and people that had been "set apart" and "consecrated" for the service of God; for example, the holy place (I Kings 8:10) and the holy of holies (Exod. 26:33), the tithe of the land (Lev. 27:30), the priests (Lev. 21:6, 7), and even the Israelites as a whole, viewed in distinction from the other nations (Exod. 19:6; Lev. 20:26; Deut. 7:6; Dan. 7:22). It is this idea which in the New Testament is applied to Christians generally. *They* are the "elect race, royal priesthood, holy nation, people for God's own possession" of the new dispensation, chosen to declare God's praises (I Peter 2:9). A saint, then, is a person whose guilt has been blotted out on the basis of Christ's substitutionary atonement, and who, consequently, by means of the power of the indwelling Spirit, strives to live to God's glory. He is one who has been *set apart* and *consecrated* for service.

Paul, then, is stating that the addressees are such people. They are saints by virtue of having been effectively called.

But now, having rejected the rendering "called *to be* saints," because it is wrong, it is but fair to point out that this very translation, though far from satisfactory, does contain one element of value. It points to the fact that a person who, by God's sovereign grace and power, has become a saint cannot rest on his laurels. On the contrary, now being a saint, he should endeavor day after day after day to live as a saint should live. This is true all the more because as long as he is still on this earth, he remains a sinner. He should do his utmost—not by his own power, for he has none, but by the power of the Holy Spirit—*to be* "holy and without blemish before him" (Eph. 1:4). If he is indeed a saint, he will also actually do this. Thus we see that even a faulty translation of Rom. 1:7 can point in the right direction.

Paul has called these Romans "the called of Jesus Christ, beloved of God, saints." "Why," we may well ask, "is he so generous in his praise for these

---

21. With minor variations one finds this translation in the commentaries on Romans authored by the following, among others: Bruce, Coltman, Cranfield, Denney, Erdman, Greijdanus, Hobbs, Murray, Ridderbos.

people and so eager to assure them that he loves them . . . and even better, that God loves them?" Probably because he knows, and they know, that he, Paul, has not founded this church. So he is, as it were, saying, "I love y o u as sincerely and deeply as if I myself had been the founder of y o u r church. And I consider myself y o u r apostle; yes, y o u r very own."

Grace to y o u and peace from God our Father and the Lord Jesus Christ.

This is the form of the salutation found in most of Paul's epistles. In Colossians and in I Thessalonians there is an abbreviation; in I and II Timothy there is an expansion, the word "mercy" having been inserted between "grace" and "peace." In Titus the word "our Savior" has been substituted for "our Lord."

What we see here in Romans, etc., is that the Greek greeting form has been combined with the Jewish form. The Greek says *Chaire!* = "Joy to you!" The Jew says *Shalom!* = "Peace!" Not only, however, have these two greetings been joined by Paul but they have at the same time been transformed into one distinctively *Christian* salutation. Note, in this connection, that *chaire* has been changed into *charis* = *grace*.

Grace, as here used, is God's spontaneous, unmerited favor in action, his freely bestowed lovingkindness in operation, bestowing salvation upon guilt-laden sinners who turn to him for refuge. It is, as it were, the rainbow round about the very throne out of which proceed flashes of lightning, rumblings, and peals of thunder (Rev. 4:3, 5). We think of the Judge who not only remits the penalty but also cancels the guilt of the offender and even adopts him as his own son.

Grace brings *peace.* The latter is both a *state,* that of reconciliation with God, and a *condition,* the inner conviction that consequently all is well. It is the great blessing which Christ by his atoning sacrifice bestowed upon the church (John 14:27), and it surpasses all understanding (Phil. 4:7). It is not the reflection of an unclouded sky in the tranquil waters of a picturesque lake, but rather the cleft of the rock in which the Lord hides his children when the storm is raging (think of the theme of Zephaniah's prophecy); or, to change the figure somewhat but with retention of the main thought, it is the hiding place under the wings, to which the hen gathers her brood, so that the little chicks are safe while the storm bursts loose in all its fury upon herself.

Now this grace and this peace have their origin in God *our* (precious word of appropriation and inclusion!) Father, and have been merited for believers by him who is the great Master-Owner-Conqueror ("Lord"), Savior ("Jesus"), and Office-Bearer ("Christ"), and who, because of his threefold anointing "is able to save to the uttermost them that draw near to God through him" (Heb. 7:25).

For further details about certain aspects of Paul's opening salutations see N.T.C. on I and II Thessalonians, pp. 37–45; on Philippians, pp. 43–49; and on I and II Timothy and Titus, pp. 49–56; 339–344.

8 To begin with, I thank my God through Jesus Christ for y o u all, because y o u r faith is being talked about throughout the entire world. 9 For God, whom I serve from the heart[22] in the gospel of his Son, is my witness, how unceasingly I make mention of y o u 10 at all times in my prayers, asking if perhaps now at last, by God's will, the way may be opened for me to come to y o u. 11 For I am yearning to see y o u, in order that I may impart some spiritual gift to y o u, so that y o u may be strengthened—12 I mean that while (I am) among y o u, we may be mutually encouraged by each other's faith, both y o u r s and mine. 13 I do not want y o u to be unaware, brothers, that many times I planned to come to y o u—but have been prevented until now—in order that I might have some fruit among y o u also, just as (I have had) among the rest of the Gentiles. 14 To both Greeks and barbarians, to both learned and unlearned,[23] I am a debtor; 15 hence my eagerness to preach the gospel also to y o u in Rome.

Paul's thanksgiving and desire to visit Rome
1:8-15

8. To begin with, I thank my God through Jesus Christ for y o u all, because y o u r faith is being talked about throughout the entire world.
The Prologue proceeds in the usual manner; that is, with the apostle's thanksgiving. See also I Cor. 1:4-9; Eph. 1:15, 16; Phil. 1:3-8; Col. 1:3-8; I Thess. 1:2-10; II Thess. 1:3-10; I Tim. 1:12-17; II Tim. 1:3-5; Philem. 4, 5.

"I thank my God." For this author God was not a philosophical abstraction but a real Friend. Cf. Ps. 25:14; James 2:23. God was the object of Paul's trust and love, the One to whom he owed everything. Was it not God who had changed this bitter persecutor into an enthusiastic promoter of the gospel? Therefore, to appreciate the meaning of the designation "*my* God" and the emotions that must have surged through the apostle's heart when he wrote this, one should read such passages as Acts 9:3-8; 27:23 ("the God whose I am, whom also I serve"); I Cor. 15:9; Gal. 1:13 f.; Eph. 3:8; and I Tim. 1:12-17.

"... through Jesus Christ." It was through him that blessings had been received (see the preceding context, verses 4-6). Therefore also through him thanksgiving must be returned. This circle must never be broken! Divine blessings descending from heaven should ascend back to heaven in the form of grateful acknowledgment. See Ps. 50:15.

"... for y o u all," not only for those whom Paul had met or with whom he had become acquainted and whom he mentions by name in 16:3-15, but for the entire congregation.

"... because y o u r faith is being talked about throughout the entire world." Cf. Col. 1:6, I Thess. 1:8. This is understandable, especially in view of the fact that Rome was the capital, the metropolis, of "the world" known to Paul. Ever so many people had contact with Rome, either directly or

---

22. Literally: in my spirit
23. Or: to both wise and foolish

through friends, relatives, business associates, etc. The fact that in the very heart of pagan Rome there were those who worshiped the true God was indeed a worthy topic for conversation, an adequate reason for joyful thanksgiving.

9, 10. For God, whom I serve from the heart [or: in my spirit] in the gospel of his Son, is my witness, how unceasingly I make mention of y o u at all times in my prayers, asking if perhaps now at last, by God's will, the way may be opened for me to come to y o u.

"God . . . is my witness." In order that the believers in Rome may know how earnestly Paul prays for them and how deeply he yearns to see them, he, for confirmation of what he writes, appeals to the omniscient God, who cannot lie, and who judges human hearts and motives. Cf. I Sam. 15:29; Jer. 11:20; II Tim. 2:13; Titus 1:2; Heb. 6:18.

"God, whom I serve from the heart." The word used in the original refers to service of a distinctly religious kind. Often it amounts to *worship* (Matt. 4:10; Luke 1:74; Heb. 9:9, 14; Rev. 7:15; 22:3), though the object of such service or worship is not always the true God who has revealed himself in Jesus Christ. In a few cases the indicated activity amounts to *idolatry* (Acts 7:42; Rom. 1:25). With Paul the object of this service is the One he calls "my God" (verse 8), or, as here in verse 9, simply "God." When the apostle states "whom I serve *in my spirit*" (thus literally), he probably means "from the heart," that is, "with sincere devotion of heart" (Calvin).

. . . (whom I serve) . . . "in the gospel of his Son." Several interpreters insert the word "preaching" or "proclaiming" between "in" and "the gospel." If questioned about this, they might appeal to verse 15: "hence my eagerness *to preach the gospel* also to y o u in Rome." Undoubtedly also here in verse 9 the reference is mainly to gospel preaching. Nevertheless, the expression "I serve God in the gospel" may well have a somewhat broader connotation. Does not Paul serve God in the gospel of his Son also *when he prays* that the seed sown may fall into good soil, *when he comforts an individual,* and, above all, *when he dedicates his entire life and all his talents to God?*

Note "the gospel *of his Son,"* for it is by means of the latter's incarnation, life, death, resurrection, ascension, coronation, intercession, and pouring out of the Spirit (Acts 2:33), that believers obtain the promised blessings.

With respect to the rest of the sentence, it is probably advisable to read this first without insertion of any comma (reserving the phrase "by God's will" for later comment). Note, therefore, the following:

". . . how unceasingly I make mention of y o u at all times in my prayers asking if perhaps now at last . . . the way may be opened for me to come to y o u."

Where shall we place the comma? Our first inclination is probably to place it after the words "how unceasingly I make mention of y o u." Our reason for wishing to place it there is that otherwise the sentence results in an apparent redundance: "unceasingly . . . at all times." With the comma placed after ". . . of y o u," the sentence would read: "God is my witness how unceasingly I make mention of y o u, at all times in my prayers asking if perhaps now at last . . . the way may be opened for me to come to y o u."[24]

Though I respect those who favor this construction, and highly regard their books, I cannot agree. By apparently solving one problem, are they not creating a bigger one? It is difficult to believe that Paul meant to convey the thought that whenever he prayed he was always asking the Lord to lead him to Rome! Besides, so construed, does not the expression "how unceasingly I make mention of y o u" hang in the air? This unceasingly making mention of these people would then be introduced by an expression that almost amounts to an oath, as if merely mentioning them, without the modifier "in my prayers," were that important!

I believe, therefore, that the comma should be placed after "in my prayers." What the apostle *is* emphasizing is that his habit of constantly including the Roman believers in his prayers has not suffered any letup.[25]

"asking if perhaps," etc. As pointed out in *Introduction V*, Paul is not at all sure that he will ever reach Rome. See also 15:31.

". . . now at last." The restless eagerness of a heart filled with love and longing causes Paul to write as he does.

". . . by God's will." It is clear from Acts 18:21; Rom. 15:32; I Cor. 1:1; 4:19; 16:7 that for Paul *Deo volente* was not an empty phrase. The constant and voluntary act of subjecting himself to God's sovereign intention for his (Paul's) life and labors was that which sustained him in all his trials. II Cor. 12:7–10 contains a striking illustration of this attitude of wholehearted, unconditional submission. The phrase sometimes heard, namely, "God willing *or not willing*," would never have proceeded from Paul's lips or occurred to his mind. The truth expressed so beautifully in passages like Rom. 8:28–39 prevented this from ever happening. *How Christ-like this attitude!* See Matt. 26:39, 42; Mark 14:36; Luke 22:41, 42.

". . . the way may be opened," that is, the opportunity may, by divine arrangement, present itself.

Why was Paul so eager to visit the church in Rome? The answer is found in verses 11–15; also in 15:24. Since this matter has been discussed in the *Introduction, Section V,* it is not necessary to elaborate.

11, 12. For I am yearning to see y o u, in order that I may impart some spiritual gift to y o u, so that y o u may be strengthened—I mean that while (I am) among y o u, we may be mutually encouraged by each other's faith, both y o u r s and mine.

" . . . some spiritual gift." Paul expresses himself very modestly here. He is

---

24. For this construction see the following, slightly varying, translations: A.R.V., N.A.S., Phillips, N.E.B.; and consult the commentaries written by (respectively): Greijdanus, Hodge, Murray, Lekkerkerker, to mention only a few.

25. For this interpretation, again with variations, see the following translations: A.V., R.S.V., N.I.V., and commentaries by Lange, Cranfield, Ridderbos, etc.

referring to spiritual strengthening in general, not to the impartation of any specific charismatic gift, such as speaking in tongues, etc.

This modesty or humility on the part of the author is also evident from the use of the passive voice: "that y o u may be strengthened," that is, by *God*.

And especially does this attractive trait—namely humility, "that low sweet root, from which all heavenly virtues shoot" (Moore)—reveal itself in the final line, in which the apostle places himself on a level with the Roman believers, by stating that his presence in Rome will mean *mutual* encouragement; as if to say, "My faith, as well as y o u r s, is in need of strengthening. Y o u will be a blessing to me; I to y o u." Says Calvin, "Note to what degree of modesty his pious heart submitted itself, so that he did not disdain to seek confirmation from inexperienced beginners. He means what he says, too, for there is no one so void of gifts in the Church of Christ who is unable to contribute something to our benefit. Ill will and pride, however, prevent our deriving such fruit from one another."

13. I do not want y o u to be unaware, brothers, that many times I planned to come to y o u—but have been prevented until now—in order that I might have some fruit among y o u also, just as (I have had) among the rest of the Gentiles.

"I do not want y o u to be unaware." This expression occurs also in Rom. 11:25; I Cor. 10:1; 12:1; II Cor. 1:8; and I Thess. 4:13. It is a kind of litotes; i.e., a figure of speech in which something is expressed and even emphasized by the negation of its opposite. For example, "not a few" probably means "many" or even "very many." So what Paul means in the present connection is, "I want y o u to take special note of the fact that. . . ."

" . . . brothers." "All men are brothers" is a common saying. Though in a certain sense this cannot be denied, it is not what Paul had in mind. He is speaking about "brothers *in Christ*," about "those who together belong to *The Family of God*." See N.T.C. on Ephesians, pp. 165–170. In the vocabulary of Paul the word "brothers" occurs with great frequency; in fact, slightly more than 100 times. In Romans it is found 14 times. The fact that what the apostle generally has in mind when he uses the term is "those who are united in a common bond of Christian fellowship" is especially clear from such passages as I Cor. 15:58; Col. 1:2; I Tim. 6:2.

Also at this point, the recognition of *The Family of God*, whose members are "brothers" and "sisters," Paul is following the teaching and example of Christ. See Matt. 12:50; Mark 3:35; Heb. 2:11.

" . . . that many times I planned to come to y o u." This can mean no less than that there had actually been several occasions when Paul had made serious plans to visit the church in Rome. When had this happened? During a previous stay in Corinth? In connection with the apostle's lengthy ministry in Ephesus? We do not know. What we do know, however, is that Paul, by writing this, is revealing to the believers in Rome that his interest in and love for them was not born yesterday. On the contrary, he has heard many reports about them, has repeatedly remembered them in his prayers, is still doing this (verse 9), is filled with tenderness toward them, and is again (as often previously) planning to visit them.

It is clear that "but have been prevented until now" is a parenthesis. What was it that had blocked these planned trips? It is possible that 15:22—especially in view of its immediately following context—points in the direction of an answer.

The sentence, "I do not want y o u to be unaware, brothers, that many times I planned to come to y o u" continues as follows: "in order that I might have some fruit among y o u also . . ." In Paul's thinking what was included in this *fruit?* Growth in spiritual knowledge? That the apostle considered this important is clear from such passages as Eph. 1:17; 4:13; Col. 1:9, 10. And certainly the fruit he himself mentions in Gal. 5:22, 23—love, joy, peace, longsuffering (or patience), kindness, goodness, faithfulness, meekness (or gentleness), self-control, and similar graces—should be added.

When Paul mentioned "fruit," could he also have been thinking about conversions to the Christian religion, whether directly from paganism, or from paganism via Judaism? Some commentators deny this. Yet, in view of I Cor. 9:22, is it at all possible to exclude this type of fruit from the harvest Paul had in mind?

What is important in this connection is to note, once again, how very close is the relationship between the mind of Christ and the mind of Paul. Did not also our Lord emphasize the necessity of fruitbearing? See John 15:1–8. Add Matt. 9:36–38; 11:28; John 4:35; 7:37, 38.

" . . . in order that I might have some fruit among y o u also, just as (I have had) among the rest of the Gentiles." It will never do to skip this statement, as if it were of no importance. Nor is it satisfactory to dismiss it after having commented that evidently the church in Rome consisted for the most part of Gentiles, though that inference is probably warranted. See *Introduction, IV.* It would appear to me that the real lesson conveyed by verse 13 is once again Paul's modesty. "Some fruit . . . among the rest of the Gentiles." What a humble manner of describing the rich and abundant harvest of families and individuals which through the instrumentality of Paul had been won for the Lord from among the Gentiles! Read Acts 13:48; 14:21–23; 16:14, 15, 31–34; 17:4, 12, 34; 18:14; 19:10, 18–20. Some of these Gentiles had been won for the Lord from the darkness of heathendom; others had been transferred out of the kingdom of darkness to that of light after having tarried first, for a little while, at the depot of Judaism, a way station where the deepest needs of the soul had failed to find ultimate satisfaction. The totality of the harvest had been enormous. And this was true without even counting *the Jews* who had been converted. "Some fruit among y o u also just as among the rest of the Gentiles!" *Paul's humility was indeed profound, an example to us all.* And of whom does that meekness, humility, and kindness remind us? See Isa. 42:1–4; Matt. 12:18–21.

Paul has just now referred to "the Gentiles" (". . . just as I have had among the rest of the Gentiles"). With respect to the Gentiles, then, he now continues:

14, 15. To both Greeks and barbarians, to both learned and unlearned, I am a debtor; hence my eagerness to preach the gospel also to y o u in Rome.

The wide variety of explanations of these words may come as somewhat of a surprise.[26] As I see it, what we have here is an example of the type of parallelism in which the second member, though repeating the thought of the first, adds something to it by way of explanation. In other words

learned and unlearned

explains

Greeks and barbarians.

Paul is writing to believers living in Rome. It is understandable, therefore, that when he uses the term *Greeks* he does not limit himself to people born in Greece. What he means is: Gentiles who were either of Greek descent or were in the habit of speaking Greek and had, at least to a certain extent, assimilated Greek culture. The very fact that the apostle is writing this epistle in Greek and takes for granted that the addressees can understand it, proves that, in the sense already indicated, the people to whom he writes could be called "Greeks."

Now, whenever a Greek-speaking person was listening to conversation carried on by a foreigner, the latter's unintelligible chatter sounded to him like *brrrbrrr*. So he would call the stranger a *barbarian*. Some of these barbarians were undoubtedly people of low intelligence or *were so regarded by the "Greeks."* However, the gospel reaches out to all, educated and uneducated, cultured and uncultured. What Paul is saying, then, is this: "It is my divine calling to preach the gospel to both Greeks and barbarians; that is, to both learned and unlearned."

There was and is *one* message for both, *one* and the same way of salvation for both. The people of Lystra were used to speaking in the Lycaonian language (Acts 14:11). Paul had brought the gospel to them. Believers in Rome were fluent in Greek. They too must hear the gospel from the lips of Paul. Had not the Lord appointed him to be "the apostle to the Gentiles" regardless of their real or assumed degree of culture? Was it not true that they *needed* to hear this gospel? Those who were still in darkness needed to hear it. Those who had been brought out of darkness into the light also needed it. To all of them Paul considered himself to be a debtor; first, because of the commission God had given him; secondly, because he him-

---

26. Though one may or may not agree with the interpretation presented by Cranfield, *op. cit.,* p. 83, his summary of five different views is both interesting and helpful.

self had been a persecutor and had been rescued by the Lord in such an unforgettably gracious manner. And so to both Greeks and barbarians, that is, to both learned and unlearned, hence also to those living in Rome, the apostle must bring the good tidings.

It is as if also at this point we hear him saying, "Woe to me if I do not preach the gospel" (I Cor. 9:16). Not only was it his inescapable duty to do this. He himself was also *eager* to do it.

Chapters 1:16—8:39

Justification by Faith

Outline

Justification by Faith

A. *Real and Necessary.*
1. *Theme.*
"The gospel is the power of God for salvation
to everyone who exercises faith."
1:16, 17

2. *The Gentiles need this justification.*
"Although they knew God, they did not glorify
him as God, or give thanks."
1:18–32

CHAPTER 1:16–32

---

16 For I am not ashamed of the gospel, for it is (the) power of God for salvation to everyone who exercises faith; to the Jew first, and also to the Greek. 17 For in it a righteousness from God is revealed from faith to faith; as it is written, "But the righteous shall live by faith."

A. *Real and Necessary.*
1. *Theme.*
"The gospel is the power of God for salvation
to everyone who exercises faith."
1:16, 17

It is of the utmost importance that this thematic passage be interpreted correctly. With a few necessary exceptions, I shall not take the time to discuss, in detail, the various views with which I cannot agree. The reader can find these conflicting theories for himself. I shall simply try to interpret the terms and/or phrases one by one, and afterward summarize the whole.

16. For I am not ashamed of the gospel . . .
The apostle was not reluctant to preach the gospel, for he loved that good news. In the preceding context Paul had made mention of "learned" (as well as unlearned) people. There must have been many philosophers in such cities as Athens, Corinth, Ephesus, and, last but not least, *Rome.* Has the apostle perhaps delayed his coming to Rome because he was ashamed of meeting these highly educated individuals?

His answer amounts to, "No, indeed!" When he writes, "I am not ashamed," etc., he probably means, "I am proud and overjoyed to receive the opportunity to preach the gospel." And why should he not be eager to proclaim the message of salvation through Christ, the news concerning "Christ Crucified . . . the power of God and the wisdom of God" (I Cor. 1:23, 24)?

. . . for it is (the) power of God for salvation to everyone who exercises faith . . .
The word "for" is again definitely in place. It is logical to say, "I am not ashamed of the gospel, *for it reveals the saving power of God.*"

Are the Romans always boasting about their power, the force by which they have conquered the world? "The gospel I proclaim," says Paul, as it were, "is superior by far. It has achieved and offers something far better, namely,

59

(everlasting) *salvation,* and this not for the people of one particular nation—for example Rome—but for everyone who exercises faith." The most urgent and imperative need of the soul is not earthly renown, but peace, joy, glory for today, tomorrow, and the never-ending future. Compared with "the power of God" how feeble the power of Rome or of any earthly host. Earthly armies *destroy.* The gospel *saves.* It is the power of God "for salvation." And what is salvation? What does *to save* mean? In Paul's writings it means:

NEGATIVELY	POSITIVELY
to rescue men from sin's:	to bring men into the state of:
a. guilt (Eph. 1:7; Col. 1:14)	a. righteousness (Rom. 3:21–26; 5:1)
b. pollution (Rom. 6:6, 17; 7:21–25a)	b. holiness (Rom. 6:1–4; 12:1, 2)
c. slavery (Rom. 7:24, 25; Gal. 5:1)	c. freedom (Gal. 5:1; II Cor. 3:17)
d. punishment:	d. blessedness:
(1) alienation from God (Eph. 2:12)	(1) fellowship with God (Eph. 2:13)
(2) the wrath of God (Eph. 2:3)	(2) the love of God "shed abroad" in the heart (Rom. 5:5)
(3) everlasting death (Eph. 2:5, 6)	(3) everlasting life (Eph. 2:1, 5; Col. 3:1–4)

Note that over against each evil stands a corresponding blessing. To be saved, then, means to be emancipated from the greatest evil, and to be placed in possession of the greatest good. The promised blessings pertain to the past, present, and never-ending future. Justification, sanctification, and glorification are all included. The state of salvation is opposed to the state of "perishing" or being "lost." Cf. Luke 19:10; John 3:16.

" . . . to everyone," regardless, therefore, of race, nationality, age, sex, social rank, degree of education or culture, etc. Cf. Isa. 45:22; John 4:42; I Tim. 1:15.

But note the significant qualification "(to everyone) *who exercises faith.*"[27] Cf. John 3:16.

And what is meant by faith? It is trust, confidence, leaning on the everlasting arms, the conviction (Heb. 11:1) that through Christ and his atoning sacrifice, my sins are forgiven, my debt is canceled; and that, having now been adopted as a child of The King,

I am in my Father's keeping,
I am in his tender care;

---

27. As far as the meaning is concerned, the far more usual rendering, "to everyone *who believes*" is certainly correct. However, it fails to retain the harmony of the original, in which the participle in verse 16 (πιστεύοντι) and the two forms of the noun in verse 17 (πίστεως, πίστιν) are cognate; that is, derived from the same stem. Moreover, when this harmony is retained in the translation, is not the meaning of the entire passage (verses 16, 17) grasped more quickly?

One encounters the same difficulty (lack of harmony) in the Latin, and naturally also in the French, Spanish, etc., translations. On the other hand, everything runs very smoothly in the German, Dutch, Frisian, Swedish, Danish, and South African renderings.

Whether waking, whether sleeping,
I am in his care.

Mrs. C. H. Morris, lines from
"When the Early Morning Breaking"

Faith is the trunk of the tree whose roots represent grace, and whose fruit symbolizes good works. It is the coupling that connects man's train with God's engine. It is the sinner's empty hand stretched out to God, the Giver. It is, from start to finish, *God's gift.* See N.T.C. on Ephesians (2:8), pp. 121-123.

... to the Jew first, and also to the Greek.
That was the divinely planned historical order. As Paul shows in chapter 4 (and to a certain extent already here in verse 16) the gospel of salvation is essentially the same in both dispensations. However, in the divine economy it was revealed first of all to the Jews. During the old dispensation they were the highly privileged nation. See Ps. 147:19, 20; Amos 3:2. Naturally that "advantage" did not immediately cease when the new dispensation was ushered in (Rom. 3:1, 2; 9:4, 5). When Jesus for the first time charged his twelve disciples, he sent them only "to the lost sheep of the house of Israel" (Matt. 10:5, 6). And when Paul carried out his mission mandate, he and his companions, wherever possible, first of all brought the gospel to the Jews.

But there came a change. It is useless to deny this, for on this subject Scripture expresses itself very clearly. Even during the old dispensation God had made it clear that salvation was not going to be limited to one nation. See Gen. 12:3; 22:18; Ps. 72; 87; Isa. 60:1-3; 61:1-3 (in the light of Luke 4); Mal. 1:11. Jesus himself opened the door more and more widely (Matt. 8:10-12; 28:19, 20; Luke 14:23; 17:11-19; 20:9-16; 24:45-47; John 3:16; 4:35-42; 10:16). Similarly, by divine direction, when the Jews refused to accept the gospel, the apostles proclaimed it to the Gentiles (Acts 13:46; 18:5, 6; 19:8, 9). By divine inspiration Paul teaches that the wall of separation between Jew and Gentile has been completely broken down (Eph. 2:11-22), and that there is no longer any distinction (Rom. 10:11, 12). Thus "also to the Greek," that is, to the person(s) influenced by Greek culture, hence to the Gentile(s), the door was opened wide. The gospel became the power of God for salvation to *every* true believer.

The question arises, "How does Paul prove that the gospel is indeed the power of God for salvation *to everyone who exercises faith?*" The answer is given in verse **17. For in it a righteousness from God is revealed from faith to faith; as it is written, "But the righteous shall live by faith."**

Taken by itself, without reference to context, the expression here rendered "righteousness from God" could be translated "righteousness of God" (see A.V.). The question then is, "What does this mean?"

How Luther struggled with this problem! How it bothered him ... until one day, rather suddenly, by divine illumination he realized that what was meant here was not God's retributive justice but the righteousness freely imputed to the sinner by God's sovereign grace, on the basis of Christ's substitutionary atonement, and made the sinner's own possession by means of God-given faith. When the great Reformer made the discovery that Rom. 1:17 speaks about God's gracious verdict of righteousness pronounced upon the believer, he experienced the happiest day in his life. In what may be termed his "Commentary on Romans" he writes:

"The sum and substance of this letter is: to pull down, to pluck up, and to destroy all wisdom and righteousness of the flesh . . . and to affirm and enlarge [prove to be large] the reality of sin, however unconscious we may be of its existence." He continues by pointing out that there have always been people, both Jews and Gentiles, who believed in the possibility of inner goodness. Of these the apostle says, "Professing themselves to be wise, they became foolish" (Rom. 1:22). Luther then shows that in Romans the apostle teaches the very opposite, namely, that the only way in which a person becomes really good is the one provided by God's righteousness. He states, "For God does not want to save us by our own but by an extraneous righteousness, one that does not originate in ourselves but comes to us from beyond ourselves, which does not arise on earth but comes from heaven."[28]

Luther's experience changed his view of the Bible. From this point on Scripture became a book of light and joy for him. It was as if he had been delivered from a dark dungeon and brought into beautiful daylight, where he could inhale the fresh, invigorating, exhilarating air. The peace of God which transcends all understanding now filled his heart and mind.

And was not Luther's experience a replica of Paul's? Read Phil. 3:1–14. What makes Romans so fascinating is the fact that it is not only the product of divine inspiration but also the precipitate of the apostle's conversion experience.

Both Luther and Calvin defined the term which in the A.V. is rendered "the righteousness of God" as indicating *the righteousness that avails before God.* And there can be no question about the fact that this kind of righteousness is indeed indicated. The question remains, "Should not something be added?" Both Reformers, in their discussions, have indeed added something. They have added that the righteousness to which Paul refers is by God freely granted or imputed to the sinner who, by the power of the Holy Spirit, accepts it—that is, appropriates Christ and all his benefits—*by faith.*

That this position is correct becomes clear when Paul is allowed to be his own interpreter. In Phil. 3:8, 9, in discussing the same subject, he writes, ". . . that I may gain Christ, and be found in him, not having a righteousness of my own, legal righteousness, but that (which is) *from* God (and rests) on faith." It is clear then that also here in Rom. 1:17 the term in question should be rendered "righteousness *from* God," meaning that God, its Au-

---

28. Martin Luther, *Lectures on Romans,* tr. of *Römerbriefvorlesung* (Vol. 56 of the Weimar edition of Luther's Works), Philadelphia, 1961, pp. 3, 4.

thor, imputes this right standing to the sinner, who accepts it by faith. *From start to finish* this righteousness is *sola fide;* that is, by faith alone. This also explains the expression "from faith to faith."[29] See Rom. 3:28. And even that faith is God's gift. It is all a matter of sovereign grace, not of works. See N.T.C. on Eph. 2:8–10.

This should not be interpreted as if *the exercise* of faith is the operation of God. *We ourselves* must accept the Triune God, as revealed in Christ Jesus. It is *we* who must exercise faith. God does not believe for us. This position is in harmony with Scripture. See John 3:16; Phil. 2:12, 13; II Thess. 2:13.[30] We should bear in mind, moreover, that not only the gift of faith is from God but so is also the power to exercise it. To him alone be the glory!

"As it is written, But the righteous shall live by faith."

In presenting this comforting doctrine Paul is not introducing something new. The words "as it is written" show that he is basing his presentation on the Old Testament. And it is indeed in that book, which for the apostle as well as for his addressees was the Bible, that *righteousness,* and therefore *salvation,* is repeatedly presented as a treasure which belongs to Jehovah. By sovereign grace he bestows it as a gift on all who *trust* in him. A few precious passages will make this clear. One of the most familiar and outstanding is surely Isa. 12:2:

"Behold, God is my salvation. I will trust and will not be afraid, for Jehovah, even Jehovah, is my strength and song; and he has become my salvation."

Note also the following:

"For thy salvation I am waiting, O Lord" (Gen. 49:18).

"Salvation belongs to the Lord" (Ps. 3:8).

"Thou art the God of my salvation" (Ps. 25:5).

"The Lord is my light and my salvation. Whom shall I fear?" (Ps. 27:1). Fear is the opposite of trust.

"O sing to the Lord a new song, for he has done marvelous things. His right hand and his holy arm have achieved salvation for him. The Lord has

---

29. The expression "from faith to faith" is too short and simple to allow for complicated interpretations. So, for example, I cannot accept Barth's view that it means "from God's faithfulness to man's faith"; or Murray's that by means of this brief phrase the apostle would be saying "only by faith are we the beneficiaries of this righteousness and every believer is the beneficiary." The most simple interpretation of such a brief expression is usually the best. According to this rule the meaning is in all probability: "from start to finish (or: from first to last) by faith." In agreement with this interpretation are also the following: Cranfield, Erdman, Harrison, Hodge, and Ridderbos.

30. Would it not seem, therefore, that Lenski, who in his commentaries has enriched the church with much excellent material, expresses himself somewhat injudiciously in his *Interpretation of St. Paul's Epistle to the Romans,* Columbus, p. 83? Read also his comments on what he calls "false Calvinistic exegesis" (p. 9).

made known his salvation. He has revealed his righteousness in the sight of the nations" (Ps. 98:1, 2).

Note close relation between *salvation* and *righteousness* both here and elsewhere.

"The Lord is my strength and my song. And he has become my salvation" (Ps. 118:14).

"I long for thy salvation, O Lord" (Ps. 119:174).

"I bring near my righteousness, and my salvation shall not tarry" (Isa. 46:13).

"My righteousness is near. My salvation has gone forth. And my arms will judge the peoples . . . My salvation will be forever. And my righteousness will not diminish . . . My righteousness will be forever, and my salvation to all generations" (Isa. 51:5–8).

"Their righteousness [or vindication] is from me, says the Lord" (Isa. 54:17).

"He has clothed me with the garments of salvation. He has wrapped me in a garment of righteousness (Isa. 61:10).

"For Zion's sake I will not be silent. And for Jerusalem's sake I will not keep quiet, until her righteousness goes forth like brightness, and her salvation like a torch that is burning" (Isa. 62:1).

Here in Rom. 1:17, "But the righteous shall live by faith," the apostle is almost literally quoting Hab. 2:4b. There are those who insist on the rendering (here in Rom. 1:17), "But the righteous by faith shall live." In other words, they connect "by faith" with "the righteous" instead of with "shall live." I have not been convinced by their arguments. Those who are interested in this question should read the footnote.[31]

---

31. The reasons that have convinced me that ἐκ πίστεως should be connected with ζήσεται, not with δίκαιος, are as follows:

a. In the Habakkuk passage (the original) the phrase "by his faithfulness" or "by his faith" is most logically connected with "he lives." See I. Lesser's rendering (in *Twenty-Four Books of the Holy Scriptures,* New York, n.d., Vol. II, p. 959), "But the righteous ever liveth in his (trustful) faith."

b. If Paul had intended to connect "by faith" with "the righteous" he would probably have written ὁ δὲ ἐκ πίστεως δίκαιος instead of ὁ δὲ δίκαιος ἐκ πίστεως.

c. The phrase ἐκ πίστεως here in verse 17b corresponds to the same phrase in the earlier part of the verse. There too it belongs to the predicate, not to the subject.

d. In Paul's epistles there is no parallel to "righteous by faith." Rom. 5:1 is not really a parallel.

e. If here in Rom. 1:17 we connect ἐκ πίστεως with δίκαιος, should we not also do this in Gal. 3:11, where the identical Old Testament passage is quoted by the same writer and for the same purpose? Now in Galatians the context makes it very clear that "shall live by faith" and not "the righteous by faith" is the meaning. This is shown by the preceding and also by the

The prophet Habakkuk appeared upon the scene of history during the reign of wicked Jehoiakim (608–597 B.C.). What bothered him was that it seemed as if wicked men were getting away with their wickedness. Jehovah apparently tolerated such evils as the exploitation of the needy, strife, contention, violence, etc. So the prophet begins to ask questions. He addresses these questions to Jehovah. He complains, objects, and waits for an answer. Habakkuk's first question amounted to this, "Why does Jehovah allow the wicked in Judah to oppress the righteous?" Jehovah answers, "Evil-doers will be punished. The Chaldeans (Babylonians) are coming." But this answer does not quite satisfy the prophet. So he asks another one, which was tantamount to this: "Why does Jehovah allow the Chaldeans to punish the Jews, who at least are more righteous than these foreigners?" The prophet stations himself upon his watch-tower and awaits an answer. The answer arrives: "The Chaldeans, too, will be punished. In fact *all sinners* will be punished . . . but the righteous shall live by his *faith.*" It is his duty and privilege to *trust,* and to do this even then when he is not able to "figure out" the justice of Jehovah's doings. In this humble trust and quiet confidence he shall truly *live,* prosper.

But Jehovah does more than merely tell the prophet that he must *exercise* faith. He also *strengthens* that faith by means of a marvelous, progressive vision. Habakkuk sees the symbol of Jehovah's presence, descending from Mt. Paran. Having descended he stands firm and shakes the earth. The tent-hangings of Cushan and Midian are trembling and are being torn to shreds. One question worries the prophet: "Upon whom is Jehovah's wrath going to fall? Merely upon the realm of nature? Upon Judah perhaps?" Finally, the answer arrives; Jehovah destroys the Chaldeans and delivers his people.

So fearful and terrifying had been the appearance of Jehovah, so alarming the sound of the tempest, of crumbling mountains, etc., that the prophet is trembling in every part of his body. Nevertheless, having witnessed that Jehovah had descended for the defense of his own people, Habakkuk no longer questions the ways of God's providence. From now on he "waits quietly." He expresses his feelings in a beautiful psalm of *trust:* "For though the fig tree shall not flourish . . . Yet I will rejoice in Jehovah, I will joy in the God of my salvation."

Paul, accordingly, could not have chosen a better prophecy from which

---

following context; for "live by faith" is there contrasted with "justified by law" and is also contrasted with "live by (doing) them." We cannot very well adopt one grammatical construction for Gal. 3:11, and another for Rom. 1:17.

f. If we translate, "He who is justified by faith (or: The righteous by faith) shall live" we are placing the emphasis where it does not belong. The entire context indicates that Paul's emphasis is on "live *by faith*" instead of "live by the works of the law."

Having carefully read and studied Cranfield's arguments in favor of the opposite position I am unable to agree. But, for the sake of fairness, I hope everyone will by all means read Cranfield, *op. cit.,* pp. 101, 102.

to quote than that of Habakkuk. The passage fits the situation exactly! In every age and in all circumstances, hence also in connection with the question, "What must I do to be accepted by God?" it remains true that "The righteous shall live by faith." "In quietness and confidence shall be y o u r strength" (Isa. 30:15).

But not only is Paul's doctrine in line with the teaching of the Old Testament—a subject on which the apostle is going to dwell in far more detail in chapter 4—it is also in harmony with the teaching of Christ during his earthly ministry. See N.T.C. on Luke 18:9–14, pp. 818–821.

To summarize, what Paul teaches here in Rom. 1:16, 17 and in Gal. 3:11 amounts to this:

> Not the labors of my hands,
> Can fulfil thy law's demands;
> Could my zeal no languor know,
> Could my tears forever flow,
> All for sin could not atone;
> Thou must save, and thou alone.

> Lines from "Rock of Ages"
> by A. M. Toplady

---

18 For the wrath of God is being revealed from heaven against all ungodliness and unrighteousness of people who are constantly attempting to suppress the truth by (their) unrighteousness, 19 because what can be known of God is plain to them, for God has made it plain to them. 20 For since the creation of the world his invisible qualities—his eternal power and divine nature—have been clearly seen, being understood through (his) works, so that these people are without excuse.

21 For although they knew God, they neither glorified him as God nor gave thanks to him, but became futile in their speculations, and their foolish hearts were darkened. 22 Although they claimed to be wise, they became fools 23 and exchanged the glory of the immortal God for an image in the shape of mortal man and of birds, four-footed animals, and reptiles.[32]

24 Therefore God, letting them follow the sinful cravings of their own hearts, gave them over to sexual immorality, so that their bodies were dishonored among themselves; 25 since they had indeed exchanged God, (who is) the truth, for a lie, and worshiped and served the creature rather than the Creator, who is blessed forever. Amen.

26 Because of this, God gave them over to passions that bring dishonor. For as well as their females [or women] exchanged natural intercourse for that (which is) contrary to nature, 27 so likewise also the males [or men] having abandoned natural intercourse with the female [or woman], were consumed by flaming passion for one another, males with males [or men with men] perpetrating shamelessness, and receiving in their own persons the due return for their deviation.

28 And since they did not deem it worthwhile to retain the knowledge of God, he gave them over to (their) worthless disposition, to do what is improper; 29 having become filled with every kind of unrighteousness, wickedness, greed, depravity; being full of envy, murder, strife, deceit, and malice. (They are) gossips, 30 slanderers, haters of God, insolent, arrogant, boastful, inventors of (novel forms of) evil, disobedient to (their) parents, 31 senseless, faithless, loveless, pitiless. 32 And although they know the ordinance of God that those who

---

32. Or: creeping things, crawling creatures.

practice such things are worthy of death, they not only continue to do them but also approve of those who practice them.

---

2. *The Gentiles need this justification.*
"Although they knew God, they did not glorify
him as God, or give thanks"
1:18–32

18. For the wrath of God is being revealed from heaven against all ungodliness and unrighteousness of people who are constantly attempting to suppress the truth by (their) unrighteousness...

What kind of people is Paul describing in 1:18–32? There are those who maintain that since the word *Gentiles* is never mentioned in this section and since at least some of the sins here catalogued were committed by Jews as well as by Gentiles, we must conclude that the apostle is here referring to unregenerate men in general, not just to Gentiles.

There is some truth in this. See on 2:1. On the other hand, is it not also true that several traits here mentioned are far more characteristic of Gentiles than of Jews? Note, for example, image worship (verse 23), and see also verses 26, 27. Moreover, to a large extent the people here described derive their knowledge of God not from special but from general revelation (verses 19, 20). Besides, 2:1 clearly marks a transition to the discussion of another group of people, namely, the Jews (see 2:17). This too seems to indicate that up to this point Paul has been speaking chiefly about Gentiles. Finally, does not 3:9 prove that the apostle had been speaking about two groups, namely, Gentiles and Jews (there mentioned in reverse order)? We conclude therefore that in 1:18–32 the reference is *mainly* to Gentiles, though it is true that not all Gentiles were guilty (or equally guilty) of the enumerated vices.

The word "For" should not be left untranslated. It indicates the relation between verses 16, 17, on the one hand, and verse 18 on the other. The reasoning is probably along this line: No other way to be saved is available than that of accepting the gospel by faith, *for* since the wrath of God rests by nature upon man, the latter is completely unable to save himself, whether by performing the works of the law or by any other means.

What is meant by God's wrath? See also John 3:36; Rom. 9:22; Eph. 5:6; Col. 3:6; I Thess. 1:10. God's *wrath* is his settled indignation. It differs from *fury,* which generally points in the direction of *rage,* sudden outbursts of anger.[33] Whenever God's wrath is mentioned in the New Testament the final manifestation of divine vengeance is either indicated or, as here, is at least in the background.

"... is being revealed ..." What is meant is that this wrath is revealed *in*

---

33. For more on this see R. C. Trench, *Synonyms of The New Testament,* Grand Rapids, 1948 (reprint), par. 37. See also below, on 2:8.

action; for example, by means of the deluge (Gen. 6–8), the destruction of Sodom and Gomorrah (Gen. 19), the plagues upon Egypt (Exod. 6–12), and the bowls of wrath (Rev. 16). In each case Scripture shows that these manifestations of wrath have their origin in *heaven*. It is God, dwelling in heaven, who vents his wrath upon the perpetrators of "ungodliness and unrighteousness."

These two concepts—ungodliness and unrighteousness—must not be viewed as completely separate entities; as if, for example, the first pertains exclusively to the religious sphere; the second only to the moral realm; or as if the first concerns merely the first table of the law; the second, the remainder of the law. Both represent sin, rebellion against God. The first views sin as want of reverence for God; the second, as want of reverence for his ordinances, his holy law. That the relation between these two is very close is shown by the fact that at the close of verse 18 *one* term, unrighteousness, covers both concepts.

". . . of people who are constantly attempting to suppress[34] the truth by their unrighteousness . . ."

Elsewhere too Scripture teaches that the wicked make an attempt to suppress the truth. The fool is constantly trying to convince himself that "there is no God." To Ps. 14:1 and 53:1 add Ps. 73:11; Rom. 2:15. Even when he is confronted with the voice of God addressing him by means of special revelation, he still refuses to capitulate. See Mark 6:20, 26, 27. In fact, as it was in the case of Herod Antipas, so generally, the more conscience warns, the more the sinner hardens himself.

But do the Gentiles really have sufficient knowledge of the truth to be considered guilty of constantly attempting to suppress it? The answer is found in the next verse:

19. . . . because what can be known of God is plain to them, for God has made it plain to them.

Even entirely apart from special revelation through the gospel, which ever so many Gentiles have never heard, God has made himself known and continues to do so by means of his general revelation in nature, history, and conscience; here, as the sequel indicates, with emphasis on God's revelation

---

34. In favor of the conative force of this pres. act. participle (κατεχόντων) are the following facts:

a. A verb which by itself suggests effort, when used in a context that implies action in progress (for example, progression in the present, or in the past as in Luke 4:42), points in the direction of *attempted* action. See E. De Witt Burton, *Syntax of the Moods and Tenses in New Testament Greek*, Chicago, 1923, p. 8.

b. Even some of those exegetes who in their *translation* have adopted the English equivalent "who suppress," etc., in their *interpretation* speak about the *efforts* of the ungodly to suppress the truth.

c. The conotative force of the participle is clear also from this fact that no less than three times (verses 19, 20, and 21) the immediate context assures us that the ungodly do not succeed in holding down or blotting out the truth. They sin against better knowledge. See also on verses 28 and 32.

In favor of the conative force of this present participle is also Cranfield, *op. cit.,* p. 112.

in *nature;* that is, in "creation." Not as if men, acting on their own initiative, could have discovered God, but, as the passage states, *God* has made known to them[35] whatever in the area of creation can be made known about him.

20. For since the creation of the world his invisible qualities—his eternal power and divine nature—have been clearly seen, being understood through (his) works, so that these people are without excuse.[36]

The little word "For" is again very meaningful. It is not only continuative but also supportive, showing that what was said in verse 19 is indeed a fact. The sentence introduced by "For" may even reflect on what was said earlier, namely, in verse 18; that is, it may be viewed as indicating why the wrath of God is being revealed against the wicked: their wicked deeds are inexcusable!

In verses 16, 17 Paul had been speaking about God's revelation *in the gospel* unto salvation. It is clear that here, in verses 19, 20 he has made the transition from special to general revelation. He is now speaking about "the things that are made," that is, about God's revelation "in his works," meaning, in *creation* or *nature.*

Note the expression "God's invisible qualities." That God is indeed invisible is taught everywhere in Scripture. Note especially the following passages:

"God himself no one has ever seen" (John 1:18).

"(the Son of his love, who is) the image of the invisible God" (Col. 1:15).

"the King of the ages, the imperishable, invisible, only God" (I Tim. 1:17).

"... seeing him who is invisible" (Heb. 11:27).

A further explanation of these invisible qualities or attributes is given in the words "his eternal power and divine nature."

---

35. ἐν αὐτοῖς can be used instead of the ordinary dative; so probably here; hence "to them." See L.N.T. (A. and G.), p. 260.

36. Several items in the Greek text require comment:

a. ἀόρατα ... καθορᾶται. The oxymoron is probably intentional.

b. καθορᾶται, third per. s. pres. pass. indicat. of καθοράω, (κατά, perfective, plus ὁράω, to see), to see clearly.

c. νοούμενα, nom. pl. n. pres. pass. participle of νοέω, to perceive, understand. The participial form is related to the noun νοῦς, which, depending on the context, can have any one of the following meanings: mind, intellect, intelligence, thought, understanding, attitude, disposition. In the present passage νοῦς must be viewed as *intellect plus* (or including) *sense of responsibility.* Man's entire mental and moral state of being is indicated. It is in that sense that νοούμενα can here be interpreted as meaning "being perceived" or "understood." As an adverbial modifier of καθορᾶται, the participle νοούμενα shows that more than merely physical vision is indicated by καθορᾶται.

d. ἀΐδιος (from ἀεί), ever-enduring, eternal.

e. εἰς τὸ εἶναι does not necessarily always introduce a purpose clause. A result clause is far more reasonable in the present connection. See Gram. N.T., p. 1003; L.N.T. (A. and G.), p. 228 (under 4e).

As to this eternal power or never-failing omnipotence, it is evident in all God's works (Ps. 111:2; 118:17; 119:27; 139:14; 145:10); in Israel's deliverance from Egypt (Exod. 20:1, 2) and in God's tender care bestowed on his people (Deut. 33:27). Again and again psalmists and prophets refer to God's mighty deeds. No one is able to stay his hand (Dan. 4:35). He does whatever he pleases, for nothing is too difficult for him (Gen. 18:14; Jer. 32:27).

In the present context, however, it is not—at least not primarily—God's mighty deeds in history that are being contemplated. The reference is rather to the works of *creation:* the works of God which *for a very long time,* in fact *ever since the creation of the universe,* have been visible to men and have made their indelible impression upon their minds.

Paul is thinking of the God who created the heavens and the earth and who establishes them by perpetual decrees (Gen. 1; Ps. 104). He is reflecting on the One who made "the Pleiades and the Orion, who turns the shadow of death into the morning, and makes the day dark with night" (Amos 5:8).

The term "his divine nature" indicates the sum of all God's glorious attributes, in the present connection especially those attributes which make and leave an impression on everybody's mind: the exhibition of God's power, wisdom, and goodness in the created universe. Such passages as Ps. 8, Ps. 19:1-6, and Isa. 40:21, 22, 26 shed further light on the subject.

The rendering "His invisible qualities . . . have been clearly seen" correctly reproduces the sense of the original, but fails to do justice to its beauty. The original (Greek), even somewhat more clearly than the usual English translation, employs a pair of words which, though resembling each other in form, express a seeming contradiction. Call it a paradox or an oxymoron if you prefer. A closer approach to the original would be: "his *unseeable* qualities . . . *are clearly seen.*"

But how is it possible to see the unseeable? Is it not true that physical eyes are unable to see God's invisible qualities? True; yet, while these eyes are observing the glories of the universe which God created, the soul, with its invisible eye, is being deeply impressed. It *clearly sees* God's power displayed in "the things that were made," that is, in God's works.

The Belgic Confession, Article I, commenting on Rom. 1:20, speaks about "the creation, preservation, and government of the universe; which is before our eyes as a most elegant book, wherein all creatures, great and small, are as so many characters leading us *to see clearly the invisible things of God, even his everlasting power and divinity,* as the apostle says, 'All these things are sufficient to convince men and to leave them without excuse.'"

". . . so that these people are without excuse." Even though they have been constantly surrounded by the evidences not only of God's existence but also of his infinite power, adorable goodness, and incomparable wisdom, they have refused to acknowledge him as *their* God, and to worship him.

Even without the benefit of such products of human invention as *micro-scope* and *telescope,* they were able to reflect on the vastness of the universe, the fixed order of the heavenly bodies in their courses, the arrangement of the leaves around a stem, the cycle of the divinely created water-works (evaporation, cloud formation, distillation, pool formation), the mystery of growth from seed to plant—not just any plant but the particular kind of plant from which the seed originated, the thrill of the sunrise from faint rosy flush to majestic orb, the skill of birds in building their "homes" without ever having taken lessons in home building, the generous manner in which food is supplied for all creatures, the adaptation of living creatures to their environment (for example, the flexible soles of the camel's feet to the soft desert sands), etc., etc. In addition to this voice of God in the works of creation there was also the voice of that same God in conscience (2:15). The evidence was overwhelming. And still no response of adoration and gratitude. Then surely their conduct is inexcusable!

21. For although they knew God, they neither glorified him as God nor gave thanks to him, but became futile in their speculations, and their foolish hearts were darkened.

Verse 21 is a clarification and amplification of verse 18 (final clause) and verse 20. It confirms the statement that by their unrighteousness these wicked people are constantly attempting to suppress the truth that has been and is continually being revealed to them, and that they are accordingly without excuse.

For, although they knew God from his works in creation, they did not glorify him: did not acknowledge him as their God and did not bestow upon him the honor and praise they owed him. Nor did they return thanks to him for the blessings they were constantly receiving. That they were the recipients of blessings in abundance is clear (Matt. 5:45; Luke 6:35; Acts 14:17). But though there are indeed *blessings* that are *common, gratitude* in return for them is not. A striking example is Luke 17:11–19.

Instead of praising God for all his benefits, these people became futile in their speculations. Instead of following the advice incorporated in a hymn:

> Lift now hearts and voices
> While our soul rejoices
> In our God above,

the minds and hearts of these people remained on a horizontal plane: they carried on a dialog with themselves. Their minds were arguing, speculating. Their hearts were void of thanksgiving and adoration. Such hearts are useless; in fact, worse than useless. Whenever people, in their conceit and ingratitude, begin to reason on their own, without constantly checking the results of their speculations with God's revelation in nature, history, conscience, and especially, whenever possible, with the Word of God, their *foolish* hearts are darkened.

Such darkness indicates mental dullness, emotional despair, and spiritual depravity.

Note the expression "their foolish hearts." In Paul's epistles the word *heart* (s. and pl.) occurs more than fifty times. The heart, according to Paul and Scripture in general, is the hub of the wheel of man's existence, the mainspring of all his thoughts, words, and deeds. It is the motive power hidden away deeply within man; so deeply, in fact, that God, he alone, knows its secrets. See Prov. 4:23; 23:7; Jer. 17:9, 10; Matt. 12:34; 15:18, 19; Luke 6:45; Rom. 8:27; I Cor. 14:25; I Thess. 2:4.

Of course, the word's exact shade of meaning in each case depends on the context. Sometimes, in Paul, when the word *heart(s)* is used, the emphasis is on the emotions or feelings (Rom. 1:24; 9:2); sometimes on the intellect (Rom. 10:6-9); and sometimes on the will (Rom. 2:5).

Now when, according to the present passage (1:21), men's hearts are darkened, it follows that whatever they feel, think, say, or do is detrimentally affected. Their minds cannot reason straight; their emotions cannot function properly, imparting peace and joy to their lives; and their wills do not even try to be in harmony with God's holy law. Note the tragic result:

22, 23. Although they claimed to be wise, they became fools and exchanged the glory of the immortal God for an image in the shape of mortal man and of birds, four-footed animals, and reptiles [or crawling creatures].

What a contrast between the *claim* and the *reality*. For a striking example read John 9:40, 41. However, the present passage refers especially to the blindness of *heathendom* and of all who imitate its foolish practices. As has been indicated, such blindness is inexcusable. It amounts to sinful folly. It is illustrated in such passages as the following:

"Let us build for ourselves a city, and a tower whose top will reach into heaven" (Gen. 11:4).

"The Syrians said, 'Jehovah is a god of the hills, but he is not a god of the valleys' " (I Kings 20:28; see also verse 23).

"Those who lavish gold . . . hire a goldsmith, who makes a god of it. They bow down; indeed, they worship it. Then they lift it upon (their) shoulders and carry it. They set it in its place, and there it stands! It does not move from its place. Though a person may cry to it, it cannot answer. It cannot rescue him from his distress" (Isa. 46:6, 7).

What stupendous folly! Said Aaron, "The people gave the gold to me. I threw it into the fire, and out came this calf!" (Exod. 32:24). Cf. verse 4: "This is your God, O Israel, that brought you up out of the land of Egypt."

And to think that people would actually give up their faith in the glory of God—the excellence of his attributes, with all this implies in blessings for those who rely on him—in exchange for the worship of idols. They exchange *the One who carries* for *those who must be carried* (contrast Isa. 63:9 with Isa. 46:1). What *fools* they have made of themselves![37]

In the enumeration: man, birds, quadrupeds, reptiles or crawling creatures ("creeping things"), *man* is mentioned first. Throughout the ages people have paid homage to *man, mortal* man at that, and have prostrated themselves before his *image* (see Dan. 3; and N.T.C. on Matthew, p. 857). The slogan has been, and in many circles is even today, "No God for a gift God gave us; mankind alone must save us."

By adding "an image in the shape of . . . birds, quadrupeds, and creeping things (reptiles, etc.)," Paul is following the order of the Creation Account (Gen. 1:20-25). Here again it is the *image* of the animal that is mentioned as the object of worship. Think of the golden calf at Sinai (Exod. 32) and the golden calves at Bethel and Dan (I Kings 12:28f.). As to birds, think of the veneration accorded by the Romans to the image of the eagle. See N.T.C. on Matthew, pp. 187, 188. And even "creeping things" were reproduced in the idolatrous imagery of the Gentiles and at one time or another were worshiped by Jewish imitators (Ezek. 8:10).

All this in spite of the fact that:

a. Such worship had been strictly forbidden by the Lord (Exod. 20:4, 5; Deut. 4:15-19; 5:8, 9). Every worship of the creature, whether directly or through an image, whether in the heavens (worship of sun, moon, stars) or on earth, had been warned against again and again.

b. By bowing down before any object other than the true and only God, those wicked and foolish enough to do this were losing much. That is brought out by the very wording of the present passage: "they became fools and exchanged the glory of the immortal God for an image," etc. This reminds us of

Ps. 106:20: "They exchanged their glory—God was Israel's glory—for the image of an ox that munches grass"; and also of

Jer. 2:11: "Has any nation ever changed (its) gods, though they were not (even) gods? But my people have changed their glory for something that is of no benefit whatever."

Even in the apocrypha such sin and folly was held up to scathing ridicule:

"An experienced woodcutter will cut down a tree that is easy to handle. Skillfully he strips off all its bark. And then, with pleasing workmanship, he makes a useful article that serves life's needs . . . But he takes a castoff piece, one that is good for nothing, a stick crooked and full of knots. He carves it with care . . . and causes it to resemble a man. Or he makes it to look like some worthless animal, giving it a coat of red paint, and with paint covering every blemish . . . Then he makes for it a suitable niche, sets it in

---

37. The *possibility* that Paul meant, "By pretending to be wise they made themselves fools," must be granted.

the wall, and fastens it with iron. He takes care that it does not fall, because he knows that it cannot help itself, for it is only an image and in need of help. Then he prays (to it) about possessions and his marriage and children . . . For health he appeals to a thing that is weak. For life he prays to a thing that is dead. For aid he entreats an object that is thoroughly inexperienced . . . He asks strength of a thing whose hands have no strength" (Wisd. of Solomon 13:11-19, abbreviated). Cf. Isa. 40:19f.

Indeed, they exchanged "the glory of the immortal God" for a mere image!

Here, in Rom. 1:23, the word *glory* does not have exactly the same meaning as it has in Ps. 106:20; Jer. 2:11, though the two connotations are not far apart. In these two Old Testament passages the designation "glory" indicates God himself. In Paul's passage it refers to God's absolute perfection and splendor, the sum-total of all his marvelous attributes. For more on this very interesting term *glory* read the footnote.[38]

God's response to the wicked course chosen by sinful men (verses 22, 23) is indicated in the next verse.

24. Therefore God, letting them follow the sinful cravings of their own hearts, gave them over to sexual immorality, so that their bodies were dishonored among themselves . . .

Note the close connection between idolatry (verse 23) and immorality

---

38. Paul uses the word δόξα, *glory,* more than seventy-five times in his epistles. Since it is a word with many different, though related, meanings, a closer study is profitable. The noun is related to the verb δοκέω; hence, has the primary meaning *opinion* (IV Macc. 5:18). It is but a small step to the meaning *good opinion* concerning someone; hence, *praise, honor, homage.*

The Hebrew *kābhōdh,* which is the most common word for *glory* in the Old Testament, has the primary meaning *weight, heaviness, burden* (Isa. 22:24); hence, *substance, wealth, dignity.* It is used to describe Jacob's *substance,* his flocks and herds (Gen. 31:1). At times the element of brightness, radiance, splendor is added to that of substance. Thus, the word is used to indicate *the brilliant physical manifestation of Jehovah's presence* (Exod. 16:7; Isa. 6:1-5).

In a study of the meaning of δόξα in Paul's epistles both the Greek derivation and use and the Hebrew background must be borne in mind. Accordingly, the different senses in which the word is used by Paul may be summarized as follows:

a. *praise, honor, bestowed on creatures or belonging to them, approbation, approval, reputation.* Here the antonym is *dishonor* (II Cor. 6:8) or *shame* (Phil. 3:19). The synonym of δόξα, so used, is τιμή (Rom. 2:7, 10).

b. *adoration or homage rendered to God.* Thus the word is used in Phil. 1:11, as is shown by its synonym *praise.* See also Rom. 3:7; 4:20; 11:36; I Cor. 10:31; etc.

c. *the thing which reflects honor or credit on someone, or the person whose virtues redound to the glory of another* (I Cor. 11:7, 15; II Cor. 8:23; I Thess. 2:20).

d. *external splendor, brightness, brilliance, or radiance* (of the heavenly bodies, I Cor. 15:40, 41).

e. *the bright cloud by which God made himself manifest, the shekinah* (Rom. 9:4).

f. *the manifested excellence, absolute perfection, royal majesty, splendor or sublimity of God* (here in Rom. 1:23, cf. verses 19, 20; II Cor. 4:6), *or of Christ* (II Cor. 3:18; 4:4), *particularly also at his second coming* (Titus 2:13; II Thess. 1:9).

g. *God's majestic power* (Rom. 6:4).

h. *the light that surrounds those who are, or have just been, in contact with God* (II Cor. 3:7).

i. *the state and/or place of blessedness into which believers will enter* (Rom. 8:18); *and Christ has already entered* (I Tim. 3:16).

j. in general, *the pre-eminently excellent or illustrious condition of something or of someone, manifested excellence, either now or in the future.*

(verse 24). Similarly in the apocryphal book Wisd. of Solomon we read: "For the idea of making idols was the beginning of fornication, and their invention was the corruption of life" (14:12).

In this connection we should bear in mind that Paul is writing this epistle from Corinth, a city notorious for its sexual immorality and debauchery. The expression "to live like a Corinthian" meant "to live a life of moral degradation." Corinth's temple counted more than a thousand lust-promoting priestesses.

The fact that no less than three times (verses 24, 26, 28) we are told that "God gave them over" is significant. In the interpretation of this shocking statement extremes should be avoided. One extreme position would be to say that as soon as these sins—idolatry and immorality—started to appear God *immediately* said, "Let them perish!" That, however, is not what Scripture teaches with respect to the manner in which God deals with sinners. Read especially Gen. 4:6, 7, and note the tender manner in which God dealt with Cain!

The woman "Jezebel" seems to have been the very embodiment of the sins mentioned in the present context (cf. Rev. 2:20 with Rom. 1:23, 24), namely, idolatry and immorality. Nevertheless, God gave her "time to repent." And even in the days of Noah, "when the wickedness of man was great on the earth, and every imagination of the thoughts of his heart was only evil continually" (Gen. 6:5), "the patience of God waited" (I Peter 3:20). Other examples of patience shown to sinners, "handing them over to Satan" *in order that this disciplinary action might lead them to repentance,* are found in I Cor. 5:5 and I Tim. 1:20. And the fact that also in the Romans 1 context God had revealed himself to the wicked, so that they might turn to him, is clear not only from the immediate context (Rom. 1:19–21) but also from 2:15.

It is not surprising, therefore, that it has been suggested that also here in Rom. 1:24, 26, 28, the divine relinquishment is of the same merciful character, a smiting *in order to heal* (Isa. 19:22).[39]

Unquestionably recognition of this divine patience is proper in connection with the study of Rom. 1:18–25. Nevertheless, justice must be done also to the other side of the picture. Mercy unrequited produces wrath. Divine patience without favorable response on the part of man results in the outpouring of divine indignation. Honesty in exegesis compels one to admit that verse 24 is part of a paragraph that is introduced by a reference to "the wrath of God" (verse 18). What the present verse (24) holds before us, therefore, is the fact that at the proper time—known only to God— impenitent sinners are by that wrath allowed to be swept away by their own sins into the pit of their vile passions. *By a positive action of God's will they are finally abandoned.*

---

39. So, for example, Cranfield, *op. cit.,* p. 121.

Speaking about the uncleanness or "impurity" (II Cor. 12:21; Gal. 5:19; Eph. 5:3; I Thess. 4:7) into which these sinners have plunged themselves "so that their bodies were dishonored among themselves" (for explanation see on verses 26, 27), Col. 3:5, 6 states, "Put to death therefore y o u r members that (are) upon the earth: immorality, impurity, passion, evil desire, and greed, which is idolatry, *on account of which things the wrath of God is coming*." Though the outpouring of this wrath in all its fulness is a matter of the future ("eschatological"), a foretaste is by the impenitent experienced even here and now. God finally abandons them, allowing them to perish in their own wickedness.

25. ... since they had indeed exchanged God, (who is) the truth, for a lie, and worshiped and served the creature rather than[40] **the Creator, who is blessed forever. Amen.**

Verse 25, which must probably be considered a modifier of verse 24, resumes the thought of verse 23. Similarly verse 26 is an elaboration of verse 24.

The fact that in verses 21–23 a reason had already been given for the divine abandonment mentioned in verse 24, by no means rules out the possibility that this reason is in essence repeated here in verse 25, especially since this verse is not a *mere* repetition but an elaboration in which a new thought is added (see the final clause of verse 25).[41]

The translation as here proposed[42] brings out the chiastic parallelism of the original:

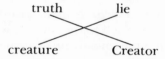

That God, the Creator, should be called "the truth" is not strange. See John 14:6(cf. Ps. 31:5; Isa. 65:16). Neither is it strange that an idol, or any creature (sun, moon, stars, etc.) that is regarded as an object of worship, should be called "a lie." Isa. 44:20 describes a sculptor, who has made for himself a "god." He reaches out and takes hold of it, but fails to ask himself, "Is there not *a lie* in my right hand?" The LXX equivalent of the Hebrew word for "lie" is ψεῦδος. The idol is "a lie" because (in the imagination of the worshiper) it promises much; however, it provides nothing!

---

40. παρά, alongside of; i.e., compared to; here: rather (than), the idea being that they worshiped and served the creature *and not* the Creator. For a similar use of παρά see Luke 18:14.

41. This, it would seem to me, is better than starting a new paragraph with verse 25. The doxology at the close of that verse is a fitting conclusion of the little paragraph—but see also Cranfield, who favors the opposite view, stating his reasons on p. 123 of his commentary.

42. Note "God (who is) the truth." (One might also say "the true God." See N.E.B.) This is better than "the truth of (or about) God," for it is clear that in this chiastic parallelism τὴν ἀλήθειαν τοῦ θεοῦ is a synonym of τὸν κτίσαντα; as is τῷ ψεύδει of τῇ κτίσει. The genitive τοῦ θεοῦ is one of *apposition*. It is not possessive.

What Paul is saying, then, is this: they (the Gentiles, etc.) *worshiped* (i.e., adored, revered) and *served* (rendered cultic service to) the creature rather than the Creator, and therefore deserved the punishment described in verse 24.

At the mention of God, the Creator, the apostle adds a doxology, strictly speaking a benediction: "who is blessed forever. Amen." Commentators remind us that this was a Jewish custom when God's name was mentioned. Nevertheless, anyone who has made a study of Paul's life, as revealed to us in his epistles and in the book of Acts, is bound to agree that for this apostle a benediction, or in general a doxology, was not uttered merely out of custom. Rather, when Paul reflects on God, to whom he owes so very much, he shrinks back in revulsion at the thought that there are those who, in their religious practices, substitute a mere creature for that wonderful God who has done so much for him, the former bitter persecutor. Every reported Pauline benediction or doxology is sincere and soulful. In addition to the benediction reported in Rom. 1:25 study also those found in Rom. 9:5; II Cor. 1:3, 11:31; Eph. 1:3f. And see Luke 1:68, I Peter 1:3. For other praise exclamations or doxologies see Rom. 11:36; 16:25–27; II Cor. 9:15; Eph. 3:20, 21.

The apostle concludes this little paragraph by adding a wholehearted and worshipful *Amen* to the benediction he has uttered just now. It is a word of solemn affirmation and enthusiastic approval. For more about this word *Amen* see N.T.C. on Matthew, pp. 290, 291, and on John, Vol. I, pp. 110, 111.

26, 27. Because of this, God gave them over to passions that bring dishonor. For as well as their females [or women] exchanged natural intercourse for that (which is) contrary to nature, so likewise also the males [or men], having abandoned natural intercourse with the female [or woman], were consumed by flaming passion for one another, males with males [or men with men] perpetrating shamelessness, and receiving in their own persons the due return for their deviation.[43]

---

43. Note τε ... τε: as ... so; not only ... but also; as well as ... so likewise. The rendering "even their women" (A.V. and some commentators) cannot be recommended.

θήλειαι, nom. pl. f. of θῆλυς, female. See also Matt. 19:4; Mark 10:6; Gal. 3:28. In certain contexts the word, however, can be rendered "woman."

χρῆσις (here acc. s. -ν), use, usefulness, but in the present context: sexual intercourse. Secular Greek also employs the term in that sense. For example Xenophon, in his ΣΥΜΠΟΣ-ΙΟΝ (*Banquet*) 8.28, writes, "Not only human beings but also gods and demigods set a higher value on friendship of the spirit than on τὴν τοῦ σώματος χρῆσιν, "use of the body," that is, sexual intercourse. Similar examples of χρῆσις in the sense of "sexual relations" can be found in the writings of Plato, Plutarch, Isocrates, etc.

ἐξεκαύθησαν, third per. pl. aor. indicat. pass. of ἐκκαίομαι, to be inflamed; only here in the New Testament. But compare I Cor. 7:9, though the "burning" mentioned there is of a different character: in a sense it is not "contrary to nature."

ὀρέξει, dat. s. of ὄρεξις, ardent longing, lust; cf. ὀρέγω, to desire eagerly, reach out after (I Tim. 3:1; I Tim. 6:10; Heb. 11:16).

ἀσχημοσύνη (here acc. s. -ν), in the New Testament used only here and in Rev. 16:15. The

The connection between verse 26 and verse 25 is the same as that between verse 24 and verses 22, 23. In each case the sin is mentioned first, then the result. Now Paul no longer dwells on sexual immorality in general, as in verse 24, but becomes specific, and focuses the attention on one of its most disgusting manifestations, namely, wilful homosexuality.

For "God gave them over" see on verse 24.

". . . to passions that bring dishonor." Here we find an echo of verse 24b: "so that their bodies were dishonored among themselves."

". . . their females exchanged natural intercourse for that (which is) contrary to nature." This "exchange" reminds us of the "exchange" mentioned in verses 23 and 25: ". . . the glory of the immortal God for an image . . .""; "God (who is) the truth, for a lie."

It is clear that the apostle is censuring the wilful practice of homosexuality or sodomy. And, indeed, Scripture does not make light of this vice. In Lev. 20:13 the death penalty is pronounced upon its perpetrators. For more information on this horrible evil read Gen. 19:4–9; Lev. 18:22; 20:13; Deut. 23:17, 18; Judg. 19:22–24; I Kings 14:24; 15:12; 22:46; II Kings 23:7; Isa. 3:9; Lam. 4:6; and see also I Cor. 6:9, 10; Eph. 4:19; I Tim. 1:10; II Peter 2:6; Jude 7.

A person's sexual orientation, whether heterosexual or homosexual is not the point at issue. What matters is what a person does with his sexuality!

According to the plain teaching of Scripture sexual intercourse was intended for a husband and his wife, for no one else! (Gen. 2:24). See also Matt. 19:5; Mark 10:7, 8; I Cor. 6:16; Eph. 5:31. All else is "contrary to God's will." It is in conflict with the Creator's intention.

It is not clear why homosexual relations between females (lesbianism) is condemned *before* illicit relations between males (pederasty). The only explanation that has any merit, as far as I can see, is the one according to which the apostle wanted to place special emphasis on the male-with-male perversion; hence, kept the condemnation of this vice for the close of the sentence, so that he would then be able to enlarge on it, since, of the two homosexual sins it was probably the most prevalent.

". . . males with males perpetrating shamelessness." Throughout the

---

word is derived from ἀ and σχῆμα; hence, "without (proper) form," deformed, shameful; and the noun as here used means shamelessness, indecent acts, improper behavior. In Rev. 16:15 it refers to a person's *shame:* that is, "private parts."

ἀντιμισθία (here acc. s. -ν). From my dissertation on *The Meaning of the Preposition ἀντί in the New Testament,* p. 81, I quote the following:

"This word is used in a favorable sense in II Cor. 6:13; in an unfavorable sense in Rom. 1:27, the only two New Testament passages in which it occurs. The fact that the ἀντιμισθία is here regarded as a "return" or requital for a certain kind of action is clearly brought out by the addition of the words ἣν ἔδει in Rom. 1:27. The ἀντιμισθία is that which was due. Moreover, the base-word itself already suggests the idea of a return. Therefore the meaning of the preposition is clear."

πλάνης, gen. s. of πλάνη, wandering; cf. *planet:* "wandering star." What is meant in the present context is, accordingly, a wandering away (or deviation) from the proper course, a perversion.

apostle uses the terms *males* and *females* (thus literally). He stresses the distinction between the sexes, as is also done in the following passages: Gen. 1:27; 5:2; Lev. 12:7; 27:3–7; Num. 5:3; Matt. 19:4; Mark 10:6; Gal. 3:28. The rendering "men" and "women" is also possible. Nevertheless, the sins here condemned are committed not only by men and women, but also, at times, by "boys" and "girls."

"... receiving in their own persons the due return for their deviation."

That this wicked practice results in a harvest of bitterness has been proved again and again and is being demonstrated every day of the year. Some of the fruits are: a guilty conscience, sleeplessness, emotional stress, depression. Moreover, such mental discord does not leave *the body* untouched. In his very interesting book *None of These Diseases,* Westwood, New Jersey, 1963, p. 60, Dr. S. M. McMillen informs us that according to a report published in 1948 two-thirds of the patients who went to a physician had symptoms caused or aggravated by mental stress.

Truly "God is not mocked. Whatever a person sows, that also he will reap. For he who sows to his own flesh [i.e., allows his old nature to have its own way] will from the flesh reap corruption, and he who sows to the Spirit [allowing the Spirit to rule over him] will from the Spirit reap life everlasting" (Gal. 6:7, 8. See also I Cor. 3:17; 6:19, 20; 10:31).

The best of all remedies against reaping the fruits of corruption is the practice of the kind of life described beautifully in such passages as Rom. 12; I Cor. 13; Gal. 5:22, 23; and Eph. 5.

28. And since they did not deem it worthwhile to retain the knowledge of God, he gave them over to (their) worthless disposition, to do what is improper...[44]

Here for the third and last time our attention is focused on the correlation between man's rejection of God and God's rejection of man. For the two previous references to this correlation see verses 24 and 26. Men's arrogance comes to the fore in the expression, "They did not deem it worthwhile to retain the knowledge of God," the very knowledge to which reference was made in verses 18–21; note especially, "For although they knew God" (verse 21). Instead of regarding this knowledge about God which they were deriving from his revelation in nature to be a precious

---

44. ἐδοκίμασαν, 3rd per. pl. aor. indicat. act. of δοκιμάζω. In certain contexts this verb means: to prove, test, examine (Rom. 12:2; I Peter 1:7; etc.). It may also mean: to approve (after testing), see fit; consider worthwhile. For this meaning see Rom. 14:22; I Cor. 16:3; and our present passage, Rom. 1:28.

ἀδόκιμον, not approved; hence, rejected, unable to pass the test, worthless, disqualified, unfit (Rom. 1:28; I Cor. 9:27; II Cor. 13:5–7; II Tim. 3:8; Titus 1:16; Heb. 6:8).

Note word-play: οὐκ ἐδοκίμασαν ... ἀδόκιμον νοῦν: they did not approve, did *not* deem (it) *worthwhile ... worthless* disposition.

On the meaning of the noun ἐπίγνωσις and the cognate verb ἐπιγινώσκω see the article by R. E. Picerelli in *E.Q.,* Vol. XLVII, April–June, 1975, pp. 85–93.

καθήκοντα, acc. pl. n. pres. participle of καθήκω (κατά plus ἥκω), to come down (to), to be becoming, proper; hence here τὰ μὴ καθήκοντα indicates the things that are not becoming, not proper; hence improper, indecent, immoral.

treasure, they were constantly attempting to suppress it (verse 18) and, as is stated here in verse 28, regarded it as a negligible entity. They did not deem it to be worthwhile to pay any attention to God and to his revelation. So they continued on their sinful way, as described in verses 21–27 (the way of idolatry and immorality). In fact, the improper things the apostle has in mind probably also covered those mentioned in verses 29–32. Note that an evil "disposition" or "mind" or "attitude" results in evil *deeds*.

29–31. ... having become filled with every kind of unrighteousness, wickedness, greed, depravity; being full of envy, murder, strife, deceit, and malice. (They are) gossips, slanderers, haters of God, insolent, arrogant, boastful, inventors of (novel forms of) evil, disobedient to (their) parents, senseless, faithless, loveless, pitiless.

The list of vices mentioned in Rom. 1:29–31 should be compared with similar lists elsewhere in Paul's writings: Rom. 13:13; I Cor. 5:9–11; 6:9, 10; II Cor. 12:20, 21; Gal. 5:19–21; Eph. 4:19; 5:3–5; Col. 3:5–9; I Thess. 2:3; 4:3–7; I Tim. 1:9, 10; 6:4, 5; II Tim. 3:2–5; and Titus 3:3, 9, 10.

Whether there were factors other than identity of authorship (for example, already existing lists) that account for this resemblance is difficult to ascertain.

The most simple and logical way to divide the twenty-one vices mentioned in Rom. 1:29–31 is to list them in three groups:

a. one group of four vices (in the original each in the dat. s.), these four being introduced by the words "having become filled with every kind of";

b. one group of five vices (all in the gen. s.), introduced by "being full of"; and

c. one group of twelve items, beginning with "gossips."[45]

The final four items in this group of twelve form a kind of sub-group, each member beginning with ἁ-privative (equal to English prefix *un, dis-*, or suffix *-less*).

The 4-5-12 grouping is also accepted by Cranfield, Murray, Ridderbos, Robertson, etc.

It will be noticed that no longer is there any specific reference to sins of sex, since that subject has been fully treated in the preceding verses.[46]

GROUP OF FOUR

unrighteousness. See on verse 18.

wickedness. This describes those people who take delight in doing what is wrong.

---

45. In the original πεπληρωμένους is in apposition with αὐτούς in verse 28. Also in apposition is the entire third group, beginning with *gossips* (literally "whisperers").

46. There is no textual justification for the insertion of the word πορνείᾳ ("fornication" A.V.) in verse 29.

greed. This is covetousness, over-reaching, the craving for more and more and still more possessions, no matter how they are obtained. At times, as in Eph. 5:3, the word applies to ravenous self-assertion in matters of sex, at the expense of others.

depravity. This is badness in general. It is hard to distinguish it from wickedness.

GROUP OF FIVE

envy.[47] This is the keen displeasure aroused by seeing someone having something which you begrudge him.

murder. Envy often leads to murder. This was true in the case of Cain who murdered Abel (Gen. 4:1–8; I John 3:12). It was true also with respect to those who demanded Christ's crucifixion (Matt. 27:18; Mark 15:10). And was it not envy that caused the brothers of Joseph to plan his death? See Gen. 37:4, 18.

strife. This refers to a quarrelsome disposition and its consequences.

deceit. This is cunning, treachery.

malice. This indicates malignity, spite, the desire to harm people.

GROUP OF TWELVE

gossips. The "whispering" slanderers are meant. They do not—perhaps do not dare to—come out in the open with their vilifying chatter, but whisper it into someone's ear.

slanderers. What the gossips do *secretly,* the slanderers do *openly.*

haters of God. The word used in the original more often refers to those who are hated by God. However, the word is also used at times, as it is here, to indicate those who hate God.

insolent. See also I Tim. 1:13. This marks overweening individuals. They treat others with contempt, as if *they* (these insolent ones) and *they alone,* amounted to anything, and all others amounted to nothing.

arrogant. These fellows consider themselves "supermen."

boastful. Such people are constantly bragging about themselves. Think of Lamech (Gen. 4:23, 24), of Sennacherib (II Chron. 32: 10–14); and of those described in Isa. 10:8–11; 14:13, 14.

inventors of (novel forms of) evil. The reference is to those who take special delight in inventing "original" methods of destroying their fellowmen.

disobedient to (their) parents. Read Exod. 20:12; Lev. 19:3; Prov. 20:20; Matt. 15:4; 19:19; Eph. 6:2.

And now the little sub-group of four:

senseless.[48] These are the people that are "void of understanding." But this is not merely a mental weakness; it is also a moral blemish. They are

---

47. Note the sound-similarity in the original between φθόνου (envy) and φόνου (murder).

48. Note assonance (in the original) between this and the next item: ἀσυνέτους, ἀσυνθέτους.

stupid because they have all along been unwilling to listen to God! See Matt. 15:16; Mark 7:18; Rom. 10:19 (cf. Deut. 32:2).

faithless. They are "not true to the covenant," hence are perfidious, not to be trusted. See Ps. 73:15; 78:57; 119:158.

loveless. The meaning is: without natural affection. It was not at all unusual for pagans to drown or in some other way to destroy unwanted off-spring. In this connection think of present-day *abortion,* for which all kinds of excuses are being invented.

pitiless. The reference is to people without mercy, cruel persons, ruthless ones. Think not only of *the robbers* in the parable of *The Samaritan Who Cared* (Luke 10), but also of *the priest* and *the Levite,* the two who "passed by on the other side."

32. And although they know the ordinance of God that those who practice such things are worthy of death, they not only continue to do them but also approve of those who practice them.

What Paul is saying is that the perpetrators of the crimes, either implied or expressed in verses 29–31, must not be regarded as being so innocent that they cannot distinguish between right and wrong. On the contrary, they know—have an awareness of the fact—that according to God's ordi-nance, his decree, those who practice such vices are worthy of death.

How do they know this? They know it because a righteous and holy God has revealed himself to them in nature (1:21) and in conscience (2:14, 15); in fact, is constantly doing this. Accordingly, they sense the fact that God will call them to account, and that continuing in their evil way will result in perdition for them. Nevertheless, in spite of this awareness, they not only continue to practice these vices and to perpetrate these crimes but even applaud others who do the same.

There are those who see a problem here; as if the apostle were saying that rejoicing to see other people engage in wickedness while you yourself abstain is even more wicked than taking part in such evil practices yourself. Having created this problem, they then try to solve it.

But is it not true that what Paul is actually saying is that those who *not only* practice these vices *but also* applaud others who engage in them are even worse than those who simply practice them? For example, a person might commit a wicked deed. Afterward he is sorry. Perhaps he even warns others. But here is another person who not only commits evil and continues to do so, but who *in addition* encourages others to copy his example, applauding them when they do so. Certainly such an individual has reached the climax of perversity.

Having reached the close of the chapter, and looking back, we should not forget that Paul's real purpose in writing it was to show that man's (here particularly the Gentile's) wickedness is so great that only God is able to rescue him. Only when man accepts the divinely appointed way of salva-tion, namely, that of embracing God by faith, can he be saved. To God alone be the glory!

Practical Lessons Derived from Romans 1

Verse 1

"Paul . . . a called apostle, one set apart for the gospel of God." It was God who called Paul and who set him apart for his special task. Does not this prove that, in the final analysis, Romans is *God's* letter addressed to the church and individual believer in every age? And does not this knowledge make the epistle even more precious?

Verse 4

"the Son of God *invested with power,* namely, Jesus Christ our Lord."
The fact that there are no limits to that power, and the additional fact that it is exercised in our interest—note "*our* Lord"—should comfort us in every trial, so that, with the author of Hebrews (2:9), we exclaim, " . . . But we see Jesus . . . crowned with glory and honor."

Verse 7

"Grace to y o u and peace," etc.
When a person becomes a Christian everything changes. Even the manner in which he greets people is transformed. See the explanation of this verse.

Verses 8, 9, 11, 15

" . . . *my* God . . . whom I serve *from the heart* . . . I *am yearning* to see y o u . . . hence my *eagerness* to preach the gospel also to y o u in Rome."
Many people get "all excited" about picnics or sports. Paul is "excited" about God. Note his enthusiasm and eagerness in the quoted expressions.

Verse 11

" . . . in order that I may impart . . ."
Paul knew that the Christian's business in life is "to impart," that is, to be a blessing.

Verse 12

"I mean that . . . we may be mutually encouraged by each other's faith, both y o u r s and mine."
The apostle is also convinced that even the lowliest child of God can impart something to him (Paul).

Verses 16, 17

" . . . to everyone who exercises faith . . . from faith to faith . . . shall live by faith."
Again and again Paul mentions faith, looking away from oneself for salvation, and looking to God to receive it as a gift.
From the Translator's Preface of my translation of Dr. Herman Bavinck's work on *The Doctrine of God* (published by that title, in paperback, Grand Rapids, 1977) I quote the following:

"'My learning does not help me now; neither does my Dogmatics; faith alone saves me.'

"These remarkable words, uttered by one of the greatest Reformed theologians, Dr. Herman Bavinck, should not be misinterpreted. They were uttered on his death-bed and did not imply that this humble child of God retracted anything that he had written, or that he was trying to express regrets. The statement simply means that a system of doctrine, however necessary and valuable, is of no avail in and by itself. It must be translated into Christian living. There must be genuine faith in the Triune God as manifested in Jesus Christ. Now, Dr. Bavinck was, indeed, a man of faith, a faith which in his case was working through love."

Verse 18

"For the wrath of God is being revealed from heaven against all ungodliness and unrighteousness . . ."

The attempt to downgrade God's wrath is foolish. That wrath should fill our hearts with joy and satisfaction, for if God's wrath did not blaze against sin, how could he be a holy God? And how would it be possible for a God lacking the quality of holiness to save us?

Besides, we insist on drastic measures against crime, and on the appointment or election of judges and officers who do not think lightly of crime. Is it consistent, then, to expect that the evil practice which fills the minds and hearts of decent men with horror and indignation should leave *God* untouched? Therefore, instead of trying to minimize the reality of God's wrath, should we not rather thank him for his marvelous plan whereby the Son of God bore the wrath of God in our stead?

Verses 21–32

"For although they knew God, they neither glorified him as God nor gave thanks to him . . . they exchanged the glory of God for an image . . . Therefore God . . . gave them over to sexual immorality . . . to passions that bring dishonor . . . They not only practice such (wicked) things but also approve of those who practice them."

Notice that sin begets sin. Apart from God's grace the sinner descends lower and lower on the ladder of evil. The lesson: *Avoid the first downward step.* By God's grace and power, keep clinging to God and to his will for our lives, as revealed in Scripture.

Summary of Chapter 1

In what may be called a Prologue or Introduction, Paul, a servant of Christ Jesus, and a called apostle, pronounces his official salutation upon the members of the church located in Rome, the empire's capital (verses 1–7).

The apostle expresses his elation over the fact that the faith of these Romans is being proclaimed everywhere, and he tells them that he is asking God to grant him the opportunity to visit them soon (verses 8–15).

He then announces what may, in a qualified sense, be termed his *theme,* namely, "the gospel is the power of God for salvation to everyone who exercises faith." In other words, justification, which is basic to salvation, is by faith alone. This great truth was by divine direction proclaimed first of all to the Jews, and is now also to be made known to the Gentiles. In confirmation of the theme Paul adds the words found in Hab. 2:4b, "But the righteous shall live by faith." All this is found in Rom. 1:16, 17.

Having stated that the way of salvation is the same for everyone, namely, by faith alone, Paul now divides the human race into two groups: Gentiles and Jews.

He first of all describes the conditions existing in the Gentile world. He shows that although God, by means of his general revelation, made himself known to the Gentiles, "they neither glorified him as God nor gave thanks to him" (verses 18-21). Instead of worshiping the one true God, they became idol worshipers (verses 22, 23). As a result God at last abandoned them (verses 24, 26, 28) to their own sinful practices, including not only wilful homosexuality (verses 24-27) but also many other vices, twenty-one of which are mentioned in verses 29-31.

The chapter closes on this dismal note: "And although they know the ordinance of God that those who practice such things are worthy of death, they not only continue to do them but also approve of those who practice them" (verse 32).

Outline (continued)

Justification by Faith

3. *The Jews also need this justification.*
"Therefore you have no excuse, O man, whoever you are,
when you pass judgment (on someone else), . . . because you,
the judge, are practicing the same things."
2:1—3:8

CHAPTER 2:1—3:8

2 1 Therefore you have no excuse, O man, whoever you are, when you pass judgment (on someone else), for at whatever point you judge the other person, you are condemning yourself, because you, the judge, are practicing the same things.
2 Now we know that God's judgment is justly pronounced[49] against those who practice such things. 3 And do you imagine—you who, though you pass judgment on those who practice these things, do the same things yourself—that you will escape God's judgment? 4 Or do you look down on the riches of his kindness, forbearance, and patience, not realizing that God's kindness seeks to bring you to conversion?
5 But by your hard and unconverted heart[50] you are storing up for yourself wrath in the day of wrath and of the revelation of the righteous judgment of God, 6 who will render to every person according to his deeds. 7 To those who, by perseverance in doing what is right, are seeking glory, honor, and immortality (he will give) life everlasting, 8 but for those who are filled with selfish ambition and who disobey the truth but obey unrighteousness (there will be) wrath and anger. 9 (There will be) affliction and distress for every human being who is an evil-doer; first for the Jew, also for the Greek; 10 but glory, honor, and peace for everyone who does what is good; first for the Jew, also for the Greek; 11 for God does not show partiality.[51]
12 For all who have sinned in ignorance of the law [or: apart from the law] will perish even though they do not know the law [or: will perish apart from the law]; and all who have sinned knowing the law [or: under the law] will be judged by the law. 13 For it is not the hearers of the law who are righteous in God's sight, but it is the doers of the law who will be pronounced righteous. 14 For when Gentiles who do not possess the law do by nature things required by the law, they are a law for themselves, even though they do not have the law, 15 since they show that the work required by the law is written on their hearts, their consciences also bearing witness, and their thoughts between themselves now accusing, now even defending them.
16 (All this will become clear) on the day when, according to my gospel, God, through Jesus Christ, will judge men's secrets.
17 Now you, if you call yourself a Jew, and rely on (the) law, and brag about your relationship to God, 18 and, being instructed out of the law, know (his) will, and approve the things that really matter;[52] 19 and if you are convinced that you are a guide for the blind, a light for those in darkness, 20 an instructor of the foolish, a teacher of the immature,[53] because in the law you have the embodiment of knowledge and truth—21 you, then, who teach someone else, don't you teach yourself? You who preach that people should not steal, do you steal? 22 You who say that people should not commit adultery, do you commit adultery? You who

---

49. Literally: is according to truth.
50. Or: hardness and unconverted heart.
51. Literally: for there is no partiality with God.
52. Or: the things that are excellent.
53. Or: of infants.

abhor idols, do you rob temples? 23 You who brag about the law, do you dishonor God by (your) transgression of the law? 24 As it is written,

"Because of y o u the name of God is being
blasphemed among the Gentiles."

25 Circumcision does indeed profit, but only if you put the law into practice. But if you are a transgressor of the law, your circumcision has become uncircumcision. 26 Therefore, if the uncircumcised man keeps the requirements of the law, will not his uncircumcision be regarded as circumcision? 27 Indeed, he who is physically uncircumcised but keeps the law will condemn you, who, though provided with the written code and circumcision, are a transgressor of the law. 28 For he is not a (real) Jew who is one only on the outside, nor is (true) circumcision something external and physical. 29 But he is a (real) Jew who is one inwardly; and (real) circumcision is a matter of the heart, by the Spirit, not by the written code. Such a person's praise is not from man but from God.

3:1 What advantage, then, does the Jew have, or what is the value of circumcision? 2 Much in every respect. First of all, they have been entrusted with the oracles of God. 3 And what if some (of them) were unfaithful? Their unfaithfulness does not nullify God's faithfulness, does it? 4 By no means! Let God be true, and every person a liar. As it is written:

"That thou mayest be proved right in thy words
And prevail in thy judging."

5 But if our unrighteousness confirms God's righteousness, what shall we say? The God who inflicts wrath is not unrighteous, is he? (I speak from a human standpoint.) 6 By no means! For then how could God judge the world? 7 (Someone might object) "If through my falsehood God's truthfulness is enhanced to his glory, why am I still being condemned as a sinner?" 8 Why not say—as we are being slanderously reported and some claim that we say—"Let us do evil that good may result"? Their condemnation is deserved.

---

3. *The Jews also need this justification.*
"Therefore you have no excuse, O man, whoever you are,
when you pass judgment (on someone else), . . . because you,
the judge, are practicing the same things."
2:1—3:8

1. Therefore you have no excuse, O man, whoever you are, when you pass judgment (on someone else), for at whatever point you judge the other person, you are condemning yourself, because you, the judge, are practicing the same things.

Many are puzzled by the word "Therefore" (or "Wherefore"). It must be admitted that its meaning is not immediately clear. The following interpretation, however, seems to be supported by the preceding context: "Since it has been established (1:18–32) that the immoral practices of the Gentiles are an abomination to God, *therefore* you, too, whoever you may be, are without excuse when you practice these same evils, the very vices you condemn in others."

The question might be asked, "But does not the description of the evil practices of the Gentiles prove that Jew and Gentile differed considerably in their manner of life?" It has already been admitted that, on the whole, that is true. See on 1:18. It is true, however, only in a certain sense. For example, the Gentiles were idolaters. But many a Jew, by means of his self-righteousness, was making an idol of *himself*. Many a Gentile refused to repent. But so, in his own way, did many a Jew. Besides, as the apostle shows in 2:21–23, many specific sins were committed by both Jew and Gentile, by each in his own way.

We now understand what the apostle means when he says, ". . . at whatever point you judge the other person, you are condemning yourself, for you, the judge, are practicing the same things." Before we leave this passage (to which we shall return again in our Practical Lessons) we must not fail to notice how closely Paul's reasoning approaches that of Jesus. See Matt. 7:1–4; Luke 6:41, 42.

2. Now we know that God's judgment is justly pronounced [or: is according to truth] against those who practice such things.

For the expression "*we* know" or "*we* agree"—that is, "*y o u*, who read or hear this, and *I*, the writer, agree"—see also 3:19; 7:14; 8:22, 28; II Cor. 5:1; I Tim. 1:8.

Though this statement is, of course, meant for everyone who reads or listens to the reading of Romans, as, in a sense, is true of everything in Scripture, it was intended especially for the Jews, specifically mentioned in verses 9, 10, 17, 28, 29; 3:1, 9. They were the very people who were always bragging about the fact that they *possessed* the "law" (God's special revelation reduced to writing, what we today call the Old Testament), as if mere *possession* made them better than any other people. So the apostle reminds them of the fact that self-righteous people will not escape the judgment. What God requires is that we *do* the things he commands.

Do these people think, perhaps, that because the hour of the final accounting has not yet arrived, they can afford to ignore the divine warnings?

"God's judgment is justly pronounced," that is, it is ever in line with absolute truth and justice. That is by no means always the case with respect to human evaluations. "I'm six feet tall," exclaimed the little boy. When his father asked him how he had arrived at this conclusion, he replied, "I found a stick as big as myself, and I divided it into six equal parts, calling each part a foot. That makes me just as tall as you are: six feet." We smile about the argumentation of the little fellow, but do we not often make ourselves guilty of similar reasoning: measuring ourselves and others by our own measuring rod? The result is often a too favorable estimate of ourselves, and a too harsh judgment of others.

The point Paul makes is that in the final analysis human judgments, whether about ourselves or about others, do not count. God's judgment, on the other hand, is inescapable:

3. And do you imagine—you who, though you pass judgment on those who practice these things, do the same things yourself—that you will escape God's judgment?

The implication is clear. II Cor. 5:10 expresses it in these words, "For we must all appear in our true character before the judgment seat of Christ, so that each one may receive what is due him for the things done (while he was) in the body, whether it be good or whether it be worthless." It is clear that no one can escape this judgment.

Paul continues **4. Or do you look down on the riches of his kindness, forbearance, and patience, not realizing that God's kindness seeks to bring you to conversion?**

One reason for a sense of security—false security, of course—has been given, namely, "Being a Jew, I am in possession of God's holy law." Now a second reason for this baseless tranquility is added, namely, "I have not been abandoned by God to a life of scandalous immorality (1:22-32); therefore it must be that God's kindness (or goodness, generosity), forbearance, and patience (or longsuffering) are still smiling upon me. He must be very pleased with me." For more on "forbearance" see on 3:25 and compare 8:32.

The apostle, on the other hand, reminds the self-righteous Jew that the purpose of God's *kindness*—here probably representing all the three previously mentioned qualities—is not at all to make him feel self-satisfied but rather to bring him to *conversion*. When the Jew reflects on the vices of the Gentiles he should bear in mind that even if it should be true that he does not have any of them, he has nothing to brag about. The absence of any number of pagan vices does not constitute even a single virtue. Not even a billion zeros make a single plus. What the Jew should do is this: he should constantly remember that God's aim in being so kind to him is to bring him to *conversion*.

The rendering *repentance* is not the best, although sorrow for sin is certainly included in what Paul has in mind. Repentance may be called the negative aspect of conversion. The positive aspect is reaching out to God by means of genuine trust and wholehearted surrender. Conversion indicates a complete turnabout: from Satan to God; from sin to holiness. See II Cor. 7:8-10; II Tim. 2:25. It is the frame of mind, heart, and will of the person who says,

> Other refuge have I none;
> Hangs my helpless soul on thee.[54]

Lines from "Jesus Lover of My Soul"
by Charles Wesley

Note the piquant contrast between the arrogant disposition of the self-righteous Jew, who resists conversion, and the kindness of God that seeks to bring him to conversion. For the divine qualities here mentioned see also the following passages: Gen. 18:22-33; Exod. 34:6; Num. 14:18; Neh. 9:17; Ps. 86:15; 103:8; 145:8; Isa. 1:18; 55:6, 7; Ezek. 18:23, 32; 33:11;

---

54. On μετάνοια (verse 4) and ἀμετανόητος (verse 5) see J. Behm's article in Th.D.N.T., Vol. IV, pp. 975-1009; B. B. Warfield, *Biblical and Theological Studies*, Philadelphia, 1954, p. 366; and W. D. Chamberlain, *The Meaning of Repentance*, Philadelphia, 1943, p. 22.

Hos. 11:8; Joel 2:13; Jon. 4:2; Mic. 7:18, 19; Nah. 1:3; Luke 13:8; II Peter 3:9. Also see N.T.C. on Luke, pp. 76, 696, 697.

5-8. But by your hard and unconverted heart you are storing up for yourself wrath in the day of wrath and of the revelation of the righteous judgment of God, who will render to every person according to his deeds. To those who, by perseverance in doing what is right, are seeking glory, honor, and immortality (he will give) life everlasting, but for those who are filled with selfish ambition and who disobey the truth but obey unrighteousness (there will be) wrath and anger.

Over against the delusion of those who were constantly condemning others but refusing to be converted (verses 3, 4) the apostle now reveals the true situation. He informs them that even though the wrath of God may not as yet have reached the Jew in the manner in which it had already been revealed to the Gentile, this does not mean that it will never be poured out on him. It merely indicates that for a while his (the Jew's) punishment is being suspended. All the while, however, that wrath is, as it were, piling up. This must be true, for the sin of the Jew is very grievous. To describe it the apostle uses the expression, "your hardness and unconverted heart." But in this case we must probably link "hardness" with "heart," as Scripture does so often. For the Old Testament see Deut. 10:16; Prov. 28:14; Ezek. 3:7; and for the New Testament Matt. 19:8; Mark 3:5; 6:52; 8:17; 10:5; John 12:40; Heb. 3:8, 15; 4:7. Thus we arrive at the phrase "your hard and unconverted heart."[55]

It should be noted that the person whom Paul addresses is himself the agent in piling up wrath for himself. Moreover, the wrath is that of God, as in 1:18, but in the present case the pouring out of this wrath is connected with, and takes place on, "the day of wrath and of the revelation of the righteous judgment of God," that is, on *the day of the final judgment.* Though some (for example, K. Barth) reject this explanation, it is supported by the following arguments.

a. The broader context (verse 16) favors it. Note, "(All this will become clear) on the day when, according to my gospel, God, through Jesus Christ, will judge men's secrets."

b. In fact, the *immediate* context (verse 6) describes this day as the one in which God "will render to every person according to his deeds." This reminds one of Matt. 16:27, "For the Son of man shall come in the glory of his Father, with his angels, and then shall he render to each according to his deeds."

c. See also the following passages:

I Cor. 3:13 ("the day")

I Cor. 4:3-5

---

55. For this construction see also Behm in the article to which reference was made in the preceding footnote; p. 1009, footnote 3.

> I Thess. 5:4 ("that day")
>
> II Thess. 1:7-10
>
> II Tim. 4:8.

The day of *wrath* (see on 1:18) is the same time the day of "the revelation of the *righteous* judgment of God." Here the truth mentioned in verse 2, namely, that God's judgment is "according to truth" is essentially repeated. Among men judgments are by no means always "righteous."

The fact that every person will be judged "according to his deeds" is taught throughout Scripture (Eccl. 11:9; 12:14; Matt. 16:27; 25:31-46; John 5:28, 29; I Cor. 3:12-15; 4:5; II Cor. 5:10; Gal. 6:7-9; Eph. 6:8; Rev. 2:23; 11:18; 20:12, 13).

The question has been asked, however, "If God judges people 'according to their deeds,' how can salvation be 'by grace alone'?" Now it should be emphasized that the line "Naught have I gotten but what I received" (James M. Gray) is thoroughly scriptural. Salvation is indeed by grace alone (Ps. 115:1; Isa. 48:11; Jer. 31:31-34; Ezek. 36:22-31; Dan. 9:19; Acts 15:11; Rom. 3:24; 5:15; Eph. 1:4-7; 2:8-10; I Tim. 1:15, to mention only a few passages). Nevertheless, again and again when Paul emphasizes divine sovereignty or saving activity he immediately links it with human responsibility (Eph. 2:8-10; Phil. 2:12, 13; II Thess. 2:13; II Tim. 2:19). Granted that man cannot perform his duties or discharge his responsibilities in his own strength, it is nevertheless he to whom a task is assigned. God does not assume this task for him. But, in his sovereign grace and love, God rewards man for his faithfulness in accomplishing what has been assigned to him. Moreover, both rewards and punishments are distributed *in accordance with the degree of faithfulness or unfaithfulness* shown by anyone. In the final analysis it is the person who makes light of the thoroughly biblical doctrine of human responsibility who has any real problem.

In verses 7, 8 Paul divides mankind into two large groups, as Jesus had done again and again (Matt. 7:24-29; 10:39; 11:25, 26; 12:35; 13:41-43; 18:5, 6; 21:28-32; 23:12; 25:29, 46; etc.).

The first group consists of all who *persevere* (Matt. 24:13; Col. 1:23; Heb. 3:14; Rev. 2:10) in doing what is right; not *right* merely in the eyes of other people, a standard of measurement which the apostle has just now condemned (verses 1-3), but right in God's eyes. These are people whose aim is high (Phil. 3:8-14). By persevering in God-glorifying deeds they are aiming to obtain *glory* (see above on 1:23, item "a" in the list of Meanings), *honor,* and *immortality,* that is, incorruptible and indestructible resurrection life in never-ending bliss, that of the new heaven and earth (Rom. 8:23; I Cor. 15:42, 50-57; I Peter 1:4; II Peter 3:13; Rev. 21:1—22:5).

On them God will bestow *life everlasting,* the totality of that life which was already in principle their portion before death. On the day of the final judgment they receive this blessing in full measure for both soul and (as far as applicable) body.

And what is life everlasting? According to Scripture it is fellowship with God in Christ (John 17:3), possession of the peace of God that transcends all understanding (Phil. 4:7), joy inexpressible and full of glory (I Peter 1:8), the light of the knowledge of the glory of God in the face of Christ (II Cor. 4:6), and the love of God poured out into one's heart (Rom. 5:5), all of this to continue forever and ever.

The second group consists of those who are filled with selfish ambition. Instead of obeying the truth, they lend their ears to whatever is God-dishonoring. For them there will be wrath and anger; that is, on the day of the final judgment and forever afterward they will be the objects of God's keen displeasure and indignation. They will always be conscious of this, and will never be able to get out from under it.[56]

The sharp contrast between the everlasting destiny of the two groups, as portrayed here in Rom. 2:7, 8, can be compared with the similarly contrasting descriptions found in the book of Revelation:

A. *The Blessedness of the Saved*

"Never again shall they be hungry, and never again shall they be thirsty. The sun shall not beat down on them nor any heat, for the Lamb, sitting in the center of the throne, shall be their shepherd. He shall guide them to springs of living water, and God shall wipe away every tear from their eyes" (Rev. 7:16, 17).

B. *The Wretchedness of the Lost*

"The sound of harpists, musicians, flute players, and trumpeters shall be heard in you never again.

A workman in any trade shall be found in you never again.

The sound of a millstone shall be heard in you never again.

---

56. For ἐριθεία see L.N.T. (A. and G.), p. 309. In addition to its occurrence here in Rom. 2:8 this word is also found in II Cor. 12:20; Gal. 5:20; Phil. 1:17; 2:3; James 3:14, 16. Its meaning is disputed. If there is a connection between this word and ἔρις, the meaning might be strife, contentiousness, faction. On the other hand, if the word is derived from ἔριθος, a hireling, the meaning would be: the spirit of a hireling; hence, selfish ambition, selfishness (cf. John 10:12). In the present passage (Rom. 2:8), since man's everlasting destiny is at stake, the concept *selfishness* or *selfish ambition,* more basic than *contention,* may well be the meaning. In support of this theory it is generally pointed out that Aristotle in a couple passages of his work *Politics* uses the word in that more basic sense.

What may well be an even stronger argument in favor of the view that ἐριθεία = *selfish ambition* is the fact that both in Gal. 5:20 and in II Cor. 12:20 ἐριθεία is used in addition to ἔρις, which would probably not be the case if the meaning were identical. Also, it has been shown (see N.T.C. on Galatians, pp. 218, 220, and on Philippians, pp. 72, 100) that the rendering "selfish ambition" suits the context in Gal. 5:20 and Phil 1:17; 2:3. It also is in line with the context in II Cor. 12:20 and James 3:14, 16.

For the difference between ὀργή and θυμός see on 1:18. If, when these two words are used in connection with *God,* there is a difference in meaning, it would probably be that ὀργή stresses the *presence* or *feeling* of keen divine displeasure or indignation, while θυμός places the emphasis on its *effusion.*

The light of a lamp shall shine in you never again.

And the voice of bridegroom and bride shall be heard in you never again" (Rev. 18:22, 23).

9–11. (There will be) affliction and distress for every human being who is an evil-doer; first for the Jew, also for the Greek; but glory, honor, and peace for everyone who does what is good; first for the Jew, also for the Greek; for God does not show partiality [or: for there is no partiality with God].

First a comment about the form, then about the meaning of this passage.

As to *form,* it is clear that the antithesis found in verses 7, 8 is reproduced here in inverted order. This is true in two respects:

a. In verses 7, 8 the obedient were mentioned before the disobedient; in verses 9, 10 the opposite is true.

b. In verses 7, 8 the description of the person (whether obedient or disobedient) precedes the mention of the reward (7b) or punishment (8b). The reverse is true with respect to verses 9, 10.

As to *meaning,* here in verses 9, 10 the fact is stressed that not what a person imagines himself to be but what he actually is in God's sight, as demonstrated by his life, his works, determines what will happen to him in the final judgment. This holds for every "soul of man," that is, for every living person.

For the evil-doer (verse 9) there will be *outward affliction* and *inward distress.* Cf. 8:35.

In connection with well-doers (verse 10), note that what according to verse 7 God's people were seeking, namely, "glory and honor and *immortality,*" is also what they receive, namely, "glory and honor and *peace.*" Here the terms "immortality" and "peace" may be viewed as being, at least to a considerable extent, synonymous. See what was said in the preceding about "immortality." The word "peace" should be interpreted in its broadest sense, as indicating salvation full and free, joyful and never-ending participation, with renewed soul and body, in all the blessings of the new heaven and earth. This, of course, includes sweet fellowship with God Triune and with all the redeemed. All this to God's glory!

Since in the order of history the Jews had received the gospel before the Greeks or Gentiles, this order—first the Jew; then the Greek—will also be taken into account in the final judgment. Neither with respect to punishment nor with respect to reward will the fact be lost sight of that the Jews had been privileged far above the Gentiles (1:16; 3:1, 2; 9:4, 5).

This, however, must not be interpreted to mean that God will deal more generously with the Jew than with the Gentile. On the contrary "God does not show favoritism" (verse 11), a lesson Peter had to learn (Acts 10:34).

We are reminded of a passage from the lips of Jesus:

"From every one who has been given much, much will be required; and from the one who has been entrusted with much, all the more will be demanded" (Luke 12:48).

12, 13. For all who have sinned in ignorance of the law [or: apart from the law][57] **will perish even though they did not know the law [or: will perish apart from the law]; and all who have sinned knowing the law [or: under the law] will be judged by the law. For it is not the hearers of the law who are righteous in God's sight, but it is the doers of the law who will be pronounced righteous.**

The statement that every person will be judged according to his deeds (verses 6–11) receives clarification and augmentation in the present passage. The apostle underscores the fact that what counts both now and in the day of the Grand Assize is not whether people have possessed the law or have heard it read to them in the synagogue or elsewhere, but whether they have conducted their lives in harmony with its requirements.

Those who have sinned in ignorance of the law—cf. I Cor. 9:21—in other words, the Gentiles, will perish even though they did not know the law. That by using the word "law" the apostle is thinking especially of the Pentateuch, even more precisely, of the law of the Ten Commandments, is clear from verses 21, 22. Cf. Rom. 13:8–10. They will perish because of their *sins*. And, on the other hand, those who were privileged to possess and/or to hear the law must not think that this fact as such will be of any benefit to them before God. On the contrary, disobeying the law which is being constantly dinned into one's ears will make condemnation so much more severe. Not those who merely hear, but those who hear *and do* will be pronounced righteous.

A word of caution is necessary at this point. It must be borne in mind that at this juncture the apostle is not drawing a contrast between justification *by faith* and justification *by the works of the law*. Those who would so interpret

---

57. Twice in one verse the original uses the word ἀνόμως. It is related to the noun ἀνομία and to the adjective ἄνομος.

The noun, as it occurs in Matt. 7:23; 13:41; 23:28; 24:12; Rom. 6:19; II Cor. 6:14; Titus 2:14; Heb. 1:9 can be rendered "lawlessness" or "wickedness." In Rom. 4:7 it has reference to lawless deeds, offenses. "The man of lawlessness" (Antichrist) is mentioned in II Thess. 2:3, and "the mystery of lawlessness" in II Thess. 2:7. I John 3:4 states that "sin is lawlessness."

The adjective ἄνομος, in the sense of *lawless*, occurs in Luke 22:37 (gen. pl.): "He was numbered with the lawless ones," that is, "with the transgressors." Note also "By the hands of lawless (or wicked) men . . ." (Acts 2:23), and cf. I Tim. 1:9. II Peter 2:8 mentions "lawless deeds."

Nevertheless, with respect to Rom. 2:12 the rendering "All who have sinned *lawlessly*" would be the worst kind of tautology, since "sin is lawlessness," as has been indicated.

How, then, must we render the *adverb* ἀνόμως? It is clear that the meaning of the noun ἀνομία or of the adjective ἄνομος, as it is used in the passages cited in the preceding, does not help any. What will help is the use of the *adjective* in I Cor. 9:21. Here the rendering "I (became) lawless [that is wicked]" would be wrong. Paul cannot have meant that he became wicked to those who were wicked. The meaning must be, "To those without law (or: not having the law) I became as one without law (or: not having the law)." That passage supplies the key to the correct translation of the adverb ἀνόμως here in Rom. 2:12. The meaning is: "All who have sinned in ignorance of the law will perish even though they did not know the law; and all who have sinned knowing the law will be judged by the law." Here the first ἀνόμως (apart from the law) can be rendered "in ignorance of the law," and the second ἀνόμως must mean, and can be freely translated "though they did not know the law."

what he is saying would be making Paul contradict himself, for the very purpose of this letter is to show that a person is not justified by the works of the law but by faith in Christ. No, the antithesis he is discussing here in 2:12, 13 is that between two groups of people: (a) those who not only hear but also obey, and (b) those who merely hear. Cf. Matt. 7:24–29. It is, of course, the former who are pronounced righteous by God. Cf. Lev. 18:5, "If you obey them [my statutes] you shall live."

So interpreted, that rule holds even for those believers who are living in the new dispensation. Precisely because they have been delivered from the curse of the law, they are all the more deeply obliged not only to hear but also to obey the gospel. By their good deeds, resulting from gratitude, they show that by God's sovereign grace and power they have given their hearts to him. In him alone do they place their trust. From him they have received their status of being righteous in God's eyes.

When Paul discusses the antithesis: justification *by faith* or *by works* he will make very clear that it is not by works but by faith that a person is justified (Rom. 3:20, 28; 4:2; Gal. 2:16; 3:11, 12). See on 3:20, 28.

14, 15. For when Gentiles who do not possess the law do by nature things required by the law, they are a law for themselves, even though they do not have the law, since they show that the work required by the law is written on their hearts, their consciences also bearing witness, and their thoughts between themselves now accusing, now even defending them.

Some translators and commentators consider verses 14, 15 to be a parenthesis.[58] One of the reasons for this construction is that verse 15 does not seem to link naturally with verse 16.

The *objections* to the idea of a parenthesis beginning with verse 14 are:

a. The connection between verses 13 and 14 is too close to justify their arbitrary separation which such a parenthesis would bring about.[59]

b. Placing parentheses around verses 14, 15 does not solve the difficulty of getting rid of the seemingly unnatural connection—or lack of connection—between verses 15 and 16.

As I see it, the solution to the problem lies in the direction pointed out by J. Denney in his comments on verse 16; *The Expositor's Greek Testament* (on Romans), Vol. II, Grand Rapids, n.d., p. 598, and by Ridderbos on the page to which reference was made in the preceding footnote. Verse 16 should be linked with the main verbs of the entire little paragraph: God's righteous judgment *will be revealed* (verse 5); all who sin under the law *will be judged* (verse 12); while those who obey the law *will be declared righteous* (verse 13), all this is to take place and to become clear "on the day when . . . God will judge men's secrets" (verse 16). Somewhat similarly Rid-

---

58. A.V. includes even verse 13 in this parenthesis.
59. So also Ridderbos, *op. cit.,* p. 62. He describes the connection between verses 13 and 14 as a *natural* one.

derbos states that for the proper understanding of verse 16 one should preface its statement with "All this will become clear." See my translation. Similar is also the rendering of verse 16 found in Phillips, namely, "We may be sure that all this will be taken into account in the day," etc. What we have in verse 16 is almost surely a case of "abbreviated expression." On this subject see N.T.C. on John, Vol. I, p. 206.

So much for *the construction* of these verses. As to *the meaning* of verses 14, 15, note the following:

Paul has just now stated that whether a person sinned in ignorance of the law or knew the law—hence, whether he be Gentile or Jew—he will be treated as a transgressor if he conducts himself in a manner contrary to God's holy law. Every person will receive a penalty or a reward commensurate with his deeds (see verse 6). This does not cancel the fact that the measure of light one has received will be taken into account. See Amos 3:2; Luke 12:47, 48.

The objection might be raised, "But is this fair to the Gentile? After all, he does not have the faintest notion about God's law. Why, then, should he be punished at all?"

As shown in verses 14, 15, this objection is not valid. Even though the Gentile does not have the law as originally written on tablets of stone (Exod. 24:12), God wrote on his heart—for this idiom see Jer. 31:33; II Cor. 3:3—what was the work required by the law. He equipped him with a sense of right and wrong. He did not permit even the Gentile to remain altogether without a testimony concerning God. Cf. Ps. 19:1–4; Acts 17:26–28; Rom. 1:28, 32. This accounts for the fact that Gentiles are "a law for themselves." By nature—that is, without prompting or guidance coming from any written code, therefore in a sense spontaneously—a Gentile will at times do certain things required by God's law. For example, he is kind to his wife and children, has a heart for the poor, promotes honesty in government, shows courage in fighting crime, etc.

What God has written on his heart finds a response in this man's conscience. As the etymology of the word, both in Greek and in English (from Latin) implies, conscience is a *knowledge along with* (or shared with) the person. It is that individual's inner sense of right and wrong; his (to a certain extent divinely imparted) moral consciousness viewed in the act of pronouncing judgment upon himself, that is, upon his thoughts, attitudes, words, and deeds, whether past, present, or contemplated. As the passage states, the resulting *thoughts* or *judgments* are either condemnatory or, in certain instances, even commendatory. For more on conscience see 9:1; 13:5.[60]

---

60. τὸ ἔργον τοῦ νόμου. For similar construction see John 6:29, where "the work of God" means the work required by God, the work that is in harmony with his will.

Note the gen. absolute συμμαρτυρούσης αὐτῶν τῆς συνειδήσεως. The question has been asked, "What is the significance of the prefix σύν in the gen. s. fem. pres. participle συμμαρτυρούσης? Does conscience bear witness along with the thoughts? Along with the people? Or

16. (All this will become clear) on the day when, according to my gospel, God, through Jesus Christ, will judge men's secrets.

The connection between this verse and the preceding context has already been discussed. The meaning of verse 16, then, is along this line, that on Judgment Day "all this"—men's thoughts, words, actions, motivations, God's evaluations—will become clear. It is on that day that God will judge not only men's open deeds but even their secrets (Eccl. 12:14; Luke 12:3; I Cor. 4:5).

A few additional matters require our attention:

a. God will judge "through Jesus Christ."

It is true that in the original the modifier "through Jesus Christ" is far removed from "God will judge," and is much closer to "according to my gospel." It is for this reason that some commentators link "my gospel" with "through Jesus Christ." They reach the conclusion that what the apostle is really saying is that it was Jesus Christ who had entrusted him with the gospel. Now the fact as such that Paul had received the gospel from Christ is not only true but is even worthy of emphasis. See N.T.C. on Gal. 1:1. But this is definitely not the thought here in Rom. 2:16. Here, as frequently, the emphasis is on the fact that God will judge mankind through his Son, Jesus Christ. A passage which, in more than one respect, parallels Rom. 2:16 is I Cor. 4:5, "Therefore judge nothing before the appointed time. Wait until the Lord comes, who will both bring to light the things hidden in darkness and will expose the motives of men's hearts." Other passages in which the truth that God judges through Jesus Christ is taught, either directly or by implication, are Matt. 25:31–36; John 5:22; Acts 17:31; II Cor. 5:10.

b. Since "the darkness and the light are both alike to God" (Ps. 139:12), it should not sound strange that God, through Christ, will judge both what was done in the darkness and what was performed in open daylight.

c. Paul adds "according to my gospel." It was the apostle's gospel because in its fulness it had been conveyed to him by the Lord, and because he, Paul, loved it. Ponder his words, "Woe to me if I preach not the gospel (I Cor. 9:16)!" The good news is not complete without the very important

---

must we assume that although originally the prefix strengthened the meaning of the verbal form, its added strength gradually faded, as happened frequently in such cases, with the result that what Paul is saying is simply this, that the conscience of these people bore witness to that which God had written on their hearts?" This explanation probably deserves the preference.

Another gen. absolute is καὶ μεταξὺ ἀλλήλων τῶν λογισμῶν κτλ. Does this have reference to thoughts between Gentile and Gentile, or to thoughts between (or among) themselves? Probably the latter, for

a. The modifier "between themselves" stands closer to "thoughts" than to Gentiles. Unless there is a sound reason to do otherwise—as is sometimes the case; see on verse 16—it is generally best to link modifiers with words that stand closest to them, especially when, as in the present case, the resulting idea makes good sense.

b. It is indeed a fact that the thoughts that fill the mind as a result of the operation of conscience operate independently; in fact, so very independently that at times the involved person *hates* these thoughts or judgments. He may even rise in rebellion against them. He may curse the thoughts with which his conscience tortures him.

item with respect to the glorious day of Christ's Return unto Judgment, a day of supreme joy for every child of God. To mention a few examples of the importance the apostle attached to that second coming note the following: Rom. 8:18–23; I Cor. 15:20–58; Phil. 3:20, 21; I Thess. 1:10; 2:19, 20; 3:3:13; 4:13–18; 5:1–11, 23, 24; II Thess. 1:5–10; 2:1f.; Titus 2:11–14.

Before leaving this important passage (Rom. 2:14–16) there is one more lesson to which I wish to call the reader's attention. That lesson is: *in our doctrinal views we should try to avoid extremes.*

Note how, by implication, Paul is teaching us this principle. He is in the process of establishing the thesis that there is only one way in which the sinner, whether Gentile or Jew, can attain to the status of being accepted by God. That way was opened by God himself. Gentiles need this "justification by faith" because "although they knew God, they did not glorify him as God, or give thanks." Jews also need it, for "they practice the same things." Both Gentile and Jew are by nature bad . . . bad . . . bad.

Yet, in the midst of this section the statement occurs, "Gentiles who do not possess the law do by nature the things required by the law." In other words, Paul is not forgetting that there is a sense in which it is legitimate to say that the unregenerate can do good.[61] God's image in man has not been completely destroyed.

This reminds us of Calvin, who similarly avoided extremes in writing about this same subject. In his *Institutes of the Christian Religion* (tr. by John Allen, Philadelphia, 1928, Vol. I, p. 264) he speaks about "the universal state of human depravity." Note also ". . . man is so enslaved by sin, as to be of his own nature incapable of an effort, or even an aspiration, toward that which is good" (p. 278). Nevertheless, he also states, "in all ages there have been some persons who, from the mere dictates of nature, have devoted their whole lives to the pursuit of virtue. . . . Some men have not only been eminent for noble actions, but have uniformly conducted themselves in a most virtuous manner throughout the whole course of their lives. But here we ought to remember that amidst the corruption of human nature there is some room for divine grace, not to purify it, but internally to restrain its operations" (pp. 262, 263).

When Aristotle gave the advice that people should eagerly render service to those in need (*The Nicomachean Ethics* IX. 6), and when he ordered that at

---

61. This follows unless one adopts the theory favored by K. Barth (going back even to Augustine), according to which the reference here in Rom. 2:14 is to Gentile Christians. See Barth's *Kirchliche Dogmatik*, Zollikon-Zurich, 1932, Vol. I, p. 332; and his *Shorter Commentary on Romans*, London, 1959, p. 36. Others who defend this view are F. Flückiger, in his article "Die Werke des Gesetzes bei den Heiden (nach Röm. 2:14ff.)," *ThZ* 1952, pp. 17–42; and Cranfield, *op. cit.,* p. 56.

Objections:

1. The passage clearly states that the Gentiles "by nature" perform these "things required by the law." This expression "by nature" must mean "before conversion."

2. The passage refers to Gentiles "who do not possess the law." This too, as 13:8, 9 and many other references indicate, cannot refer to Christians.

his death some of his slaves should be set free, was he not, in a sense, doing good? Does not the Old Testament record generous deeds performed by such Gentiles as Cyrus (Ezra 1:1–4; 5:13–17), Darius (6:1–12), and Artaxerxes (7:11–26)? Note what Ezra says about the deed of the latter (7:27, 28). II Chron. 24:20–22 does not leave the impression that King Joash was a child of God. Nevertheless, II Chron. 24:2 states, "And Joash did that which was right in the eyes of Jehovah all the days of Jehoiada the priest."

When the city clerk of Ephesus quieted the rioters (Acts 19:35–41), was not that to a certain extent a good deed? When Romans of high standing protected the apostle Paul (Acts 23:12–30; 27:43), was not that commendable? And the deed of those "barbarians" who "showed unusual kindness to Paul and those with him, building a fire and welcoming all because it was raining and cold" (Acts 28:2), was not also that a manifestation of "goodness"?

To be sure, man is by nature "totally depraved," in the sense that depravity has invaded every part of his being: mind, heart, and will. If he is to be saved it is God who must save him. Man cannot save himself. This, however, does not and cannot mean that he is "*absolutely* depraved," as bad as he can be, as bad as the devil himself. Did not also Jesus teach that there is a sense in which even the unconverted "do good"? See Luke 6:33.

The lesson Paul teaches—namely, *Avoid Extremes!*, should be taken to heart.

The remainder of chapter 2 can be divided into the following units:

a. A description of Jewish self-exaltation (verses 17–20), leading to:

b. A series of questions for self-examination. Paul asks how the Jews dare to accuse the Gentiles of sins they themselves commit (verses 21–23).

c. A grave accusation (verse 24).

d. A portrayal of the contrast between the true and the merely nominal Jew; and between heart circumcision and literal circumcision (verses 25–29).

A. *A Description of Jewish Self-Exaltation*

17-20. Now you, if you call yourself a Jew, and rely on (the) law, and brag about your relationship to God, and, being instructed out of the law, know (his) will, and approve the things that really matter [or: the things that are excellent]; and if you are convinced that you are a guide for the blind, a light for those in darkness, an instructor of the foolish, a teacher of the immature [or: of infants], because in the law you have the embodiment of knowledge and truth...

Although the Jews were uniquely privileged, enjoying advantages above all others, they did not seem to realize that these blessings implied obligations. Many of these people, instead of using their superior endowments to help those in need, merely bragged about their prerogatives. This attitude of boastfulness found expression in various ways, as will be indicated.

First of all, they bragged about the very fact that they were Jews, probably thinking, "Since we are Jews, we are better than everybody else." Was it
not true that a Jew had a right to consider himself a member of the chosen
race? Read Exod. 19:6; Deut. 10:15; Isa. 43:20, 21.

Now Paul is not altogether condemning pride of race or of nationality.
Did not Mordecai, probably with a feeling of pride, proclaim, "I am a Jew"?
See Esther 3:4. However, it makes a universe of difference in what spirit
and with what purpose a person says this. Does he mean, "By God's sovereign, unmerited grace I am a worshiper of the only true God, and I regard
it my high privilege to make all my wants and wishes known to him, and to
dedicate my life completely to him and his cause. Therefore I cannot and
will not bow down before, and pay homage to, anyone or to anything else"?
That was undoubtedly the spirit in which Mordecai told people that he was
a Jew. But when a person says, "I am a Jew," implying, "Therefore I am
better than you. Listen carefully to me, and do whatever I say," he is *placing
confidence in himself,* not in God.

". . . and rely on (the) law." Here again we must bear in mind that there is
a sense in which relying or resting on God's law is the right thing to do. Is
not God's law the standard according to which a person's conduct should be
regulated? And did not the Psalmist "take delight" in God's law? Read Ps.
119. However, the Jews whom Paul had in mind were committing a twofold
error with respect to relying on the law: (1) the mere possession of, and
instruction in, the law gave them a sense of security and superiority; and (2)
they believed that by means of a strenuous and continued effort to obey
that law they could, as it were, earn salvation.

". . . and brag about your relationship to God," as if this relationship—if,
in any given case, it even existed—had been brought about by good deeds!

Here, for the first time in Romans the apostle uses the verb *to boast* or *to
brag.* The word used in the original[62] is in the New Testament almost
confined to the writings of Paul. It occurs five times in Romans (2:17, 23;
5:2, 3, 11), twice in Galatians (6:13, 14); once in Ephesians (2:9); once in
Philippians (3:3); but by far most frequently in the Corinthian correspondence: five (perhaps six) times[63] in I Corinthians, and no less than
twenty times in II Corinthians. So all in all Paul uses this verb 34 or 35
times. It is also found in James 1:9; 4:16.[64]

At times this verb is used in a favorable sense; for example, ". . . far be it
for me *to glory* except in the cross of our Lord Jesus Christ" (Gal. 6:14).

---

62. Here καυχᾶσαι, 2nd per. s. pres. indicat. (for καυχᾷ) of καυχάομαι, to boast or brag
(about), exult, glory, or take pride in.

63. Six times if this verb is authentic in I Cor. 13:3.

64. The cognate noun καύχημα occurs ten times in Paul's letters; once in Heb. 3:6; while
καύχησις also is found ten times in the writings of Paul; once in James 4:16. The compound
κατακαυχάομαι is found only in Rom. 11:18; James 2:13; 3:14. See also R. Bultmann,
Th.D.N.T., Vol. III, pp. 648–654.

There is such a thing as glorying in the Lord (II Cor. 10:17) or in Christ Jesus (Phil. 3:3). The apostle is even able to glory in his weaknesses, for when he is weak, then (in the Lord) he is strong (II Cor. 12:9, 10).

Often, however, the verb is used in an unfavorable sense. For example, the Corinthians were *boasting* or *bragging* about *men*, almost as if they owed their salvation to *them* (I Cor. 1:12, 29). So Paul tells them, "No more boasting about men!" (I Cor. 3:21; cf. 4:7). "Let him who boasts, boast in the Lord" (II Cor. 10:17). But although glorying or exulting in the Lord is wonderful, bragging about one's close relationship to God, as if its attainment had been a human achievement, is very sinful. And this is what the Jews whom Paul had in mind were doing.

". . . and being instructed out of the law, know (his) will, and approve the things that really matter . . ."

Though it is possible to construct "being instructed out of the law" solely with "approve the things that really matter," I can see no reason why this *instruction out of* (hence, based on) *the law* should not also be linked with "know (his) will." Certainly both the knowledge of God's will and the ability and desire to rank essentials above non-essentials, resulted from being "catechized" in the law. On "being catechized" or "instructed" see also N.T.C. on Luke 1:4, p. 62.[65]

As a result of being catechized in the law, the Jew was supposed to be able and desirous to approve the things that really mattered. He regarded himself as a person who knew the difference between essentials and non-essentials, preferring the former. Instead of "and approve the things that really matter" or "the essential things," the rendering "and approve the things that are excellent" is also possible. In *meaning* these two translations differ only slightly. See N.T.C. on Phil. 1:10.

What Paul is saying, then, is this, "If you call yourself a Jew, and rely on the law . . . and, being instructed out of the law, know (his) will, and approve the things that really matter. . . ." He now adds, "and if you are convinced that you are a guide for the blind," etc.

Note the four parallel items:

(1) *a guide for the blind.*

Physical blindness is mentioned with great frequency in Scripture. See, for example, Lev. 21:18; 22:22; Deut. 15:21; 28:28, 29; II Sam. 5:6; Zeph. 1:17; John 5:3. It was due to various causes, among which may well have been unsanitary environment, venereal disease, lack of eye care immediately after birth. During the days of Christ's sojourn on earth he restored sight to many a blind person (Matt. 9:27-30; 11:5; 12:22; 20:30-34; Mark 8:22-26; 10:46-52; Luke 7:21; John 11:37). Jesus also instructed his audiences to treat blind people with special kindness, inviting them to their banquets, etc. (Luke 14:13, 21).

---

65. The verb χατηχέω is used also with reference to instruction in *the gospel*. See Acts 18:25; Gal. 6:6. In Acts 21:21 the sense is *to inform*.

Guides were needed to lead the blind (II Kings 6:19; Matt. 12:22). They must be *reliable* guides. See Deut. 27:18.

It is understandable that by an easy transition, probably already evident in Deut. 27:18, physical blindness became the symbol of intellectual, moral, and spiritual blindness (Isa. 42:19; 56:10; Rom. 11:7, 8; II Cor. 4:4; I John 2:11). Note especially the impressive transition from the one (physical) to the other (spiritual) in John 9:1, 7, 39-41.

Very sad indeed was the condition of spiritually blind *people* if they were being led by similarly blind *guides* (Matt. 15:14; 23:16-24; and cf. Luke 6:39).

When, therefore, Paul now writes, "If you are convinced that you are a guide for the blind," is he not implying, "Be sure that you are a reliable guide!"? We can understand that many a Jew, instructed in temple and/or synagogue, must have regarded himself as being indeed a capable guide for those not equally *privileged* (?).

(2) *a light for those in darkness*

The Bible of the Jews was and is a mission book, from beginning—"In your seed shall all the nations of the earth be blessed" (Gen. 22:18)—to end—"From the rising of the sun even to its setting my name shall be great among the Gentiles" (Mal. 1:11). And in between beginning and end we read "I have appointed you as a light for the Gentiles" (Isa. 42:6). See also Isa. 9:2; 49:6; 58:8; 60:3.

To a certain extent the Jews understood this. Living in the midst of a pagan environment—especially during the captivity, but to some extent even earlier and in a sense also again during the days of Christ's sojourn on earth—they not only defended themselves against heathen attacks upon their monotheism but even carried the war into the enemy's camp by attacking the polytheism and the wickednesses, especially sexual perversity, of the Gentiles. The holy books too were translated into languages which the Gentiles could understand. To a certain extent, therefore, the Jews were a blessing for the surrounding nations. Many a pagan found Christ by means of the stepping stone of the synagogue, for it was here that Jesus and later on his apostles, especially Paul, proclaimed the gospel of salvation. See N.T.C. on Mark, *The Synagogue During New Testament Times*, pp. 74-77.

That is one side of the picture. The other side is described by Jesus in Matt. 23:15, in these words, "Woe to y o u, scribes and Pharisees, hypocrites! because y o u travel about on sea and land to make a single proselyte, and when he has become one, y o u make him twice as much a son of hell as y o u are yourselves." It was not so much the purpose of scribes and Pharisees to change a Gentile into a Jew; no, he must become a full-fledged, legalistic, ritualistic, hair-splitting Pharisee, one filled with fanatic zeal for his new salvation-by-works religion. As Jesus implies, soon this new convert would even out-Pharisee the Pharisees in bigotry, for it is a fact that new converts frequently outdo themselves in becoming fanatically devoted to their new faith.

With all this in mind, it will be easier to understand Paul's remark, "and *if* you are convinced that you are . . . a light for those in darkness. . . ."

(3) *an instructor of the foolish*

What Paul probably meant was, "If you are convinced that you have been endowed with so much wisdom and knowledge that you are thoroughly qualified to teach those (in your estimation) foolish know-nothings . . ."

(4) *a teacher of the immature*

A rendering that merits consideration and may well be correct is "a teacher of *babes* [or infants]." See I Cor. 3:1; Eph. 4:14; Heb. 5:13. It is easy to understand that a Jew, having been drilled in the knowledge of the law from his youth might deem himself thoroughly capable of imparting instruction to Gentiles; or, if he considered that a task for his teachers, the scribes (cf. Matt. 23:15), and would prefer not to approach too closely to those who in his eyes were unclean, he could at least teach recent converts (to Judaism) from paganism. Paul adds, "having in the law the embodiment [or repository] of knowledge and truth." That the law of God, minus the load of man-made restrictions and modifications, was indeed a priceless and inexhaustible treasure cannot be denied. The law of the Ten Commandments, the entire Pentateuch, even better the entire Old Testament, was indeed a source of knowledge (Ps. 119:66) and truth (Ps. 119:142).

If now for a moment we summarize what Paul is saying—"If you are convinced that you are a guide for the blind, a light for those in darkness, an instructor of the foolish, a teacher of infants, because in the law you have the embodiment of knowledge and truth . . . ," does it not seem that Calvin was right when he characterized this part of Paul's sentence as being tinged with ridicule? The apostle is probably saying, "If you think you are really so learned and wise and capable, is it not high time that you begin to examine *yourself*?"

B. *A Series of Questions for Self-Examination*

21-23. . . . you, then, who teach someone else, don't you teach yourself? You who preach that people should not steal, do you steal? You who say that people should not commit adultery, do you commit adultery? You who abhor idols, do you rob temples? You who brag about the law, do you dishonor God by (your) transgression of the law?

First a word about the *construction* of this passage. It is held by some that verses 17-23 contain a number of anacolutha, that is, statements in which the grammatical construction with which the sentence begins is not completed: the condition (or protasis) does not have the expected conclusion (or apodosis). The answer is that though, strictly speaking, there is some truth in this assertion, in the broader sense the charge is untrue. What Paul is saying amounts to this, "If you present yourself as a person who relies on God and his law, and even teach others the meaning of this law and impress upon them that they should live in harmony with it, how is it that you yourself do not practice what you preach?"

Another matter touching on construction is this, "Should verse 23 be translated as a *statement* (so, for example, N.E.B. and Cranfield), or as a *question*?" The original allows either. Those who favor the first alternative base their opinion on the fact that verse 24 is a confirmation—note γάϱ—of that which precedes. But how can it be a *confirmation* of a *question*?

On the surface this reasoning sounds convincing. But is it? Verse 23 can still be regarded as a question if in connection with verse 24 the very real possibility of abbreviated discourse is kept in mind. See N.T.C. on John, Vol. I, p. 206. The sense of verse 24 would then be, "(I ask this question) for because of y o u the name of God is being blasphemed among the Gentiles."

Moreover, the reason I, along with most translators, favor the idea that verse 23 is a question is that both in form and content it harmonizes with the four preceding lines (about teaching, stealing, committing adultery, and robbing temples).

It is interesting to note how precisely Jewish sources agree with the implied charges made here by Paul. The question, "You who teach others, don't you teach yourself?" is found again and again in rabbinical writings. Note the following: "You have many a man who teaches himself but does not teach others, many a man who teaches others but does not teach himself, many a man who teaches himself and others, and many a one who teaches neither himself nor others" (S.BK. III, p. 107).

For instances of stealing that occurred among the "learned ones" see the same source, again p. 107; for adultery, pp. 109-111—sometimes of a very scandalous nature among the rabbis!—; and for the robbing of temples, pp. 113-115.

That the life of many a scribe and/or Pharisee was not in keeping with his teaching, and certainly not in harmony with God's holy law as found in Scripture, is brought out clearly by Jesus (Matt. 23; Mark 7:9-13; Luke 11:37-52).

It is asserted at times that there is no proof in Scripture that Jews could be legitimately charged with the crime of robbing temples. However, is there not certain evidence which might indirectly point to its actual occurrence? Note the following:

If something resembling this evil had never occurred or had never been in danger of occurring, why would it have been so sternly forbidden in Deut. 7:25? Moreover, does not the fact that according to Acts 19:37 the city clerk at Ephesus, in quieting a tumultuous crowd, asserted, "Y o u have brought these men [Paul and his traveling companions] here, *though they have neither robbed temples* nor blasphemed our goddess," indicate that such *sacrilege* (temple robbery) was not altogether unheard of? Besides, why would Paul have mentioned it here in 2:22 if in this respect the Jews were completely innocent?[66]

---

66. Add to all this the reference to temple robbery in Josephus, *Antiquity* IV.207. Without corroborative value but too interesting to pass by in silence is the mention of temple robbery in

Paul's final question is, "You who brag about the law, do you dishonor God by (your) transgression of the law?" The very question shows that the apostle realized that among his Jewish opponents there was a sharp contrast between theology and practice, between doctrine and life. To attain acceptance with God on the basis of obedience to his law, such obedience must, of course, be perfect, a goal unattainable here on earth. In fact, with respect to Paul's opponents the very opposite was true, as he now indicates by means of

C. *A Grave Accusation*

24. As it is written, "Because of y o u the name of God is being blasphemed among the Gentiles."

The quotation is based on Isa. 52:5. It is an adaptation of the LXX version[67] of that passage. The context, however, is somewhat different in the two cases. The Old Testament passage takes into consideration the assumption on the part of the Gentiles that when a nation is conquered and deported, its god has also been conquered. So the conquered nation is blasphemed along with its god. Cf. Ezek. 36:20. Here in Rom. 2:24 the Gentiles are represented as reasoning: the people (Israel) behave wickedly; therefore their god must be wicked also, for people resemble their god.

The two instances are alike, however, in this respect: in both cases Israel had failed to be what according to Rom. 2:19 it pretended to be, namely, a light for those in darkness. It was for that reason that Israel was deported and its God mocked. It was also for that reason that God's name was in Paul's day being blasphemed among the Gentiles.

D. *A portrayal of the contrast between the true and the merely nominal Jew; and between heart circumcision and literal circumcision*

25-27. Circumcision does indeed profit, but only if you put the law into practice. But if you are a transgressor of the law, your circumcision has become uncircumcision. Therefore, if the uncircumcised man keeps the requirements of the law, will not his uncircumcision be regarded as circumcision? Indeed, he who is physically uncircumcised but keeps the law will condemn you, who, though provided with the written code and circumcision, are a transgressor of the law.

Paul has already shown that the Jews cannot build the castle of their confidence on the fact that they, and not the Gentiles, were in possession of

---

a fictitious story fabricated by an anti-Semite. According to this fairy tale, reported by Josephus (*Against Apion* I.310, 311), a group of condemned Jewish lepers, having been sent to the desert so that they might perish there, start out on a trip to the land that was later called Judea. Arrived, they build here a city which was called *Ierosyla* (Jerusalem), that is, according to this thoroughly corrupt etymology, "the town of temple robbers!"

On the serious side see the treatment of the verb ἱεροσυλέω and of the noun ἱερόσυλος by G. Schrenk in Th.D.N.T., Vol. IV, pp. 255-257.

67. δι' ὑμᾶς διὰ παντὸς τὸ ὄνομά μου βλασφημεῖται ἐν τοῖς ἔθνεσιν.

the law, in which they had received instruction. He now proceeds to prove that neither can they base their sense of security on the circumstance that they, and not the Gentiles, have been circumcised. Paul argues that circumcision unaccompanied by obedience to God's holy law is of no value. The same is true, of course, with respect to the water of baptism and with respect to the bread and wine in holy communion. As signs and seals these things have value, but only when accompanied by obedience. A circumcised person who is a transgressor of the law is equal to an uncircumcised individual.

The converse is also true: an uncircumcised man who in a certain sense (see on 2:14) keeps God's law is, in God's sight, equal to a circumcised person.

This causes Paul to address his Jewish opponent as follows: "Indeed, he who is physically uncircumcised but keeps the law *will condemn* you, who, though provided with the written code and circumcision, are a transgressor of the law."[68] Here again, as always, Paul agrees with Jesus. See Matt. 12:41, 42; Luke 11:31, 32.

Paul is summarizing here. What he is saying is that neither of the two grounds on which Jews often based their confidence—the possession of the law or the fact of having been circumcised—sufficed for salvation. He has already enlarged on the first point, having shown that the Jews he has in mind have not kept the law (see verses 13, 17-24). In fact, *no one* can keep the law in all its details. No one is by nature even true to its underlying principles.

Now the apostle shows that also the second ground of confidence is insecure: a circumcision that is merely outward is not any better than is the observation of the mere letter of the law. The letter kills; the Spirit imparts life (Rom. 7:6; II Cor. 3:6).

---

68. Note καὶ κρινεῖ ἡ ἐκ φύσεως ἀκροβυστία τὸν νόμον τελοῦσα σὲ (2:27a); meaning: "and the physically uncircumcised keeping the law will condemn [or judge] you," which can be interpreted as an elliptical conditional sentence: "and if the physically uncircumcised person keeps the law, he will condemn you," which, in turn, can be transposed into, "And [or Indeed], he who is physically uncircumcised but keeps the law will condemn you." See also footnote 119.

διὰ γράμματος καὶ περιτομῆς. Note various interpretations that have been given to διά as used here:

(1) because, while Gram. N.T. (Bl.-Debr.), par. 223, p. 119.

(2) manner and means shading off into one another, Gram. N.T., p. 583.

(3) accompanied by, with the advantage of, A. T. Robertson, *Word Pictures,* New York and London, 1933, Vol. IV. p. 340.

(4) attendant circumstance, Cranfield, p. 174.

It would seem that *means* (or *agency*) and *concession* (though) are both implied in this sentence. The thought is somewhat compressed, as happens often both in writing and in speaking. A.R.V. reads, "you, who *with* the letter and circumcision art a transgressor of the law." Notice "with" (hence, attendant circumstance). But, again, does not such a "with" imply "though"? We sometimes hear the expression, "*With* all his learning, he can be so foolish." Does not this "with" have the meaning "in spite of having" or "though he has"? So also in Rom. 2:27b many translations have adopted "though" or "even though" as being the best rendering of the Greek in this particular case. I agree.

Is it not clear that what Paul is actually doing is preparing the reader or hearer for the foreceful affirmation or re-affirmation of the *theme*, "Apart from the righteousness freely granted by God no one can ever attain to the state of being accepted by God"? See Rom. 1:17; 3:21-24; 5:1; etc.

A very important conclusion and climax follow:

28, 29. For he is not a (real) Jew who is one only on the outside, nor is (true) circumcision something external and physical. But he is a (real) Jew who is one inwardly; and (real) circumcision is a matter of the heart, by the Spirit, not by the written code. Such a person's praise is not from man but from God.[69]

Paul's opponents among the Jews were building their hope for eternity on the mere fact that they were Jews, and therefore, as they thought, God's chosen people. This reminds us of the days of John the Baptist when these people were similarly resting their case on the parallel circumstance that they were "Abraham's seed" (Matt. 3:9; John 8:33, 39).

Paul, on the other hand, draws a sharp distinction between Jew and Jew: (a) the person who is a Jew outwardly only; that is, a Jew by virtue of physical or biological descent, nothing more; and (b) the individual who is a Jew not only outwardly but also inwardly; that is, a Jew to the eyes of the One before whom the secrets of men's hearts and lives are an open book (Ps. 139:1-6; Rom. 2:16; Heb. 4:13).

Similarly he draws a distinction between (a) merely physical circumcision, the excision of the male's prepuce, in strict compliance with "the written code," the letter of the law (cf. Gen. 17: 10-13; Lev. 12:3); and (b) circumcision that concerns the heart: the removal (in principle) from that heart of whatever is evil; heart renewal (cf. Lev. 26:41; Deut. 10:16; 30:6; Jer. 4:4; 9:26; Ezek. 44:7), which is the work of the Holy Spirit (Rom. 7:6; II Cor. 3:6, 18; Gal. 5:16-23).[70]

Concerning the Jew who is one also on the inside, and whose heart has accordingly been circumcised by the Holy Spirit, Paul says, "Such a person's praise is not from man but from God." This is a play on words, one that goes back all the way to the book of Genesis:

"She [Leah] conceived again and gave birth to a son, and she said, 'This time I will *praise* the Lord.' Therefore she named him Judah" (Gen. 29:35).

"*Judah,* your brothers will *praise* you." (Gen. 49:8).

---

69. This is surely a striking example of abbreviated discourse. The words printed in brackets are *implied*. I agree here with Cranfield, p. 175.

οὐ γὰρ ὁ ἐν τῷ φανερῷ ['Ιουδαῖος] 'Ιουδαῖός ἐστιν, οὐδὲ ἡ ἐν τῷ φανερῷ ἐν σαρκὶ [περιτομὴ] περιτομή [ἐστιν]. ἀλλ᾽ ὁ ἐν τῷ κρυπτῷ 'Ιουδαῖος ['Ιουδαῖός ἐστιν], καὶ περιτομὴ καρδίας ἐν πνεύματι οὐ γράμματι [περιτομή ἐστιν], οὗ ὁ ἔπαινος οὐκ ἐξ ἀνθρώπων [ἐστιν] ἀλλ᾽ ἐκ τοῦ θεοῦ.

70. Verse 29 should not be rendered "by the spirit," as if the human spirit were meant: for:
(1) after "of the heart" this would be redundant; and
(2) as has been indicated, such renewal is in Scripture ascribed to the Holy Spirit.

The word JEW, derived from JUDAH, means PRAISED.[71]

As is clear from Scripture, many of the Jews praised *themselves* (Rom. 2:17-20) and were eager to receive praise from *men* (Matt. 6:1-8, 16-18; 23:5-12). Therefore, they did not deserve to be called "Jews," for, according to Rom. 2:29, a genuine Jew is one whose praise does not come from men but from God.

At this point in the explanation of Romans some commentators hurry to point out that when Paul places such emphasis on the fact that the only real Jew is the one who is a Jew inwardly, he cannot mean that there are no rich blessings in store for the Jews as a people, believers and unbelievers alike. To substantiate their position they refer to Rom. 9:1—11:36. Would it not be better to wait with drawing conclusions from that remote section until we come to it? For the present all we know is that the apostle affirms that "he is not a (real) Jew who is one only on the outside . . . but he is a Jew who is one inwardly . . . whose praise is not from men but from God." That Paul also uses the term *Jew* in a more general, physical sense is clear. He has done this in 1:16; 2:9, 10, 17, 28, is about to do it again (3:1), and will do it once more in 10:12.

Accordingly, using the term "Jew" in that more general sense, the apostle continues:

3:1. What advantage, then, does the Jew have, or what is the value of circumcision?

At this point Paul seems to be hearing an objection. It is as if someone is saying, "If, in order to amount to something, one has to be a Jew inwardly, and must have experienced the circumcision of the heart, then is there any advantage in being a Jew in the broader literal sense, or in having been physically circumcised?" Is there *any* advantage at all in belonging to the Jewish nation?

Paul answers, **2. Much, in every respect. First of all,[72] they have been entrusted with the oracles of God.**

Among the many passages showing that the Jews as a people received privileges above all other nations are the following: Ps. 147:20; Isa. 5:5, 6; Amos 3:2, 3; Matt. 22:1-8; Luke 13:6; 14:16, 17, 24; *and especially Rom. 9:4, 5, where the apostle returns to this subject and enlarges on it.*

When Paul mentally calls the roll of Jewish prerogatives, one item tops all others, namely, the fact that to the Jews, and to no other nation, was accorded the unique privilege, the high honor, of being the custodians of the *oracles* of God, that entire special revelation to Israel which consisted not only of commandments, but also of predictions and promises.

All of this had been entrusted to the Jews, to be accepted by faith, obeyed (as far as applicable), held in honor, and transmitted to others.

---

71. The Hebrew word for Judah is יְהוּדָה and for Jew יְהוּדִי. These forms are clearly connected with the Hiph'il of יָרָה, to throw, though the nature of the connection is obscure.

72. It is impossible to determine whether γάρ is authentic.

Privileges imply duties; honors go hand in hand with responsibilities. Could it be truthfully stated that Israel had shouldered these responsibilities? That it had been faithful to its trust? If not, what then? Says Paul:

3, 4. And what if some (of them) were unfaithful?[73] **Their unfaithfulness does not nullify God's faithfulness, does it? By no means. Let God be true, and every person a liar. As it is written:**

"That thou mayest be proved right in thy words
And prevail in thy judging."

That Israel as a people had been blessed with many advantages cannot be questioned. But does this fact, considered by itself, guarantee a rosy future? Not necessarily. If the Jews expect God's special blessing, they better be faithful to their trust. If they fail to be a blessing to the nations, a light to the Gentiles, their future is dark.

Illustration: A youth enrolls in college. He has the following advantages over many others: he comes from a rich family, so that paying room and board, tuition, etc., is no problem. He enjoys excellent health, and is even blessed with above average intelligence. The college he attends rates very high. His teachers are the best. In spite of all these advantages he never graduates. Why not? Because he does not make the most of his opportunities. He fritters away his time, is lazy, unfaithful to his trust.

As 2:21–23 has shown, something similar was true with respect to Israel. It too, in spite of all its special privileges, had become unfaithful to its trust, and because of this disloyalty God's name was being blasphemed among the Gentiles (2:24). As a people, therefore, unless it should experience a radical change of heart, it could not look forward to a glorious future.

Does Paul mean that *all* the Jews were doomed? He does not. Very tactfully and mercifully he states (here in Rom. 3:3) that "some" of them

---

73. Granted that in this passage τὴν πίστιν τοῦ θεοῦ means God's faithfulness, there is considerable difference of opinion with respect to the meaning of the verb ἠπίστησαν and the noun ἀπιστία. Some believe that in this passage the noun means both lack of faith and lack of faithfulness (Greijdanus). Others accept "lack of faith" (Sanday and Headlam). Among translators who have adopted this view are A.V., A.R.V., N.A.S., Berkeley, Norlie, N.I.V. Among those who favor "were unfaithful" (=untrustworthy) for the verb, and "unfaithfulness" for the noun are, among commentators, etc.: Bultmann, Th.D.N.T., Vol. VI, p. 208; L.N.T. (A. and G.), p. 84, Bruce, Hodge, Lenski, Ridderbos, Van Leeuwen and Jacobs. Among translators who support this view are Beck, Williams, Phillips, R.S.V., N.E.B., Weymouth, Moffatt, Good News for Modern Man, Jerusalem Bible, Dutch (Nieuwe Vertaling).

There is certainly room for difference of opinion, and, as Cranfield and others have pointed out, there is a very close connection between "lack of faith" and "lack of faithfulness." He who lacks faithfulness also lacks faith. Yet, I too favor the translation "were unfaithful . . . unfaithfulness." Reason: it agrees best with the present context in which God's faithfulness is contrasted with human ἀπιστία. Though the meaning of the same word in other passages of the same epistle is important, is not the immediate context even more important? Besides, not only does verse 3 point in this direction, because here the unfaithfulness of men is contrasted with God's faithfulness, but so does also verse 4, where divine veracity is synonymous with the preceding divine faithfulness, and where human mendacity reminds one of similar human unfaithfulness.

110

were unfaithful. It would seem that even now he is distinguishing between "Israel" and "Israel" (cf. 9:6). In another passage where the apostle uses the word "*some*" once in each of four successive verses, this indefinite designation seems to amount to "most" (I Cor. 10:7–10; cf. verse 5). But here in Rom. 3:3 he does not indicate the proportion. He simply writes, "What if some of them were unfaithful?" And he adds, "Their unfaithfulness does not nullify God's faithfulness, does it?"

Does he mean then, "In spite of their unfaithfulness God will still grant them a glorious future, because they are Jews"? Probably not. His real meaning seems to be this: "Since God is faithful, those Jews who are faithful to him, and therefore to that which has been entrusted to them, will certainly receive the fulfilment of his promises."

But the God who is faithful to his *promises* is also faithful to his *threats*. Divine faithfulness is a priceless comfort for the faithful, an earnest warning for those in danger of becoming unfaithful, and a harbinger of doom for those who continue to be untrustworthy. Cf. II Tim. 2:11–13.

The very suggestion that God might become unfaithful causes the apostle to shudder. He exclaims, "By no means" (or "Let it not be," "Perish the thought," "God forbid"). This expression occurs often in Paul's epistles— including Rom. 3:31; 6:2, 15; 7:7; 9:14; 11:1, 6— and elsewhere.

By adding, "Let God be true (cf. Ps. 119:9, 160; Jer. 10:10) and every person a liar (Ps. 116:11)," Paul places divine veracity (akin to faithfulness) and human mendacity (an ally of unfaithfulness) over against each other, in sharp contrast, and prays that full recognition be accorded to the former. *Human mendacity and unfaithfulness, far from nullifying divine faithfulness, causes it to stand out in bold relief.*

Paul adds words taken from Ps. 51:4b (=LXX 50:6b).

In order to understand the relevancy of this quotation for Paul's purpose we should see it on the basis of its background.

David had sinned grievously. He had committed adultery with Bathsheba, the wife of Uriah. When he had discovered that Bathsheba had become pregnant, he had, in a very deceitful manner, brought about the death of Uriah, and married Bathsheba. Then the Lord had sent Nathan the prophet to David. By means of a parable about a rich man who had deprived a poor man of his one and only "little ewe lamb," he had elicited from the lips of David the words, "As the Lord lives, the man who has done this deserves to die." Nathan's response had been, "You are the man." Result: David's deep sorrow and his admission, "I have sinned against the Lord." See II Sam. 11, 12.

In Psalm 51 David again confesses his sins and says,

"Against thee only have I sinned and done that which is evil in thy sight." In the words quoted here in Rom. 3:4b he adds, "(I confess this in order) That thou mayest be proved right in thy words And prevail in thy judging" (Ps. 51:4b).

It is clear, therefore, that David's aim was to make his confession as frank, open, and unconditional as possible, in order that on the dark background of his own unrighteousness God's righteousness in judging him would stand out the more clearly. David wants God to triumph!

Faulty and perverse human reasoning now registers an objection which Paul, almost apologizing for even paying attention to it, immediately knocks down:

5, 6. But if our unrighteousness confirms God's righteousness, what shall we say? The God who inflicts wrath is not unrighteous, is he? (I speak from a human standpoint.)[74] By no means! For then how could God judge the world?

It is clear that not only the words of Paul in Rom. 3:4a but also those of David in 3:4b quoted from Ps. 51, make God's righteousness stand out on the dark background of human sin. As the dark shadows in Rembrandt's (misnamed) *Night Watch* causes the spots of light to explode all the more brilliantly, so man's unrighteousness accentuates God's righteousness.

The opponent now raises an objection which amounts to this: "On the basis of your doctrine, Paul, since man's unrighteousness brings out more sharply God's righteousness, should not the Almighty be happy about that turn of events? Is he not unfair when, instead, he inflicts wrath on man?"

With another "Perish the thought" (or "By no means") the apostle, filled with holy indignation, crushes this wicked type of reasoning. It is as if he were saying, "What? God unfair? How do you even dare to suggest this? It is agreed, is it not, that God is qualified to judge and actually will judge the world? Well, then, how could he be unfair? Shall not the Judge of all the earth deal justly?" (Gen. 18:25).

7, 8. (Someone might object) If through my falsehood God's truthfulness is enhanced to his glory, why am I still being condemned as a sinner? Why not say—as we are being slanderously reported and some claim that we say—Let us do evil that good may result? Their condemnation is deserved.

Here are two rhetorical questions followed by a brusque appraising answer.[75]

---

74. The Greek reads κατὰ ἄνθρωπον λέγω, both here and in Gal. 3:15, "I speak from a human standpoint." I Cor. 9:8 (with λαλῶ for λέγω) has the same meaning. Note also ἀνθρώπινον λέγω, "I speak in human terms" (Rom. 6:19). With respect to the meaning of somewhat similar phrases in I Cor. 3:3 and I Cor. 15:32 opinions vary.

75. The grammatical construction of verse 8, beginning with "Why not say" is probably as follows:

a. After the opening words καὶ μὴ insert λέγομεν or something similar.

b. The parenthesis enclosed within the rhetorical question of verse 8 begins with the first καθὼς and ends with λέγειν.

c. ὅτι is recitative. For various ways in which this little word is used see N.T.C. on John, Vol. I, p. 54.

d. ὧν refers to τινες.

There is a close connection between verses 5, 6 and verses 7, 8. Compare:
"If our unrighteousness confirms God's righteousness..." (vs. 5)

with

"If through my falsehood God's truthfulness is enhanced..." (vs. 7).

In both cases the attack upon God's rectitude or righteousness is repulsed, his honor maintained.

However, there are also minor differences:

(1) Note the change from *our* unrighteousness (verse 5) to *my* falsehood... why am *I*, etc. However, the first person plural returns in verse 8.

(2) In verses 7, 8 the attention shifts from the condemnation of the attack on God's righteousness to the condemnation of the perversion of the doctrine of salvation by grace. Hence there is also a close connection between 3:7, 8 and 6:1.

Compare:
"Let us do evil that good may result" (3:8)

with

"Let us continue in sin that grace may increase" (6:1).

The opponents speak as if, when Paul taught that a person is saved by grace, he meant, "Go ahead and sin to y o u r heart's content, in order that grace may have a chance to do its work!"

For more on this terribly destructive perversion of sound doctrine see on 6:1 f.

The apostle concludes by saying, "Their condemnation is deserved." He means, "Those who flaunt this slogan will receive a just retribution. The people who so wickedly misrepresent the doctrine we proclaim will get what they deserve."

Practical Lessons Derived from Romans 2:1—3:8
A. From Chapter 2

Verse 1

"At whatever point you judge the other person, you are condemning yourself." According to a Dutch proverb,[76] "He who compares himself with another person is generally easy on himself."

Verse 3

"Do you imagine that you will escape God's judgment?"
There are all kinds of ways in which the guilty person tries to escape punishment: (a) fleeing to another country and living there under an assumed name; (b) instead

---

76. "Die zich aan een ander spiegelt, spiegelt zich zacht."

of making an excuse, immediately changing the subject so that the opponent in his excitement begins to defend himself; (c) placing himself in the hands of "a lawyer who has never lost a case." At times such tricks work, at least for a while. But one can never escape *God's* judgment, and that is what counts. Is "escape" then entirely impossible? The only real way is, "Confess. Ask forgiveness. If possible, make restitution. By God's grace begin a new life."

Verse 4

Verse 4 mentions "the riches of God's kindness, tolerance, and patience." Who can read the following passages without being overcome with emotion and gratitude? See Gen. 4:6, 7; 18:22, 23; 39:5; Ps. 36:6; 145:9, 15, 16; Isa. 1:18; 55:1, 6, 7; 57:15; Jer. 31:31–35; Lam. 3:22, 33; Ezek. 18:23, 32; 33:11; Hos. 11:8; Jonah 4:10, 11; Mic. 7:18, 19; Zeph. 3:17; Matt. 5:43–45; 11:25–30; Luke 6:35 (see also N.T.C. on Luke, p. 76); John 3:16; 7:37; Acts 14:16, 17; Rom. 8:31–39; II Cor. 5:20, 21; 8:9; I Tim. 4:10; Heb. 4:16; Rev. 22:17. The reading of this or a similar list of passages has often helped children of God while they were passing through valleys of doubt, as every pastor can testify.

Verse 5

"You are storing up for yourself wrath." If the national debt of the United States of America would be reduced by a billion dollars a year, how long would it take to pay it off? Each hour, minute, and even second the sinner is increasing the pile of his debt . . . unless, by God's sovereign grace and power, he surrenders himself to Christ and discovers that "Jesus paid it all." What a "joy unspeakable and full of glory!"

Verse 13

"It is the doers of the law who will be pronounced righteous." Good works have never saved anybody. Yet without them no one has a right to claim that he is a Christian. The believer does the works of the law "out of gratitude for salvation received as God's free gift."

Verse 15

". . . their conscience also bearing witness . . ." If conscience forbids you to do something, you should not do it. But be sure to send conscience to school, the school of the Bible. If conscience allows you to do something, does that necessarily mean that the contemplated action is right?

Verse 16

"God, through Jesus Christ, will judge men's secrets." By means of wiretapping, concealed microphones, hidden cameras, and many other devices secrets are being uncovered. Potential enemies are discovering that the nature and extent of their armor is no longer a secret. Yet, in spite of all detection equipment some secrets remain undiscovered. Not, however, before the eyes of God. Read Ps. 139. Add Heb. 4:13. Is this a dreadful thought? Could it be a source of comfort? Read John 21:17.

Verses 17-23

The apostle urges the Jews to examine themselves. Yet, again and again certain psychologists tell us that self-examination is "morbid," may lead to a dangerous guilt complex, etc. *To a certain extent* these psychologists are right. What is the solution? Study Psalm 51.

Verses 28, 29

Following the example of Matthew Henry, we can read these verses as follows, "For he is not a Christian who is one only on the outside, nor is (real) baptism something external and physical. But he is a Christian who is one inwardly; and (real) baptism is a matter of the heart, by the Spirit, not by the written code. Such a person's praise is not from man but from God."

B. From 3:1-8

Verse 3

"Their unfaithfulness does not nullify God's faithfulness, does it?" Comment on:
1. God's faithfulness . . . a frightening thought.
2. God's faithfulness, a source of comfort.

Verses 5-8

In a certain state an amendment was proposed that would have legalized casino gambling (in a specified district). The proponents argued that if this amendment passed, huge profits would result for the benefit of education, etc. These people argued as did those whom Paul denounces in Rom. 3:5-8. In what respect? See Commentary.

Summary of Chapter 2:1—3:8

Having shown that *the Gentiles* are the objects of God's wrath because of their sinful practices, the apostle now directs his attention to *the Jews*, and states that they are without excuse when they practice some of the very evils they condemn in others. Let not the Jew think that because he has not been abandoned by God to a life of most scandalous immorality, God must be very pleased with him. Rather, let him take to heart the fact that God's kindness toward him should bring him to conversion (2:1-4).

Paul continues, "But by your hard and unconverted heart you are storing up for yourself wrath in the day of wrath and of the revelation of the righteous judgment of God, who will render to every person according to his deeds . . . and who does not show partiality" (verses 5-11).

"All who have sinned in ignorance of the law will perish even though they did not know the law, and all who have sinned knowing the law will be judged by the law. For it is not the hearers of the law who are righteous in God's sight but it is the doers. . . ."

The apostle then reveals that even the Gentiles, who do not have the written law, do have a conscience which at times condemns and at times commends them. God will take all this into consideration. He will judge with absolute fairness, not showing any partiality. All this will become clear on the day of the final judgment, when God, through Jesus Christ, will judge men's secrets (verses 12–16).

The next paragraph may be condensed into this one big question, "Do you, who are a Jew, really practice what you preach?" More in detail, Paul asks, "Do you, who call yourself a Jew and rely on (the) law . . . and consider yourself a light for those in darkness, try to live in accordance with the law?" . . . "You, then, who teach someone else, don't you teach yourself; you who preach that people should not steal, do you steal?" etc. He concludes this section with the accusation, "As it is written [see Isa. 52:5] 'Because of y o u [i.e., y o u r wickedness] the name of God is being blasphemed among the Gentiles" (verses 17–24).

The Jew was of the opinion that because he had the law and had been circumcised, all was well for time and eternity. Paul answers, "Circumcision does indeed profit, but only if you put the law into practice . . . He is not a (real) Jew who is one only on the outside, nor is (true) circumcision something external and physical. But he is a (real) Jew who is one inwardly; and (real) circumcision is a matter of the heart, by the Spirit, not by the written code. Such a person's praise is not from man but from God." (verses 25–29).

At this point the apostle seems to hear an objection. It is as if someone is saying, "But Paul, do you mean that the Jews have no advantages, the most priceless of them being that the oracles of God have been entrusted to them?" (3:1, 2).

The question naturally arises, "But what if some of the Jews are unfaithful to that trust? Their unfaithfulness will not nullify God's faithfulness, will it?" Paul answers, "By no means. Let God be true, and every person a liar. As it is written,

"'That thou mayest be proved right in thy words
And prevail in thy judging.'"

Since God is faithful, those Jews who are faithful to him and to their trust will certainly receive the promised goods. Human unfaithfulness, far from invalidating divine faithfulness, causes it to stand out in bold relief; just as, for example, David, by means of his wholehearted confession (Ps. 51), caused God's righteousness in judging him to shine forth all the more brilliantly on the dark background of the adulterer's own sinfulness. See II Sam. 11, 12.

This answer, however, leads to the question, "Since this is true, namely, that man's unrighteousness brings out more sharply God's righteousness, should not God be happy about that turn of events, instead of inflicting wrath on man for his sins?" This question is asked first in 3:5 and then, in a slightly different form, in verse 7. In both cases it amounts to, "Does not the end—namely, the revelation of God's glorious attributes—justify the means, namely, man's sinfulness?"

Paul's answer is, "Perish the thought, and let the people who so wickedly misrepresent our gospel receive the punishment they deserve" (verses 3-8).

Outline (continued)

Justification by Faith

4. *Accordingly,*
"There is no one righteous, not even one."
"All have turned aside."
3:9–20

5. "But now, apart from law, a righteousness from God has been revealed . . . a righteousness through faith in Jesus Christ."
3:21–31

CHAPTER 3:9-31

9 What then? Are we any better? Not at all, for we just previously made the charge that Jews and Greeks alike are all under (the power of) sin.   10 As it is written:

"There is no one righteous, not even one;   *Eccl. 7:20*
11   there is no one who understands;
       there is no one who is searching for God.
12 All have turned aside; together they have become worthless;
       there is no one who does what is right;
       there is not even one."   *Ps. 14:3; 53:1-3.*
                                                                     LXX:13:1, 3; 52:2-4.
13 "An open grave is their throat;
       with their tongues they practice deception."   *Ps. 5:9; LXX:5:10.*
    "The poison of vipers is under their lips."   *Ps. 140:3; LXX:139:4.*
14   "Their mouth is full of cursing and bitterness."   *Ps. 10:7: LXX:9:28.*

15 "Swift (are) their feet to shed blood;
16   ruin and misery mark their ways,
17 and the way of peace they have not known."   *Isa. 59:7, 8.*
18   "There is no fear of God before their eyes."   *Ps. 36:1; LXX:35:2.*

19 Now we know that whatever the law says, it speaks to those (who are) within the pale of the law, that every mouth may be silenced, and the entire world may be exposed to the judgment of God.[77]   20 Therefore by law works no flesh[78] will be justified in his sight, for through law (comes) consciousness of sin.

---

4. *Accordingly,*
"There is no one righteous, not even one."
"All have turned aside."
3:9-20

9a. What then? Are we any better?

These words present problems. Interpretations vary widely.[79]

---

77. Or: may stand guilty before God.
78. Or: mortal being.
79. First, there is the question of the Greek text. Should we read προεχόμεθα or προεχώμεθα? Since the former has by far the strongest textual support, and there are no reasons to reject it, I accept it as being authentic. In view of οὐ πάντως, it is clear that both Τί οὖν and προεχόμεθα should be followed by the Greek question mark (;).
The next question is, "What does the verb προεχόμεθα (not to be confused with

119

The meaning, "Do we excel?" or "Are we any better?" suits the present context, in view of the fact that the status of both Gentiles (1:18–32) and Jews (2:1–3:8), a very deplorable status indeed, has been described.

The next question is, "What does *we* mean?"

As many translators and interpreters see it, the meaning is, "We Jews." But this position is vulnerable:

a. The apostle has already indicated, and this in some detail, that Jews are not better than Gentiles. See 2:1, 17–24. Why, then, should he now be raising this question again?

b. Paul has been referring to the Jew(s) in the *third* person (1:16; 2:9; 3:1), and will do so again (9:4; 10:1; 11:20; etc.); and see above, p. 21. He has also *addressed* the typical Jew, using the second person (2:17f.). In the entire preceding discussion (1:1–3:8) he has never identified himself with the Jews. Never has he said, "we Jews." What sound reason is there for supposing that he does so here in 3:9?

Moreover, he probably does not mean, "In comparison with others, do the Jews have any outward advantages or privileges?" for on this subject he has already made himself very clear (3:1, 2). The present context indicates that the reference now is to *superior standing with God.*

Accordingly, the true meaning must be, "Do we—I, Paul, and y o u, believers in Rome—excel?" Or, more broadly, "Do we, believers in Christ (in general), excel? Are we better than all other people? Do we have a superior standing with God?"

This interpretation is supported also by the following considerations:

a. It is clear that the pronoun "we" implied in the immediately preceding sentence (verse 8: ". . . as *we* are being slanderously reported, and as some claim that *we* say") refers to the believer, Paul, and those associated with him; therefore refers to "believers."

b. It is also clear that in the immediately following line (verse 9b: ". . . for *we* just previously made the charge") this "we" refers to Paul, the believer.

The conclusion would seem to be clear. What the apostle is asking is this,

---

προερχόμεθα) mean?" Very little help is available from other sources. In the New Testament this verb occurs nowhere else. See, however, Josephus, *Against Apion* II. 186. But Rom. 3:9 uses the middle voice. Is the meaning then "Do we *hold* something *in front* of ourselves for protection?" "Do we have a defense?"

Or should we ascribe a *passive* meaning to this middle; hence, "Are we being excelled?" It would be very difficult to fit either of these meanings into the present context.

Is it possible, then, that this middle form must be given an active meaning? The answer sometimes given is, "No example has been found that this verb, in its middle form, has an active meaning." But when the applicable examples are so few and far between, such a verdict has little, if any, value. More significant is the fact that use of a middle form in an active sense is by no means infrequent in Koine Greek or in Paul's epistles. See Gram. N.T. (Bl.-Debr.), par. 316, p. 165. The sense may therefore very well be "Do we excel?" "Are we any better?" So interpreted, the prefix πρό is that of *precedence.* The total meaning, justifiable also from the point of view of etymology, may well be, "Do we possess any priority?" In the present context this would amount to, "In the eyes of God do we hold a superior standing of righteousness?" Or more simply, "Are we any better?"

"*By nature*—or *of ourselves*—are we, Christians, better than all other people?" We have a right *in our explanation* to add the words "by nature," for the apostle has not yet expounded, in any detail, what we become "by grace." For that doctrine see 3:21 f. The fact that *by nature* everyone is a "child of wrath" is clear from Eph. 2:1–3.[80]

Continued: **9b. Not at all, for we just previously made the charge that Jews and Greeks alike are all under (the power of) sin.**

Paul's "Not at all" is decisive.[81] He has indeed shown that the Jews are sinners, and as such are lying under the sentence of condemnation (2:1–3:8). He has proved this also with respect to the Greeks or Gentiles (1:18–32). Accordingly, the entire human race is condemnable before God. That means, therefore, that basically the same applies to the apostle himself and to all those who serve the Lord with him, for[82] they too belong to this sin-laden, guilt-burdened human race. *By nature* all are under (the power of) sin.

For additional substantiation of this charge the apostle, in a manner that is both artistic and convincing, introduces a chain of Old Testament passages. If he has borrowed this mode of argumentation from the rabbis, that surely cannot be held against him. Fact is that the material he quotes is relevant, well-chosen, inspired.

On the formal side, it is clear that the quotation-chain (verses 10b–18) has three strophes or stanzas. The first strophe (verses 10b–12) consists of two sets of three lines; the second (verses 13, 14) has two sets of two lines, and so does the third (verses 15–18).

The quotations are not all *ad verbum* (literal) but are all *ad sensum* (according to meaning).

By far the most of the quoted material is from the Psalms, though the Prophets (Isaiah) and the Writings (Ecclesiastes) are also represented. Does not this indicate that Paul regarded not only the historical but also the poetical and the prophetical books of the Old Testament as being inspired?

Turning now to the material contents of this chain of proof, we note that the opening strophe is as follows:

10-12.   As it is written:
"There is no one righteous, not even one;
there is no one who understands;
there is no one who is searching for God.

---

80. In this interpretation I agree with Greijdanus, *op. cit.*, p. 171, against Ridderbos, *op. cit.*, p. 76. As mentioned previously, in essence I agree also with Lekkerkerker. See p. 20.

81. Though it is true that οὐ πάντως can mean either (a) not altogether, not in every respect; or (b) not at all, the *radical nature of the explanatory and confirmatory quotations in verses 10–18 favors the latter sense.* Here I agree with Ridderbos (*op. cit.*, p. 76), as against Cranfield (*op. cit.*, p. 190), Greijdanus (*op. cit.*, p. 171) and J. A. C. Van Leeuwen and D. Jacobs, *Korte Verklaring der Heilige Schrift*, Kampen, 1932, p. 43.

82. I can see no good reason for interpreting γάρ as here used in any other sense than as meaning *for.*

> All have turned aside; together they have become worthless;
> there is no one who does what is right;
> there is not even one."

It is clear that the argument which intends to demonstrate the universality of sin builds up to a climax.

The very first strophe shows that Paul is not describing this or that particular race or class of people but men in general. The picture he draws is dismal: no one is righteous; in fact, no one understands his deplorable condition. And no one is even trying to understand, is even searching for God, the Source of all wisdom and knowledge.

But are there no exceptions? Paul answers, "There is no one ... no one ... no one ... no one ... not even one."

He makes all this even more emphatic by interspersing the five negatives with one positive statement, "*All* have turned aside" (from God and his law), etc. Is not this *all* an echo of the one in verse 9 ("Jews and Greeks alike are *all* under the power of sin")?

To make his argument convincing the apostle now descends to particulars. He speaks about the evil *throat* (voice), *tongue, lips, mouth:*

13, 14. "An open grave is their throat;
> **With their tongue they practice deception."**
> **"The poison of vipers is under their lips.**
> **Their mouth is full of cursing and bitterness."**

It must be borne in mind that Paul is attempting to prove that *by nature* all people, without exception, are under the power of sin. In order to do so, what specific type of sinfulness will he select as an illustration? Will he remind his listeners or readers of the gross immorality that marked the heathen world? Cf. 1:24, 26, 27. He will not, for in that case many a Jew and perhaps even this or that Gentile might object, "But I, for one, am not guilty!"

Guided by the Holy Spirit, the apostle wisely selects *the sin of the tongue* to illustrate the universality of human sinfulness, for with respect to *this* evil who can truthfully say, "I am not guilty?"[83] On this subject of sinful human speech see also Ps. 39:1; Prov. 10:19; 17:27; Matt. 5:22, 37; 10:19, 20 (and parallels); Titus 3:2; James 1:19, 26; 3:1–12; I Peter 3:10.

Since a tree is known by its fruit, and a man by his deeds, Paul stresses the viciousness of the evil throat by showing how it operates. Quoting from Ps. 5:9 he describes the throat as "an open grave." He is probably thinking of a huge, cruel monster, ready to devour its victims; yes, even to devour them *unawares*. On a human plane this destruction may even take place by means of flattery, "the smooth tongue" of Ps. 5:9, the one that practices deception.

The final line of verse 13, "The poison of vipers is under their lips" is an

---

83. In this connection I wish to call the reader's attention to L. B. Flynn's book, *Did I Say That?*, Nashville, 1959. It is very interesting and instructive.

exact quotation of the LXX version of Ps. 140:3 (LXX 139:4).[84] The emphasis continues to be on the perfidious manner in which people, *acting from motives that lie outside of the sphere of God's sovereign grace,* try to destroy their intended victims. Their words may be very flattering, but watch out: the speakers cannot be trusted. They resemble vipers which "under their lips," at the base of their fangs, are equipped with sacs filled with deadly poison. Examples: Saul (I Sam. 18:17); David; *yes even David* (II Sam. 11).

Still continuing in the same vein, that is, emphasizing the deceitful nature of human speech, the "chain" continues in verse 14, with a quotation from Ps. 10:7 (LXX 9:28), "Their mouth is full of cursing and bitterness." In the Psalm from which these words are quoted the context again very definitely stresses *the treacherous manner* in which a person will at times try to "use" and abuse his fellowmen. Note such expressions as "he lurks in secret, lies in wait, crouches." Truly, deceptive is man's heart! See Jer. 17:9.

Thus interpreted, the reference to "cursing and bitterness" may well mean that in the process of attempting to deceive their neighbors people will at times perjure themselves; that is, they will pronounce *bitter curses* upon themselves, to be poured out if what they say turns out not to have been true. For example, a merchant will say to a potential customer, "May I drop dead on this very spot if I have not shelled out more for this article than I ask you to pay for it." In expressing this wish he is, of course, insincere.[85]

Since the second strophe dealt with men's *speech,* it is logical that the final one, in its first three lines, would describe men's life and conduct, their *actions.*

15–18.   **"Swift (are) their feet to shed blood;**
      ruin and misery mark their ways,
    and the way of peace they have not known.
    There is no fear of God before their eyes."[86]

A long and still continuing series of wars and murders proves that the first three lines of this final stanza are true today as well as in Isaiah's time.

---

84. In both places—LXX and here in Rom. 3:13—the original reads: ἰὸς ἀσπίδως ὑπὸ τὰ χείλη αὐτῶν.

85. Another interpretation, favored by several commentators, divides the *cursing* and the *bitterness* between the perpetrator and the victim: the former utters curses, the latter experiences bitterness. But at this point is not this separation of two nouns connected by *and* rather unnatural?

86. ὀξεῖς, nom. pl. m. of ὀξύς, sharp (cf. *acute*); Rev. 1:16; 2:12; 14:14, 17, 18; 19:15; and in connection with time: quick, swift.

In the New Testament σύντριμμα occurs only here. The cognate verb συντρίβω means *to rub together;* hence, to bruise, crush, destroy. See N.T.C. on Luke 9:39 (p. 524). We use the expression "to rub each other the wrong way." It is understandable that the noun σύντριμμα means destruction, ruin.

With respect to the derivation of the word ταλαιπωρία unanimity is lacking, though to *tole*rate (bear, endure) that which is *poro*tic (in the sense of forming a hardness or callus) may point in the right direction. The word occurs also in James 5:1. It means hardship, suffering, distress, misery. The related adjective ταλαίπωρος is found in Rom. 7:24; Rev. 3:17.

See Isa. 59:7, 8. The ruin and misery brought about by these explosions of human wrath are evident everywhere.

The basic reason for this deplorable situation is expressed in the final line, "There is no fear of God before their eyes" (Ps. 36:1). The *consistent* operation of the fear of God in human hearts would have brought about a yearning for the reconciliation of man with God and with his fellowmen.

The conclusion of this section is found in verses 19, 20, beginning as follows:

19. Now we know that whatever the law says, it speaks to those (who are) within the pale of the law . . .

Since in the preceding series of quotations the apostle has never quoted from the Decalog or even, in general, from the Pentateuch, but only from the Psalms, Prophets, and Writings, it is clear that the term "the law" must refer to the Old Testament as a whole. Such passages as John 10:34; 15:25; and I Cor. 14:25 illustrate a similar use of the expression "the law."

If, in the present case, there is any real difference in meaning between "says" and "speaks," it would be that "says" refers to what is said, and "speaks" draws attention to the act of speaking.

With respect to the phrase "those (who are) within the pale of the law" there is a wide difference of interpretation. Here are a few samples:

a. *the Jews.* Thus J. P. Lange, *Commentary on the Holy Scriptures,* (translated and edited by P. Schaff), Grand Rapids (reprint), 1869, p. 121; also Ridderbos, *op. cit.,* p. 79.

b. *all who have the Old Testament,* including the believers in Rome. That view is expressed by Lenski, *op. cit.,* pp. 239, 240, who correctly stresses the fact that Paul is not just writing to Jews, but to the Roman Christians.

c. *everybody, the whole world.* Thus Greijdanus, *op. cit.,* p. 177; and Murray, *op. cit.,* p. 106.

d. *everybody, but with special application to the Jews.* For this interpretation see, for example, C. R. Erdman, *Epistle of Paul to the Romans,* Phila., n.d., p. 50; and G. B. Wilson, *Romans, A Digest of Reformed Comment,* Edinburgh, 1977, p. 56.

I believe c.—everybody, the whole world—most adequately expresses what Paul had in mind. It is true that the phrase "those (who are) within the pale of the law" might cause us to think exclusively of the Jews. However, does not the law, God's Word, have a message for all? And does it not have authority over all, and a claim on all, whether they be believers or unbelievers? And does it not concern all, without exception, whether they be Jews or Gentiles by race?

Besides, words must be interpreted in light of their context, which is as follows: **that every mouth may be silenced, and the entire world may be exposed to the judgment of [or: may stand guilty before] God.**

It is clear that the apostle is no longer thinking exclusively about Gentiles or Jews. No, he is summarizing his argument, combining the conclusions to which he has arrived in connection with Gentiles (1:32), Jews (2:21-24), everybody, including even believers (3:9) as they are by nature. He repeats the verdict expressed earlier. See especially 3:9–12.

The figure used is dramatic, fear-inspiring, unforgettable. Everybody is standing in front of God, the Judge. The records are read, and as it were one by one the accused are given an opportunity to answer the charges made against them. However, their guilt having been exposed, they have no answer. Their mouths are silenced, stopped.

Conclusion: **20. Therefore by law-works no flesh [or: mortal being] will be justified in his sight, for through law (comes) consciousness of sin.**

In somewhat different phraseology the thought of Ps. 143:2 ("Do not bring thy servant into judgment, for no one living is righteous before thee") is here reproduced.[87] Cf. Job 9:2.

Paul's argument is irrefutable. By the works of the law no one can ever be justified in God's sight. Why not? Consider, for a moment, what the law demands. Nothing less than this, that a person love God "with all" his heart, soul, mind, and strength, and that he love his neighbor as he loves himself (Matt. 22:37–40; Mark 12:29–31; Luke 10:27). The apostle has shown that it is exactly this love that was lacking on the part of both Gentile (note: "neither gave thanks," Rom. 1:21) and Jew (note: "hard and unconverted heart," 2:5). He has made clear that *every person* stands condemned before God (3:19).

He stands condemned because of his sins of commission, but also because of his sins of omission (1:21, 28; 2:21; 3:11; cf. Matt. 25:41–43); not only because of his sins open and public, but also because of the evil he commits in secret (Rom. 2:16). He is damnable in God's sight not only because of what he says and does (Rom. 3:13–17), but even because of what he *is* (3:9, 10); that is, because of his sinful *state*.

Only one conclusion is possible therefore. Man is doomed, doomed, doomed. His condition is one of thorough hopelessness and despair. And the law, with its demand of nothing less than moral and spiritual *perfection* (cf. Lev. 19:2), a state to which man, in his own power, can never attain, creates in him a dreadful, mortifying sense of sin; hence, a presentiment of doom, total and everlasting.

21 But now, apart from law, a righteousness from God, attested by the law and the prophets, has been revealed,   22 namely, a righteousness from God which, through faith in

---

87. Note the Hebraisms: (a) A word for word rendering of the Hebrew text would be, ". . . for not is righteous before thy face all living being." The LXX version (of Ps. 142:2b) is: ὅτι οὐ δικαιωθήσεται ἐνώπιόν σου πᾶς ζῶν. Note "not . . . all" in the sense of "no." (b) For "all living being" Paul has substituted "all flesh," which is frequently used in the Hebrew text of the Old Testament to indicate mankind considered in its frailty and insignificance, as contrasted with God viewed in his greatness and majesty.

The various meanings of the word σάρξ in Paul's epistles are summarized on p. 217.

For δικαιωθήσεται πᾶσα σάρξ see also Gal. 2:16, where the same expression is used without the addition ἐνώπιον αὐτοῦ ("before him" or "in his sight").

Jesus Christ, (comes) to *all* who exercise faith—for there is no distinction, 23 since all have
sinned and fall short of the glory of God— 24 being justified freely by his grace through the
redemption (accomplished) in Christ Jesus; 25 whom God designed to be, by the shedding of
his blood, a wrath-removing[88] sacrifice, (effective) through faith. (God did this) to demonstrate
his justice, because in his forbearance he had treated past sins with indulgence.[89] 26 (So he
did it) to demonstrate his justice in the present time, that he might be just and the One who
justifies the person who has faith in Jesus.

27 What room, then, is left for boasting?[90] It is excluded. On what basis? Of works? No, but
on the basis of faith. 28 For we maintain that it is by faith that a person is justified, apart from
law works. 29 Or is God (the God) of Jews only? Is he not (the God) of Gentiles also?
Certainly, of Gentiles also; 30 seeing that there is only one God, who will justify the circumcised by faith, and the uncircumcised through that same faith. 31 Do we then invalidate the
law through our (insistence on)[91] faith? By no means. On the contrary, we uphold the law.

---

5. "But now, apart from law, a righteousness from God has been
   revealed ... a righteousness through faith in Jesus Christ."
   3:21–31

**21. But now, apart from law, a righteousness from God, attested by the
law and the prophets, has been revealed ...**

Dark and dismal is man's condition. This darkness and despair is unfathomable and universal. It envelops all.

Then suddenly a light, the very light which previously had flickered for a
brief moment (1:16, 17), comes streaming in. Hope revives.

This light, this ray of optimism, comes not from below but from above. It
is "a righteousness from God." It is he who comes to the rescue. It is he who
condescends to save those who had made themselves thoroughly unworthy
of being saved. And, being God, he does this—of course!—without sacrificing his righteousness or lifting the demands of his law. This is the *light* of
his glorious gospel. Study such passages as Isa. 9:1 (cf. Matt. 4:16); 49:6b;
58:8; 60:1, 3, 19, 20; Mic. 7:8; Luke 1:78, 79; 2:32; John 1:9; 8:12; Acts
13:47; Eph. 5:8, 9; Rev. 22:5.

Why God did this is a mystery we shall never be able *fully* to understand.
Such love is infinite and incomprehensible. See what the apostle says about
it in Rom. 5:6–8, and how in II Cor. 9:15 he pours out his heart in gratitude
and adoration by exclaiming, "Thanks be to God for his indescribably
precious gift!" What took place when (to speak in human terms) in the
quiet recess of eternity God Triune decided to deliver man from the
greatest evil and to place him in possession of the greatest good, to do this
at *such* a price (II Cor. 5:21), is a matter so marvelous and sublime that in
his epistle to the Ephesians the apostle prays that the readers (or hearers),
being rooted and established in love, may be strong, in unison with all the

---

88. Or: propitiatory.
89. Or: had overlooked past sins.
90. Literally: Where, then, is boasting?
91. Or: teaching about.

saints, *to grasp* the breadth, length, height, and depth of *the love of Christ which* (in all its dimensions) *can never be grasped* (3:14-19)! This too is a matter "angels desire to look into" (I Peter 1:12). It is the most glorious paradox one can imagine.

Here in Rom. 3:21 Paul states, "But now"—that is, at this present time (verse 26; cf. 5:9), this very strategic moment in the history of redemption, in Gal 4:4 called *the fulness of the time*—"a righteousness *from God* has been revealed." This righteousness goes into effect "apart from the law," which can only mean that it was not, and cannot be, earned by men's obedience to God's law. It was and is a righteousness "apart from *the works* of the law." Cf. Rom. 3:28; 4:6-8; Gal. 2:16, 21; 3:10-13; Eph. 2:9; Phil. 3:9; II Tim. 1:9; Titus 3:5.[92]

Is Paul presenting a new doctrine, something never heard of? On the contrary, he is speaking about "a righteousness attested by the law and the prophets."[93] The apostle has already quoted Hab. 2:4; see Rom. 1:17. Undoubtedly he also has in mind other passages; such as Gen. 15:6; Ps. 32:1, 2; see Rom. 4:3, 7, 8. And see N.T.C. on Luke, p. 125.

Continued: **22, 23. namely, a righteousness from God which, through faith in Jesus Christ, (comes) to *all* who exercise faith—for there is no distinction, since all have sinned and fall short of the glory of God— ...**

In substance Paul here repeats what he has stated in 1:16, 17. He is not forgetting his *theme*. In the former passage he had declared, "The gospel . . . is (the) power of God for salvation to everyone who exercises faith . . . For in it a righteousness from God is revealed from faith to faith . . ." He now adds that the object of this faith is *Jesus Christ*. Cf. Matt. 1:21; John 3:16; 14:6; Acts 4:12.

With great emphasis the apostle repeats the thought of 1:16b, namely, that this righteousness is granted to *all* those—and *only* to those—who put this faith into practice; that is, to all true believers in Jesus Christ. It makes no difference whether a person is rich or poor, young or old, male or female, educated or uneducated, Jew or Gentile. All need this righteousness and can obtain it only through faith in the Savior, in and through whom the Triune God reveals himself.

There is no distinction. Since *all,* everybody in the entire world, have sinned and therefore fall short of or lack the glory of God, no one should base his hope for acceptance with God on his own goodness. God's law demands perfection, and no one is any longer perfect in God's sight. The apostle has explained this in some detail; first with respect to the Gentiles (1:18-32); next with respect to the Jews (2:1-3:8). He has summarized it in 3:9-20.

All people have sinned and fall short—or are falling short—of God's

---

92. This does not mean that the law has no place in the plan of redemption. See on 3:31.
93. For this designation of what we today call the Old Testament see also Matt. 5:17; 7:12; 22:40; Luke 16:16; Acts 24:14; 28:23.

glory. When man transgressed God's command he lost the earlier blessings; specifically, the divine *approval* resting upon him, hence also freedom of access to God. See Gen. 3:8.[94]

24, 25a. . . . being justified freely by his grace through the redemption (accomplished) in Christ Jesus; whom God designed to be, by the shedding of his blood, a wrath-removing sacrifice, (effective) through faith.

---

94. With respect to the meaning of καὶ ὑστεροῦνται τῆς δόξης τοῦ θεοῦ commentators differ widely. Here are four views:

a. All men fail to render to God the glory they owe him. The divine standard for human life, the ideal of perfection, remains far above and beyond the reach of anyone. See W. H. G. Thomas, *St. Paul's Epistle to the Romans*, Grand Rapids, 1946, p. 112.

Though the thought here expressed is true, as has been indicated previously (3:10–18), and in his very practical and devotional commentary Thomas adds a valuable illustration, this is probably not what Rom. 3:23b means, for in that case would not Paul have inserted an additional verbal form? Would he not have written, "All fall short of *doing* everything to God's glory"? See I Cor. 10:31.

b. The term "glory of God" refers to the future heavenly glory. So sure is Ridderbos (*op. cit.*, p. 84) that this is the correct interpretation that he states, "Nothing else can be meant by it."

It is true that there are several Pauline passages in which "glory" or "glory of God" refers to the believers' future reward. See, for example, Rom. 2:7; 5:2; 8:18, 30; I Cor. 15:43; II Cor. 4:17; Col. 1:27; 3:4; II Tim. 2:10. Nevertheless, it is important to take note of the fact that here in Rom. 3:23b Paul uses the present tense. He says that because of the entrance of sin all men *are falling short* of God's glory. If he had been thinking of the glory awaiting God's children in heaven, would he not have used the future tense?

c. Just as by redemption a person is transformed into the image of God (II Cor. 3:18), so previously by means of the fall he became destitute of that perfection which is the reflection of God's glory. He lost what he once possessed. The term "the glory of God" as used in Rom. 3:23b therefore means "conformity to God's image." See Murray, *op. cit.*, p. 113; and John Knox, *The Interpreter's Bible*, Vol. IX, p. 430. Closely related is the view of E. F. Harrison, *The Expositor's Bible Commentary*, Grand Rapids, 1976, p. 41, according to which the term in question refers to the privilege man originally enjoyed of having direct communion with God. What man originally enjoyed in Paradise was lost through sin. Or, as Van Leeuwen-Jacobs (*op. cit.*, p. 53) point out, because of the fall man can no longer approach God directly but must stand from afar (Exod. 20:18, 21; Num. 4:15; 17:13, etc.). See also U. Wilckens, Th.D.N.T., Vol. VIII, p. 596. According to that article Paul may be referring to the glory with which Adam was originally invested.

Insofar as this theory interprets the phrase "glory of God" as a reference to a privilege (or privileges) man enjoyed in the state of rectitude but has lost through the entrance of sin, I agree with it. The words "All have sinned *and*—probably meaning *and as a result*—are falling short of the glory of God" certainly seem to point in that direction.

Is it possible, however, that the apostle may have been thinking first of all of something else which man once had but now lacks? This introduces us to the next theory:

d. The term "glory of God" means "glory imparted by God." It refers to "glory" in the sense of *approval, approbation, praise.* (For the various senses in which the term δόξα is used by Paul see above, p. 74.) Supporting this theory are C. Hodge, *A Commentary on the Epistle to the Romans*, Grand Rapids, 1886, p. 140; J. Denney, *op. cit.*, p. 610; C. R. Erdman, *op. cit.*, p. 52; and in a sense R. C. H. Lenski, *op. cit.*, p. 249. Also R. Knox, who translates, ". . . all alike are unworthy of God's praise."

The objection raised against this theory, namely, that in that case Paul would have used a preposition, would have written παρὰ θεοῦ (cf. John 5:44; II Peter 1:17) is not very convincing; for:

(1) Without using a preposition *John* can refer to "praise coming from God" (12:43). If John, why not Paul?

(2) When Paul refers to "*righteousness* coming from God," he at times does this without

Note the various elements of this important passage:

a. *being justified*

Here, for the first time in Romans, the verb *to justify* is used in a positive context in order to set forth the doctrine of justification by faith.[95]

It is easy to go astray here in interpreting Paul's thought. By combining the beginning of verse 24 with the closing words of verse 23 the result is, "... all have sinned and fall short of the glory of God, being justified freely by his grace," etc. Is Paul actually saying, then, that all sinners are being justified; therefore, are being saved? Has Paul suddenly become a universalist?

The writer of this commentary remembers hearing a minister say from the pulpit, "In the end everybody will be saved. I have hope even for the devil." Omitting the part about the devil, was that minister in line with Paul?

But this cannot be, for in 1:16, 17 and 3:22 the apostle insists that the "righteousness from God" is a blessing bestowed on those who exercise faith, on no one else.

What is the solution? Probably this: when in verse 22a Paul declares that God's righteousness extends to all who exercise faith, there is, as it were, an interruption. It is as if someone (a Jew perhaps?) is asking, "Only to those, Paul? Not also to us who, though we do not share your faith in Jesus Christ, have tried very hard to please God by means of our effort to live in harmony with his law? Are we no better than other people? *Is there no distinction between us and others?*"

The answer to this parenthetical question—as has already been shown—is, "There is no distinction, since all have sinned and fall short of the glory of God" (22b, 23).

Returning now to the main line of thought, "a righteousness from God which, through faith in Jesus Christ (comes) to *all* who exercise faith" (verse 22a), the apostle continues, "being justified freely by his grace through the

---

using a preposition (Rom. 1:17; 3:21, 22). If he can do this with the word "righteousness," why not with "glory"?

(3) What may well be the strongest argument in favor of interpreting Paul to mean that as a result of man's sin he is falling short of, or lacking, the divine approbation or praise is this, that in these earlier chapters of the epistle, and to some extent even later, the apostle is operating with a series of concepts such as sin, condemnation, righteousness, justification. Into this series—think especially of justification—the concept *approbation* fits very naturally.

I therefore believe that verse 23 means "All have sinned and as a result are now in a state in which they are falling short of (or are lacking) what they possessed before the fall, namely, the inestimable blessing of having the approval of God resting upon them."

This implies the truth mentioned under theory c, for how can I say, "God approves of me" without at the same time also saying, "Therefore I have freedom of access to him"? Hence, while, as I see it, theory d. is to be preferred, theory c. comes very close and is probably implied.

95. Earlier use of the verb δικαιόω in Romans:

2:13, in connection with a contrast between doers and merely hearers.

3:4, in the sense of divine vindication ("that thou mayest be proved right").

3:20, negatively, to indicate the impossibility of salvation by works.

redemption (accomplished) in Christ Jesus" (verse 24). Not everybody but only those who exercise faith, the genuine believers, receive the great blessing of justification.[96]

When used, as here in Rom. 3:24, in the dominant forensic sense, *to justify* means *to declare righteous;* and *justification* may be defined as *that gracious act of God whereby, on the basis solely of Christ's accomplished mediatorial work, he declares the sinner just, and the latter accepts this benefit with a believing heart.* In defense of this definition see not only the present context (Rom. 3:24-30) but also 4:3, 5; 5:1, 9; 8:30; Gal. 2:15, 16; 3:8, 11, 24; 5:4; Titus 3:7. *Justification stands over against condemnation.* See Rom. 8:1, 33, 34.

Justification is a matter of *imputation* (reckoning, charging): the sinner's guilt is imputed to Christ; the latter's righteousness is imputed to the sinner (Gen. 15:6; Ps. 32:1, 2; Isa. 53:4-6; Jer. 23:6; Rom. 5:18, 19). While *justification* is a matter of *imputation, sanctification* is a matter of *transformation.* In justification the Father takes the lead (Rom. 8:33); in sanctification the Holy Spirit does (II Thess. 2:13). The first is a "once for all" verdict, the second a lifelong process. Nevertheless, although the two should never be identified, neither should they be separated. They are distinct but not separate.

b. *freely*

The word used in the original means "as a gift"; in other words, without payment made by the one who receives it; without any human merit. See I Tim. 1:9; Titus 3:4. If the sinner is to be *declared righteous* at all, it will have to be *freely,* for, as has been shown in the preceding, as measured by the standard of God's requirement (Lev. 19:2; Matt. 22:37 and parallels), human merit is impossible. Man cannot earn the great and basic blessing of justification. He can only accept it as a gift (Isa. 55:1).

c. *by his grace*

Grace is God's love directed toward the *guilty,* just as his *mercy* is that same love directed toward *those in misery.*[97] It is easy to understand that "freely" and "by his grace" go together.

d. *through the redemption (accomplished) in Christ Jesus*

The word *redemption* (Greek ἀπολύτρωσις) occurs ten times in the New Testament (Luke 21:28; Rom. 3:24; 8:23; I Cor. 1:30; Eph. 1:7, 14; 4:30; Col. 1:14; Heb. 9:15; 11:35). In those passages in which the term is used, as here in Rom. 3:24, in its full spiritual sense, it indicates deliverance, by

---

96. The fact that δικαιούμενοι is in the nominative but πάντας is in the accusative is no valid objection to the proposed construction, for this is not at all unusual when the modifier is so far away from the word or phrase it modifies, especially when such a nominative introduces a new clause.

97. For more on *grace* see N.T.C. on Luke, pp. 181, 182.

means of the payment of a ransom, from the guilt, punishment, and power of sin.[98]

This redemption was accomplished *in,* probably meaning "in connection with," Christ Jesus, the Anointed Savior. Most translators have adopted this or a very similar translation, namely, *"in* Christ Jesus." Some, however, prefer *"by* Christ Jesus." The Greek allows either. In favor of "in" or "in connection with" is the fact that in verses 23, 24 "God" is clearly mentioned as the Author of the believers' redemption. Not to Jesus alone but to God Triune should be accorded the praise and glory for man's deliverance from sin and its consequences. It was accomplished or brought about in and through Christ Jesus; that is, by means of his voluntary suffering and death on the cross.

e. *whom God designed to be . . .*[99]

This *design* points back to the divine eternal counsel. In that counsel or decree Christ Jesus was designed to be the One through whom the plan of

---

98. It must be granted that in such a passage as, for example, Rom. 8:23 the deliverance indicated by this noun does not in and by itself include the idea of the payment of a ransom.
99. The root meaning of the verb προτίθημι, of which the form here used, προέθετο, is the third per. s. 2nd. aor. indicat. middle, is *to set before;* which, in the middle voice becomes *to set before oneself.* It is easy to understand that one may set something before oneself in a twofold sense: (1) for public display; (2) for mental consideration; to plan (something) for oneself; Dutch: *zich (iets) voornemen.* Most translators prefer (1). However, in favor of (2) *to plan, purpose, design,* the following facts should be borne in mind:
   In both of the other instances in which this verb is used in the New Testament, Rom. 1:13 ("many times *I planned* to come to y o u") and Eph. 1:9 ("which *he purposed* for himself") the sense is clearly telic. If there, why not here? Also note that wherever in the New Testament the cognate *noun* πρόθεσις is used, except when it occurs in connection with showbread (the consecrated unleavened loaves placed on a table in the Holy Place), the meaning is *purpose:* "with steadfast purpose" (Acts 11:23); "supposing that they had obtained their purpose" (Acts 27:13); "called according to his purpose" (Rom. 8:28); "in order that God's purpose according to election might stand" (Rom. 9:11); "having been foreordained according to the purpose of him who accomplishes all things according to the counsel of his will" (Eph. 1:11); "according to the eternal purpose which he formed in Christ" (Eph. 3:11); "who saved us . . . according to his own purpose and grace" (II Tim. 1:9); and "You, however, followed my purpose" (II Tim. 3:10).
   In favor of a telic rendering here in Rom. 3:25a are also Origen, Ambrosiaster, Chrysostom, Oecumenius, Lagrange, Fritzsche, Robertson, Phillips ("appointed," cf. Jerusalem Bible), N.E.B. ("designed") and Cranfield.
   In support of the rendering *presented, set forth, put forward,* or something similar, it has been argued that this meaning fits better into a context which speaks of the *demonstration* of God's justice (3:25, 26), and that it parallels the words of Paul in Gal. 3:1 ("Jesus was openly displayed"). But it is not clear how it can be convincingly argued that a verb indicating the demonstration of *God's* justice parallels a verb referring to the shedding of *Christ's* blood. Besides, the grammatical construction in the two cases differs radically. And Gal. 3:1 certainly belongs to a different type of context than the first clause in Rom. 3:25.
   In order to justify a meaning for the Greek verb which it has nowhere else in the New Testament, and which differs substantially from the sense of the cognate noun in *all* comparable New Testament instances of its use, stronger arguments will have to be presented. On this question see also the fine remarks of Cranfield, *op. cit.,* Vol. I, pp. 208–210.

salvation would be realized. Christ Jesus and his people can never be separated. Note such parallel passages as Eph. 1:4, 7, 10, 11.

f. *by the shedding of his blood, a wrath-removing or propitiatory sacrifice*[100]
Blood represents life (Lev. 17:11; Matt. 20:28, cf. 26:28; John 10:11, 15). The words "by the shedding of his blood" refer to Messiah's voluntary sacrifice of his life in the place of those whom he came to save. Cf. Isa. 53:10–12.

Though it is being constantly denied, there is indeed such a thing as the wrath of God that rests on the sinner and must be removed if he is to be saved. See Rom. 1:18; 2:5, 8; 3:5; 5:9; 9:22; Eph. 2:3; 5:6; Col. 3:6; I Thess. 1:10; 2:16; 5:9; Rev. 6:16, 17; 11:18; 14:10; 16:19; 19:15.

When atonement is rendered, God's wrath is removed. Rom. 3:25a mentions a wrath-removing or propitiatory sacrifice, namely, Christ Jesus himself. It was he who *gave*—voluntarily offered—his blood; hence his life; hence himself (I Tim. 2:6) for his sheep, bearing the wrath of God *in their stead,* thereby causing them to be reconciled to God.

There are many passages which teach this truth, either as a whole or in part: Isa. 53:4–8, 12; Matt. 20:28; 26:28; Mark 10:45; 14:24; Luke 22:20; Acts 20:28; I Cor. 10:16; 11:25; II Cor. 5:20, 21; Eph. 1:7; 2:13; Col. 1:20; I Peter 1:18, 19; 2:24; I John 1:7; 5:6; Heb. 9:11, 12, 15, 23–28; Rev. 1:5; 5:9; 7:14; 12:11; 13:8.

The Greek word for which I have chosen the English equivalent "wrath-removing (or propitiatory) sacrifice," in the LXX (Greek translation of the Old Testament) indicates the blood-sprinkled lid of the ark of the covenant. This is the "mercy seat" (A.V.) or "atonement cover" (N.I.V.). See Exod. 25:17, 18; Lev. 16:2, 3; etc. In all, the word occurs more than twenty times in the Pentateuch, most often in Exodus. In the description of tabernacle furniture (Heb. 9:1–5) it is logical to believe that verse 5 similarly refers to this *cover*. However, although the same Greek word is found also in Rom. 3:25, it is understandable that most translators—there are exceptions—hesitate to call Christ Jesus either a "mercy seat" or an "atonement cover." "Wrath-removing sacrifice," "sacrifice of atonement" (N.I.V.),[101] or simply "propitiation" (A.V., A.R.V.) is better. See also I John 2:2; 4:10.

g. *(effective) through faith*
Christ's propitiatory sacrifice does not go into effect automatically. If a person wishes to obtain this great blessing—the turning away of God's

---

100. The phrase "by the shedding of his blood" should probably not be construed with "faith," resulting in the rendering "faith in his blood." It is true that ἐν τῷ αὐτοῦ αἵματι directly follows πίστεως; and it is also true that grammatically (ἐν plus the dative to indicate faith's object) is not as unusual as some maintain. (See, for example, Gal. 3:26; Eph. 1:15; Col. 1:4; I Tim. 3:13; II Tim. 1:13). But it is also a fact that a modifier does not always stand close to the word it modifies. Moreover, with Paul the object of faith is a person, not a thing.

101. To help the reader the N.I.V. adds this valuable footnote: "(God presented him) as the one who would turn away his wrath, taking away sin."

wrath, forgiveness, acceptance with God—he must exercise genuine faith in Christ, in and through whom God Triune reveals himself.

The indispensability of faith has been pointed out before (1:8, 16, 17; 3:22) and will be emphasized again (3:26, 28, 30; 4:3, etc.). Without faith no one can please God (Heb. 11:6). To be saved a person needs faith, *God-given* faith (Eph. 2:8).

By works, human effort, or earnings no one has ever been saved or will ever reach everlasting, heavenly glory (3:9–20).

> Not what my hands have done
> Can save my guilty soul;
> Not what my toiling flesh has borne
> Can make my spirit whole.
> Not what I feel or do
> Can give me peace with God;
> Not all my prayers and sighs and tears
> Can bear my awful load.
>
> Thy grace alone, O God,
> To me can pardon speak;
> Thy power alone, O Son of God,
> Can this sore bondage break.
> No other work save thine,
> No other blood will do;
> No strength save that which is divine
> Can bear me safely through.
>
> Horatius Bonar

By way of summary it can be pointed out, therefore, that justification, as taught by Paul, is in no sense whatever the work of man. On the contrary, it is:

a. God's gift (Rom. 5:15–18)

b. the product of his grace (3:24; 4:16; 5:15)

c. free (5:16)

d. not of works (3:20)

e. the opposite of condemnation (8:1, 33, 34)

f. that which deprives man of every reason for boasting (3:27)

g. appropriated by faith, even that faith being God-given (Eph. 2:8).

That this doctrine of justification by faith is in accord with the teaching of the Old Testament will be shown in Romans 4.

That it also is in harmony with the teaching of Christ will be indicated in a moment (see the next paragraph). Add Luke 18:14.

All this is contrary to Rome's doctrine, for while Rome certainly teaches that Christ, by means of his atonement, supplied the meritorious basis for our justification, the predisposing cause must be supplied by ourselves; that is, by our hope, faith, love, contrition, etc. In his doctoral dissertation *Attrition and Contrition at the Council of Trent,* Kampen, 1955, p. 227, G. J. Spykman made the following excellent observation:

"Trent in effect made saving grace dependent upon what the penitent does or fails to do, be it in ever so refined form. . . . Not only grace but also good works contributed to justification, it held." He further points out that this "flatly contradicts Christ's invitation, 'Come to me all ye that labor and are heavy laden, and I will give y o u rest'" (Matt. 11:28–30).

25b, 26. (God did this) to demonstrate his justice, because in his forbearance he had treated past sins with indulgence. (So he did it) to demonstrate his justice in the present time, that he might be just and the One who justifies the person who has faith in Jesus.

How did it happen that, according to God's plan from eternity, nothing could keep Jesus from shedding his blood as a propitiatory sacrifice? The answer is: This happened in order to prove or demonstrate that God had not been unfair or unjust when, in his *forbearance* (cf. 2:4, and see on 8:32), he had treated with indulgence—had "passed over," "overlooked"—for the time being the sins of his people committed in earlier days; that is, during the old dispensation. When God's Son suffered and died, he did so to atone for the sins of *all* who had accepted or were going to accept him by a living faith; that is, for *all* believers in *both* dispensations. The merits of the cross reach backward as well as forward. By not allowing the earlier sins to be left forever unpunished but loading them on Christ (Isa. 53:6), God demonstrated that he was, is, and forevermore will be *just*. And since he is just, who can deny that he, he alone, has a right to be, and actually is, the justifier of all who repose their trust in *Jesus*?[102]

Note the following:

a. Again, as frequently in Romans, we are told that the wonderful blessing of justification is for that person, for him (her) alone, who has *faith* in Jesus.

b. "In *Jesus*." That must mean the Jesus of history, the One who was born in Bethlehem, was crucified, rose again, and ascended to heaven. The claim that it is possible to believe in a Christ who is not the Jesus of history to which Scripture bears testimony is false!

27. What room, then, is left for boasting? It is excluded. On what basis?[103] Of works? No, but on the basis of faith.

Paul has made clear that no one, whether Gentile or Jew, can achieve acceptance with God, hence salvation, by means of his own works or boasting (see on 2:17) or on the basis of the privileges he has received (3:3, 4, 9). Nevertheless, it is characteristic of certain people to boast or brag. See Mic.

---

102. For a different translation and interpretation of the closing words of verse 26: δικαιοῦντα τὸν ἐκ πίστεως Ἰησοῦ, see Cranfield, *op. cit.*, pp. 201, 213.

103. Or: principle.

The word νόμος does not always have the same meaning. In Rom. 2:12 f. it refers to *the Pentateuch*, with emphasis on the Decalog, as is clear from 2:21, 22. In 3:19 the reference is to *the Old Testament* as a whole. In 8:2 (cf. 7:23) the apostle is thinking of an *actuating principle*. Here in 3:27 the meaning seems to be *basis, norm, standard, principle*.

3:11; Matt. 3:9; Rom. 2:17, 23; 4:2; I Cor. 1:29; Phil. 3:3. Paul may have been thinking especially of the Jews in this connection. All such boasting is senseless and sinful, for "no one is righteous, not even one" (Rom. 3:10). "All have sinned and fall short of the glory of God" (3:23). So, there simply is no room for boasting. Very decisively Paul states. "It is excluded," meaning, "Once for all it has been banished."[104]

On what basis has it been thrown out? On the basis of works perhaps? Of course not. Constant reflection on meritorious (?) accomplishments makes a person proud, not humble. This sinful habit *en*courages rather than *dis*courages boasting.

It is the doctrine of justification, hence salvation, *by faith,* which implies that there is no room whatever for bragging. For faith is a *gift* of God, as is also salvation considered in its entirety. Not even the tiniest part of it is a product of man's ingenuity. See Eph. 2:8, 9. This truth, when applied to the heart by the Holy Spirit, convinces a person that whatever good he possesses has been received (I Cor. 4:7), and that he who boasts should boast in the Lord (I Cor. 1:31).

The right to brag has been excluded. On the basis of faith it has been ruled out. So, in support of verse 27, and to summarize, Paul again states what *in essence* he has said before (1:17; 3:22–24, 26) and is going to reiterate (5:1; 9:30–33; 10:5–13):

28. For we maintain that it is by faith that a person is justified, apart from law works.

Here, by implication, the two conceivable methods of being saved are set over against each other in a sharp antithesis. According to the first, a person is saved by obeying God's law (which to the Jew meant: as interpreted and expanded by tradition). According to the second, he is saved by faith. All "glorying" is excluded. It is by faith that it has been excluded. According to the first, justification, therefore also salvation, is the product of human merit; according to the second, of divine grace.

Paul here, as well as everywhere else, definitely endorses the second proposition. He rejects the first. No wonder, for he who stresses *works* expects salvation to come from within; that is, *from below.* He who emphasizes *faith* looks away from himself to God, and expects salvation to come from him; that is, *from above.*

When, in his translation of the New Testament Luther reached this passage he rendered it as follows, "So halten wir nun dafür, dass der Mensch gerecht werde ohne des Gesetzes Werke, allein durch den Glauben," that is, "So we hold that a person is justified without works of the law, through faith alone." For this addition of the word *alone* he was severely criticized. His answer was:

"If your papist makes much useless fuss about the word *sola, alone,* tell

---

104. Note ἐξεκλείσθη, third per. s. aor. indicat. pass. of ἐκκλείω, to shut out, exclude.

him at once: Doctor Martin Luther will have it so . . . Are they [the Papists] doctors? So am I. Are they learned? So am I. Are they preachers? So am I. Are they theologians? So am I . . . Therefore the word *alone* shall remain in my New Testament, and though all papal donkeys get furious, they shall not take it out."[105]

Luther should not have inserted this word. And the critics should not have raised such a storm of protest about it, for, after all, when Paul states that it is by faith that a person is justified, apart from law works, does he not actually mean "by faith alone"?

This position, of course, does not exclude works of gratitude, *the fruit* of faith, as the apostle makes very clear, both in Romans (6:1–14; 7:4–6; 8:12–14; ch. 12, etc.), and in other epistles (Gal. 5:22–26; Eph. 2:8–10; I Tim. 2:1–6; Titus 2:11–14).

Hymn writers have caught the true meaning of Rom. 3:28 and similar passages:

> My hope is built on nothing less
> Than Jesus' blood and righteousness;
> I dare not trust the sweetest frame,
> But wholly lean on Jesus' name.
> On Christ, the solid Rock, I stand;
> All other ground is sinking sand.
>
> Edward Mote

In close connection with the thought of verse 28 Paul continues:
29, 30. Or is God (the God) of Jews only? Is he not (the God) of Gentiles also? Certainly, of Gentiles also; seeing that there is only one God, who will justify the circumcised by faith, and the uncircumcised through that same faith.

If it were true that works in conformity with the law were required as a condition upon the fulfilment of which salvation was based, then Gentiles, living apart from the law, would have no chance to be saved. God would be the God of the Jews only. The Gentiles would have to look elsewhere for salvation; perhaps to some other God? The apostle definitely rejects this suggestion. He affirms that there are not two Gods, one for the Jews, and one for the Gentiles. In harmony with what he has said previously (see especially such passages as 2:25f.; 3:22) and is going to say a little later (10:12, 13), and in thorough agreement also with the teachings of Jesus (Matt. 8:10–12; John 3:16; 10:14–16; 17:20, 21), the apostle here strongly affirms that there is only *one* God (cf. Deut. 6:4; Isa. 45:5) and only *one* way of salvation for both Jew and Gentile, for circumcised and uncircumcised (Gen. 22:18; Isa. 45:22; Rom. 4:9–12). See also footnote 119.

It is hard to see how, by inspiration of the Holy Spirit, Paul could have expressed the "no distinction" truth in clearer language. It takes but little

---

105. See Luther's *Sendbrief vom Dolmetschen*, Erl.-Frkf. ed. Vol. LXV, p. 107f.

imagination to sense how the entire Roman congregation, gathered for worship, whether in one meeting place or in several, must have rejoiced when this epistle, with its emphasis on unity (cf. Eph. 2:11-17) was read. The notion according to which even today God recognizes two groups in which he takes special delight—the Jews and the church—finds no support either here or anywhere else in Scripture. What *does* find support is Paul's passage found in Eph. 4:4-6:

"There is one body and one Spirit, just as also y o u were called in one hope which y o u r calling brought y o u; one Lord, one faith, one baptism; one God and Father of all, who is over all and through all and in all."[106]

The apostle closes this section with the words of verse

31. Do we then invalidate the law through our (insistence on) faith? By no means. On the contrary, we uphold the law.

There are those who say that 3:31 should have been 4:1; in other words, that it belongs to and introduces the material of the fourth chapter. They take the term "the law" as used here in 3:31, to be the equivalent of "Scripture" in 4:3. Moreover, it has already been admitted that the term *law* does at times have that significance.

However, there are two main objections against directly connecting with chapter 4:

a. No clear connection can be shown between the substance of 3:31 and the opening paragraph of chapter 4.

b. The very wording of 3:31—Note "Do we, *then*," etc.—clearly indicates that this passage reflects on that which *precedes*.

What the apostle is saying amounts to this: "Since by law-works no mortal will ever be justified (3:20), and since it was *apart from the law* that a righteousness from God has been revealed (verse 21), and since, therefore, a person is justified *by faith, apart from the works of the law* (verse 28), are we depriving the law of its value?"

"Do we then invalidate the law through our (insistence on) faith?"

Paul's answer is very abrupt and decisive, "By no means. On the contrary, we uphold the law."

The forceful character of the answer must probably be explained in light of the fact that there were those who were saying, "Let us do away with the law. All we need is faith. Let us continue in sin, that grace may abound." See on 3:8 and 6:1.

If anyone should ask the further question, "In which way, Paul, do you uphold the law by your emphasis on justification by faith?," he would undoubtedly refer that individual to the contents of Rom. 3:20; 7:7, 8, 13; Gal. 2:19; 3:21, 24.

The doctrines of (a) justification, hence salvation, by faith and (b) that of the usefulness of God's law, coincide beautifully; for "through law comes

---

106. Though it is true that in verse 30 ἐκ indicates source; and διά probably intermediate agency, the distinction should be considered a rhetorical device, with no further significance.

consciousness of sin." And this very consciousness, when it is sanctified by the Holy Spirit, causes one to cry out for help and deliverance. That deliverance is fully supplied whenever a sinner surrenders his life to God; that is, when by genuine God-given faith he welcomes into his heart and life the Lord Jesus Christ, with the word of committal:

> Nothing in my hand I bring,
> Simply to thy cross I cling.

It is in this way that the Scriptures—hence also Paul and his companions—*uphold the law* while teaching and insisting on the doctrine about *faith*.

To every sincere believer the doctrine of justification by faith is a very precious treasure. To realize for one's own soul what this glorious truth means can be a very thrilling and unforgettable experience. We have already seen what the discovery of this marvelous theme meant for Paul (see pp. 28, 29) and for Luther (pp. 61, 62). When John Bunyan read Rom. 3:24 it was as if he heard God saying to his deeply troubled, guilt-stricken soul, "Sinner, thou thinkest that because of thy sins and infirmities I cannot save thy soul, but behold my Son is by me, and upon him I look, and not upon thee, and I will deal with thee according as I am pleased with him."

Is it possible that we have become so used to the expression "forgiveness of sins" that it has lost most of its meaning for us? Do we reflect on the fact that these sins are infinitely more heinous in God's sight than they are to us? That he nevertheless blots them out once and for all, lovingly assuring us, "I will forgive y o u r iniquity, and y o u r sin will I remember no more"? Yes, he forgives even though, in order to do this, he, because of the demand of his perfect righteousness, had to punish them in his Son, the One whom he loved as God alone can love!

But justification implies more, much more, than forgiveness. The heavenly Father, having canceled our debt, then as it were lovingly throws his arms around us (cf. Luke 15:20), and tells each of his pardoned ones, "You are *my* son, *my* daughter, my very own. And being my child, you are also my heir" (Rom. 8:17).

Think of it, "Heirs of God" are we and "joint-heirs with Christ," united with him by a bond of love that can never be severed!

So amazing and so abounding is God's love for us that never shall we be able to measure it. Throughout all eternity the mysteries of that love, infinite in number, will continue to be revealed to us. And we shall glorify him:

> By the sea of crystal, saints in glory stand,
> Myriads in number, drawn from every land.
> Robed in white apparel, washed in Jesus' blood,
> They now reign forever with the Lamb of God.

Unto God Almighty, sitting on the throne,
And the Lamb victorious, be the praise alone.
God has wrought salvation, he did wondrous things;
Who shall not extol Thee, Holy King of Kings?

William Kuipers
(based on Rev. 15:1–4)

Practical Lessons Derived from Rom. 3:9–31

Verses 9, 10

"What then? Are we any better? Not at all. . . . There is no one righteous, not even one." When the new minister arrived, he was told, "Your work here will be easy, for we are all good people." So he preached on the text, "Reliable is the saying, and worthy of full acceptance, that Christ Jesus came into the world, sinners to save, foremost of whom am I" (I Tim. 1:15).

Verses 21, 22

"But now . . . a righteousness from God, attested by the law and the prophets, has been revealed, namely, a righteousness from God which, through faith in Jesus Christ, comes to *all* who exercise faith. . . ." Here something old is added to something new:

a. something old, for the righteousness here indicated, had been proclaimed long ago in the law and the prophets. Abraham, David, Habakkuk, etc., had borne testimony to it.

b. something new, for not until now—that is, very recently—Jesus Christ had entered this realm of sin and woe, had offered himself as a sacrifice for the sins of his people, had been raised from the dead, and ascended to heaven, having purchased salvation for all who place their trust in him.

The old and the new belong together: it was Jesus who, by means of his active and passive obedience, obtained for all who surrender themselves to him, "righteousness from God," hence salvation full and free.

So the old and the new are actually *one*. The idea that the Old Testament is for the Jews, the New Testament for the church, is in need of re-examination. To a considerable extent it should be discarded. He who thinks lightly of the Old Testament does not understand Paul, nor the Bible.

Verses 24, 25

". . . being justified freely by his grace through the redemption (accomplished) in Christ Jesus . . . the shedding of his blood." Those who think that they can be saved apart from "redemption through the blood of Christ" are committing a tragic error.

Verse 25

". . . a wrath-removing sacrifice." Then alone is it possible to do justice to the comforting truth of God's love (Jer. 31:3; John 3:16) when this love is seen in its relation to God's wrath.

Verse 27

"What room, then, is left for boasting? It is excluded."

Heaven will be filled with boasting . . . *in the Lord!* The redeemed "are casting their crowns before the throne, while they say, 'Thou art worthy, our Lord and God, to receive glory and honor and power. . . .'" (Rev. 4:10, 11).

In a sense this song already begins on earth, with the words:

> Thou art, O God, our boast, the glory of our power;
> Thy sovereign grace is e'er our fortress and our tower.
> We lift our heads aloft, for God our shield is o'er us;
> Through him, through him alone, whose presence goes before us,
> We'll wear the victor's crown, no more by foes assaulted,
> We'll triumph through our King, by Israel's God exalted.

> Versification (of Ps. 89:17, 18)
> by William Kuipers

Summary of Chapter 3:9-31

By means of a chain of Old Testament passages Paul adduces the evidence for the proposition that by nature everybody is under the power of sin, and that accordingly "there is no one righteous, no, not one." This being true, it follows that the attempt to gain salvation by performing works of obedience to God's law will fail. "Therefore by law-works no flesh [mortal being] will be justified in his sight, for through law comes consciousness of sin" (3:9-20).

However, when for the sinner things begin to look very dark, the light of the gospel suddenly breaks through the gloom and dispels it: "But now, apart from law, a righteousness attested by the law and the prophets has been revealed, namely, a righteousness from God." This righteousness, in order to be effective in the life of a person, must be appropriated by faith in Jesus Christ. This rule holds for everybody: Gentile and Jew alike, "for there is no distinction, since all have sinned and fall short of the glory of God" (verses 21-23).

The price paid by the Savior for the justification of those who place their trust in him, and through him in God Triune, was immeasurably heavy. It amounted to no less than the shedding of Christ's blood, that is, the offering up of himself. This meant that the full burden of wrath was transferred from his people to himself, so that he, Lord Jesus Christ, bore it in their stead. All this took place in harmony with God's design from eternity. What Jesus offered was therefore a voluntary wrath-removing sacrifice, made effective in the lives of God's children by means of their God-given faith. Not until a person welcomes Christ into his heart and life by genuine, humble trust and self-surrender, does God pronounce him to be just; that is, free from every speck of guilt and therefore also bound to receive all the other blessings that are included in the term *salvation.*

Although it is true that this heavy penalty was not paid by Christ immediately upon the entrance of sin, and that accordingly throughout the entire old dispensation God treated with indulgence the sins of his people, punishment could not be delayed indefinitely. Divine justice had to be satisfied. During Christ's entire life on earth and especially at Calvary the heavy price was paid: "God did not spare his own Son but gave him up for us all" (Rom. 8:31). God did this "to demonstrate his justice in the present time, that he might be just and the One who justifies the person who has faith in Jesus" (3:24–31).

Outline (continued)

Justification by Faith

B. *Scriptural.*
1. *The Example of Abraham.*
"What does the Scripture say? Abraham believed God,
and it was reckoned to him for righteousness."
4:1–12

2. *This example shows
that God's promise is realized through faith, not works.*
"Therefore what was promised came by faith, in order
that it might be a matter of grace."
4:13–25

CHAPTER 4

4 1 What then shall we say that Abraham, our forefather according to the flesh, has discovered? 2 For if Abraham was justified on the basis of works, he has something to boast about. But from God's point of view he has no reason to boast.[107] 3 For what does the Scripture say? "Abraham believed God, and it was reckoned to him for righteousness." 4 Now to the one who works, his wages are not reckoned as a favor but as a debt.[108] 5 On the other hand, to the person who does not work but rests his faith on him who justifies the ungodly, his faith is reckoned for righteousness; 6 just as David also pronounces a blessing upon the person to whom God reckons righteousness apart from works:
7 "Blessed (are) those
    whose transgressions are forgiven,
    whose sins are covered.
8 Blessed is the man
    whose sin the Lord will never reckon (against him)."
9 Is this blessing then [pronounced] only upon the circumcised, or also upon the uncircumcised? For we are saying, "To Abraham his faith was reckoned for righteousness." 10 Under what circumstances then was it so reckoned? Not after he had been circumcised, but while he was still uncircumcised.[109] 11 And he received the sign of circumcision as a seal of the righteousness by faith which he had while still uncircumcised, so that he might be the father of all who have faith but have not been circumcised, in order that righteousness might be reckoned to them; 12 and also the father of those circumcised people who not only are circumcised but also walk in the footsteps of the faith our father Abraham had (even) before he was circumcised.

B. *Scriptural.*
1. *The Example of Abraham.*
"What does the Scripture say? Abraham believed God,
and it was reckoned to him for righteousness."
4:1–12

1. What then shall we say that Abraham, our forefather according to the flesh, has discovered?[110]

In the preceding paragraph (3:21–31) Paul has been proclaiming a righteousness *from God,* and therefore valid before God and not dependent

---

107. Literally: but not before God.
108. Or: not as a gift but as an obligation.
109. Literally: While being in circumcision, or (while being) in uncircumcision? Not in circumcision but in uncircumcision. See footnote 119.
110. There are textual variants. Some MSS. omit the word εὑρηκέναι, which, however, does not seriously affect the central meaning of the passage. Others place this perf. act. infinitive

in any way on human merit. He has stated that the law and the prophets had already borne witness to this righteousness (3:21). It is this point which he is now going to develop.

It should be observed that, in doing so, the apostle does not try to make matters easy for himself. He attacks the proponents of the opposite view—salvation on the basis of human merit—at the very fortress in which they deem themselves to be the strongest, namely, the story of Abraham, that great patriarch who, according to the thinking of the Jews, had *earned* his way into God's good pleasure. Paul asks, "What then shall we say that Abraham, our forefather according to the flesh, has discovered?" He probably means, "What was it he discovered with respect to the manner in which a person enters into right relation with God?"

Note "Abraham, *our* forefather." Among authors who believe that the church of Rome consisted mainly of Jews there are some who appeal also to this passage. Their argument is that when Paul, being himself a Jew, calls Abraham "our forefather," he must mean that those whom he addressed were mainly Jews.[111] But by no means all who are of the opinion that the Jews predominated in that church use Rom. 4:1 in support of their contention, the reason being that such a "proof" (?) is very weak indeed; and this for the following reasons:

a. Abraham was the father not only of Jews but also of Ishmaelites and Edomites; hence even in the physical sense he was the father of Jews *and Gentiles.*

b. The very purpose of Paul in Rom. 4 was to show that in a sense Abraham was the father not only of Jews but also of Gentiles. See 4:11, 12.

c. In I Cor. 10:1 the apostle states, "*Our* ancestors were all under the cloud and all passed through the sea," but he could not have meant that the Corinthians he was addressing were mostly Jews. See I Cor. 12:2, ". . . when y o u were *pagans. . . .*"

d. As any unabridged *dictionary of the English language* indicates, the word *our* is not always used in the strictly literal sense "belonging to us." It can also mean "of interest to us," or "pertaining to the subject we are

---

after ἡμῶν. See Hodge, *op. cit.,* pp. 162, 163. The meaning would then be, "What did Abraham attain κατὰ σάρκα; that is, in a fleshly or carnal manner?" One might say, "in his own power." But not only is the textual support for this variant weak—see textual apparatus Grk.N.T. (A-B-M-W)—but this thought is also out of line with the context. The apostle is not discussing the subject of Abraham's "discovery" or even "attainment" *after the flesh.*

There is also the variant πατέρα instead of προπάτορα. But it is natural to assume that the rareness of the word προπάτορα (acc. s. of προπάτωρ) occurring only once in the New Testament, as contrasted with the frequency of the shorter one, which covers several pages in Moulton and Geden's *Concordance,* caused someone to start the process of substituting the latter for the former. Moreover, does not the fact that the longer word occurs only once point to its authenticity at this place?

The best procedure would seem to be to leave the Greek text exactly as given in the Greek New Testament to which reference has just been made.

111. The question, "To whom did Paul address Romans?" has been discussed earlier. See pp. 20-23.

discussing," etc. In the present context Paul, in referring to "Abraham, our forefather," may well have been thinking of him as "that distant ancestor of interest to all of us."[112]

What, then, had this forefather discovered with respect to the subject in question?

The apostle feels that he has a right to bring up this example of Abraham.

2a. For[113] if Abraham was justified on the basis of works, he has something to boast about.

A few lines earlier (3:27) Paul has drawn the conclusion that since justification—hence also salvation in general—is by faith alone, and faith is God's gift, every reason for human boasting is excluded. However, having been thoroughly drilled in Pharisaic doctrine, he knows that his *opponents* will immediately cite the example of Abraham as proof positive that the factor of *works,* and therefore *human merit,* cannot be entirely excluded when the question is asked, "How do people obtain acceptance with God?" Moreover, if there is really such a thing as human *merit,* then is there not also a basis for human *boasting?*—What follows therefore in chapter 4 is Paul's powerful defense of the proposition, expressed earlier (3:20, 27, 28), that justification is *by faith,* not by works.

By the Jewish teachers and their followers Abraham was considered the only righteous man of his generation. Moreover, they held that it was for that very reason that he had been chosen to be the ancestor of the holy nation. He was considered the first of seven men who, by their *merits,* brought back the Shekinah (cloud of light, cf. Exod. 24:15, 16), so that it could take up its abode in the tabernacle. We are told, moreover, that Abraham began to serve God at the age of three, and that his righteousness was made complete by his circumcision and his anticipatory fulfilment of the law.

Note also the following words from *The Prayer of Manasseh* 8, "Therefore thou, O Lord, God of the righteous, hast not appointed repentance for the righteous, for Abraham, Isaac, and Jacob, who did not sin against thee, but thou hast appointed repentance for me, who am a sinner."

The Book of Jubilees, probably dating from the second century B.C., minimizes the weaknesses of the patriarchs, and contains the statement, "Abraham was perfect in all his deeds with the Lord, and well-pleasing in righteousness all the days of his life (23:10).

Special note should be taken of the fact that the rabbis were not at all

---

112. The possibility must also be granted that the apostle meant, "the forefather of myself and my fellow-Jews." Even if he meant that, this would not prove that the members of the Roman church were mostly Jews.

113. γάρ can best be regarded as explaining the relevance of the question of verse 1 with respect to Abraham. This is another case of abbreviated expression. See N.T.C. on John, Vol. I, p. 206. More fully expressed, the meaning is probably, "I refer to Abraham *for* what is said about him proves that justification is by faith, not by works."

afraid of referring to Gen. 15:6 in defense of their doctrine of justification and salvation on the basis of human works and merit; witness this statement:

"Our father Abraham became the heir of this and of the coming world simply by the merit of the faith with which he believed in the Lord; as it is written, 'He believed in the Lord, who counted it to him as righteousness.' "[114]

It is clear therefore that *by appealing to Gen. 15:6 in defense of the doctrine of justification and salvation purely by faith the apostle was making use of the very passage which by the rabbis was regarded as supporting the opposite view.*

Paul's rejection of this doctrine of *merit* is clear-cut. He writes: **2b–5. But from God's point of view he [Abraham] has no reason to boast. For what does the Scripture say? "Abraham believed God, and it was reckoned to him for righteousness." Now to the one who works, his wages are not reckoned as a favor but as a debt. On the other hand, to the person who does not work but rests his faith on him who justifies the ungodly, his faith is reckoned for righteousness...**

What Paul is saying amounts to this:

Our opponents appeal to Gen. 15:6 in support of their doctrine of justification by works, by human merit. As they see it, Abraham was justified by works. But where, in Gen. 15:6 is even *one* word said about work or merit? According to Gen. 15:6 God bestowed righteousness on Abraham as a free gift. Abraham rested his faith on the gracious Giver, who "reckoned" the patriarch's faith for righteousness. More fully expressed this means that God counted for righteousness *that which Abraham appropriated by faith,* namely, the *righteousness* of Christ. That the apostle had this in mind he makes clear in this very chapter—see verses 6, 11 and 25—and in the next (5:6–21). See also II Cor. 5:21.

The Lord "reckoned" or "considered" or "counted" this "ungodly individual," yes this sinner, namely, Abraham, to be that which in and by himself he was not, namely *just.* The Lord was able to do this, without in any way becoming unjust, because of the certainty that the Coming Messiah would by means of his voluntary sacrifice secure this great blessing for Abraham and for all those who share Abraham's faith. In this connection read Isa. 53, especially verses 4–6, 8, 12 (material with which Paul was thoroughly acquainted; see Rom. 4:25; 5:19; I Cor. 15:3). On the question whether Abraham himself "saw Christ's day" see N.T.C. on John 8:56 (John, Vol. II, pp. 64–66).

I favor this interpretation, with its emphasis on Abraham's *faith,* for the following reasons:

a. In Gen. 15:6 the emphasis is entirely on Abraham's *faith.* No mention is made at all of his work or merit.

---

114. See S.BK. III, p. 186 ff.; 199 ff.; Mekilta on Exod. 14:31; Sanday and Headlam, *op. cit.,* pp. 100, 101, 330–332; Lekkerkerker, *op. cit.,* Vol. I, p. 164.

b. In Rom. 4:2–5 two forms of the verb *to exercise faith, to believe,* occur; so does the cognate noun *faith* (once).

c. To sharpen this emphasis on faith the passage (in verses 4, 5) even implies that Abraham belonged to the class of people who do not work (to obtain their salvation), and who accordingly earn no wages. God owes them nothing!

d. The Hebrew verb, a form of חָשַׁב (Gen. 15:6), in Rom. 4:3 rendered ἐλογίσθη, "was reckoned," is frequently used to indicate what a person, *considered by himself,* is not, or does not have, but is reckoned, held, or regarded to be, or to have. Examples: Gen. 38:15; I Sam. 1:13; Job 13:24. So also here (Gen. 15:6; Rom. 4:3) to Abraham is ascribed or imputed that which he does not himself possess. It is *graciously reckoned* to him because of the righteousness of Another. It is conferred on those who *trust* in God for their justification and salvation.[115]

e. In the parallel passage (Gal. 3:6–9) the emphasis on *faith* (in the sense already explained) is very strong:

"(It is) even as recorded: 'Abraham *believed* [rested his *faith* in] God, and it was reckoned to him for righteousness.' Know then that those who are of *faith*, it is they who are sons of Abraham. Now Scripture, seeing that it was by *faith* that God would justify the Gentiles, preached the gospel beforehand to Abraham, (saying): 'In you all the nations shall be blessed.' Therefore those that are of *faith* are blessed with Abraham, the man of *faith.*"

From start to finish, *therefore, right standing with God* is God's gift. It is appropriated by *God-given faith* (Eph. 2:8; see N.T.C. on Ephesians, pp. 120–123). To God therefore belongs all the glory. For human boasting there is no room whatever.

Between verses 1–5 and verses 6–8 there is a close connection. The earlier passage made reference to Abraham, upon whom God graciously conferred the blessing of *right standing* with the Almighty, *justification.* The immediately following lines describe the blessedness of those whose transgressions are forgiven. Now forgiveness is a very important part of justification. Also note how often a form of the verb *to reckon* occurs in verses 1–5. There is an echo of this in verse 8.

6–8. ... just as David also pronounces a blessing upon the person to whom God reckons righteousness apart from works:
"Blessed (are) those
   whose transgressions are forgiven,
   whose sins are covered.
Blessed is the man
   whose sin the Lord will never reckon (against him)."
There are those who believe that, influenced by his earlier training under Gamaliel (Acts 22:3), Paul, in combining a reference to Abraham

---

115. See also H. W. Heidland on λογίζομαι, Th.D.N.T., Vol. IV, pp. 284–292.

(Gen. 15:6) with a reference to David (Ps. 32:1, 2a), is making use of one of the seven rules of interpretation formulated by Hillel, namely, the rule called *Analogy*, which allows one passage to be joined to another if the same word occurs in both (here the word "reckoned"), the purpose being that the meaning of the word in the first passage will then apply also to its use in the second. However that may be, in the present case this carryover in meaning is certainly legitimate, since the universe of discourse, namely, gracious imputation of righteousness, has not changed.

Note the following:

a. The words of Ps. 32:1, 2a are quoted here. David is jubilant. Why? Because he knows that *his* transgressions[116] have been forgiven,[117] *his* sins covered.[118] See Ps. 32:1–5; especially verse 5b.

If the sins to which this Psalm refers are those in connection with Bathsheba, which may well be the case, the historical background of Ps. 32 would be the same as that of the words quoted in Rom. 3:4. See on that passage.

However, David is thinking not only of the pardon he himself received. The very words, "Blessed (are) *those* whose transgressions are forgiven, whose sins are covered. Blessed is *the man*," etc. indicate that he includes in his beatitude all those who have received a similar blessing.

b. The main point here stressed is that the forgiveness, granted and experienced, was the result not of human work but of divine grace. In this respect Abraham and David have something in common. Both are the recipients of God's sovereign, unearned favor.

c. In verse 5 of the immediately preceding section (verses 1–5) Paul used the expression "faith is reckoned for righteousness," meaning, "God counted for righteousness that which Abraham (or anyone who similarly places his trust in God) appropriated by faith, namely, the righteousness of Christ." This explanation is confirmed in the present section (verses 6–8); note the words, "the person to whom God reckons righteousness apart from works" (verse 6). In both cases, therefore, it is in the final analysis not faith considered by itself but the righteousness of Christ which is imputed to the sinner who, in genuine faith, has fled to God for refuge.

d. It has been shown that Abraham was declared righteous, justified, though he had not earned this blessing by the performance of any good work. Here, in verses 6–8, David pronounces a blessing upon contrite, conscience-stricken sinners, penitent wrongdoers. In both cases human

---

116. Literally: acts of lawlessness, law-violations, and in that sense *transgressions*.

117. Greek ἀφέθησαν, third per. pl. aor. pass. indicat. of ἀφίημι. This is the only passage in which Paul uses the verb ἀφίημι in the sense of to *forgive*. He does, however, use the noun ἄφεσις, forgiveness (Eph. 1:7; Col. 1:14). For the wide range of meaning which the verb has in the New Testament see N.T.C. on Luke, pp. 271, 364 (respectively on Luke 4:39 and 6:42).

118. ἐπεκαλύφθησαν, from ἐπικαλύπτω, *to cover*, same construction as the preceding verb. In the favorable sense, as here, of "blotting out" sin, the Hebrew original on which this Greek verb is based is found also in Ps. 85:2. There is, however, also an unfavorable sense in which sin can be covered (or concealed). See Job 31:33; Prov. 28:13.

works do not enter into the picture; only God's work of grace does. Far from pronouncing "blessed" those who have performed good deeds, David pronounces a blessing upon those whose transgressions were not laid to their account.

e. Justification transcends forgiveness. It includes but also goes beyond pardoning, as the very exclamation "Blessed" ("O the blessedness of") hints. The truly "blessed" person is not only conscious of having been pardoned. He rejoices with "joy unspeakable and full of glory" because he is able to say, "God has accepted me as his son, his daughter. He loves me." For evidence see this same Ps. 32:10. Cf. Ps. 103:11-13; Rom. 8:1, 16, 17.

f. In verse 7 David, by inspiration, is represented as pronouncing a blessing upon *those* whose transgressions have been forgiven, *on them all.* In verse 8 he individualizes this pronouncement. This time the singular is used, "Blessed is *the man*—that is, *the person*—whose sin the Lord will never reckon (against him)."

To speak about blessings granted to many is fine and necessary. Nevertheless, for any particular person these favors become real only then when he is able to say, "O God, thou art *my God*" (Ps. 63:1).

9-12. Is this blessing then (pronounced) only upon the circumcised, or also upon the uncircumcised? For we are saying, "To Abraham his faith was reckoned for righteousness." Under what circumstances then was it so reckoned? After he had been circumcised, or while he was still uncircumcised? Not after he had been circumcised, but while he was still uncircumcised. And he received the sign of circumcision as a seal of the righteousness by faith which he had while still uncircumcised, so that he might be the father of all who have faith but have not been circumcised, in order that righteousness might be reckoned to them; and also the father of those circumcised people who not only are circumcised but also follow in the footsteps of the faith our father Abraham had (even) before he was circumcised.

Paul now returns to Gen. 15:6. In light of his interpretation of Ps. 32:1, 2a his further remarks about the Genesis passage take on added significance. It now becomes clear that when, in the sense already explained, Abraham's faith was reckoned for righteousness, this was indeed an inestimable blessing, a blessing all the more significant because the patriarch could not have earned it. Moreover, as the reference to Ps. 32:1, 2a has shown, the blessing was not only for Abraham but also for David, and . . . for any others? For the circumcised and also for the uncircumcised? For the Jews and also for the Gentiles?[119]

---

119. The words περιτομή and ἀκροβυστία, both of which occur several times in Rom. 4:9-12, have a wide range of meanings. They can refer to a state or condition (respectively that of circumcision and uncircumcision) but can also indicate an individual or even a people. Besides, these words and their Hebrew equivalents can be used in a figurative or spiritual sense (Deut. 10:16; 30:6; Jer. 4:4; Rom. 2:29; Phil. 3:3; Col. 2:11). In any given case the correct English equivalent is determined by the context.

Standard Jewish doctrine answered, "Only for the circumcised."[120] Even in the early church Jewish converts to Christianity found it difficult to shake off their nationalistic prejudices: "Some men came down from Judea to Antioch and were teaching the brothers, 'Unless y o u are circumcised according to the custom taught by Moses, y o u cannot be saved.'" (Acts 15:1). If any further proof is needed see Rom. 2:25–27; Gal. 5:2, 6, 12; 6:12–15; Phil. 3:2, 3. Paul's question, "Is this blessing then (pronounced) only upon the circumcised or also on the uncircumcised?" is therefore understandable.

Paul's response is masterful. It should constantly be borne in mind that he is writing by inspiration. He proves that *Abraham's faith*—meaning "the righteousness of Christ appropriated by faith"—*was reckoned or imputed to Abraham for righteousness* not after he had been circumcised but *while he was still uncircumcised!* It was then already that Abraham was declared righteous in God's sight.

This very significant chronological observation becomes clear from a study of the following references:

a. Abraham was ninety-nine years of age when he was circumcised (Gen. 17:24).

b. On that same day Ishmael was also circumcised (Gen. 17:25).

c. Ishmael was then thirteen years of age (Gen. 17:25).

d. When God made his covenant with Abraham (Gen. 15:18), and "Abraham believed the Lord, and it was reckoned to him for righteousness" (Gen. 15:6), Ishmael had not yet been conceived (Gen. 15:2, 3; 16:4).

Conclusion: between the moment when the blessing of Gen. 15:6 was pronounced upon Abraham and the day he was circumcised there must have been an interval of at least about fourteen years. An even longer interval is possible. According to Jewish chronology the gap was one of twenty-nine years (S.BK. III, p. 203). A considerably shorter period than fourteen years is impossible.

Accordingly, it was upon the still uncircumcised Abraham, who in that respect resembled a Gentile, that the promise was given, the blessing pronounced. This proves that circumcision has nothing to do with being declared righteous.

If any unbelieving Jews heard these words, they must have been shocked. Even some Christians from among the Jews must have been startled.

We are told that Abraham received "the sign of circumcision," meaning: the sign, namely, circumcision.[121] Being a "sign," it signifies or indicates a fact. *Sign* and *thing signified* are generally closely related. Thus in the present case the *cutting away* of the foreskin suggests and symbolizes the *excision* of the guilt and pollution of sin; hence, justification and, closely connected with it, sanctification.

Circumcision was also a *seal.* To Abraham it was a guarantee of the

---

120. See S.BK., p. 203.

121. περιτομῆς must be interpreted as a gen. of apposition.

trustworthiness of God's promise. It meant that this patriarch could depend upon it that in the way of faith, and the obedience resulting from faith, the righteousness of Christ was reckoned or imputed to him.

Signs and seals are very valuable. To be sure, it is possible to overestimate their significance. In and by themselves these signs—in the old dispensation the bloody ones of circumcision and Passover; in the new, the unbloody ones of baptism and the Lord's Supper—do not bring about justification or, in general, salvation. However, they do indeed signify and seal it in the manner already indicated. And is not that a source of comfort? The rainbow does not save mankind from being swallowed up by a flood, but it does signify and seal that God will never again drown the human race. The wedding ring does not bring married bliss, but what married person, who loves his (her) marriage partner, would ever think of doing away with the ring that means so much to him (her)? Indeed, signs and seals must not be underestimated. See Exod. 4:24-26; Josh. 5:1-12; II Kings 23:21-23; Acts 2:38, 39; I Cor. 11:23 f. They have great educational and psychological value. *But neither should they be overrated!*

Paul clings to his subject. Therefore, what he really emphasizes is this, namely, that Abraham received *the sign of circumcision as a seal of the righteousness by faith which he had while still uncircumcised!*

These words "while still uncircumcised," with slight variations, are found in three succeeding verses: 10, 11, 12. It is as if Paul wanted to din into the ears of the uncircumcised Gentiles this enormous truth: "Believe in the Lord Jesus Christ. Don't hold back. Don't hesitate to place y o u r undivided trust in this marvelous Savior, the Revealer of God Triune. The fact that y o u have not been circumcised cannot prevent y o u from being saved. God is calling y o u. He is calling y o u *now*. It was while Abraham was still uncircumcised that God made his covenant with him. He stands ready to do the same for y o u."

It is clear, therefore, that Abraham, to whom the righteousness of Christ was reckoned or imputed before he had been circumcised, and to whom, once he had been circumcised, God repeated his gracious promise again and again, is the spiritual father, the head of the procession, of two *sub*-groups: (a) all who have faith but have not been circumcised; and (b) all who not only have been circumcised but also have and exercise faith, showing this to be true by following "in the footsteps of the faith Abraham had (even) before he was circumcised." These two *sub*-groups constitute *one large group of believers,* Abraham being the father of them all (verse 16).

This also indicates that circumcision is not essential to salvation.

It is maintained at times that neither is it a deterrent or excluding factor.[112] If this means, as it probably does, that the fact that a person has been circumcised does not *necessarily* prevent him from being saved, I fully agree, for this is what Rom. 4:12 clearly teaches.

---

122. Murray, *op. cit.,* p. 139.

What the apostle stresses again and again in his epistles is that, as far as being saved is concerned, circumcision makes no difference, amounts to nothing (I Cor. 7:19; Gal. 5:6; 6:15; Col. 3:11). But does this not also imply that if too much is made of circumcision—or today, of baptism—as if in some sense salvation were dependent upon it, it might in certain cases indeed become an excluding factor? Note what Paul says in Gal. 5:2:

"Now I, Paul, say to y o u that if y o u let yourselves be circumcised, Christ will be of no value to y o u at all." I feel sure that the author of the fine commentary to which I just now referred would have agreed with me.

This subject has practical significance for every age, including the present. Previously the importance of signs and seals has been established. See p. 151. (It should not be lost sight of, however, that the bloody signs and seals have been replaced by the unbloody ones.) Just now the danger of overestimating their value has been signalized. The reason for stressing the fact that both extremes should be avoided is that even today the Church administers sacraments: baptism and the Lord's Supper. With respect to these, too, extremes should be avoided. Rushing in to drop some water on a dying child's forehead, fearing that otherwise it might not enter heaven at death, makes no sense. On the other hand, the custom of some, needlessly to postpone baptism, is also not to be recommended. Both extremes are unbiblical.

Signs and seals do not save automatically. In this connection note how careful the apostle is. Here in Rom. 4:12 he first tells believers from the Gentiles (the uncircumcised) that, according to God's plan, Abraham became "the father of all who have faith but have not been circumcised." Then he adds, with respect to believers from the Jews, who, even after their conversion to Christ were prone to attach too great a value to the sign (Acts 15:1), "and also the father of those circumcised people who not only are circumcised *but also follow in the footsteps of the faith our father Abraham had (even) before he was circumcised.*" It is *life*—cf. "*living* for Jesus"—that is emphasized.

It would be difficult to overestimate the significance of Rom. 4:9–12. The passage means that with one stroke of the pen the entire huge wall of separation between Jew and Gentile was razed to the ground. Moreover, the promise made to Abraham, when God established his covenant with him (Gen. 15:6, 18; 17:7; 22:15–18), is still in effect,[123] and has significance for all believers and their families.[124]

---

123. For more on this see my booklet *The Covenant of Grace,* Grand Rapids, 1978, especially pp. 21-25.

124. Attention should be focused on a few points of grammar in verses 11, 12:

First of all note εἰς τὸ εἶναι αὐτόν . . . εἰς τὸ λογισθῆναι αὐτοῖς: there is no reason to subtract anything from the full telic sense. But purpose does not exclude (but here certainly includes) result.

δι' = διά expresses attendant circumstance, as in 2:27.

Τοῖς before στοιχοῦσιν. We translate, ". . . those who not only are circumcised *but also follow* in the footsteps . . ." It is difficult to explain this τοῖς. Many say nothing about it. Others are sure

13 For it was not through (the) law that Abraham or his seed received the promise that he would be heir of the world, but through righteousness resulting from faith.   14 For if those who live by law are heirs, faith is deprived of its value and the promise is rendered worthless; 15 for the law produces wrath, but where there is no law there is also no transgression.

16 For this reason what was promised came by faith, namely, in order that it might be a matter of grace, and in order that the promise might be certain of fulfilment[125] for all the seed, not for those who only live by the law, but for those who also live by the faith of Abraham (who is the father of us all,   17 as it is written, "Father of many nations have I made you"), in the presence of God on whom he rested his faith, the God who imparts life to the dead, and calls things that are not as though they were.

18 Against all hope, Abraham in hope believed, so that he became the father of many nations, in agreement with what had been told him, "So shall your seed be."   19 And without weakening in faith he took note of the fact that his own body was as good as dead—since he was about a hundred years old—and that Sarah's womb was also dead.[126]   20 Yet he did not waver in unbelief with respect to God's promise, but was strengthened in faith, giving glory to God,   21 being fully persuaded that what God had promised he would be able to perform. 22 That is why it was reckoned to him for righteousness.

23 Now the words, "It was reckoned to him," were written not for him alone,   24 but also for us to whom it is to be reckoned, to us who rest our faith on him who raised Jesus our Lord from the dead,   25 who was delivered up for our trespasses and was raised for our justification.[127]

---

2. *This example shows
that God's promise is realized through faith, not works.*
"Therefore what was promised came by faith, in order
that it might be a matter of grace."
4:13-25

Paul continues his demonstration of the fact that the doctrine of justification by faith, not through the works of the law, is indeed not a novelty but has its foundation in the Scriptures; that is, in what today we call the Old Testament.

In the preceding paragraph (4:1–12) he has already shown that *according to Scripture,* attaining the status of *righteousness in the eyes of God* is a matter not of works and merit but of faith and therefore of grace. Also, that it has nothing to do with circumcision. In fact, Abraham was pronounced righteous long before he was circumcised. Therefore Abraham should be regarded as the father or spiritual leader of all true believers, circumcised or not.

---

that someone made a mistake. The possibility that a very early copyist erred must be granted. The text is well attested, however, so that on that score there is no solution. What then? As I see it, Ridderbos, though not completely solving this puzzle, provides what may well be the best answer. See his comments, *op. cit.,* pp. 95, 96, 98, 99. He points to the fact that in verse 16 we find a similar construction (τῷ before ἐκ πίστεως) "which raises the question whether for Paul this kind of connection was as unusual as for his commentators."

125. Or sure, firmly grounded, unshakable.
126. Or: he considered his own body . . . and the deadness of Sarah's womb.
127. Instead of *for . . . for,* one may substitute *on account of . . . on account of.*

In the present paragraph (verses 13-25) this idea that divine grace, not human effort, is the basis upon which rests the building of salvation full and free is made to stand out even more clearly by the emphasis that is placed on *the divine promise*. That word *promise*—at times indicating the divine declaration itself, then again its effectuation or realization (the promised blessing)—occurs here for the first time in Paul's epistle to the Romans. The idea that the God of the covenant is the God of the promise is repeated several times (verses 13, 14, 16, 20, 21). This promise, moreover, is of *world-embracing* significance. It affects not only *all* true believers, Jew and Gentile alike, but also causes its influence to be felt in every age, past, present, and future. For this world-embracing application of the divine promise verses 11, 12 have already prepared us.

13-15. For it was not through (the) law that Abraham or his seed received the promise that he would be heir of the world, but through righteousness resulting from faith. For if those who live by law are heirs, faith is deprived of its value and the promise is rendered worthless; for the law produces wrath, but where there is no law there is also no transgression.

As the Jews saw it, the promise made to Abraham was to be realized through obedience to the Mosaic law. The rabbis even maintained that long before the law was promulgated from Sinai, Abraham already had a thorough knowledge of it and obeyed it in all its details.[128]

Over against this the apostle states that the promise was given to Abraham considered as a man of faith in his God, and that it was a result of this faith that righteousness had been reckoned or credited to him. Works or merit had nothing to do with the promise or its fulfilment. Obedience to the law was not in the picture, for the promise was made to Abraham many years before the law had been promulgated. Cf. Gal. 3:16-18.

Note the words, ". . . Abraham or his seed received the promise that he would be "heir of the world," that is, that, as a *gift* from God he would *obtain* "the world."[129] But what does that mean?

In answer to this question it may be well, first of all, to point out that God's promise to Abraham contained the following items:

a. title to the land of Canaan (Gen. 12:7; 13:14, 15, 17; 15:7; 17:8). This item is spelled out in some detail in 15:18-21.

b. the assurance that in number his seed would be as the dust of the earth (13:16; 15:5; cf. 18:18).

The book of Exodus shows us that the promise of an abundant posterity was realized. The book of Joshua shows us that also the land of Canaan became the possession of Abraham's descendants.

Before we proceed to item c. it should be pointed out that the conclusion drawn by many, namely, that *today*, because of item a., the entire land of

---

128. S.BK. III, pp. 186 ff.; 199-201; 204 ff.
129. On the meaning of the word κληρονόμος see W. Foerster, Th.D.N.T., Vol. III, pp. 781-785.

Canaan, in its widest dimensions, really belongs to the Jews, is unwarranted. Every fairminded person regrets the persecutions the Jews have endured, wants them to enjoy the full measure of security to which they are entitled, and is relentlessly opposed to every manifestation of anti-Semitism. But all this is no excuse for ignoring the fact expressed so clearly in Jer. 18:9, 10.

This brings us now to the next item:

c. the guarantee that in Abraham's seed all the *families of the earth* will be blessed. Gal. 3:16 states that it is in Christ, the real *Seed,* that all those who embrace him will be blessed. Gal. 3:29 adds, "And if y o u are Christ's, then y o u are Abraham's seed, heirs according to promise."

It is in light of such passages as these that we will have to interpret the passage that Abraham or his seed received the promise that he would be *heir of the world* (Rom. 4:13), "father of many nations" (verses 17, 18). And is it not also true that Abraham and all who by sovereign grace constitute his seed do actually in a sense own the universe? Do not all things work together for good for those who love God and are called according to his purpose (Rom. 8:28), so that Paul can say, "All things are y o u r s" (I Cor. 3:21)? Rightly interpreted, therefore, Abraham, to whom the righteousness of Christ was imputed, was "heir of the world." The same was and is true, of course, with respect to all those who have a share in Abraham's faith. If the Lord is *their* God, which is the very essence of the covenant of grace (Gen. 17:7), all is well.

It is understandable that if, instead, those people who believe that strenuous efforts to obey the law in all its details will save them, were right, then faith—reliance for salvation not on self but on God—would have lost its value. Also, on that basis no one would ever be saved, for the law demands perfection, which no sinner is able to render. Therefore the promise would be rendered worthless, for under those circumstances it could never be fulfilled.

Paul had tried very hard to be saved by the law. He had failed miserably (Acts 22:3, 4; Gal. 1:13; Phil. 3:4-7). Having been "snatched as a brand from the fire," he now understood that "the law produces wrath." It *condemns* the sinner, pronounces a curse on all those who do not comply perfectly with its demands (Deut. 28:58 f.). Rom. 8:3 impresses this lesson upon us in very touching manner. The law cannot enable a person to fulfil its demands; hence cannot save anyone: "For what the law could not do, God did by sending his own Son."

When God had come to Abraham with his covenant promise, the law had not yet been promulgated, as mentioned in the preceding. Therefore conscious transgression of that law was also, in a sense, impossible: "Where there is no law there is no transgression." As a result God had provided ample room for *the promise* to function.

16, 17. For this reason what was promised came by faith, namely, in order that it might be a matter of grace, and in order that the promise

might be certain of fulfilment for all the seed, not for those who only live by the law, but for those who also live by the faith of Abraham (who is the father of us all, as it is written, "Father of many nations have I made you"), in the presence of God on whom he rested his faith, the God who imparts life to the dead, and calls things that are not as though they were.

In line with what the apostle has just now been saying about the manner in which God carries out his plan of salvation, namely, by not insisting that in order to be saved the sinner must earn his own entrance into the kingdom of heaven, but by providing a solution in which grace would triumph, he now states that the reason the promised salvation came *by faith* was that it might be *a matter of grace*.[130] This also implies that the promise, "I will be their—or y o u r—God," hence the promise of salvation full and free, would be certain of fulfilment, sure, firmly grounded, and unshakable. If the fulfilment of the promise had been dependent on human effort, so that salvation would have been the product of perfect obedience to the demands of God's law, this fulfilment would never have been attained. But now that it is a matter of grace, hence a matter of God's eternal and effective plan, its realization in the lives of all God's people is assured.

And what a source of comfort this is! That is why, it is with such gusto that the congregation, gathered for worship, professes its faith by breaking out into the words of Ps. 89:

> I sing of mercies that endure,
> Forever builded firm and sure,
> Of faithfulness that never dies,
> Established changeless in the skies.[131]

Anonymous

The immediately following words (16b) present a problem. After "to the end the promise might be sure to all the seed," the A.V. has: "not to that only which is of the law, but to that also which is of the faith of Abraham, who is the father of us all." Almost all modern translations agree in affirming that the apostle has in mind two groups of people to whom the promise is made sure. According to Hodge (*op. cit.*, p. 192) these two are, respectively, believing Jews and believing Gentiles.

Now one objection to this construction is that in the immediate

---

130. In view of the almost immediately following ἵνα, it is best to interpret διὰ τοῦτο as pointing forward; hence, "For this reason ... namely, in order that."

131. Or, with no less enthusiasm, in the Dutch services one will hear:
Gij toch, Gij zijt hun roem, de kracht van hunne kracht;
Uw vrije gunst alleen wordt d'ere toegebracht;
Wij steken 'thoofd omhoog, en zullen d'eerkroon dragen,
Door U, door U alleen, om 'teeuwig welbehagen;
Want God is ons ten schild in 'tstrijdperk van dit leven,
En onze Koning is van Isrels God gegeven.

context—see verses 11, 12—Paul has indicated that he regards Abraham as the father of *all* believers, both Gentiles and Jews. It is therefore hard to see how the words "that which is of the faith of Abraham" (or "those who live by the faith of Abraham") could refer to Gentiles only; all the more so in the light of the appended clause "who is the father of us all."

Besides, the place which the little word "only" (Greek μόνον) occupies in the sentence would seem to indicate that Paul is not thinking of two groups for which the promise has validity, but of one group only. He is saying, "that the promise might be certain of fulfilment *for all the seed, not for that by the law only but also by the faith of Abraham,* thus literally; meaning: *not for those who live by the law only but for those who also live by the faith of Abraham;* or "not for those who only live by the law but for those who also live by the faith of Abraham," etc.[132]

The promise, then, is certain of fulfilment for one group only, namely, for that true seed, those people who, while honoring God's law (cf. 3:31), rest their faith on God, as did Abraham. All of them, whether Gentiles or Jews, "are blessed with Abraham, the man of faith" (Gal. 3:9). See also Gal. 3:29, "And if y o u belong to Christ, then y o u are Abraham's seed, heirs according to promise." What the apostle says here in 4:16 resembles what he has stated in 4:11, 12.

Abraham is here called "the father of us all." In verse 11 he is called "the father of all who believe." The apostle is evidently determined to see to it that the readers or hearers will understand that God does not recognize two separate groups on whom his special favor rests, but only one group, consisting of all genuine believers, whether they be Gentiles or Jews. In verse 17 he even adds evidence from the Old Testament, "Father of many nations have I made you" (Gen. 17:5).

Now it must be admitted that in the Genesis passage the words "many nations" apply to Abraham's natural posterity. In the physical sense this patriarch was indeed the father of many nations or peoples: of the Ishmaelites (Gen. 17:20) as well as of Isaac and his descendants (Gen. 21:1–3); and through Isaac, of the Edomites as well as of the Israelites (Gen. 25:21–25; ch. 36); in fact even of the seed of Keturah (25:1f.).

Shall we say, then, that *the apostle,* in speaking about Abraham's *spiritual* fatherhood, and in this context directing our attention to Gen. 17:5, is committing an error? But who would dare to take the position that the Holy Spirit lacks the right to take an Old Testament passage and give it an application different from that which it had in its original setting? However, in the present instance we do not have to make use of this argument, for even in the Genesis passages a reference to spiritual fatherhood is not

---

132. On this construction see also Greijdanus, *op. cit.,* Vol. I, p. 238; and Ridderbos, *op. cit.,* pp. 98, 99.

altogether wanting. Note that in Gen. 12:3 Abraham is told that in and through him all the families of the earh *will be blessed.*[133]

Beautiful is the expression "the faith of Abraham . . . in the presence of[134] God on whom he rested his faith." It describes the great patriarch as one who was the recipient of vivid experiences of the divine Presence. The father of all believers was filled with profound reverence; yet also with filial trust.

Paul further describes the object of Abraham's faith as "the God who imparts life to the dead." The reference is to the One who revived Abraham's power to beget, and Sarah's ability to bear. See verses 18, 19.[135] Paul may also have been thinking about the resurrection of Jesus, for when he describes God as the One who imparts life to the dead, he is by means of that statement professing also his own faith. Moreover, see 4:24, 25.

What is the meaning of "and calls things that are not as though they were"? Of these words there are several interpretations. The worst one is probably that volunteered by the leader of a certain sect. According to a newspaper report, when this person was caught in the act of telling an untruth, his excuse was, "What of it? Does not Scripture state that even God calls things that are not as though they were?"

The most reasonable explanation may well be that which refers this expression to the activity of the Almighty during the week of creation, when, according to Isa. 48:13, he *called into being* or *summoned* that which beforehand did not exist, namely, "the foundations of the earth" and "the heavens," probably representing the entire work of creation.

The main thrust of Paul's argument is this, that it was by *faith* in the Almighty and All Faithful God, and not by works, that Abraham received the fulfilment of the promise.

18-22. Against all hope, Abraham in hope believed, so that he became the father of many nations, in agreement with what had been told him, "So shall your seed be." And without weakening in faith he took note of the fact that his own body was as good as dead—since he was about a hundred years old—and that Sarah's womb was also dead. Yet he did not waver in unbelief with respect to God's promise, but was strengthened in faith, giving glory to God, being fully persuaded that what God had promised he would be able to perform. That is why it was reckoned to him for righteousness.

The character of Abraham's faith is set forth in a very striking manner.

---

133. For this passage (Gen. 12:3) a spiritual overtone or implication is also recognized by G. Ch. Aalders, *Korte Verklaring, Genesis,* Kampen, 1949, Vol. II, p. 63.

134. ϰατέναντι, closely related to ἔναντι, is the LXX equivalent of the Hebrew לִפְנֵי. See my dissertation, *The Meaning of the Preposition* ἀντί *in the New Testament,* pp. 68–70.

135. There are those who, in this connection, also mention the sparing of Isaac's life (Gen. 22). Heb. 11:17–19 may offer some support for this idea. However, Rom. 4:19 makes no reference to this incident. Its relevance at this point is therefore rather uncertain.

Note the following:

a. "Against all hope, Abraham in hope believed."

Basically *hope* means the expectation of something desirable. In the present case the object of hope was the fulfilment of God's promise that Abraham would have a son, in whose line the precious promise of God—"I will be your God . . . in your *seed* all the nations of the earth will be blessed . . . So shall your seed be"—would attain fulfilment.

A time arrived when *humanly speaking* this hope seemed impossible of realization. Nevertheless, "against all hope," that is, in spite of the fact that the birth of the child of promise appeared to be impossible, Abraham "in hope"—here the persuasion that God would be faithful to his promise—continued to trust in God. Result: the hope was fulfilled so that, through his son Isaac, Abraham became "the father of many nations" (see on verse 17).

b. "He did not waver . . . but was strengthened in faith. . . ."

Years passed, and still the promise had not been fulfilled. Bravely the patriarch faced the fact that he was now about a hundred years of age, that "his own body"—here with special reference to his reproductive capacity—was as good as dead,[136] and that Sarah was barren. Nevertheless, he not only continued to exercise faith in God and his promise but was even strengthened in his faith. That this is what actually happened is evident from the fact that when God repeated the promise to him in his very advanced age—"Sarah your wife will indeed bear you a son" (Gen. 17:19)—and ordered all the male membes of his household to be circumcised (Gen. 17:9-14), Abraham immediately glorified God by obeying this command (Gen. 17:23-26). And because of the fact that he thus glorified God he was strengthened in his faith. And since this faith expected everything from God, completely relying on him, it could be, and actually was, "reckoned to him for righteousness."

When a pastor presents to his congregation this account of Abraham's marvelous unwavering faith, it may well be that some people will become discouraged, thinking, "If God requires such faith as this, namely, that a man way past the age of begetting children, with a wife whose womb is *dead,* must believe God's promise that he is going to have a child, that this child will be a boy, and that this very wife, and not some other woman, will give birth to him, then there is no hope for me. When it comes to simple, steadfast faith, the kind of trust that takes hold of God *under any and every circumstance of life,* what a struggle I often experience!"

Close study of Scripture, however, should convince such a person that though, in a sense, Abraham's faith did not waver and was even

---

136. The reading ἤδη νενεϰρωμένον, with retention of ἤδη, is subject to a considerable degree of doubt. It would seem to have a slight edge over the reading without ἤδη. The verbal form is the acc. s. neut. perf. pass. participle of νεϰρόω, to put to death; in pass., as here, to be impotent, as good as dead.

strengthened, this cannot mean that he did not experience a struggle. He did! That is clearly implied in Gen. 17:18 (and perhaps even in 17:17, though with respect to that verse interpreters are divided). But God immediately reassured him (Gen. 17:19), and it was in that sense that Abraham's faith did not waver and was even strengthened. Every pastor should therefore point his congregation to the Savior who, in answer to the prayer of the struggling soul, and in co-operation with the teaching of the Word, will strengthen and reassure. An excellent hymn in this connection is:

> When I fear my faith will fail, Christ will hold me fast.
>
> A. R. Habershon

That these precious passages of Scripture were meant for every age is shown in the verses which conclude this chapter of Romans:

23-25. Now the words, "It was reckoned to him," were written not for him alone, but also for us to whom it is to be reckoned, to us who rest our faith on him who raised Jesus our Lord from the dead, who was delivered up for our trespasses and was raised for our justification.

" . . . not for him alone but also for us." That the words of Scripture were written not solely for the contemporaries of the respective authors but also for later generations is taught in both testaments (Ps. 78:1-7; Rom. 15:4; I Cor. 9:10; 10:11; and in a sense II Tim. 3:16). So also the experiences of God's children were to be related to later generations (Gen. 18:19). Today, an age in which for many the study of history has become a lost art, this reminder should serve a good purpose. What Paul is saying is that we too are vitally concerned with this story about Abraham, and with the manner in which the righteousness of Christ was imputed to him. Is it not true that we too are the ones to whom it is to be reckoned? Are not we included in the family of those who rest our faith on him who raised Jesus our Lord from the dead?

Note that Paul's attitude toward Jesus Christ is one not only of profound reverence ("Lord"), but also of deep gratitude, heart-warming love ("Our"). When the apostle wrote the words "Jesus our Lord" he was not just rattling off a few titles. No, this is the Paul of Gal. 2:20, the one who said, "the Son of God loved me and gave himself up for me."

Reflecting, then, on God's omnipotence and love employed in the interest of his people, Paul includes his addressees and himself in the circle of those who rest their faith on the One *who raised Jesus our Lord from the dead.*

The long list of references which indicate that The Twelve (often represented by Peter) and Paul were convinced not only of the fact that Jesus had risen from the dead but also that *God* had raised him—see Acts 2:24, 32; 3:15, 26; 4:10; 5:30; 10:40; 13:30, 33, 34, 37; 17:31; I Cor. 6:14; 15:15; II Cor. 4:14; Gal. 1:1; Eph. 1:20; Col. 2:12; I Thess. 1:10 (cf. Heb. 13:20; I Peter 1:21)—is significant. Does it not seem as if these passages are calling attention to the fact that God the Father must have been satisfied with the atoning sacrifice Jesus had offered?

Paul continues with words that have been, and continue to be, the occasion of much controversy, a controversy that centers in a little Greek word of three letters (διά), which can be translated "for" or "because of," or "on account of."

The controversial passage concerns "Jesus our Lord," and the dispute is focused on the clause "who was delivered up *for* our trespasses and was raised *for* our justification."

Some maintain that because these two clauses—(a) delivered up for our trespasses, (b) raised for our justification—are parallel, therefore if the first *looks back* (is retrospective), the second must do the same. Or if the first *looks forward* (is prospective), the second does likewise. See Murray, *op. cit.*, p. 154 f. That author chose the second of these alternatives: Jesus was delivered up in order to atone for our sins and was raised in order that we might be justified. A somewhat similar view can be found in Denney's commentary, *op. cit.*, p. 622. To be fair to these authors, both of whom have written commentaries that are worthy of serious study, their books should be consulted on this question.

It is interesting to notice that A. Schlatter, who also proceeds from the idea that διά must have the same meaning in both clauses, reaches the opposite conclusion. As he sees it, both are retrospective: because we fell, Jesus was condemned; because we had been justified, he arose.[137]

Is it true, indeed, that we are compelled to choose between these two alternatives? Probably not. There is a third possibility, namely, that while basically the little word may have the same meaning in both clauses, namely, may indicate causality, this causality could still look backward in the first clause, forward in the second. In fact, even in the almost immediately preceding line (verses 23, 24) it is clear that the first διά (the one in verse 23: "*for* him") looks backward, to Abraham; the second (in verse 24, "*for* us") looks forward. So also here "He was delivered up *for*, or *on account of*, our trespasses" *looks backward* and means that our trespasses made it necessary for him to be delivered up, while "(he) was raised *for*, or *on account of*, our justification" *looks forward* and indicates that he was raised in order to assure us that in the sight of God we are indeed without sin. In other words Christ's resurrection had as its *purpose* to bring to light the fact that all those who acknowledge Jesus as their Lord and Savior have entered into a state of righteousness in the eyes of God.[138] The Father, by raising Jesus from the dead, assures us that the atoning sacrifice has been accepted; hence, our sins are forgiven.

Before we leave this precious passage (Rom. 4:25) we must point out that here again the close connection between the Old and the New Testament is revealed. The words "who was delivered up [or: over to death] for our

---

137. A. Schlatter, *Gottes Gerechtigkeit, Ein Kommentar zum Römerbrief*, Stuttgart, 1952, p. 173.
138. On this debate with respect to the meaning of διά I have not been able to find anything better than that which is offered by S. Greijdanus, *op. cit.*, pp. 251, 252; and by Ridderbos, *op. cit.*, p. 104. Both of these are excellent.

trespasses" are a strong reminder of what is found in Isa. 53, where in verses 4, 5, 6, 8, 11, and 12, in one way or another, Messiah's *vicarious suffering* is described and predicted.[139]

That the truth with respect to the believers' justification, solely of grace and by faith, is a treasure so precious that nothing—no, nothing!—can top it, Paul confesses when, in jubilation of spirit, he exclaims:

"Nevertheless the things that once were gains to me these have I counted loss for Christ. Yes, what is more, I certainly count all things to be sheer loss because of the all-surpassing excellence of knowing Christ Jesus my Lord, for whom I suffered the loss of all things, and I am still counting them refuse, in order that I may gain Christ, and be found in him, *not having a righteousness of my own, legal righteousness,* but that (which is) through faith in Christ, the righteousness (which is) from God and is by faith..." (Phil. 3:7-9).

Among the many precious truths held before us in this fourth chapter of Romans is certainly also this outstanding one, namely, that the comforting doctrine of justification not by works but by faith is firmly rooted in Scripture (the Old Testament), as the example of Abraham proves.

Practical Lessons Derived from Romans 4

Verse 1

"What then shall we say that Abraham has discovered?" See also verses 3, 9, and 10. A hint for speakers: keep alive the interest of your audience by asking questions... but do not overdo this.

Verse 6

"Blessed are those whose transgressions are forgiven... whose sins are covered." The reference to David is certainly apt, for if ever a man received righteous standing with God without having *earned* it, it was David. But because of the sovereign grace of his God his sins were forgiven, blotted out. Moreover, as Ps. 32 proves, that same blessing is bestowed upon every truly penitent sinner.

Verse 11

"And he received the *sign* of circumcision as a *seal* of the righteousness by faith...."

Because God is love (I John 4:8) and takes delight in saving sinners (see Isa. 1:18; Ezek. 18:23, 32; 33:11; Hos. 11:8; Matt. 11:28-30; John 7:37; Rev. 22:17), he strengthens his promises by means of signs and seals.

---

139. In fact, in the LXX version of Isa. 53 the very expression "deliver" in the sense of "deliver up to death" occurs twice (verses 6 and 12). Translated into English, verse 6 in the LXX reads, "And the Lord delivered him up for our sins." Verse 12 reads, "And on account of their sins he was delivered up." But in that verse the Hebrew reads differently, "And he made intercession for the transgressors."

Verses 16–18

"Abraham . . . the father of us all; the father of many nations." In God's kingdom there is no room for racial prejudice. All believers constitute one family, *Abraham's* Family; in an even deeper sense, *"God's* Family" (Eph. 3:14, 15).

Verse 18

"Against all hope, Abraham in hope believed." There is a kind of hope that has no real foundation, no anchor. Abraham's hope was firmly anchored, namely, in God's unfailing promise. See Heb. 6:19, 20; 11:1; and sing "We Have an Anchor" by Priscilla Owens.

Verse 21

". . . being fully persuaded that what God had promised he would be able to perform."

Points of Contrast Between the Divine Promise and Human Promises

a. God's promise is always right. Human promises are sometimes wrong.

b. God's promise is substantial; in fact, priceless. Human promises are often trivial.

c. God never forgets his promise. People frequently forget.

d. God—hence also Jesus—fulfils his promise. In this respect, too, people often fail. But as to the Lord, is it not true that what he grants is often even more than what he promised? Cf. Matt. 28:7 (or Mark 16:7) with Luke 24:34, 36.

Summary of Chapter 4

Having set forth the truth that the state of righteousness in God's sight cannot be achieved by means of human works but is God's gift, the apostle now, in harmony with 4:21, elaborates on the fact that this representation is not a novelty but is thoroughly scriptural.

In this connection he fixes the attention of the hearer and/or reader on the manner in which Abraham obtained this great blessing: "Abraham believed God, and it was reckoned to him for righteousness" (Gen. 15:6). He comments, "Now to the one who works, his wages are not reckoned as a favor but as a debt. On the other hand, to the person who does not work but rests his faith on him who justifies the ungodly, his faith is reckoned for righteousness." God counted for righteousness that which Abraham appropriated by faith, namely, the righteousness of Another, that is, of Jesus Christ, which was imputed to Abraham. Cf. Rom. 4:6, 11, 25; 5:6–21; cf. Isa. 53:4–6, 8, 12.

By means of a quotation from Ps. 32 the apostle proves that what was true with respect to Abraham holds for *all* believers: "Blessed (are) those whose transgressions are forgiven, whose sins are covered."

Returning to Gen. 15:6, Paul asks, "Is this blessing then pronounced only upon the circumcised or also upon the uncircumcised?" He shows that it was long before Abraham was circumcised that his faith was reckoned for righteousness. As a result Abraham became "the father of *all* believers";

that is, of those uncircumcised as well as of those circumcised; in other words, of Gentile as well as of Jewish believers (verses 1–12).

In close connection with the immediately preceding, Paul now emphasizes the importance of God's *promise* and its fulfilment. It was not through the law that Abraham received the promise. Human works or merit had nothing to do with it. It was *faith* in the *promise* that mattered. Cf. Gal. 3:9, 29. God *promised* Abraham that he would be "the father of many nations," therefore "heir of the world" (Gen. 17:5). Abraham did not waver in unbelief but was strengthened in faith. He rested his faith on him "who imparts life to the dead, and calls things that are not as though they were." In view of the fact that Abraham was almost a hundred years old and Sarah was barren, this faith of Abraham was indeed remarkable. The patriarch believed that whatever God promised he would also do. Moreover, the words "It was reckoned to him for righteousness" were meant not only for him but for all who rest their faith on God, the One who "raised Jesus our Lord from the dead."

The Savior "was delivered up for our trespasses and was raised for our justification." This probably means that our trespasses made it necessary for Jesus to be delivered over to death, and that he was raised to life in order to assure us that his vicarious sacrifice had been accepted. As a result believers are, in the very sight of God, without sin and therefore righteous (verses 13–25).

By means of corroborative evidence from the Old Testament Paul has made clear that the comforting doctrine of justification—hence salvation—by faith, on the basis of God's sovereign grace, is indeed thoroughly scriptural.

Outline (continued)

Justification by Faith

C. *Effective.*
1a. *It produces the fruit of* **peace** *and its concomitants:*
freedom of access, exultation, firmly anchored hope: assurance
of complete salvation.
"Therefore, having been justified by faith, we have peace
with God through our Lord Jesus Christ."
5:1–11

1b. *The certainty and copiousness of salvation confirmed by the parallel*
Adam—Christ
Correspondence and Contrast
"But where sin increased, grace increased all the more."
5:12–21

CHAPTER 5

5 1 Therefore, having been justified by faith, we have peace with God through our Lord Jesus Christ, 2 through whom we have also gained access by faith into this grace in which we stand, and we exult in the hope of the glory of God. 3 And not only this, but we even exult in our sufferings, because we know that suffering brings about perseverance; 4 perseverance, proven character; proven character, hope. 5 And this hope does not disappoint, because God's love has been poured out into our hearts by the Holy Spirit who was given to us.

6 For while we were still powerless, at the appointed time Christ died for the ungodly. 7 Now a man will scarcely die for a righteous person, though for a good person someone might possibly dare to die. 8 But God demonstrates his own love for us in this, that while we were still sinners Christ died for us.

9 Since, then, we have now been justified by his blood, we shall much more be saved through him from (God's) wrath. 10 For if, while we were enemies, we were reconciled to him through the death of his Son, much more, having been reconciled, shall we be saved through his life! 11 And not only this, but we also exult in God through our Lord Jesus Christ, through whom we have now already received our reconciliation.

C. *Effective.*
1a. *It produces the fruit of **peace** and its concomitants:*
freedom of access, exultation, firmly anchored hope: assurance
of complete salvation.
"Therefore, having been justified by faith, we have peace with God
through our Lord Jesus Christ."
5:1-11

Under the general heading *Justification by Faith, Exposition* (1:16-11:36) Paul has shown that this justification is *necessary and real* (1:16—3:31), as well as *scriptural* (chapter 4). In chapters 5-8 he demonstrates that it is also *effective, fruitful.*

It is clear that in Paul's thinking chapters 5, 6, 7, and 8 belong together. The fruits of justification are set forth in all of them. In addition, in its final verse each of these four chapters contains the phrase "through (or *in*) Jesus Christ (or Christ Jesus) our Lord."

The kind of fruit varies from chapter to chapter. Here, in 5:1-11, the attention of the hearer and/or reader is focused first of all on *peace*. In connection with it mention is also made of freedom of access, exultation, and hope, a hope that is firmly anchored and amounts to certainty with respect to salvation.

167

By means of the parallel Adam-Christ (verses 12–21) the *certainty* and especially the *copious character* of salvation receive further elucidation.

1, 2. Therefore, having been justified by faith, we have peace with God through our Lord Jesus Christ, through whom we have also gained access by faith into this grace in which we stand, and we exult in the hope of the glory of God.[140]

The apostle has reached a new phase in the discussion of *justification by faith*. He now simply assumes that he himself and those addressed have received and are enjoying this marvelous gift. It is from this fact, viewed as a startingpoint, that the discussion now moves forward.

The various units composing verses 1 and 2 may be grouped as follows:

a. "Therefore, having been justified by faith..."

The reasons implied in this "Therefore" are found in the first four chapters; especially in 3:21–4:25.

---

140. At the very beginning of this paragraph we encounter a difficulty. Did Paul say, and did Tertius (16:22) write, "*We have* peace," or "*Let us have* peace"? Among translators and commentators there is a sharp division of opinion with respect to this question. Fact is that the underlying Greek text is not uniform. Textual evidence in support of the subjunctive ἔχωμεν is strong. This form is supported by Sinaiticus and Vaticanus (original hand in both cases), and further by Alexandrinus, Ephraemi Rescriptus, Codex Bezae, etc., as well as by many cursives and patristic citations. Several ancient versions, too, as well as more recent translations, show that their authors accept this reading. Some writers express themselves very forcibly, as if the opposite view, favoring the indicative ἔχομεν, is entirely impossible. See, for example, Robertson, *Word Pictures,* Vol. IV, p. 355; and Lenski, *op. cit.,* pp. 333, 334. Among others who, in one sense or another, also favor the subjunctive ("Let us have peace," "Let us continue to have peace," "Let us live in peace," "Let us enjoy peace," or something similar) are Berkeley, Goodspeed, Moffatt, N.E.B.

But the indicative ἔχομεν, "we have," also has considerable support. In fact, the Wyman fragment, to which a very early date (latter part of the third century A.D.) has been ascribed, has the indicative ἔχομεν.

Among translations favoring the indicative are A.V., A.R.V., N.A.S., Beck, R.S.V., N.I.V. At times one possibility is recognized in the text, the other in a footnote or margin.

As to still another attempt to do justice to the original, namely, "Let us enjoy the peace we have," or something similar (see Murray, *op. cit.,* p. 159), I can see no justification for this compromise.

I accept the indicative. In addition to the evidence furnished by the third-century fragment mentioned above, two considerations have led me to adopt this reading:

a. At the time the New Testament was written the Greek letters o and ω were beginning to be pronounced alike and at times were used interchangeably. In this connection note also the variant διώκομεν for διώκωμεν in Rom. 14:19, where the spelling with the two omegas deserves the preference, a reverse application of the same pronunciation and writing peculiarity found in 5:1.

b. The logic of the context here in Rom. 5:1 strongly favors the indicative. Justified people *have* peace with God (Eph. 2:14–18). They do not say, "Let us have peace." The immediately following clause, "through whom we have also gained access by faith into this grace in which we stand" is a statement of *fact,* and, as shown by the word *also,* implies that the immediately preceding words similarly express a *fact.* "We have peace... we have also gained access." Note the series of indicatives which follows: "... we exult... we even exult... we know, etc." Does not all this clearly indicate that in 5:1 the hortatory part of this section—see 6:1 f., 6:15 f., 7:7 f., 8:31 f.—has not yet begun?

b. "...we have peace with God..."

For the meaning of the term *peace* see on 1:7; 2:10. As 5:10, 11 makes clear, in 5:1 the basic meaning of peace is *reconciliation* with God through the death of his Son. This implies the removal of divine wrath from the sinner, and the latter's restoration to divine favor.

The fact that *objective* peace is here in the foreground does not mean, however, that the *subjective* enjoyment of this great blessing is absent from Paul's mind. How could he even think about the cause without reflecting on the effect, namely, the condition of rest and contentment present in the hearts of those who know that the sins of the past have been forgiven, the evils of the present are being overruled for good, and future events cannot bring about separation from God's love? The mention of this "peace which passes all understanding" (Phil. 4:7) makes the transition to the next item very natural:

c. "...through our Lord Jesus Christ, through whom we have also gained access by faith into this grace in which we stand..."

It was Christ's blood, representing his entire vicarious sacrifice, which brought reconciliation, and it was his Spirit which brought to the hearts of all true believers appreciation of that which redemption through blood had accomplished. So it was indeed through the person and work of the Savior, appropriated by faith, that access into this state of grace—that is, the state of justification—had been effected. Moreover, access to this state of grace implies confident access to the Father (Eph. 2:8; 3:12) and to his throne of grace (Heb. 4:16).

It is "our Lord (Owner, Master) Jesus (Savior) Christ (Anointed)" who, having paid his people's debt, introduces them to the Father. It is he who not only "makes intercession" for them (Rom. 8:34) but, even more meaningfully, "ever lives to make intercession" for them (Heb. 7:25). And if even his intercession for them while he was still on earth was filled with comfort (read John 17), can his pleading for them, now that he has returned to heaven, *clothed with the merits of his accomplished redemption,* be less precious and effective?

d. "...and we exult in the hope of the glory of God."

This "glory of God" indicates the marvelous salvation God has in store for those who place their trust in him. See such passages as the following: Rom. 2:7; 8:18, 30; I Cor. 15:43; II Cor. 4:17; Col. 1:27b; 3:4; II Tim. 2:10. For the meaning of the Greek word here rendered "exult" see on 2:17. Undoubtedly what Paul has in mind is, "We do not, like certain selfrighteous people, *brag* about our own accomplishments, but we place all our confidence in God. In him *we greatly rejoice.*"

> On Christ, the solid Rock I stand,
> All other ground is sinking sand.
>
> Refrain of "My Hope Is Built"
> by Edward Mote

169

Actually, however, the apostle does not say, "We exult in the glory of God," but "We exult in *the hope of* the glory of God." In light of Col. 1:27 the meaning is probably, "We rejoice greatly when we reflect on *the solid basis for the expectation* of future bliss." See N.T.C. on Col. 1:27. In principle we have this blessedness here and now; in perfection, at Christ's return.

Paul continues, **3, 4. And not only this, but we even exult in our sufferings, because we know that suffering brings about perseverance; perseverance, proven character; proven character, hope.**

Here "*in our sufferings*" means "*in the midst of and because of*" the tribulations we experience in carrying on the work of the Lord. Cf. Rom. 8:35-39; I Cor. 4:9-13; II Cor. 1:4-10; 11:23-30 (the long list); 12:7-10; Gal. 6:17; II Tim. 3:11, 12 (to the extent in which that passage reflects on earlier events).[141]

But how was it possible for the apostle to exult in sufferings? How can suffering—here probably especially tribulation for the sake of Christ and the gospel—be regarded as a blessing? For a somewhat detailed answer see N.T.C. on Philippians, pp. 90, 91. Be sure also to examine Heb. 12:5-11, and in the Old Testament Ps. 119:67, 71; Jer. 31:18.

To all this add II Cor. 12:7-10. Note especially verse 9, "My grace is sufficient for you, for my power is made perfect in weakness."

In this connection two facts should be borne in mind:

a. An afflicted believer's own *weakness,* by way of contrast, serves to magnify God's *power.*

b. It is exactly when the sufferer recognizes that he is weak but God is strong and ready to help that he will seek help from above. Since this help is sufficient, his faith will be strengthened. Thus *suffering brings about perseverance.*

Although it is true that perseverance (strength *to bear up under* plus the persistent application of this strength) is basically the result of the operation of the Holy Spirit in the hearts and lives of God's children, it implies human action. It is by no means a passive quality. The person who has it *perseveres.* He holds on to what he has (Rev. 2:25), is faithful even to the point of death (Rev. 2:10).[142]

Perseverance produces proven character, that is, character that has sustained *the test* to which it was subjected.[143]

---

141. Sometimes reference is also made to II Tim. 4:14-17. This is permissible if it be borne in mind that when Paul wrote Romans *he* could not have been thinking of suffering that was experienced at a later time.

142. For the word ὑπομονή, by Paul mentioned first in Rom. 2:7, next here in 5:3, 4, see also 8:25; 15:4, 5; II Cor. 1:6; 6:4; 12:12; Col. 1:11; I Thess. 1:3; II Thess. 1:4; 3:5; I Tim. 6:11; II Tim. 3:10; Titus 2:2; Heb. 10:36; 12:1; James 1:3, 4; I Peter 1:6; and see its various occurrences in Revelation, beginning with 1:9.

143. On δοκιμή and related words see W. Grundmann's article in Th.D.N.T., Vol. II, pp. 255-260.

With respect to this "test" see Zech. 13:9, "I will refine them like silver and test them like gold." Just as the refining fire of the goldsmith frees gold and silver from the impurities which in the natural state cling to them (cf. Isa. 1:25; Mal. 3:3), so also the patient endurance or perseverance of God's children purifies them, that is, by the operation of the Holy Spirit brings about "proven" character, a character that has successfully sustained the fiery test.

It is immediately clear that consciousness, on their part, of the fact that they have sustained the test, so that God's approval rests on them, will strengthen their *hope. Proven character brings about hope.* So, in this example of chain reasoning we are back to the *hope* mentioned in verse 2.

5. And this hope does not disappoint, because God's love has been poured out into our hearts by the Holy Spirit who was given to us.

Note the masterful transition from *faith* (verses 1, 2) to *hope* (verses 2, 4, 5), to *love* (verse 5). This is the sequence found also in I Cor. 13:13. (In I Thess. 1:3 the sequence is faith, love, hope.)

There are people without hope (Eph. 2:12; I Thess. 4:13). There are also those who cling to illusory or deceptive hope (Prov. 11:7; Acts 16:19). But those who have been justified by faith and have been reconciled with God cherish the kind of hope that does not disappoint (Ps. 22:5). Their hope is firmly anchored in God's redeeming love. Another way of expressing the same thought is this: their hope is moored to the throne of grace, that is, to that which is "within the veil," where Jesus is seated at God's right hand (Heb. 6:19, 20). He is living forevermore to intercede for his people (Heb. 7:25).

Moreover, God's love is not rationed out drop by drop. On the contrary, by the Holy Spirit it is "poured out" into the hearts of the redeemed; in other words, it is supplied freely, abundantly, copiously, lavishly, as is true with respect to God's gifts in general (Num. 20:8, 11; II Kings 4:1–7; Ps. 91:16; Isa. 1:18; 55:1; Ezek. 39:29; Joel 2:28, 29; Zech. 12:10; Matt. 11:27–30; 14:20; 15:37; Luke 6:38; John 1:16; 3:16; Acts 2:16–18; 10:45; 14:17; 17:25; Rom. 5:20; I Cor. 2:9, 10; II Cor. 4:17; Eph. 1:8; 2:7; James 1:5; Rev. 22:17). "He giveth and giveth and giveth again." See N.T.C. on John, Vol. I, pp. 88, 89 ("grace upon grace").

In fact, the Holy Spirit, who is the Dispenser of God's gifts, is also himself God's gift to the church (John 14:16; 15:7).

Over against the opinion of some it should be emphasized that the expression "the love of God" cannot mean "our love for God." How could such thoroughly inadequate love ever be the basis of hope that does not disappoint? The reference is clearly to God's own love, as verse 8 proves. See also Rom. 8:35; II Cor. 13:13.

Now all this sheds light on the glorious character of justification by faith. This divine deed whereby the sinner who flees to God for refuge is declared righteous is often compared to that which happens in a courtroom. It has accordingly been called a *forensic* action. It is indeed that, but, considered in its most comprehensive sense, it is far more than that. Note contrast:

The earthly judge	God as Judge
a. finding the accused "not guilty" acquits him; or finding him guilty sentences him.	a. finding the accused guilty—as is always the case—blots out his guilt, on the basis of the work accomplished by God's Son, the Guilt Bearer.
b. dismisses him from the courtroom and has no further dealings with him.	b. through his Spirit *pours his love into his heart* and adopts him as his own son or daughter.

But the comparison should be carried one step farther, for even human adoption is not an adequate illustration of divine adoption. In human adoption the parents would like to transmit something of their own character or spirit to that adopted child. Sometimes this succeeds to a degree; sometimes not at all. But when God adopts he also plants his own Spirit into the adoptee's heart, transforming him or her into God's own image (Rom. 8:15).

6–8. For while we were still powerless,[144] at the appointed time Christ died for the ungodly. Now a man will scarcely die for a righteous person, though for a good person someone might possibly dare to die. But God demonstrates his own love for us in this, that while we were still sinners Christ died for us.

In this passage Paul states the reason for saying that God poured his love into the hearts of sinners. He tells us that he was justified in making this assertion because "while we were still powerless," that is, helpless, totally unable to rescue ourselves from the effects of the fall, Christ, motivated by sovereign love and not by any human merit or accomplishment, died for us, the ungodly.

The unique character of this love becomes apparent when we consider the fact that while for a righteous person a man will scarcely die—though, by rare exception, it might after all happen that for such a good person someone would dare to die, God, on the other hand, demonstrates *his own* love in this remarkable way, namely, that while we were still in our helpless and sinful state Christ died for us.

In connection with this explanation note the following:

a. The "ungodly" people of verse 6 are the "sinners" of verse 8, namely, those sinners for whom Christ died, the "beloved of God, saints" of 1:7.

b. The distinction between "a righteous person" and "a good person" should not be pressed, as if the apostle were saying that for a person who is

---

144. Though Grk.N.T. (A-B-M-W) favors εἴ γε . . . ἔτι textual support for ἔτι γὰρ . . . ἔτι is not any weaker. Moreover, the double ἔτι would seem to link more logically with the preceding verse. Is it not possible that the other readings arose out of an attempt to get rid of the double ἔτι? The repetition of ἔτι may have resulted from the apostle's intention to place special stress on the all-surpassing eminence of God's love.

merely "righteous" it would be almost impossible to find someone who would die, but for a "good" person, or benefactor, it might under exceptional conditions be possible to find a substitute who would be willing to offer his life. This is over-interpretation. We should adhere to the one basic point Paul is making, and not obscure the thought by introducing unwarranted distinctions. Room should be left for stylistic variation.[145]

c. What Paul is saying is that God's love, as revealed in Jesus Christ, is both unprecedented and unparalleled. No merit from our side could have moved Christ to die for us, for he died for us "while we were still sinners." Moreover, he died for us "at the appointed time," that is, at the time appointed by *God* (cf. Mark 1:15; Gal. 4:4), not by *us*.

This death was unparalleled with respect to the marvel of the implied condescending and pardoning grace. Christ died for those who were bad, bad, bad! In them there was no goodness that could have attracted this love. In the death of Jesus for sinners God demonstrates "his own" sovereign love. See Isa. 1:18; 53:6; 57:15; Dan. 9:17–19; I John 4:10.

d. Note the word "demonstrates," *present* tense. Although it is true that for Paul, at the time he wrote this letter, as well as for us today, the death of Christ was an event that had occurred in the past, its lesson remains an ever *present* and glorious reality.[146]

e. Note "his own love for us."[147]

f. Though it is true that no less than four times in these three verses Paul uses a preposition (ὑπέρ) which has a very wide range of meaning, stretching all the way from *about* or *concerning* (cf. περί) to *in the place of* (cf. ἀντί), and which frequently means "for," "in behalf of," "for the sake of," "in the interest of," it would seem that here in Rom. 5:6–8 this little word, though not by itself meaning "in the place of" *implies* as much. Does not the context (see verses 9, 10) indicate that *by means of the shedding of his blood* Christ removed from us God's wrath? See also N.T.C. on Galatians, p. 130; on Philippians, pp. 82, 83; and on I and II Timothy and Titus, pp. 375, 376.

9, 10. Since, then, we have now been justified by his blood, we shall much more be saved through him from (God's) wrath. For if, while we were enemies, we were reconciled to him through the death of his Son, much more, having been reconciled, shall we be saved through his life!

---

145. The idea that δικαίου and ἀγαθοῦ (verse 7) are neuter and indicate things or qualities conflicts with the very personal context (see verses 6 and 8).

146. For the verb συνίστημι the following meanings are worthy of consideration:

(1) intr.: to stand by or with (Luke 9:32); to hold together (Col. 1:17); to be composed of, to be formed out of (II Peter 3:5).

(2) tr.: to confirm, bring out clearly, prove, demonstrate (Rom. 3:5; 5:8; II Cor. 7:11; Gal. 2:18).

(3) to commend, in the favorable sense (Rom. 16:1; II Cor. 4:2; 6:4; 12:11); in the unfavorable sense (II Cor. 3:1; 5:12; 10:12). In II Cor. 10:18 the word *commend* is used first in the unfavorable, then in the favorable sense.

147. It is natural to construe εἰς ἡμᾶς (verse 8) with ἀγάπην. See Eph. 1:15 ("love for all the saints"); and cf. Col. 1:4; I Thess. 3:12; II Thess. 1:3.

The relation between verses 9, 10 and the immediately preceding context is as follows:

We will not be disappointed in our hope, for, in Christ, God loves us so deeply that the Savior *died* for us while we were still sinners. If, then, we were justified by that *death*—or that blood—of Christ, much more shall we be saved from any future outpouring of God's wrath.

Now the details:

a. Verses 9 and 10 run parallel. The first concerns our legal standing with God; the second, our personal relationship to him. Each of the two statements is in the form of an *a fortiori* argument: if God did the greater, will he not *even more readily* do the lesser?[148]

b. "justified by his blood."

The demands of God's justice must be satisfied. See Isa. 1:27; 53:5; Rom. 8:4. Here in Rom. 5:9, as in 3:24, the relation between justification and Christ's *death* is indicated: our justification required Christ's *eternal* (not in time but in quality) death (cf. Luke 24:26, 27). In 4:25, on the other hand, the relation described is that between justification and Christ's *resurrection*.

Blood points to *sacrifice, offering*. For more on Christ's death as an offering, a voluntary sacrifice, see such passages as Isa. 53:7, 10, 12; John 10:11, 15; I Peter 2:21–24.

c. "saved through him from God's wrath."

For this divine wrath see on Rom. 1:18. The deliverance from this wrath, by Christ's mediatorial work, and therefore by Christ himself, refers to our not having to endure the outpouring of the divine vengeance on the day of the final judgment. See I Thess. 1:10; 5:9; II Thess. 1:5–10.

d. ". . . if, while we were enemies . . ."

The word *enemies* must be understood in the passive sense: so regarded by God, because as yet we had not been reconciled to him.

e. ". . . we were reconciled to him through the death of his Son."

Believers are those who, by God's grace, have attained a standing of righteousness in relation to God's holy law; in other words, they have been *justified*. God's law no longer condemns them. But not only is this true. What is now added is that God also *loves* them. His heart goes out to them. He has made friends of enemies.

It should be emphasized that reconciliation—as well as justification—is a divine act. It is God, not man, who brings about reconciliation, the change from enmity to friendship.

However, just as it is true that justification requires faith on man's part—God-imparted and God-sustained faith, to be sure, but human faith nevertheless—so also reconciliation requires obedience on man's part. Here too it is true that such obedience is God's gift. Nonetheless, it is man

---

148. For other instances of this kind of reasoning see in Romans the following verses: 5:15, 17; 8:32; 11:12, 24; and elsewhere: Matt. 6:30; 7:11; 10:25b; II Cor. 3:11; Heb. 12:9, 25.

who obeys the exhortation, "Be reconciled with God" (II Cor. 5:10). God's relation to man is not the same as that of a carpenter to the block of wood to which he is applying his skill, nor does it resemble the ventriloquist's relation to his dummy.

Preachers are in danger of becoming onesided, unbalanced. There are those who stress divine initiative and action at the expense of human responsibility and action. There are also those who do the very opposite. Scripture avoids both extremes. The right view is found in such passages as Phil. 2:12, 13; II Thess. 2:13. See also Luke 22:22; Acts 2:23.

f. "... saved through his life"

It is the resurrected, living, and exalted Son of God who, through his Spirit, carries to completion in our hearts and lives the work of salvation.

g. "much more ... much more"

If God justifies and reconciles to himself enemies, he will *certainly* save friends.

11. And not only this, but we also exult in God through our Lord Jesus Christ, through whom we have now already received our reconciliation.

The structure of this sentence reminds one of verse 3 ("And not only this, but ..."). In view of the context the meaning is probably, "Not only shall we be saved (verse 10b), but even now we exult." See 5:2, 3. Rejoicing in God because of blessings both present and future reminds one of the words, "In this y o u greatly rejoice ... with joy inexpressible and full of glory" (I Peter 1:6, 8).[149]

Not all glorying or boasting can be recommended, however. As Rom. 2:17, 23 had indicated, Jews were boasting or bragging about the fact that they, in distinction from all other nations, possessed God's holy law. In the church at Corinth there were people who bragged about Christian leaders (I Cor. 3:21), and about special gifts or attainments (II Cor. 11:18). And in his letter to the Galatians Paul refers to men who bragged about the number of Gentiles they had "converted" (caused to be circumcised, Gal. 6:13). Does that sound up-to-date?

Over against all such sinful leaping for joy Paul informs the Romans, "We exult in God through our Lord Jesus Christ." And indeed, if, in speaking about the blessed results of Christian labor, one constantly keeps his attention focused on Jesus Christ, God's Chosen Servant, who was the very opposite of a boaster (Matt. 12:18–21; Phil. 2:5–8), and derives all his power from *him,* all will be well.

This is the One, says Paul, "through whom we have now already received our reconciliation." For those who, in faith and humility leap for joy when they consider the blessings they have already received there are even more glorious blessings in store in the hereafter.

No wonder that, in connection with blessings received through Jesus

---

149. For the various meanings of the verb καυχάομαι see on 2:17.

175

Christ, Paul is able to say, "Let him who boasts, boast in the Lord" (I Cor. 1:31; II Cor. 10:17).

---

12 Wherefore, just as through one man sin entered the world, and death through sin, and so death spread to all mankind, since all sinned— 13 for before the law (was given) sin was in the world. But sin is not taken into account when there is no law. 14 Nevertheless, death reigned from (the time of) Adam to (that of) Moses, even over those who did not sin by transgressing an express command, as did Adam,[150] who is a type of him who was to come.

15 But the free gift is not like the trespass. For if, by reason of the trespass of the one the many died, much more did God's grace and the gift that came by the grace of this one man, Jesus Christ, overflow to the many! 16 Again, the gift (of God) is not like (the result of) one man's sin. For the judgment followed one sin and brought condemnation, but the free gift followed many trespasses and brought justification. 17 For if by the trespass of the one, death reigned through that one, much more will those who receive the overflowing fulness of grace and of the gift of righteousness reign in life through the One, Jesus Christ.

18 Consequently, as one trespass resulted in condemnation for all men, so also one act of righteousness resulted for all men in justification issuing in life. 19 For just as through the disobedience of the one the many were made sinners, so also through the obedience of the One will the many be made righteous.

20 Moreover, the law came in besides, in order that the trespass might increase. But where sin increased, grace increased all the more, 21 in order that, as sin reigned in death, so also grace might reign through righteousness to bring everlasting life through Jesus Christ our Lord.

1b. *The certainty and copiousness of salvation confirmed by the parallel*
Adam—Christ
Correspondence and Contrast
"But where sin increased, grace increased all the more."
5:12–21

That there is a close connection between 5:1–11 and 5:12–21 is clear. In both of these sections the thought that is stressed is that salvation for time and eternity is through Jesus Christ. According to 5:1–11 it is through him that believers have been justified and have found peace, reconciliation with God. To this idea of certainty of salvation through Christ, Paul now, in verses 12–21, adds the thought that grace more than offsets sin. It not only nullifies the effects of sin, it also bestows everlasting life.

Paul's reasoning may at first seem somewhat difficult to follow. He starts a sentence but does not complete it. He begins by saying, **12. Wherefore, just as through one man sin entered the world, and death through sin, and so death spread to all mankind, since all sinned,** and then, instead of completing this statement, he first of all enlarges on one of its elements, namely the universality of sin. Not until he reaches verse 18 does he return to the sentence he started to write. He reproduces its thought in a modified form: "Consequently, as one trespass resulted in condemnation for all,"

---

150. Literally: "after the similitude of Adam's transgression" (A.V.).

and then he finally, in substance, completes the sentence as follows, ". . . so also one act of righteousness resulted for all men in justification issuing in life."[151]

Now it should be admitted that such a break in grammatical structure is in line with Paul's style and personality. See N.T.C. on Luke, p. 6. Yet it is not today, nor has it been in the past, an unusual style phenomenon.

For example, a minister, making an announcement to his congregation, regarding a picnic, might start out as follows:

"Since tomorrow we'll all be attending the church picnic. . . ."

He wishes to continue with, "We urge all to come early and to bring along food enough for your own family and, if possible, even something extra for poor people who may wish to join us."

But before he can even say this he notices that his words about a church picnic *tomorrow* are being greeted with skepticism. So, instead, he continues as follows:

"I notice that some of y o u are shaking y o u r heads, thinking that there can be no picnic tomorrow. Let me therefore assure y o u that the early morning prediction about a storm heading our way has been canceled. A new forecast was conveyed to me just minutes before I ascended the pulpit. According to it, the storm has changed its course and beautiful weather is expected for tomorrow. So we urge all to come early, etc."

With all this in mind, the various elements of verse 12, and also the verse viewed as a unit, may be interpreted as follows:

a. "*Wherefore*," that is, in view of the fact that, through his sacrificial death and resurrection life, Jesus Christ has brought righteousness, reconciliation (peace), and life, etc. See 5:1–11.

b. "just as through one man sin entered the world . . ."

The one man is obviously Adam. See verse 14. Cf. Gen. 2:16, 17; 3:1–6. In what sense is it to be understood that through Adam's fall sin entered the world? Only in this sense that gradually, over the course of the years and centuries, those who were born inherited their sinful nature from Adam, and therefore committed sins? Without denying that this indeed happened, we must nevertheless affirm that there was a far more direct way in which "through one man sin entered the world." On this same third

---

151. Not all agree with the idea that what we have here is an anacoluthon (change in grammatical construction). See, for example, Lenski, *op. cit.*, pp. 358, 359. He finds the "conclusion" of the sentence in the very first verse, which he translates, "even so the death went through to all men since all did sin." Objections:

a. His translation of καὶ οὕτως (verse 12b) is "even so," as if this marks the beginning of the conclusion of the sentence. But it is clear from three instances in this very chapter (18, 19, 21) that Paul would then have written οὕτως καί, not καὶ οὕτως. See also Rom. 6:4; 11:31; I Cor. 12:12, etc.

b. Logic, too, is entirely on the side of those who believe that not until verse 18b does the apostle write what may be regarded as the apodosis or conclusion of the sentence begun in verse 12. *The one man, Adam,* through whom sin entered the world, points to *the One, namely, Jesus Christ,* through whom many will be made righteous.

missionary journey, not very long before Paul composed Romans, he wrote letters to the Corinthians. In one of them (I Cor. 15:22) he says, "As in Adam all die, so in Christ shall all be made alive." In Rom. 5:15 he writes, "By reason of the trespass of the one the many died." He obviously means that *the entire human race was included in Adam,* so that when Adam sinned, all sinned; when the process of death began to ruin *him,* it immediately affected *the entire race.*

Scripture, in other words, in speaking about these matters, does not view people atomistically, as if each person were comparable to a grain of sand on the seashore. Especially in this present day and age, with its emphasis on the individual, it is well to be reminded of the truth expressed in the words which, in a former generation, were impressed even upon the minds of children:

> In Adam's Fall
> We Sinned All

Moreover, when we bear in mind that this very chapter (5) teaches not only the inclusion of all those who belong to *Adam*—that is, of the entire human race—in Adam's *guilt,* but also the inclusion of all who belong to *Christ,* in the *salvation* purchased by his blood (verses 18, 19; cf. II Cor. 5:19; Eph. 1:3-7; Phil. 3:9; Col. 3:1, 3), and that this salvation is God's free gift to all who by faith are willing to accept it, we shall have nothing to complain about.

c. "and death through sin, and so death spread to all mankind . . ."

Solidarity in guilt implies solidarity in death, here, as in I Cor. 15:22, with emphasis on *physical* death. Sin and death cannot be separated, as is clear from Gen. 2:17; 3:17-19; Rom. 1:32; I Cor. 15:22. In Adam all sinned; in Adam all died. The process of dying, and this not only for Adam but for the race, began the moment Adam sinned.

d. "since all sinned."[152]

In all probability this refers to sins all people have themselves committed after they were born. Such personal sinning has been going on throughout the centuries. Paul is, as it were, saying, "I know that *one* man, and in him all men, sinned, for if this were not true how can we account for all the sinning that has been going on afterward?"

This interpretation gives to the word *sinned* the meaning it has

---

152. ἐφ' ᾧ = ἐπὶ τούτῳ ὅτι, for this reason that; hence *because, since;* here probably to be interpreted inferentially ("I draw this inference because," or simply "since").

Among other meanings that have been assigned to this expression the following are, perhaps, the most important:

(1) the antecedent of ᾧ is θάνατος. This makes no sense.

(2) the antecedent of ᾧ is ἑνὸς ἀνθρώπου. The meaning would be that everybody sinned *in* the first man, Adam. Doctrinally this is sound, and, as was shown, is even taught in verses 12 and 15. Yet, unless there are very good reasons for doing so, we should not link ἐφ' ᾧ with an antecedent that is so far removed from it. Besides, it is not clear that ἐφ' = ἐπί should be interpreted to mean ἐν.

everywhere else in Paul's epistles. Why should "all sinned" mean one thing (actual, personal sins) in Rom. 3:23, but something else in 5:12? Besides if here in 5:12 we explain the words *all sinned* to refer to the fact that all sinned *in Adam,* would we not be making the apostle guilty of needless repetition, for the sinning of all "in Adam" is already implied in this same verse; note "through one man sin entered the world."[153]

To these two reasons for believing that this interpretation of the words "since all sinned" is the right one, a third can be added: it now becomes clear why Paul did not, at this point, complete the sentence beginning with "Wherefore," but went off on a tangent. The statement "since all sinned" could easily arouse disbelief, especially in the minds of those who attached great importance to the proclamation of the law at Sinai. The question might be asked, "If *to sin* means *to transgress the law,* how can Paul say that since the time of Adam *all* sinned? Until the giving of the law at Sinai there was no law, and therefore no transgression of the law, no sin." The apostle considers this possible objection to be of sufficient importance to justify the break in grammatical structure to which reference was made in the beginning of the explanation of verse 12 (see p. 176). Paul answers as follows:

13, 14. ... for before the law (was given) sin was in the world. But sin is not taken into account when there is no law. Nevertheless, death reigned from (the time of) Adam to (that of) Moses, even over those who did not sin by transgressing[154] an express command, as did Adam, who is a type of him who was to come.

In confirmation of the statement "all sinned," including even those people who lived on earth during the period Adam to Moses, Paul reasons as follows:

Sin was indeed in the world even before Sinai's law was given, as is shown by the fact that death, sin's punishment, ruled supreme during the period Adam to Moses. The apostle may have been thinking, among other things, about the deluge, which destroyed almost the entire population of the world. Yes, death reigned even over those who did not sin by transgressing an expressed command, as did Adam. See Gen. 2:16, 17. So, it is clear that even during the period Adam to Moses sin was indeed taken into account. Though *Sinai's* law, with its expressed commands, did not as yet exist, *there was law.* Here the apostle was undoubtedly thinking about what he had written earlier in this very epistle (2:14, 15). And this law, with death as punishment for wanton transgressors, was indeed applied (see Rom.

---

153. It is clear that on this point I am not in agreement with Murray, *op. cit.,* Vol. I, pp. 182–186. His position is that the clause cannot refer to actual, personal sins. As is clear, my own position resembles more closely that of E. F. Harrison, *op. cit.,* p. 62, according to which, while in verse 12, considered as a whole, the emphasis on original sin is primary, with reference to the clause in question personal sins are not entirely excluded.

One more point: I hope no one will conclude that because on this question I do not agree with Murray, I am a Pelagian!

154. For the noun παράβασις (here gen. s. -βάσεως) see footnote 157 on p. 180.

1:18–32). That there was law follows from the fact that there was sin. If there had been no law there would have been no sin.[155]

In introducing Adam, the transgressor of an expressed command, the apostle states, "who is a type of him who was to come."

Having said this, is Paul able now at last, to finish the sentence he began in verse 12? Not yet, for calling Adam a type of the One who was to come,[156] that is, of Christ, could easily lead to misunderstanding. Adam, whose fall resulted in incalculable misery for the human race, and Christ, the world's Savior (John 4:42; I John 4:14; cf. I Tim. 4:10), how is it possible to mention these two in one breath? How can Adam be a type of Christ? This Paul must first explain.

How can there be any *resemblance* between Adam and Christ? Nevertheless, there *is* resemblance; for just as it is true that Adam imparted to those who were his that which belonged to him, so also Christ bestows on his beloved ones that which is his. It is in this respect that Adam foreshadows Christ. For the rest, however, *the parallel is one of contrast,* a fact which the apostle sets forth as follows:

15–17. But the free gift is not like the trespass. For if, by reason of the trespass of the one the many died, much more did God's grace and the gift that came by the grace of this one man, Jesus Christ, overflow to the many! Again, the gift (of God) is not like (the result of) one man's sin. For the judgment followed one sin and brought condemnation, but the free gift followed many trespasses and brought justification. For if by the trespass of the one, death reigned through that one, much more will those who receive the overflowing fulness of grace and of the gift of righteousness reign in life through the One, Jesus Christ.

In these verses Paul shows that the parallel Adam-Christ is mainly one of *contrast,* in the sense that Christ's influence for good *far outweighs* Adam's effectiveness for evil: the free gift is "not like the trespass,"[157] that is, is far more effective than the trespass.

---

155. Paul's reasoning is so lucid, and the harmony between 5:13, 14 and his earlier statements (1:18–21; 2:14, 15), so clear, that I cannot understand the comments of John Knox (*The Interpreter's Bible,* Vol. 9, p. 464).

156. On Christ, "the Coming One" see N.T.C. on John, Vol. I, pp. 77–79; also J. Sickenberger, "Das in die Welt Kommende Licht," *ThG,* 33 (1941), pp. 129–134.

157. The noun παράπτωμα indicates a sin in the sense of a deviation from the path of truth and righteousness, a fault. The word occurs in Rom. 4:25; 6 times in chapter 5: verses 15 (twice), 16, 17, 18, 20; twice in chapter 11 (verses 11, 12); and further, once each in II Cor. 5:19; Gal. 6:1; Eph. 1:7; 2:1, 5; and twice in Col. 2:13. For the rest, in the New Testament it is found only in the clarification of the fifth petition of the Lord's Prayer, Matt. 6:14, 15 (twice), and in a similar passage in Mark (11:25, 26). For more on its meaning, in distinction from other words for sinning, see Trench, *op. cit.,* par. lxvi.

A παράπτωμα may be rather mild, so perhaps in Gal. 6:1, but may also be very serious. Thus, in Rom. 11:11 Israel's rejection of the gospel is called a παράπτωμα.

See also W. Michaelis, Th.D.N.T., Vol. VI, pp. 170–172. The παράβασις of Adam (Rom. 5:14) was a *transgression* of a distinct commandment. That same noun occurs also in Rom. 2:23; 4:15; Gal. 3:19; I Tim. 2:14; Heb. 2:2; 9:15.

By way of introduction to the further interpretation a few matters should be kept in mind:

a. The apostle uses the word *many* in a twofold sense. In its first use ("the many died") it indicates all of Adam's physical descendants. At the close of that same verse ("overflow to the many") it indicates all those who belong to Christ. This reminds one of Isa. 53:11, 12; Matt. 20:28; Mark 10:45.

b. Verse 12 has shown that Adam was responsible for bringing into the world two evils: sin and death. The apostle deals with both of these in turn: with Adam's sin or *trespass* (verses 15, 16), with *death* (verse 17). He conceives of them as being intimately related, and therefore at times mentions both in one breath.

It is understandable that Paul can say that by reason of *Adam's trespass* the many died. These *many* are those designated in 5:12 as "all mankind" (literally *all human beings, everybody*). Cf. I Cor. 15:22. But, in connection with the work of God in Christ, for God's children this evil has been *more than* canceled out. For them God's grace and his gift of salvation changed death into its very opposite. Death became a *gain* (Phil. 1:21)! Moreover, as to *sin*, when grace entered, it more than merely returned man to his former state of innocence. It bestowed on him *righteousness* (verse 17), and *life* (verse 18), that is, *everlasting life* (verse 21). For the glorious content of this term see above, on 2:7.

Again, in Adam's case a single sin was involved, a sin that resulted in condemnation. But Christ, by his work of redemption, made provision for the forgiveness not only of that one sin but also of all those that followed from it. His sacrifice *sufficed* for them all, and in fact *was efficacious* for all the sins committed by those who, by sovereign grace, were to place their trust in him. For them *condemnation was replaced by justification.* See on 1:17; 3:24; 5:1.

Paul now turns more especially to the subject of *death.* This time, after repeating that death resulted from the trespass of the one, Adam, he mentions *the reign* of death, the powerful and destructive sway it exercises over the affairs of human beings. In harmony with his thoughts on the supremacy of grace (the "much more" doctrine), the apostle now points out that in the case of believers the reign of *death* is not merely replaced by the reign of *life* but by a reign so inexpressibly glorious that those who participate in it will themselves be kings and queens. All this is the result of "the overflowing fulness[158] of grace[159] and of a righteousness that is God's gift to them through the One, Jesus Christ," that is, through his person and work.

---

158. Note περισσεία (here acc. s. -v) a περί-compound, probably basically indicating water that rises so high that "all around" it overflows its borders. See also II Cor. 8:2; 10:15; James 1:21.

159. Grace is God's love revealed to the undeserving. For a detailed word study of the word χάρις see N.T.C. on Luke, pp. 181, 182.

When the apostle has thus taken care of the difficulties that had to be cleared up before he was able to complete the thought begun in verse 12, he now, by means of somewhat varying phraseology, in verse 18a gives the gist of the earlier verse—so that essentially verse 18a amounts to verse 12, and then, in verse 18b brings this thought to a conclusion. In somewhat different wording the entire thought is repeated in verse 19.

18, 19. Consequently, as one[160] trespass[161] resulted in condemnation for all men, so also one act of righteousness resulted for all men in justification issuing in life. For just as through the disobedience of the one the many were made sinners, so also through the obedience of the One will the many be made righteous.

As the word "consequently" indicates, not only is Paul now returning to the thought expressed in verse 12; he is summing up the argument of the entire paragraph (verses 12-17). The present passage places over against each other *one* trespass, namely, that of Adam (Gen. 3:6, 9-12, 17), a trespass here called "the disobedience of the one," and *one* act or deed of righteousness, called "the obedience of the One," that One being Jesus Christ. Cf. Phil. 2:8. Since in the preceding context Paul has no less than three times mentioned Christ's death for his people (verses 6, 8, 10; cf. verses 7 and 9), it is certain that also here in verses 18, 19 the reference is to that supreme sacrifice. However, we should not interpret this concept too narrowly: Christ's voluntary death represents his entire sacrificial earthly ministry of which that death was the climax.

We can understand that one trespass resulted *for all men* in condemnation, but what does the apostle mean when he states that also *for all men* one act of righteousness resulted in life-imparting justification? If in the first case "all men" means absolutely everybody, does not logic demand that in the second instance of its use it has the same meaning? The answer is:

a. The apostle has made very clear in previous passages that salvation is for believers, for them alone (1:16, 17; 3:21-25, etc.).

b. He has emphasized this also in this very context: those alone who "receive the overflowing fulness of grace and of the gift of righteousness" will reign in life (verse 17).

c. In a passage which is similar to 5:18, and to which reference has been made earlier, the apostle himself explains what he means by "all" or "all men" who are going to be saved and participate in a glorious resurrection. That passage is:

"For as in Adam all die, so in Christ all will be made alive. But each in his own turn: Christ, the firstfruits; afterward those who are Christ's, at his

---

160. There are those who interpret ἑνός to refer to one *person*, namely, Adam. They translate "one man's misdeed." But in that case would not the apostle have used the article, as he did in verse 17? However, the difference in translation and interpretation is of little importance, since in any case Paul is speaking about the one act or deed of the one person over against the one act or deed of the other.

161. See footnote 157.

coming" (I Cor. 15:22, 23). Here it is clearly stated that the "all" who will be made alive are "those who are Christ's," that is, those who belong to him.

But though this answer proves that when Paul here uses the expression "all" or "all men" in connection with those who are or will be saved, this "all" or "all men" must not be interpreted in the absolute or unlimited sense, this still leaves another question unanswered, namely, "Why does Paul use this strong expresssion?" To answer this question one should carefully read the entire epistle. It will then become clear that, among other things, Paul is combating the ever-present tendency of Jews to regard themselves as being better than Gentiles. Over against that erroneous and sinful attitude he emphasizes that, as far as salvation is concerned, *there is no difference between Jew and Gentile.* The reader should carefully study the following passages in order to see this for himself: 1:16, 17; 2:7–11; 3:21–24, 28–30; 4:3–16; 9:8, 22–33; 10:11–13; 11:32; 15:7–12; 16:25–27. As concerns salvation, says Paul, "There is no distinction. God shows no partiality." *All men* are sinners before God. *All* are in need of salvation. For *all* the way to be saved is the same.

In a day and age in which, even in certain evangelical circles, the unbiblical distinction between Jew and Gentile is still being maintained and even emphasized, it is necessary that what God's Word says about this, particularly also in Paul's epistle to the Romans, be pointed out.

Note that in verse 18 we are told that the one trespass resulted in *condemnation* for all, but that the one act of righteousness resulted in justification issuing in *life.* This shows that justification not merely overturns the verdict of "guilty," setting aside the sentence of doom, but also opens the gate to life. For this concept of *life*—cf. verses 17 and 21—see above on 2:7.

Also in verse 19 Paul does not say, "Just as through the disobedience of the one the many were made sinners, so also through the obedience of the One will the many be made innocent or sinless," but ". . . will the many be made *righteous.*" To be sure, this basically means "*to be declared* righteous." However, when God declares someone righteous, does that action ever stand all by itself? See the explanation of 5:5.

20. Moreover, the law came in besides. In order that the trespass might increase. But where sin increased, grace increased all the more . . .[162]

Paul has been speaking about Adam and Christ, type and antitype. Adam transgressed a specific command, as has been shown. That happened long before the pomulgation of Sinai's law. Now even before this there was law, as the explanation of 5:13 has shown. But at Sinai the Mosaic law came in besides "in order that the trespass might increase." That was the divine intention in giving this law.

This cannot mean that God became the cause of sin's increase. It means that it was God's will and purpose that in light of his demand of perfect love

---

162. Note ὑπερεπερίσσευσεν, 3rd per. s. aor. indicat. of ὑπερπερισσεύω, to superoverflow, abound all the more, increase all the more. The use of this verb points to Paul as the author. See N.T.C. on I and II Timothy and Titus, p. 75.

(cf. Matt. 22:37–40; Mark 12:29–31; Luke 10:27) man's consciousness of sin might become sharpened. A vague awareness of the fact that all is not well with him will not drive man to the Savior. So the law acts as a magnifying glass. Such an instrument does not actually increase the number of dirty spots on a garment. It makes them stand out more clearly and reveals *many more* of them than one can see with the naked eye. Similarly the law causes sin to stand out in all its heinousness and ramifications. In connection with this see also Rom. 3:20; 7:7, 13; Gal. 3:19.

Moreover, this increase in the knowledge of sin is very necessary. It will prevent a person from imagining that in his own power he can overcome sin. The more he, in light of God's law, begins to see his own sinfulness and weakness, the more also will he thank God for the manifestation of his grace in Jesus Christ. Result: where sin increases, grace increases also. Not as if these two forces, sin and grace, were equal. On the contrary, grace not only pardons; as verse 21 shows, it does far more: it brings "everlasting life through Jesus Christ our Lord!" Truly, where sin increases, grace increases *all the more!*

Among the many hymns that bring out this glorious truth there are these two: (a) Charles Wesley's "O For a Thousand Tongues," containing the line, "He breaks the power of canceled sin"; what an incisive combination of two mighty products of God's grace, namely, justification and sanctification; and (b) Julia H. Johnston's "Grace Greater Than Our Sin."

Since the apostle often makes mention of God's law, as also in the present passage, it may be useful to give a brief summary of the functions of this law, as indicated in Paul's epistles and elsewhere in Scripture. Undoubtedly one or more references can easily be added to each of the following:

a. to serve as a source of man's knowledge of sin and to sharpen his consciousness of sin (Rom. 3:20, etc., as has been indicated).

b. to fix the sinner's attention on the far greater power of God's grace in Jesus Christ, and to lead him to the Savior (Rom. 5:20; Gal. 3:24).

c. to serve as a guide for the expression of the believer's life of gratitude to God's honor (Ps. 19:7, 8; 119:105; Rom. 7:22).

d. to function as a bridle, restraining sin (I Tim. 1:9–11).

There is, of course, a very close connection between these various functions.

The purpose of "grace abounding" is expressed in the following unforgettable words: **21. ... in order that, as sin reigned in death, so also grace might reign through righteousness to bring everlasting life through Jesus Christ our Lord.**

What a strikingly beautiful close to this chapter! There are seven concepts, as follows:

a. *sin*

This is, first of all, *the sin of Adam,* here viewed as our representative, whose guilt, due to the solidarity of the human race, is imputed to us all, a fact to which all the *personal sins* of human beings bear witness. See especially verses 12, 15, 17.

b. *reigning*
When Adam fell, it seemed as if sin was about to triumph completely. However, according to God's plan, grace intervened, and in the case of all God's children, triumphed over sin. See verses 12–14 for the reign of sin; verses 15–19 for the triumph of grace.

c. *death*
Sin brought condemnation and death; first of all physical death, but also spiritual and eternal death. Sin and Death are personified: Sin being, as it were, the Sovereign; Death, his Viceroy. For the moment (think of Adam's fall) it seemed as if Sin would be able to claim the victory. See verses 12, 14. But note the next item:

d. *grace*
Grace meets sin head-on and defeats it. See verses 15–17, 20.

e. *righteousness.*
Not a righteousness provided by man but a righteousness imputed by God. It was through this righteousness that grace triumphed over sin. See 1:17; 3:21–24; 5:17.

f. *everlasting life*
When the sinner is clothed with the righteousness provided by God, he is on his way to everlasting life (verse 18), the glorious life in the new heaven and earth; a life which, in principle, is given to him even here and now. For this concept see on 2:7.

g. *Jesus Christ our Lord*
See verses 14, 15, 17, 19. It must not be forgotten that apart from the immeasurably marvelous sacrifice of "Jesus Christ our Lord," a sacrifice revealing a love which, in all its dimensions, surpasses all human understanding, grace would never have been able to conquer sin and death.

The unifying thought, as it were tying together all these seven concepts, is this, "Where sin increased, grace increased all the more," namely, the grace embodied in the supreme sacrifice of our Lord Jesus Christ, and revealed to us through him.

In reviewing this entire chapter what amazes us is Paul's limitless assurance, his radiant optimism. Here is a man who until rather recently has been subjected to all the afflictions mentioned in II Cor. 11. He is about to set out for Jerusalem, Rome, Spain. That was the plan. Whether he will ever be able to carry out that plan or any part of it he does not know, though he does know that perils confront him (Rom. 1:10, 13; 15:30–32). Also he knows that he has a story to tell. His heart is filled with a flame, the flame of love: God's love for him, his love for God. Others *must* hear the story! We feel like saying, "What a man, this apostle Paul!" But if we said that we would be doing what he does not want us to do. So, in the very spirit of Paul we sing, or/and turn to a musical instrument and play AMAZING GRACE!

ROMANS 5 IN POETRY

In order to put some spirit into the study of a chapter, more than one approach may help to make it part and parcel of a person's life. In addition to

a. *Careful exegesis,* which is basic to every sound approach,

b. *Practical lessons* may be added or interspersed,

c. The chapter, as a whole or in part, may be *acted out,* if it lends itself to this approach, or it may provide the topic for

d. A *debate.* Again, it may be illustrated with

e. *Pictures.* An even different approach would be the composition of

f. A *poem,* which *in an interpretive manner,* reproduces the contents of the chapter, verse by verse. I suggest the following for chapter 5:

Verses

1, 2
Therefore, since we've been justified
By *faith,* we've peace with God, and side
With him in Christ, through whom we gain
Access by faith, and we'll remain
In this same grace in which we stand.
With joy we *hope* to reach the land
Where God his glory will display
When darkness changes into day.

3–5
And sufferings, too, we greet with cheer
Because they make us persevere
And mold our character, and then
This character builds hope again,
A hope that disappoints us ne'er;
For through his Spirit, which is e'er
Our portion, did our gracious God
His *love* so richly spread abroad.

6–8
The time was ripe and we were weak
And even godless, when to seek
The lost, yes many, far and wide,
Christ Jesus came and for us died.
It rarely happens that a man
For someone who is righteous can
Be found to die. But though it's rare
Yet for a good man one might dare
To give his life. But God above
Showed his incomparable love
In that, while we were sinners still
Christ died for us. Such was his will.

186

9, 10   Hence, since we've now been justified,
And Jesus for our sins has died,
We know that we shall surely be
From future wrath forever free.
For if the greater deed God wrought
For those who then were in his thought
Still enemies, then will not he
The lesser do, and readily?
Will he who woos the enemy
Not bless a friend, whoe'er he be?
If through Christ's *death* we friends became
Of God, then all the more the name
Of Christ, the *Living* One, will save
And make us conquerors o'er the grave.

11   'Tis good these happenings to record
But better still is to the Lord
To render joyful songs of praise
For having made us friends through grace.

12   'Twas through one man that sin began
And also death through this one man.
In this one man did all men sin,
And through this sin did death begin.

13, 14   Now, long before God's law was given,
Sin filled the world and cried to heaven.
From Adam until Moses when
The writing of God's law began,
Death ruled supreme on every hand,
Though breaking God's express command,
As Adam did, that wicked deed
None could soon afterward repeat.
Now Adam, type of Christ was he,
Since each one mankind's Head would be.

15–17   Far stronger than man's sin is grace,
Far more effective in its place:
One fearful sin laid many low,
But grace made many overflow.
God's judgment condemnation brought;
Christ's blood justification bought.
One sin, and judgment came to stay,
But grace wiped all our sins away!
Now if the trespass of the one
Brought *death* to each and everyone,
Then *how much more* will they be blessed
On whom God's grace and righteousness
Has been bestowed! Through him, the Door,
They'll enter *life* forevermore.

18, 19   Just as a single sin plunged all
Of Adam's seed into the fall,
The condemnation, so one deed

187

Of righteousness fulfilled the need
Of the whole world. All who believe
Justification will receive.
As one man's disobedience caused
The many to be counted lost,
So, too, One Man's submissiveness
Will bring to many righteousness.
20, 21   The law came in besides. 'Twas so
The sense of sin might keener grow.
But when that consciousness increased,
Grace topped it, and this never ceased.
Result was this: O'er death reigned Sin,
But all the while Grace ruled within
The heart, as Conqueror in the strife,
Bringing, through Christ, eternal life!

Practical Lessons Derived from Romans 5

Verse 1

"Therefore, having been justified by faith, we have peace with God through our Lord Jesus Christ." This peace is:
a. the gift of God's love
b. the smile of God reflected in the heart of the believer
c. the heart's calm after Calvary's storm
d. the firm conviction that he who spared not his own Son will surely also, along with him, freely give us all things (Rom. 8:32)
e. the sentinel who mounts guard over the hearts and thoughts of God's children (Phil. 4:7).

Verses 1, 2

"Therefore, having been justified by faith, we have peace with God . . . access by faith . . . and we exult in the hope of the glory of God."

This implies that with respect to *believers: past* sins are forgiven, *present* access to the throne of grace is assured, and *future* glory is guaranteed. These are *priceless* values, obtained "without money and *without price* (cost)," as far as *they* are concerned.

For a cap and bells our lives we pay,
Bubbles we buy with a whole soul's tasking,
'Tis heaven alone that is given away,
'Tis only God may be had for the asking.

Lowell,
"Vision of Sir Launfal"

Verse 3

"We even exult in our sufferings." This cheerful statement becomes even more meaningful when we bear in mind that it was uttered by one who had already experienced a lengthy series of most bitter agonies for the sake of Christ. See I Cor.

188

4:11–13; 15:30–32a; II Cor. 11:24–32. Cf. Rom. 8:35. Such exultation in suffering is possible because of the truths expressed in Rom. 8:18, 28.

Verses 6–8

"... Christ died for the ungodly. Now a man will scarcely die for a righteous person ... But God demonstrates his own love for us in this, that while we were still sinners Christ died for us." Paul is amazed by his reflection on *such* love. It is as if he were saying, "Just think of it: God loves the unlovable! Why, even for a righteous person one would hardly want to die. But Christ died for the *un*righteous, the *un*godly!"

Verses 9, 15, 17, 20

"... much more ... much more ... much more ... all the more. ..." First of all study the picture of gloom drawn by Paul in Rom. 3:10–18. Does it prove that Paul was a pessimist? Now read 5:9, 15, 17, 20. Note how the very author who has given us the darkest picture of mankind, buried in sin, is, nevertheless, the most optimistic. It is as if he were saying, "Mankind's sinfulness is indeed frightening; but God's grace is far more powerful and wonderful than mankind's sinfulness is terrible.

The apostle was an optimist, and this was not because of what sinners are by nature but because of what God's grace is able to make of them. Should not every preacher—in fact, every true believer—imitate Paul in this respect?

Summary of Chapter 5

This chapter consists of two main sections: A and B. In A we are shown that the basic result of justification by faith is *peace* with God. Other blessings are associated with it. In B the main emphasis is on the generous character of the salvation provided by God.

A. (verses 1–11)

Paul has reached a new phase in the discussion of justification by faith. He begins to fix the attention of the hearers-readers on the favorable effects resulting from justification. First of all he mentions "peace with God through our Lord Jesus Christ." As 5:10 makes clear, this peace is basically "reconciliation with God through the death of his Son." Associated with this peace are such other blessings as access to God by *faith* and a joyful looking forward to the marvelous salvation God has in store for those who have placed their trust in him. Even present suffering for the sake of Christ and his kingdom cannot dim the luster of the glory that is to come and in principle is being experienced even now. In fact, such suffering is really a link in the chain of blessings: suffering, perseverance, proven character, firmly anchored *hope*. This hope is kept alive and strengthened by God's *love* "poured out into our hearts by the Holy Spirit" (verses 1–5).

Christ's timely death for the "ungodly" is a demonstration of God's love. By way of rare exception someone might be willing to sacrifice his life for a worthy person, but God demonstrated *his own* love by means of Christ's death for us while we were still *sinners* (verses 6–8).

Not only has our legal standing been changed from "guilty" to "righteous," i.e., from condemnation to justification, but our personal relation to God has also changed. Through Christ's death former enemies were changed into friends. It was God himself who brought about this *reconciliation*. Now if God has reconciled to himself *enemies*, he will certainly save *friends*. Believers need not become alarmed about any future divine wrath. With a view to all these blessings, present and future, even now "we exult in God through our Lord Jesus Christ" (verses 9–11).

B. *(verses 12–21)*

In a sentence beginning with verse 12, recaptured (as to essence) in verse 18a, and completed in verse 18b, the apostle states, "Just as through one man sin entered the world, and death through sin, and so death spread to all mankind, since all sinned; that is, as one trespass resulted in condemnation for all men, so also one act of righteousness resulted for all men in justification issuing in life."

"In Adam's fall we sinned all." Adam, by means of his transgression of an express divine command, involved all mankind in his sin and guilt. The entire human race is viewed as being already "in" Adam. Moreover, being involved in *sin* implies being involved in *death*. The reality of sin did not depend on the establishment of the Mosaic law. Even during the period Adam-Moses sin was taken into account, for God's law had been written in man's heart (cf. 2:14, 15). This explains why it is right to state that death reigned from Adam to Moses, even over those who did not sin by transgressing an express command, as did Adam (see Gen. 2:16, 17; 3:1–6). In this connection Paul calls Adam "a type of him who was to come," Adam being considered the head of fallen humanity; Christ, the head of redeemed humanity (verses 12–14).

In the remainder of the chapter the apostle shows that as all men were included in Adam, so also "all men," that is, all those who belong to Christ, whether they be Jews or Gentiles by race, are included in Christ. The parallel Adam-Christ is, however, mainly one of contrast, as now becomes very clear. Paul says, "For if, by reason of the trespass of the one the many died, much more did God's grace, and the gift that comes by the grace of this one man, Jesus Christ, overflow to the many." Adam's transgression brought condemnation. Christ's voluntary sacrifice of himself for his people brought justification issuing in life. Moreover, grace is ever far more effective than sin. "Where sin increased, grace increased all the more." Did grace merely offset sin and death, so that mankind returned to the state of innocence, that of Adam before the fall? On the contrary, grace changed death into a gain, substituted righteousness for sin, and everlasting life for death. All this "through Jesus Christ our Lord" (verses 15–21).

Outline (continued)

Justification by Faith

2a. *It produces the fruit of* **holiness.**
"We who died to sin, how can we any longer live in it?"
6:1–14

2b. *Who Is Y o u r Master? Sin or God?*
"But now, freed from sin and made servants of God, the benefit y o u reap leads to holiness, and the outcome is life everlasting. For the wages of sin is death, but the free gift of God is life everlasting in Christ Jesus our Lord."
6:15–23

CHAPTER 6

6   1 What shall we say then? Shall we go on sinning in order that grace may increase? 2 By no means! We who died to sin, how can we any longer live in it? 3 Or don't y o u know that all of us who were baptized into Christ Jesus were baptized into his death? 4 So then we were buried with him through baptism into death, in order that, just as Christ was raised from the dead through the glory of the Father, so we too might walk in newness of life.

5 For if we have become united with him in a death like his, we shall certainly also be united with him in a resurrection like his.[163]   6 For we know that our old self was crucified with him, so that the body of sin might be destroyed, that we should no longer be slaves of sin— 7 because the one who died is freed from sin.   8 Now if we have died with Christ, we believe we shall also live with him;   9 since we know that Christ, having been raised from the dead, no longer dies. Death no longer exercises lordship over him.   10 For the death he died, he died to sin once for all; but the life he lives, he lives to God.   11 So then y o u yourselves should also consider yourselves dead to sin but alive to God in Christ Jesus.

12 Accordingly, do not let sin reign in y o u r mortal bodies, to make y o u obey their passions.   13 And do not offer the parts of y o u r bodies to sin, as weapons of wickedness, but instead offer yourselves to God, as those who were brought from death to life, and offer y o u r bodily parts to him, as weapons of righteousness.   14 For sin shall no longer be lord over y o u, because y o u are not under law but under grace.

2a. *It produces the fruit of* **holiness.**
"We who died to sin, how can we any longer live in it?"
6:1–14

Chapter 6 introduces a new subject. Not that there is a sudden break. But there is a difference, a transition from one fruit of justification, namely, peace with God, to another, *holiness.*

Sin, mentioned frequently in chapter 5, is mentioned even more often in chapter 6. And in this connection the emphasis turns away from the believer's legal *status* to his spiritual-moral *condition.* The new line of thought centers about such concepts as holiness, living a new life, dying to sin, living to God.

Nevertheless, chapters 5 and 6 are closely related, just as closely as are justification and sanctification. The God who declares the sinner just at the same time, and in close connection with it, pours the sanctifying Spirit into his heart, producing holiness.

---

163. Literally: in the likeness of his death . . . (in the likeness) of his resurrection.

A very practical consideration contributed to the writing of chapter 6. With warm enthusiasm Paul had been proclaiming the riches of God's grace. To many people, especially Jews and those former pagans who had embraced Judaism, his emphasis on divine grace as the one and only source of salvation was something new. It seemed to some of them as if this preacher-missionary-writer was minimizing the value of works. They reasoned, "If works mean so little, why perform them at all? Besides, if grace is everything, why not sin flagrantly, lustfully, in order to give grace the opportunity to operate (to use a colloquial expression, 'to do its thing')?" Chapter 6 is Paul's pointed and animated reply to this fantastic distortion of his divinely inspired presentation of the doctrine of sin and grace.

As was true with respect to chapters 4 and 5, so also chapter 6 readily divides itself into two parts. In verses 1–14 Paul points out that it would be impossible for believers to continue to *live in* sin: those who have died to sin are alive to God in Christ Jesus. In verses 15–23 the apostle, by implication, asks the question, "Who is y o u r Master? Is it Sin or God"

1. What shall we say then? Shall we go on sinning in order that grace may increase?

It will be recalled that already in 3:8 Paul briefly combats this distortion of the doctrine of grace. Here, in chapter 6, his refutation is more detailed.

It should be emphasized that we are not dealing here with a merely theoretical objection to the doctrine of grace. In fact, though some of those who asked this question may indeed have intended it to be interpreted as an objection to Paul's teaching, others were not *objecting* at all. They were rather pleased with Paul's doctrine (as they interpreted it), and were saying, "Let us go on sinning that grace may increase."

When *Peter* states that some of Paul's teachings were being distorted (II Peter 3:16), he may well have been thinking of this particular attempt to twist the meaning of the words used by his "dear brother," the apostle to the Gentiles. We know, at least, that what made *Jude* change his mind about the contents of a letter he had planned to write was the fact that "certain individuals had turned (the doctrine of) the grace of God into a license for immoral living" (Jude 4).

Every age has produced its quota of such deceivers. An example that occurs to the mind immediately is that of the Russian monk Rasputin. For a while he was a very influential favorite of Emperor Nicholas II. His doctrine seems to have been, "The more a person sins, the more grace he will receive. So sin with gusto."

Another and far more recent example from life: this man was an ardent evangelist. One of his favorite passages was taken from this very chapter of Romans, "Y o u are not under law but under grace" (verse 14). He spoke persuasively, drawing large crowds. However, his immediate neighbor never went to hear him. When someone asked that neighbor, "How is it that we never see you in his audience?" the answer was, "Because I happen to know that his back yard is filled with stolen property."

Paul's response to the question, "Shall we go on sinning that grace may increase?" is, **2. By no means! We who died to sin, how can we any longer live in it?**

The very suggestion that the end justifies the means, that grace may be produced by living in sin, is so thoroughly obnoxious to Paul that he answers it by making use of one of his characteristic, blunt rejection formulas, "By no means." See on 3:4, p. 111. For a Christian, continuing to *live in* sin is not only impermissible, it is impossible! To be sure, Paul knows that even a believer commits acts of sin until the day of his release from this earthly existence. See 7:14f. But in the apostle's theology this circumstance does not provide a valid reason for easy living. See on 6:15. Moreover, the notion that a child of God should voluntarily give sin an opportunity to operate, that he should actually encourage it, produces a revulsion in Paul's heart. He is disgusted with the very suggestion!

He reminds his readers that something decisive has taken place in his and in their lives. By the grace of God *they had died to sin;* that is, they had renounced allegiance to their sinful selves and to all the allurements and enticements of this sinful world. Cf. Col. 3:3, "For y o u died, and y o u r life is hid with Christ in God." All this had happened when they had been converted, had professed their faith, and had been baptized. So Paul continues:

3, 4. Or don't y o u know that all of us who were baptized into Christ Jesus were baptized into his death? So then we were buried with him through baptism into death, in order that, just as Christ was raised from the dead through the glory of the Father, so we too might walk in newness of life.

When Paul asks, "Don't y o u know that," etc.? he reminds us of the style of the Master. See especially John 3:10; 19:10; but compare also such passages as Matt. 12:3, 5; 19:4; 21:16, 42; 22:31; Luke 6:3, to mention only a few. The question shows too that although Paul had not himself established the church of Rome, he takes for granted that the practical significance of Christ's death for Christian living is a matter on which his readers could be expected to be thoroughly informed. See also on 7:1, p. 214.

The apostle assumes that those (including himself) who had listened to the public preaching of the gospel or who by any other means had been converted, had publicly confessed their faith and had been baptized. See Matt. 28:19; Acts 2:37, 38; 9:18. He now asks, "Don't y o u know that all of us who were baptized into Christ Jesus were baptized into his death?"

To be baptized "into Christ Jesus" implies to be brought into personal relation to the Savior. For similar expressions see Matt. 28:19 ("baptizing into the name of the Father and of the Son and of the Holy Spirit"); I Cor. 1:13 ("baptized into the name of Paul"); and 10:2 ("baptized into Moses"). Paul, accordingly, points out that baptizing people into Christ Jesus implies baptizing them into—i.e., in connection with the sacrament of baptism bringing them into personal relationship with—Christ's *death,* so that this

195

death becomes meaningful to them, teaching them that by it the *guilt* of their sins had been removed, and that they had received power to fight and overcome sin's *pollution*.

On the surface the statement, "*We were buried with him* through baptism *into his death*" may seem confusing, as if burial precedes death. Besides, how is it possible for any person to be *buried* into another's *death?* However, when we bear in mind the context, the difficulty disappears, as will be shown:

The dangerous doctrine of the antinomians was leading people astray. This sinister heresy caused Paul to emphasize the necessity of making a complete break with the sinful life of the past. So he says, "We were buried into his—i.e., Christ's—death; that is, by the power of the Holy Spirit we were made to delve down deeply into the meaning of that marvelous death. In fact, so deeply did we, with heart and mind, bury ourselves into it that we began to see its glorious meaning for our lives. Therefore we reject and loathe the terrible wicked slogan, *Let us continue to live in sin in order that grace may increase.*"

Through baptism and reflection on its meaning these early converts, including Paul, had been brought into a very close personal relationship with their Lord and Savior and with the significance of his self-sacrificing death. The meaning of that death had been blessed to their hearts by the Holy Spirit.

Paul now also reminds his readers that Christ was raised from the dead through "the glory"—here meaning "the majestic power" (see on 1:23, p. 74) —of the Father.

Since the Savior's beloved ones are "in him," the relationship being very close and inseparable (John 10:28; 17:24; Rom. 8:35-39; Col. 3:3), it follows that included in the purpose of his resurrection was this goal: "that we might walk in newness of life,"[164] a life dedicated no longer to sin but to the glory of God Triune.

It must be understood that *Christ's resurrection* from the dead must be given its full meaning, as that great event which led to his saving activity in heaven (Rom. 8:34; Eph. 1:20-23; Heb. 7:25).

For *walking*, in the sense of *conducting oneself* or *living*, see such passages as the following: Gen. 17:1; Exod. 16:4; Ps. 56:13; 101:2; 119:1; Rom. 4:12; 8:1, 4; 13:13; 14:5; I Cor. 3:3; II Cor. 5:17; Gal. 5:16, 25; Eph. 2:10; 3:6-19.[165]

---

164. Note ὥσπερ ... οὕτως, "just as ... so we too." The parallel is, however, one of analogy, not identity. Christ's resurrection was physical; the believer's resurrection here indicated is spiritual. It concerns newness of life. Also, the first is the cause of the second.

Note also καινότητι. In this case the full, distinctive meaning must probably be assigned to the implied καινός (not here νέος). The emphasis is on quality, not time.

165. There are those who believe that the expression "buried with him through baptism into death ... raised from the dead" shows that baptism should be by immersion. For a defense of this view see A. T. Robertson's article on *Baptism*, I.S.B.E., Vol. I, pp. 385-388. For the

5. For if we have become united with him in a death like his, we shall certainly also be united with him in a resurrection like his.

The close connection between verses 3, 4 and verse 5 is indicated by the word *For*. Hence, the idea of some, that verse 5 refers to the future bodily resurrection of believers must be rejected.[166] Verse 5 repeats the thought of the immediately preceding context, namely, the believers' union with Christ in (a) his death and (b) his resurrection, considered respectively as the source of (a) their death to sin, and (b) their resurrection to newness of life. But it also *adds* something to the thought expressed in the preceding. Note the word *certainly*.

The meaning of verse 5, then, is as follows, "For if we have become united with Christ in a death like his, so that his death brought about our death to constantly living in sin, we shall *certainly* also be united with him in a resurrection like his; that is, then surely his (bodily) resurrection (understood in its most comprehensive sense, as explained above, see p. 196) will bring about our spiritual resurrection; that is, our walking in newness of life." The *emphasis* Paul placed on this fact must be ascribed to the ominous character of the antinomian heresy.[167]

6, 7. For we know that our old self was crucified with him, so that the body of sin might be destroyed, that we should no longer be slaves of sin—because the one who died is freed from sin.

The wicked error of the antinomians, a subject which has been on the apostle's mind from the very beginning of this chapter, and to which he also alluded previously, helps to explain verses 6, 7. What Paul is saying is this: instead of wallowing in sin in order that grace may increase, we should bear in mind that such a course would defeat the very purpose of our lives as believers.

Paul says, "For we know," thereby appealing to that which could be assumed as common knowledge among believers, including the addressees. The important fact with which they were assumed to be familiar was this: that our old self (lit. "our old man") was crucified with Christ. This old self is the person we once were, our human nature considered apart from grace. When the apostle now states that this old self was crucified with Jesus, it is clear that he again proceeds upon the basis of the believers'

---

opposite view see John Murray, *Christian Baptism,* Philadelphia, 1952, especially pp. 29–33. On two points there should be agreement:

a. Immersion is indeed an entirely proper and beautifully symbolic mode of adult baptism.

b. In Rom. 6:3, 4 (cf. Col. 2:11, 12) Paul's chief topic is not *the proper mode of baptism* but the effects of, and responsibility arising from, union with Christ.

166. Use of the future ἐσόμεθα cannot save that erroneous theory. Is it not natural to think of *newness* of life in future terms?

167. Whether σύμφυτοι is derived from συμφύω, which seems probable, and therefore basically means *grown together;* or from συμφυτεύω, hence *planted together,* makes little difference. What matters most is not the derivation of the word but its resultant connotation *in the present context,* namely, *united.* On this see also Cranfield, *op. cit.,* Vol. I, pp. 306, 307.

solidarity with Christ. Just as he considers all human beings as present "in Adam" (cf. 5:12, 17, 19), so he views all believers as being present "in Christ." Therefore, in a sense, when Christ died on the cross, his true followers all died there with him. We are reminded of Gal. 2:20:

"I have been crucified with Christ, and it is no longer I who lives, but Christ who lives in me; and that (life) which I now live in flesh I live in faith, (the faith) which is in the Son of God, who loved me and gave himself up for me." The passing of time has nothing to do with this. Since Scripture regards us as already present in Adam, it can also view us as ever being present in Christ.

The purpose and result of our solidarity with Christ in his crucifixion is "so that the body of sin might be destroyed," that is, that, by means of Christ's crucifixion and our crucifixion with him, this destruction might take place. With the expression "body of sin" (verse 6, cf. "old self," also verse 6; and see also "I," 7:14) is probably meant the person in his entirety, viewed as controlled by sin. It is clear that the reference is to human nature apart from regenerating grace.

Does Paul mean then that in this present life the believer can reach such a degree of holiness that he does not commit any sin? He does not, neither is that fallacy taught anywhere else in Scripture. See Matt. 6:12; Rom. 7:14–25; James 3:2; I John 1:8. But there is a vast difference between (a) committing a sin and (b) constantly living and delighting in sin. By the power and grace of the Holy Spirit a person can indeed reach the point where he no longer desires to be a slave of sin. For a synonym of this phrase "slaves of sin" see II Peter 2:19, and note the words of Jesus as reported in John 8:34. See N.T.C. on John, Vol. II, p. 53.

To all this, Paul now adds, ". . . because the one who died is freed from sin." In light of the context the meaning would certainly seem to be, "The person who has by God's sovereign grace been regenerated and converted, so that he no longer delights in sin but rather fights it, can be assured of the fact that God has, on the basis of Christ's atonement, forgiven his sins, with the result that he is now truly *free, justified* in God's sight."

However, several commentators, in their attempt to explain this passage, immediately point to the familiar rabbinical (and more general) rule according to which "death pays all debts."[168] An appeal is frequently made to the fact that Paul had been trained under the famous Jewish teacher Gamaliel (Acts 22:3) and was therefore well acquainted with rabbinical lore.

Now it need not be denied that in a formal manner the apostle may indeed here and there reveal the results of this earlier training. According to Scripture by no means all of the teaching of the rabbis was bad. Study the following passages: Matt. 23:1–3; Mark 12:28–34; Acts 5:34–39; 23:8, 9.

Does this mean, then, that when Paul states his views with respect to such

---

168. See S.BK., Vol. III, p. 232.

subjects as speaking in tongues, qualifications for ecclesiastical office, the position of women in the church, etc., we are justified immediately to dismiss that with which we do not happen to agree, basing our negative attitude on the supposition that Paul's views on such matters were influenced by the rabbis?

But such reasoning is hardly fair. A thorough examination of Paul's epistles reveals that on ever so many important subjects he had by the study of Scripture and the illumination of the Holy Spirit arrived at a position that differed substantially from that of the rabbis. See, for example, the following passages: Rom. 2:9, 14, 15, 17–29; 3:9, 20, 21 f.; chapters 4, 5; 7:6; 9:8, 11; 10:3; 11:7; 14:17; 15:9–12; I Cor. 1:22–24; 3:16; 7:19; 9:20; 10:25; 15:1 f.; II Cor. 3:14; 5:20, 21; 11:22 f.; Gal. 1:6 f.; 2:19–21; 3:1 f., 24; 5:2–4; 6:12–16; Eph. 2:8–10, 11–22; Phil. 3:2 f.; Col. 1:24 f.; 2:11, 12, 16 f.; 3:11; I Tim. 1:3, 4; 4:1 f.; 6:13–16; II Tim. 2:8; Titus 3:4 f.; and see especially I Thess. 2:14–16. Besides, one cannot very well endorse a low estimate of Paul's statements and still cling to the view that Paul wrote by inspiration.

In the present instance the appeal to the quoted rabbinical rule helps little if at all in the interpretation. The apostle refers, of course, to "death to sin," the determination (followed by action) by God's grace and power no longer to live in sin. When a person no longer feels at home in sin he can be sure of the fact that he has been freed from the guilt of sin and that even the power which sin has been wielding over him is on the way out.[169]

It was the desire to live this kind of *new* life that caused people to come forward in order to be baptized. The *water* of baptism, by whatever method it is applied (immersion, pouring, sprinkling) symbolizes and seals the *cleansing* power of the Spirit (Ezek. 36:25; I Cor. 6:11; Eph. 5:26; Heb. 10:22). It symbolizes and seals what *God* has done and is doing, and, as a result, incorporation of the person into the fellowship of God and of his church. On the error of underestimating the significance of the sacraments see above, p. 152; of overestimation, p. 151.

8, 9. Now if we have died with Christ, we believe we shall also live with him; since we know that Christ, having been raised from the dead, no longer dies.

If we died with Christ, that is, if, as a result of Christ's death for us, we died to sin, we shall also *spiritually live* in fellowship with him, and this not only in the hereafter but here and now. Cf. verses 3 and 5. We know that such living *with him* is possible because he, having died, was raised from the dead, never again to die. Death could not hold him (Acts 2:24), for it no longer exercises lordship over him.

Those who, during Christ's pre-Golgotha ministry, were by him raised from the dead, died again. According to heathen mythology certain deities

---

169. I agree, accordingly, with Cranfield, *op. cit.*, Vol. I, p. 311, that the rabbinic rule to which reference was made is singularly inappropriate as a confirmation of Rom. 6:7.

are constantly dying and rising. Not so Jesus. **Death no longer exercises lordship over him.** Having been raised, he lives forevermore (Rev. 1:18), and we with him. This *we believe:* we know it to be true!

10. For the death he died, he died to sin once for all; but the life he lives, he lives to God.

Without the assurance that Christ's death was a once-for-all death, believers would lack the comfort they need for this and the future life. Does not that comfort consist exactly in this that they can sing, "We serve a *living* Savior"?

It was through his death that Jesus conquered death. Having done so, he was able to say to John, an exile on the island of Patmos, "I was dead, but behold I am alive forevermore, and I hold the keys of Death and Hades" (Rev. 1:18).

Very significant is the expression, "He died to sin once for all." This surely implies that the blood and body of Christ cannot be offered again. Jesus offered himself "once for all for the sins of his people" (Heb. 7:27; see also 9:12; 10:10). No second offering is necessary or even possible! For this once-for-all self-sacrifice see also I Peter 3:18.

Christ's life on earth before his death was conditioned by sin, sin not his own but his people's. Read Isa. 53. Cf. Matt. 20:28; Mark 10:45.

Therefore, once sin had been atoned for, he now lives to God. Of course, his entire life, also that which preceded Golgotha, had been devoted to the glory of his heavenly Father. In his high-priestly prayer he was able to say, "I glorified thee on earth, having accomplished the work thou gavest me to do" (John 17:4). But once this task had been accomplished, he was able to live to God *in an unhampered manner,* that is, without having to carry the burden of his people's sin. It is in that sense that Paul is able to say, "But the life he lives, he lives to God."

In a sense—but only *in a sense*—one might say, "After his resurrection and ascension Jesus returned to the life with the Father as it had been before he left the riches and the glories of heaven to suffer for man's sin." See John 17:5. Scripture does not tell us much about that life. Here are a few glimpses:

> When he established the heavens, I was there;
> > When he set a circle upon the face of the deep.
> When he made firm the skies above,
> > When the fountains of the deep became strong,
> When he gave to the deep its boundary,
> > That the waters should not transgress his commandment,
> When he marked out the foundations of the earth;
> > Then I was at his side as a master craftsman;
> And I was daily his delight,
> > Rejoicing always in his presence.

Prov. 8:27–30

If this refers to Christ, "the Wisdom of God," the reference is indirect.

In the beginning was the Word, and the Word was face to face with
God, and the Word was God. He himself was in the beginning face to
face with God.   *John 1:1, 2*

. . . he was rich. . . .   *II Cor. 8:9*

We should bear in mind, however, that there was at least this difference
between *then* (the time before Christ's humiliation) and *now* (after his
humiliation): he returned to heaven carrying with him the merits of his
fully accomplished redemption! Thus it is that the life he now lives he lives
to God; not, however, forgetting his people; note Heb. 7:25.

**11. So then y o u yourselves should also consider yourselves dead to
sin but alive to God in Christ Jesus.**

At this point doctrine makes way for exhortation. What has been established, namely, that believers are in principle dead to sin and alive to Christ,
must become the abiding conviction of their hearts and minds, the take-off
point for all their thinking, planning, rejoicing, speaking, doing. They
must constantly bear in mind that they are no longer what they used to be.
Their lives from day to day must show that they have not forgotten this.
They are "in Christ": chosen "in him" (Eph. 1:4), redeemed "in him" (Eph.
1:7), living "in him" (Gal. 2:20; Phil. 1:21; II Tim. 3:12). Christ's righteousness has been imputed to them. *His Spirit has been poured out into their
hearts.* In a sense it is true that when Christ died, they died with him. When
he arose, they arose with him. Cf. II Cor. 5:14, 15.

What may well be the best commentary on Rom. 6:11 is Paul's own: "If
then y o u were raised with Christ, seek the things that are above, where
Christ is, seated at the right hand of God. On the things that are above set
y o u r minds, not on the things that are upon the earth. For y o u died, and
y o u r life is hid with Christ in God. When Christ (who is) our life is
manifested, y o u also will be manifested with him in glory" (Col. 3:1–4).

**12. Accordingly, do not let sin reign in y o u r mortal bodies, to make
y o u obey their passions.**

Although it is true that believers are no longer constantly living in sin,
this does not mean that sin has ceased to be an opposing force in their lives,
a reality to be taken into account. See 7:14f.

No one acquainted with the story of David would deny that he was
indeed a child of God; in fact, "a man after God's own heart" (I Sam.
13:14). In ever so many ways Scripture proves this point.[170] Nevertheless,
at times he allowed sin to bear sway in his mortal body.[171] And David is no
exception. It is therefore understandable that the apostle urges believers
constantly to be on guard against this great danger of surrendering to evil

---

170. See my *Survey of the Bible,* pp. 98–101.
171. On this point, therefore, I share Cranfield's criticism of Murray's exegesis; see Murray,
op. cit., pp. 226, 227; Cranfield, *op. cit.,* pp. 316, 317.

passions, passions which, as also in the case of David, are often associated with the body and its functions, a body which, in man's fallen state, tends toward sin and death (hence "*mortal*" bodies).[172]

Paul becomes more specific as he continues, **13. And do not offer the parts of y o u r bodies to sin, as weapons of wickedness, but instead offer yourselves to God, as those who were brought from death to life, and offer y o u r bodily parts to him; as weapons of righteousness.**

What Paul means by "parts of y o u r bodies" is made clear by such passages as 12:4, 5, where these "parts" are clearly bodily *members;* while I Cor. 12:12–24 makes specific mention of such bodily "parts" as foot, hand, ear, eye, nose (actually "sense of smell"), head, unpresentable parts and presentable parts of a person's body. The expression "parts of y o u r bodies" therefore refers to bodily limbs, members, and organs.

What Paul is saying then is this, "Do not continue to put y o u r bodily parts at the disposal of sin, as weapons of wickedness. Stop doing this; and instead, right now, completely and decisively, put yourselves at *God's* disposal. Offer yourselves to him!"[173]

Note also the distinction between (a) "Do not offer *the parts of y o u r bodies*" and (b) "offer *yourselves,*" instead of (b) "offer those bodily parts." Devotion and consecration to God must be personal, wholehearted. Was it not God who, in his great love and kindness, had brought these people out of death into life?

Instead of *weapons* many prefer *instruments* or *tools* or *implements.*[174] Though something can be said in favor of that rendering, the arguments in support of the rendering *weapons* are probably stronger:

a. In *all* the other instances of the use of this word in the New Testament ὅπλα means *weapons, armor.* See John 18:3; Rom. 13:12; II Cor. 6:7; 10:4.

---

172. Almost all translations have retained the word *body* (or pl. *bodies* because the apostle is addressing more than one person; so also R.S.V., Phillips, Williams, Beck, etc.) here in verse 12. Calvin (*op. cit.,* p. 230) thinks the reference is to *man's degenerate state;* Cranfield translates *mortal selves* (*op. cit.,* pp. 296, 316, 317). Hodge (*op. cit.,* p. 319) would retain "body" as the organ in which sin manifests itself; so would Lange (*op. cit.,* p. 209).

The choice is difficult, perhaps due to the almost infinitely close relationship between soul and body. In Rom. 12:1; Phil. 1:20 the word σῶμα seems to refer to the entire personality. But, as Murray reminds us (*op. cit.,* p. 227) it is possible that "body" here in 6:12 is viewed in contrast with "spirit," as it is in Rom. 8:10, 11, and if that be true the rendering *body* (or *bodies*) also here in 6:12 would be correct. To this I would add that the rendering "bodies" also harmonizes better with "parts of bodies" in verse 13.

173. By means of this explanation I have tried to bring out the distinction between the continuative present imperative παριστάνετε and the aorist imperative παραστήσατε, forms, respectively, of παριστάνω (late form) and παρίστημι (original form of the same verb).

174. Nearly all modern, and even many of the older *translators* favor "instruments" or a close synonym as the equivalent of the original ὅπλα. *Commentators* (both English and other), on the other hand, prefer a more distinctly military term; for example, *weapons.* So Barth, Brunner, Denney, Lange, Lekkerkerker, Lightfoot, Meyer, Ridderbos, Sanday and Headlam, Schlatter, Van Leeuwen and Jacobs, Wilson. Among English *translations* in support of *weapons* are: Phillips, Montgomvery (*The New Testament in Modern English*). In support of *weapons* are also the following translations: Dutch (both old and new), German, Swedish, Frisian.

b. Here in Rom. 6:13 the context also points in that direction. Sin (personified) is pictured here as the dictator who demands military service, exacts soldierly obedience, and provides soldier's rations. See verses 12, 14, and 23.[175]

c. The description of a believer's life under the symbolism of a soldier is typically Pauline. See such passages as the following: I Cor. 9:7; II Cor. 6:7; Eph. 6:10–20; I Thess. 5:8; II Tim. 2:3; etc.

The whole includes the parts. When individuals offer themselves to God, their "bodily parts" constitute a portion of this offering. Result: weapons of righteousness replace weapons of wickedness. This *righteousness* indicates uprightness of conduct, the very opposite of wickedness. Cf. Eph. 6:13.

The reason Paul gives for this exhortation is: **14. For sin shall no longer be lord over y o u, because y o u are not under law but under grace.**

Law is able to do many things: it commands, demands, rebukes, condemns, restrains, even points away from itself to Another. There is, however, one thing law can never do. *It cannot save.* "By law-works will no flesh be justified" (Gal. 2:16). Does this mean then that the exhortations directed to believers in verses 12 and 13 are useless? Does it mean that everyone has to perish in his sins? The answer is found in Rom. 8:3, and it is an encouraging answer indeed, in complete accord with the passage we are now considering. Note how despair is replaced by hope, darkness by light: "For what the law was powerless to do . . . God did by sending his own Son . . . in order that the righteous requirements of the law might be fulfilled in us . . ." That sending of the Son is the very essence of God's grace. And this grace not only pardons but also cleanses. *Grace dethrones sin. It destroys sin's lordship and enables the believer to offer himself, and whatever pertains to him, in loving service to God!* The child of God is able to do this because he is *not under law but under grace,* since in his infinitely condescending love and mercy Christ has redeemed him from the curse of the law, having become a curse for him (Gal. 3:10–14). Truly, "there is now no condemnation for those who are in Christ Jesus" (8:1). The context (note "sin shall no longer be lord over y o u") may well imply an even closer connection with the thought of 7:1–6. See on that passage, and note especially "in order that we might bear fruit for God . . . so that we serve in newness of (the) Spirit." Cf. 8:5, 6.

---

15 What then? Shall we sin because we are not under law but under grace? By no means! 16 Don't y o u know that when y o u offer yourselves to someone to obey him as slaves, y o u are slaves of the one y o u obey; whether of sin, leading to death, or of obedience, leading to righteousness? 17 But thanks be to God: y o u were slaves of sin, but y o u wholeheartedly obeyed the pattern of teaching to which y o u were delivered; 18 and having been set free from sin, y o u have entered the service of righteousness.

19 I am speaking in human terms because of the weakness of y o u r flesh. For just as

---

175. Whether the word "wages" in verse 23 has this military connotation is not entirely certain. See on that verse.

formerly y o u enlisted y o u r bodily parts in the service of impurity and lawlessness for the promotion of lawlessness, so now enlist them in the service of righteousness for the promotion of holiness. 20 For when y o u were slaves of sin, y o u were free from the control of righteousness. 21 What benefit did y o u then obtain? Things of which y o u are now ashamed, for their outcome is death! 22 But now, freed from sin and made servants of God, the benefit y o u reap leads to holiness, and the outcome is life everlasting. 23 For the wages of sin is death, but the free gift of God is life everlasting in Christ Jesus our Lord.

2b. *Who Is Y o u r Master? Sin or God?*

"But now, freed from sin and made servants of God, the benefit y o u reap leads to holiness, and the outcome is life everlasting. For the wages of sin is death, but the free gift of God is life everlasting in Christ Jesus our Lord."
6:15–23

15a. What then? Shall we sin because we are not under law but under grace?

In verse 14 Paul had assured believers that they are not under law. (For explanation of this statement see on 7:1; pp. 214, 215.) Does that mean then that they are at liberty to sin? When the law, erroneously viewed as means of salvation, ceases to exist, does this imply that the law as standard of perfection, that is, as the expression of God's will for our lives, also ceases to exist and/or to operate, so that, as a result it is permissible to commit a sin here and a sin there?[176]

Not for a moment is Paul willing to grant even this concession to the antinomians. His answer is: **15b, 16. By no means! Don't y o u know that when y o u offer yourselves to someone to obey him as slaves, y o u are slaves of the one y o u obey; whether of sin, leading to death, or of obedience, leading to righteousness?**

At this point the curt and decisive "By no means" of verse 2 returns. Sin has a tendency to enslave the sinner. The first time he lies, he may be horrified; the second time, only somewhat shaken; the third time lying seems far more natural and easy. At last the sin of telling untruths has him in its grasp. For other sins the story is similar. At last this person is living in sin, has become enslaved by it. See N.T.C. on John 8:34 (Vol. II, p. 53). The result of this process, when continued to the end, is death. Cf. verse 23, and see also 5:12; 8:13. Paul does not specify whether he means physical, spiritual, or everlasting death. Is it reasonable to leave out any of these?

The opposite of sin is obedience, namely, to God. This leads to righteousness, both of state and condition. Cf. I Sam. 15:22; Rom. 4:3; James 2:20–24.

What the apostle is saying, then, is this: no man is free, in the sense of being absolutely independent, "his own boss." He has a Master. That Master is either Sin or God.

17, 18. But thanks be to God: y o u were slaves of sin, but y o u

---

176. Note difference between ἐπιμένωμεν, 1st per. pl. pres. (continuative) subj. of ἐπιμένω in verse 1; and ἁμαρτήσωμεν, aor. subj. of ἁμαρτάνω here in verse 15.

wholeheartedly obeyed the pattern of teaching to which y o u were delivered; and having been set free from sin, y o u have entered the service of righteousness.[177]

Note the following:

a. "Thanks be to *God!*" Paul does not praise the Roman church for having turned to God; he *thanks God* for having brought them where they are today. See also 7:25; and cf. I Cor. 15:57; II Cor. 2:14; 8:16; 9:15; I Peter 2:9. Nevertheless, he also generously acknowledges that these people "wholeheartedly," that is, not merely formally but with zeal, had obeyed "the pattern of teaching," that is, the gospel or sound doctrine, as it was being proclaimed everywhere in the Christian community, both now and later (I Tim. 1:10; II Tim. 1:13; 4:3; Titus 1:9; 2:1).[178]

b. "(the pattern) to which y o u were delivered."

There are those who consider "But y o u . . . delivered" to be a *gloss* (unauthentic insertion), and that Paul simply dictated the words, "Y o u were slaves of sin, but y o u have been set free." But anyone who has devoted years to the study of Paul's epistles knows that if this reasoning were correct, one would have to find hundreds of glosses in these writings. The apostle's sentence structure is often rather involved.

Paul does not say, ". . . the pattern of teaching *which y o u accepted*," but (ascribing all the honor to *God*) "to which y o u were delivered."[179]

c. "and having been set free from sin, y o u have entered the service of righteousness."

---

177. Though many interpreters admit that the term δοῦλος and its verbal cognates (see verses 16–22) can be rendered *servant* and *to render service*, as well as *slave* and *to be enslaved*, there is no unanimity with respect to the translation of these words in the verses indicated. Some throughout prefer *servant* and *render service*.

It is true that something can be said in favor of *slave*. In a sense even deeper than that which pertains to ordinary slaves and their earthly masters, believers have been bought with a price and are therefore owned by their Master (I Cor. 3:23; 7:22), on whom they are completely dependent, and to whom they owe undivided allegiance. They are totally committed to him. If by thus defining the concept *doulos* its meaning were exhausted, and if our word *slave* conveyed nothing of a sinister nature, the translation *slave* throughout, for *doulos*, might be unobjectionable. But as Paul uses the term, a *doulos*, in the spiritual sense, is one who ministers to the Lord with gladness of heart, in newness of spirit, and in the enjoyment of perfect *freedom*, as verse 18 shows (cf. verse 22; 7:6), receiving from God a glorious reward (verses 22, 23). Love and good will toward God and man fill the heart of this *doulos*. See Gal. 5:13; Eph. 6:7.

However, with the English word *slave* we immediately associate the ideas of involuntary service, forced subjection, and (frequently) harsh treatment. It is probably for this reason that, in addition to those who here in Rom. 6:16–22 throughout prefer *servant*, etc. (A.V., A.R.V., Phillips, Berkeley) and those who consistently use *slave*, etc. (Goodspeed, R.S.V., N.A.S., N.I.V.), there are also those who, while not altogether avoiding *slave*, etc., render verse 18b, ". . . y o u have entered the service of righteousness," and verse 22 "and having entered the service of God" (thus, for example, Dutch Nieuwe Vertaling, ". . . zijt gij in dienst gekomen van de gerechtigheid . . . en in den dienst van God gekomen."). In the main, I have followed that same course. See also N.T.C. on Philippians, p. 110, footnote 92.

178. The word used in the original for "pattern" is τύπος (here acc. s. -v): visible impression, mark, image, pattern; cf. *type*.

179. The verb παραδίδωμι, of which παρεδόθητε is a form (2nd per. pl. aor. indic. pass.), has a wide range of meanings, for which see N.T.C. on Luke 22:4 (p. 967). In the present case it

For the believer freedom never means laziness. It always means opportunity for rendering service. Notice that slaves to sin enjoy (?) a liberty not
worthy of the name (see verse 20). On the contrary, those who have entered
the service of righteousness enjoy true liberty, namely, freedom from sin;
not, however, in the sense that they never commit any sin, but in the sense
that Sin is no longer their Master!

Having stated that those who had accepted the gospel had exchanged
their state of *slavery to sin* to that of *service of righteousness,* Paul continues:
**19. I am speaking in human terms because of the weakness of y o u r
flesh, that is, y o u r human nature.**[180]

When Paul in verses 17, 18 spoke of those who had at one time been
slaves of sin but had subsequently become servants of righteousness, he
was, of course, using an illustration; namely, that of someone who had been
transferred from one master to another. So now, in verse 19, he explains
that the reason for the use of this illustration was their weakness to grasp
these great spiritual truths.

The people whom Paul addresses had made remarkable progress, intellectual, moral, spiritual. For this see above, p. 25. But although this progress was encouraging, they were still far from having reached the goal of
maturity. That is why Paul used this illustration, taken from familiar
human relationships. Cf. Gal. 3:15. It frequently happened that a person
enslaved to one master was transferred to another, whose slave or servant
he would then become. What Paul desires, therefore, is that these Romans,
having formerly been enslaved to their master Sin, will, with a commitment
that is no less total, serve their new Master, namely, Righteousness, sin's
opposite. Undoubtedly, reflecting on this apt illustration, would help them
to do so.

Verse 19 continues as follows: **For just as formerly y o u enlisted y o u r
bodily parts in the service of impurity and lawlessness for the promotion
of lawlessness, so now enlist them in the service of righteousness for the
promotion of holiness.**

The thought of verse 13 reappears here in a slightly different form. Note
the condition "Just as formerly . . . ," followed by the conclusion, "so
now . . ." But this parallel includes an antithesis: former impurity and lawlessness are contrasted with *the exhortation* that those who had formerly
practiced these vices should now enlist their "bodily parts" (as in verse 13)
in the service of righteousness, for the promotion of holiness.[181]

---

probably has nothing to do with the authoritative passing down of tradition from one generation (or one witness) to the next, but simply means that the members of the Roman church had
by God been transferred from one master to another. So also Cranfield, *op. cit.,* Vol. I, p. 324.
For the opposite view see Ridderbos, *op. cit.,* pp. 139, 140.

180. For the various meanings of the word σάρξ see footnote 187, on p. 217.

181. Though some regard ἁγιασμός (here acc. s. -v) to mean *sanctification,* which is probably
the meaning in such passages as I Thess. 4:3, 4, 7; II Thess. 2:13; I Tim. 2:15, here in Rom.
6:19 the *qualities* or *conditions* of impurity and lawlessness are contrasted with those of righteousness and holiness. If the first pair does not indicate processes neither does the second.

Note the emphasis here, and in this entire chapter, on *holiness,* the attitude and manner of life that is opposed to sin and dedicated to the service of God. Moreover, as before, in verse 13, so also here, even the bodily parts participate in this active promotion of holiness.

The reason for the exhortation of verse 19b, showing why this command is so necessary and urgent, is given in verses **20, 21. For when y o u were slaves of sin, y o u were free from the control of righteousness. What benefit did y o u then obtain? Things of which y o u are now ashamed, for their outcome is death!**[182]

The meaning is clearly this: To be slaves of sin means to be enemies of righteousness; to be enemies of sin means to be friends of righteousness. To be devoted to both sin and righteousness at the same time is impossible. Compare the words of Jesus, "No one can serve two masters; for either he will hate the one and love the other, or he will be devoted to one and look down on the other" (Matt. 6:24).

As to the "fruit" or "benefit" those people formerly obtained from their slavery to sin, Paul says it consisted of things of which y o u are now ashamed. He was probably thinking of such things as evil thoughts leading to evil words, issuing in evil deeds, resulting in evil habits. Cf. 1:24f. In light of the gospel and of the worship of the one true God, who reveals himself in Jesus Christ, they are now ashamed of their former walk of life. No wonder, for the outcome or final result of such a course of behavior is death. Cf. Gal. 5:22; Eph. 5:9.

What a contrast between the past and the present! From the contemplation of the disgraceful conduct of the past Paul now, with joy and gratitude, turns to the description of the present: **22. But now, freed from sin and made servants of God, the benefit y o u reap leads to holiness, and the outcome is life everlasting.**

What a contrast!

Formerly bondage	Now freedom
Formerly slaves of sin	Now servants of God

---

182. The proper punctuation of this verse is uncertain. If the first nine words (τίνα . . . . . . ἐπαισχύνεσθε) must be construed as one continued question, which could be rendered, "What fruit (or benefit) did y o u then obtain from the things of which y o u are now ashamed?" the closing five words, "for their outcome is death," do not follow naturally. By omitting γάρ from the translation the entire passage may become somewhat easier to read and understand. However, this too is no solution. Verse 21 seems to parallel verse 22, in the following manner:

Verse 21

What *benefit?* Things of which y o u are now ashamed . . . their *outcome* death.

Verse 22

The *benefit* leads to holiness . . . . . . the *outcome* life everlasting.

The best punctuation would therefore seem to be the one which does justice to this parallel construction, and which at the same time results in an intelligible interpretation of the entire verse. It is for these reasons that I have adopted the punctuation that appears in my translation. On the parallel between verses 21 and 22 see also Ridderbos, *op. cit.,* p. 142; and on the resulting translation see Cranfield, *op. cit.,* pp. 321, 327, 328.

Formerly vice	Now holiness
Formerly shame	Now peace of mind
Formerly death	Now life, even life everlasting.

The chapter ends with the unforgettably glorious sentence: **23. For the wages of sin is death, but the free gift of God is life everlasting in Christ Jesus our Lord.**

With this climactic conclusion compare similarly triumphant endings of chapters 8, 9, 12, 13, and 16. Note also how the contrasts of verse 22 are here continued. Here, in verse 23, the contrast is that between:

| wages | and | free gift |
| death | and | life everlasting |

The phrase "wages of sin" means wages paid by sin. Similarly "free gift of God" means free gift bestowed by God.

Death in all its forms, physical, spiritual, everlasting, is what the sinner has earned by his sin. As to life everlasting, it is a gift, entirely free. O yes, it has been earned; not, however, *by* the sinner, but by Christ Jesus *for* the sinner.

Whether the word *wages,* as used here in 6:23, is a military term has been debated. It should be frankly admitted that at times the word is used in a non-military context. It is not surprising, therefore, that in view of the master-slave context (verse 16f.) it has been argued that here in verse 23 the apostle views sin as a slave-master, not as a general who provides soldier's rations.

This argument may, however, not be as strong as it may sound. Consider also these other facts:

a. As is generally admitted, the word used in the original[183] indicates ration, pay; especially soldier's pay. That is the more usual meaning of the word.

b. Even in the New Testament in two of its three other occurrences ("*Soldiers* too were asking," Luke 3:14; "What *soldier* ever serves at his own expense?" I Cor. 9:7) the military sense is clear. And even in the remaining passage where this word is used (II Cor. 11:8) Paul, who throughout his epistles frequently employs figures drawn from the life of the soldier, may very well be using "a bold military metaphor." (See P. E. Hughes, *The Second Epistle to the Corinthians (New International Commentary)*, Grand Rapids, 1962, p. 385).

It would seem, therefore, that all in all the opinion that the word *wages* has here a military sense, so that Sin is viewed as the General who pays out these wages, has a slight edge.

---

183. ὀψώνιον (here nom. pl. -α), from ὄψον, cooked food, plus ὠνέομαι, to buy.

"But the free gift of God is life everlasting." What a marvelous climax! What a comforting truth! The sinner who has fled to God in Christ for refuge receives the most for the least: life everlasting for nothing!

Life everlasting; that is, fellowship with God in and through Christ Jesus (John 17:3); the light of the knowledge of the glory of God in the face of Christ Jesus (II Cor. 4:6); the love of God poured out into one's heart by the Holy Spirit; the peace of God that transcends all understanding (Phil. 4:7), all this and far more forever and ever! All this is experienced "in intimate union" with Christ Jesus. Beautifully Paul closes the chapter with the language of faith-appropriation: *our* Lord!

Practical Lessons Derived from Romans 6

Verse 1

"What shall we say then? Shall we go on sinning in order that grace may increase?"

We are saved not by works but by grace. That was Paul's doctrine. His opponents reacted as follows, "Since we are saved by grace, a grace that specializes in forgiving sin, let us sin all the more, in order that grace may abound." This misrepresentation was by no means innocent. It was an intentional, wicked distortion, a heartless mockery. Cf. Luke 23:36, 37. The distorters were guilty of lifting a few lines out of the totality of Paul's doctrine and basely twisting them. Unbiased study of the apostle's teaching shows that according to his inspired presentation justification by faith immediately implies living a life of gratitude, and therefore of holiness, to the glory of God Triune. In fact Paul places no less emphasis on consecrated living than on grace. See Rom. 1:21; 2:7, 10; 5:3–5; 6:12–14, 16, 19, 22; ch. 12; 13:10–14; I Cor. 13; Gal. 5:22–24; Eph. 2:8–10.

The later history of the church furnishes many other examples of willful distortion of a preacher's words. See Acts 17:1–7. How often has not Calvin's doctrine been misrepresented as if it were totally devoid of the milk of human kindness? Congregations should be warned against this evil.

Verse 4

"So then we were buried with him through baptism into death, in order that, just as Christ was raised from the dead through the glory of the Father, so we too might walk in newness of life."

Easter Sunday had arrived. As usual on that day, the church was crowded. But not a word was said about Christ's physical resurrection. Of course, in a "liberal" church what else could one expect? But even in conservative preaching, where the resurrection of the Savior is clearly proclaimed and is even presented as the basis for the hope and certainty of the believers' resurrection, is it always made clear to the congregation that a further and equally important purpose of our Lord's glorious triumph over death was "so we might walk in newness of life"?

Verse 12

"Accordingly, do not let sin reign in y o u r mortal bodies, to make y o u obey their passions." This passage shows that true theology is a matter not merely of doctrine but also of life. It does not confine itself to the revelation of that which God has done for us, though that is basic. It also stresses what we, by his grace and power, should do in return. It not only *teaches* but also *pleads* lovingly and earnestly.

Verse 17

"But thanks be to God: y o u were slaves of sin, but y o u . . . have entered the service of righteousness." Note how in chapter 6 doctrinal *exposition* (verses 1–10), *exhortation* (verses 11–16 for the most part), and *encouragement* (verse 17) follow each other: an example for all of us.

Verse 23

"For the wages of sin is death, but the free gift of God is life everlasting in Christ Jesus our Lord."

The choice is between these two: death and life. Though, to be sure, Scripture recognizes degrees of punishment and of glory, there is no neutral territory between death and life. Moreover, for rational beings there is no opportunity to avoid making a choice. And the contrast between the two destinies is immeasurable. Therefore this passage is so very important. The right choice should be made. It should, moreover, by the grace of God, be renewed every day.

Summary of Chapter 6

Justification, the basic blessing for every sinner who places his trust in Christ, implies union with the Savior, a union with him not only in his death but also in his resurrection. "For if we have become united with him in a death like his, we shall certainly also be united with him in a resurrection like this." Now being partakers of Christ's resurrection implies *holiness,* for it was the risen and exalted Christ who poured out upon the church his Holy Spirit, the Spirit of sanctification.

This means, of course, that those people who tried to use the doctrine of justification by faith as an excuse for leading a sinful life were dangerous heretics. Their slogan, "Let us go on sinning in order that grace may increase," was an inexcusable and horrible distortion of the doctrine proclaimed by Paul. Therefore he exhorts the members of the Roman church as follows, "Do not allow sin to reign in y o u r mortal bodies . . . but offer yourselves to God, as those who were brought from death to life, and offer y o u r bodily parts to him, as weapons of righteousness. For sin shall no longer be lord over y o u, because y o u are no longer under law but under grace" (verses 1–14).

The sinister character of the antinomian heresy fills the soul of the apostle with such horror that for the moment he does not stop to give a further explanation of the statement, "Y o u are no longer under sin but under grace." He will, however, return to that subject a little later. See 7:1 f.; 8:1 f. For the present he continues to combat the soul-destroying heresy to which reference was made. He now points out that not only the sinful *life* should be avoided but so should even yielding to individual sins, for they have a tendency to make slaves out of those who fail to combat them. If allowed to gain the mastery over a person, they will lead him on to death. Paul is happy to be able to state, however, that those whom he addresses have abandoned their slavery to sin. They have exchanged death for life everlasting. He closes this chapter by saying, "For the wages of sin is death, but the free gift of God is life everlasting in Christ Jesus our Lord" (verses 15–23).

Outline (continued)

Justification by Faith

3a. *It produces the fruit of* **liberty:**
freedom from the law.
"We have been released from the law."
7:1–6

3b. *The sinner's relation to God's Law, in the light of Paul's*
own experience and that of others like him.
"In the absence of law sin is dead. Once I was alive apart from law; but
when the commandment came, sin sprang to life and I died."
7:7–13

3c. *Paul's own experience and that of others like him*
(continued):
The wretched man's struggle and victory.
"Wretched man that I am! Who will rescue me from this body of death?
Thanks be to God through Jesus Christ our Lord."
7:14–25

CHAPTER 7

7   1 Or do y o u not know, brothers—for I am speaking to those who know law—that the law has authority over a person (only) as long as he lives? 2 For example, by law a married woman is bound to her husband as long as he is alive; but if her husband dies, she is released from the law in so far as it binds her to her husband. 3 So then, if, while her husband is still alive, she marries another man, she will be called an adulteress; but if her husband dies, she is free from the law, so that she is not an adulteress if she marries another man.

4 So, my brothers, y o u too were made dead to the law through the body of Christ, so that y o u might belong to another, even to him who was raised from the dead, in order that we might bear fruit for God. 5 For when we were in the flesh, the sinful passions stimulated by the law were active in our members, so that we bore fruit for death. 6 But now, having died to that by which we were held fast, we have been released from the law, so that we serve in newness of (the) Spirit, not in oldness of (the) letter.

3a. *It produces the fruit of* **liberty:**
freedom from the law.
"We have been released from the law."
7:1–6

It is clear that Paul continues his discussion of the fruits of justification. Among them he had already considered *peace* (chapter 5) and *holiness* (chapter 6). This time he adds *freedom,* namely, from bondage to law, the glorious *liberty* enjoyed by the children of God. Cf. Rom. 8:21; II Cor. 3:17.

Previously in this same epistle Paul had mentioned freedom from *sin.* He had linked it to freedom from *law.* He had written, "For sin shall no longer be lord over y o u, because y o u are not under law but under grace" (6:14). Then, without first explaining what he meant, he had asked and answered the question, "Shall we sin because we are not under law but under grace?" (6:15). As has been pointed out, there was a very practical reason why the answer to that question was urgent, and could not be postponed. Therefore the entire sixth chapter was devoted to it. Note its climax, "For the wages of sin is death, but the free gift of God is life everlasting in Christ Jesus our Lord." *The glorious doctrine of justification by faith must not be used as an excuse for the practice of sin!*

This shows why the apostle had not yet been able to answer such questions as, "In what sense is it true and how did it come about that we are not

213

under law but under grace?" "For what purpose were we released from bondage to law?" It is to these questions that he now gives an answer.

1. Or do y o u not know, brothers—for I am speaking to those who know law—that the law has authority over a person (only) as long as he lives?

Surely a believer is not "free from the law" in every conceivable sense! He loves God's law. Did not the author of Ps. 119—to mention only that one psalm—grow ecstatic when he reflected on the wonders of God's law? Among his many enthusiastic statements are the following:

"Open my eyes that I may behold wondrous things out of thy law" (verse 18).

"O how I love thy law. It is my meditation all the day" (verse 97).

"Rivers of water run down my eyes because they do not observe thy law (verse 136).

"Great peace have they who love thy law" (verse 165).

However, a distinction must be made. The author of Ps. 119 regards God's law as the expression of his wise, good, and merciful will. As such, for the believer the law is a rule of gratitude, answering the question of Ps. 116:12.

But the term "law" can also be used as indicating a code that must be adhered to in order to obtain salvation, "a statute wielding authority and demanding absolute obedience." It is in that sense that the apostle obviously here uses the term. Add to this the fact that the Jewish religious leaders had buried the original law of God under a load of oral traditions: minute, hair-splitting regulations touching just about every human activity and sphere of life. This was the law about which Jesus had said, "Y o u have made the word of God null and void for the sake of y o u r tradition" (Matt. 15:6). Since, according to the teaching of the rabbis, these oral traditions, as to their basic contents, had by God been given to Moses and handed down from generation to generation, it is understandable that ever so many people, in learning about them, had become filled with fear. The *law* had become an unbearable yoke (Acts 15:10).

Accordingly, what the apostle is now telling the membership of the Roman church is that from this yoke—in fact, even from Sinai's unadulterated written law regarded as a means whereby, through obedience, one can earn salvation—they have been released.

Note the tactful manner in which Paul conveys this cheering news. He asks, "Do y o u not know . . . ?" In other words, "Y o u should know, should y o u not?" Cf. I Cor. 6:2, 9, 16, 19. See also on Rom. 6:3, p. 195.

The next word—"brothers"—should not be passed by unnoticed. As here used, it is an affectionate term of address. Previously Paul has used it only in 1:13. Careful examination of all the instances of its occurrence in this epistle shows that whenever the apostle employs this term *in addressing* his readers, he is deeply moved. He is writing about a subject which emotionally affects him. He, as it were, embraces those whom he addresses with his arms of love. In this light examine also the use of this same word in 1:13; 8:12; 10:1; 11:25; 12:1; 15:30; 16:17. In each case the subject discussed is one filled with emotion. So also here, in connection with 1:1, 4, we can probably assume that Paul had heard that some of the members of the Roman church entertained doubts about the doctrine of salvation by grace alone. Therefore, by means of this term of endearment, he is, as it were, wooing them back, tenderly pleading with them to put aside their doubts.

When he adds, "I am speaking to those who know law," the word *law* can perhaps be given its broadest meaning; for according to *any* law, whether Hebrew, Greek, Roman, etc., death ends obligations and attachments, dissolves ties, releases bonds. But if Paul was actually thinking of any specific law system, it must have been the Mosaic, with which, of course, not only the Jews were well acquainted, but so were also those people who were Gentiles by race; in other words, all the members of the Roman Church. See above, p. 23. To them all the principle that the law has authority over a person (only) as long as he lives was well known and would win immediate consent.

What Paul is implying, then, is this: when a person is dead—in the present case dead *to the law*—he is free from its authority, released from its domination.

To fortify his argument the apostle now uses an illustration:

2, 3. For example, by law a married woman is bound to her husband as long as he is alive; but if her husband dies, she is released from the law in so far as it binds her to her husband. So then, if, while her husband is still alive, she marries another man, she will be called an adulteress; but if her husband dies; she is free from the law, so that she is not an adulteress if she marries another man.

Little need be said about the illustration as such. It speaks for itself. According to Scripture marriage is a very solemn bond. It is for life (Gen. 2:22–24; Mal. 2:13–16). This implies that if, while the husband is still living, the wife rejects him and marries another man, she will be called[184] an adulteress.[185]

But although marriage is for life, it does not extend beyond life, the (feigned?) position of the Sadducees notwithstanding. See Luke 20:33, 34. Therefore after the death of her husband no law would prevent this woman from remarrying.

So far the illustration. Matters become a little more difficult when we inquire into the point it wishes to bring out. For example, if we should say

---

184. Note χρηματίσει, third per. s. fut. indicat. intransit. of χρηματίζω. The word has a rich variety of meanings: act. to warn (Heb. 12:25); pass. to be warned (Matt. 2:12, 22; Heb. 8:5; 11:7); to be directed (Acts 10:22); to be revealed (see N.T.C. on Luke 2:26, pp. 175, 176); here (Rom. 7:3) and in Acts 11:26, to be called, styled, branded.

185. Here the still living husband's faithfulness is assumed. Otherwise the rule implied in Matt. 5:32 (see N.T.C. on Matthew, p. 305) would apply.

that in this illustration the husband consistently indicates the law, and the married woman consistently the believer, we would soon reach a blind alley. For in that case the law would have to die before the believer could be made free. But nowhere does Paul teach that the law dies or is put to death. Quite the opposite: it is *we* who are put to death. It is *we* who therefore die (Rom. 7:4; Gal. 2:19).

Accordingly, in our attempt to interpret these words we should concentrate on just *one* item, namely, *the third of comparison*. It is this: as it is a *death* that dissolves the marriage bond, so it is also a *death* that dissolves the legal bond; i.e., the bondage to law. The marriage bond is dissolved by the death of one of the marriage partners (in this case the husband); the legal bond is broken by the believers' involvement in Christ's death; in other words, by the believers' death. Yes, we, the believers, have indeed died with Christ, in the sense which has already been explained in connection with 6:8. See above, p. 199. Once this third of comparison is grasped, there is no further difficulty. Paul's own clarification, moreover, follows in verse.

4. So, my brothers, y o u too were made dead to the law through the body of Christ, so that y o u might belong to another, even to him who was raised from the dead, in order that we might bear fruit for God.

Several points stand out in this strikingly beautiful passage:

a. We have already commented on "my brothers." See above, pp. 214, 215.

b. "Y o u too were made dead" or "were put to death."[186]

It was *God* who not only planned salvation but also carried out this plan. It was *he* who so loved the world that he gave his only Son in order that everyone who believes in him should not perish but have life everlasting (John 3:16); *he* who did not spare his Son but delivered him up for us all (Rom. 8:32). See also Isa. 53:4, 10; II Cor. 5:21. It was *through the body of Christ Crucified* that our indebtedness to the law was completely paid off, so that, as a result, believers were made dead to the law, the latter's "bill" having been fully paid.

c. In Paul's illustration it was stated that when the husband died, the wife was released from the marriage bond, and given the right to marry someone else. That part of the figure may also have been in the apostle's mind when he wrote, ". . . that y o u might belong to another, even to him who was raised from the dead . . ." Since the relation of the Christian to the Christ is very close, release from the law must mean union with Christ, the Risen One. See Col. 3:3.

d. This union or marriage is not unfruitful. Note: "in order that we might bear fruit for God."

Our Exalted Lord, through the outpouring of his Spirit, enables believers to do this. In the Pauline epistles, and in Scripture as a whole, great emphasis is placed on fruitbearing. The reference is to the fruit of good

---

186. I can see no good reason for weakening the meaning of ἐθανατώθητε, 2nd per. pl. aor. indicat. passive of θανατόω, to put to death.

attitudes, aspirations, words, and works; to all of these directed to the glory of God Triune. Among Pauline passages mentioning or implying fruitbearing see Rom. 1:13; 6:21, 22; Gal. 5:22, 23; Eph. 2:10; 5:9; Phil. 4:8, 9, 17; Col. 1:6; Titus 3:1. For the rest of Scripture see Ps. 1:3; 92:14; Prov. 11:30; Jer. 17:8, 10; Matt. 7:17; John 15:1-8.

e. Note the shift from the second person to the first: "so that *y o u* might belong to another . . . in order that *we* might bear fruit for God." This same peculiarity appears also in such passages, among others, as the following: Rom. 6:14-16; 8:11-13; 13:11-14.

Explanation: Paul is himself deeply involved in the truths about which he writes. The doctrine of sovereign grace grips him, causes his heart to beat faster, his eyes to fill with tears of gratitude. So again and again he shifts from *y o u* to *we*. Is a sermon really good if it lacks this feature?

5, 6. For when we were in the flesh, the sinful passions stimulated by the law were active in our members, so that we bore fruit for death. But now, having died to that by which we were held fast, we have been released from the law, so that we serve in newness of (the) Spirit, not in oldness of (the) letter.

The expression "when we were in the flesh"[187] means "when basically we were governed by our sinful human nature." By "the sinful passions (cf. 6:6; Col. 2:11) . . . active in our members," are probably meant such emotions as lust, anger, hatred, ill will, jealousy, envy, unreasonable fear, etc. Although these and similar passions pertain to a person's heart and mind, they express themselves physically: the jealous eye, the clenched fist, the hateful gesture, etc. Cf. 6:12, 13. The unbridled gratification of passions, so that those who nourish them produce the fruit indicated in Gal. 5:19-21, results in death. Cf. 6:21. Contrast "fruit for God" (verse 4) with "fruit for death" (verse 5).

For the answer to the question, "How is it to be understood that these sinful passions are stimulated by the law?" see on verses 7-13.

But now, says Paul, a great change has occurred. By means of our death—a death with Christ; hence a death to sin, which held us in its grip—we were released or discharged from the law.

---

187. In Paul's epistles the word σάρξ (flesh) has the following meanings:
  a. the chief substance of the body, whether of men or of animals (I Cor. 15:39);
  b. the body itself, in distinction from the spirit, mind, heart (Col. 2:5);
  c. earthly existence (Gal. 2:20; Phil. 1:22, 24);
  d. a human being, viewed as a weak, earthly, perishable creature (I Cor. 1:29; Gal. 2:16). This usage depends heavily on the Hebrew. Cf. Isa. 40:6, "All flesh is grass," etc.
  e. physical descent or relationship (Rom. 9:8);
  f. the human nature, without any disparagement (Rom. 9:5);
  g. human worth and attainment, with emphasis on hereditary, ceremonial, legal, and moral advantages; the self apart from regenerating grace; anything apart from Christ on which one bases his hope for salvation (Phil. 3:3);
  h. sinful human nature: the human nature viewed as the seat and vehicle of sinful desire (Rom. 7:5, 25; 8:3-9, 12, 13; Gal. 5:16, 17, 19; 6:8).

What he means is that *basically* our lives are no longer governed by our sinful nature. And since Christ, by means of his vicarious death, paid the debt we owed to the law, we are now no longer under the law's domination and curse.

This does not remove the fact that sin still exercises considerable influence over us, as 7:14–25 will indicate, but *basically* there has been a tremendous change.

The result[188] of all this is that we now serve (God) in newness of the Spirit, no longer in oldness of the letter, that is, the legal code. There used to be a time when we thought that by strict obedience to the external code—the Mosaic *written law,* as interpreted by tradition—we could be saved. But now, having been set at *liberty,* we serve (see 6:15–23) in newness of the Spirit. According to Gal. 3:3; 4:6; 5:18; II Cor. 3:17 that Spirit is the Author of our liberty. Paul's thought seems to be that this Spirit guides believers in their effort to live lives of gratitude for salvation received as the product of God's sovereign grace. The Spirit guides and enables them to live such lives.

What the apostle is saying, then, is that the glorious prophecy of Jer. 31:31–34 is being realized in the lives of himself and those addressed.

When Paul closes this section by writing, "so that we serve in newness of (the) Spirit, not in oldness of (the) letter," he places the *new* over against the *old* (as he does also in II Cor. 5:17; Eph. 4:22–24; Col. 3:9, 10); and the *Spirit* over against the *letter* (as in Rom. 2:29; II Cor. 3:6). Hence, he is contrasting true liberty—the blessing bestowed on all those who have become "free from the law," in the sense explained—with the bondage of those still enslaved by the law. As always, so also at this point, his teaching is in line with that of the Master. See Matt. 9:14–17 (Mark 2:18–22; Luke 5:33–39); and compare II Cor. 3:17 with John 8:36.

---

7 What shall we say then? Is the law sin? Not at all! On the contrary, I would not have come to know sin, had it not been through the law. For I would not have known what it meant to covet if the law had not said, "You shall not covet." 8 But sin, grasping the opportunity afforded by the commandment, produced in me coveting of every variety. For in the absence of law sin (is) dead. 9 Once I was alive apart from law; but when the commandment came, sin sprang to life and I died. 10 And I found that the very commandment which was intended to bring life, in reality brought death.[189] 11 For sin, grasping the opportunity afforded by the commandment, deceived me, and through the commandment killed me. 12 So then, in itself the law is holy, and the commandment holy and righteous and good.

13 Did that which is good then become death to me? Not at all! But sin, in order that it might stand out as sin, produced death in me through that which is good, in order that through the commandment sin might become thoroughly sinful.

---

188. Note ὥστε expressing result.

189. Literally: And there was found for me the commandment, the one for life, this very one for death.

3b. *The sinner's relation to God's Law, in the light of Paul's own experience and that of others like him.*

"In the absence of law sin is dead. Once I was alive apart from law; but when the commandment came, sin sprang to life and I died."

7:7–13

7, 8. What shall we say then? Is the law sin? Not at all! On the contrary, I would not have come to know sin, had it not been through the law. For I would not have known what it meant to covet if the law had not said, "You shall not covet." But sin, grasping the opportunity afforded by the commandment, produced in me coveting of every variety. For in the absence of law sin (is) dead.

The apostle had made several statements which might lead thoughtless people to believe that the law itself was a sinful thing. Had he not made mention of "the sinful passions stimulated by the law"? (7:5). See also 5:20 and 6:14.

So in the present section (see especially verse 12) the writer makes very clear the fact that, considered in and by itself, the law is not at all sinful. On the contrary, it is exactly God's holy law—with special reference here to the Ten Commandments—that reveals sin in all its gruesomeness. It does this in order that people may earnestly wage war against sin.

This does not mean that without the written law sin is impossible. Even those who are without that law do sin, as 1:18–20; 2:12, 14, 15; 5:12–14 prove. It means that apart from the written law the terrible, soul-destroying character of sin would not have been known.

By nature people have only a dim awareness of their sinfulness. To be sure, they are often deeply conscious of *the other person's* guilt. At times they even reprimand the other person while at the same time committing the very sin they condemn.

Examples from life:

a. The following words were spoken by a (very guilty) husband to his wife, after several hours of pastoral counseling: "Well, I'll forgive you; but I'll never forget what you did to me!"

b. Mother reprimanding her little son: "I have told you at least a million times not to exaggerate!"

The very existence of the written law makes *sin,* that is, (in this case) transgression of that law, possible. We should also bear in mind that the only exclusively positive command of the Decalog is, "Honor your father and your mother," etc. Do not all the other commands, namely, "You shall not have any other gods before me," "You shall not kill," "You shall not commit adultery," etc., suggest to *sinners* that they do the very thing that is forbidden?

What strikes us in reading Rom. 7:7–13 is the fact that, in discussing this subject of transgressing God's written law, Paul no less than ten times refers to *himself.* There are those who believe that Paul is here using the first person singular *in a general sense,* hence not in an autobiographical manner.[190]

Calvin did not share that view, and I believe Calvin was correct in taking that position. Paul—unlike Mark and the author of the epistle to the Hebrews—is not in the habit of hiding his identity. Again and again, throughout his epistles, definitely including Romans, he reveals himself, telling us how a certain matter has affected, or is affecting, him personally, what *he* is doing, intends to do, is experiencing, or has experienced: Rom. 1:8–16; 6:19; 7:1; 9:1–3; 11:11–13; 12:1–3; 15:14–32. Note how the pronouns "I," "my," and "me" are also liberally sprinkled throughout the Greetings section (16:1, 2, 3, 4, 7, 8, 9, 11, 13, 17, 19, 21, 23). It is therefore natural to believe that also here (7:7–13) the apostle is actually speaking about himself. He is recounting how the law "killed" him, that is, how it struck down this self-righteous Pharisee.

Not as if the events he records were in every respect peculiar to him. Undoubtedly, they must be viewed as being, *to a certain extent,* the experience of all those who from the notion of salvation by human merit are brought to the conviction of salvation by grace alone.

Now Paul informs us that he never would have come to know sin had it not been through the law; specifically that he would not have known what it meant *to covet* if the law had not said, "You shall not covet."

It is not surprising that it was especially this tenth commandment that stopped Paul in his tracks. The other commandments, superficially interpreted, forbid transgressions that are, or seem to be, of a more or less external character; especially those of the second table. In this connection read the story of "the rich young ruler" (Matt. 20:18–20, with parallels in Mark and Luke). But the tenth commandment strikes directly at the very root of sin, namely, man's sinful *heart,* his evil *desire.*

Perhaps the covetousness here forbidden is a hankering for things that are sinful in themselves. Or it may be an inordinate yearning for things which, *used with moderation,* would not be sinful but might even be useful (e.g., sports). Or it may be that which is specifically mentioned in the commandment, namely, a craving to deprive a neighbor of anything at all that belongs to him.

Now Paul mentions the fact that sin, grasping the opportunity[191] afforded by the commandment, produced in him coveting *of every variety.* As to the different ways in which sinful coveting may express itself, note the following: The parents of the human race coveted the forbidden fruit (Gen. 3:6); Joseph's brothers, the position of their father's favorite (Gen. 37:4); Achan, a beautiful Babylonian garment and other objects included

---

190. Cranfield, *op. cit.,* p. 351.

191. ἀφορμήν, acc. s. of ἀφορμή (=ἀπό, from, and ὁρμή, impulse, incentive), place from which one starts out, base of operations, springboard; and so: pretext (II Cor. 11:12); occasion (II Cor. 5:12; I Tim. 5:14); opportunity (Rom. 7:8, 11; Gal. 5:13).

in the spoils of Jericho (Josh. 7:21); Ahab, Naboth's vineyard (I Kings 21:1 f.); Amnon, Tamar (II Sam. 13:1); Absalom, the crown (II Sam. 15:1 f.); Ananias and Saphira, prestige (Acts 5:1 f.); Simon the Sorcerer, magical healing power (Acts 8:18 f.); Demas, "this present world" (II Tim. 4:10); and Diotrephes, ecclesiastical pre-eminence (III John 9).

Moreover, as is true of every commandment, so also this one must not be interpreted too narrowly. Jesus has made this clear in such passages as Matt. 5:21 f.; 5:27 f.; 5:31 f.; 5:33 f.

Along this line the Heidelberg Catechism (Lord's Day XLIV, Q. and A. 113) gives us a meaningful interpretation of the tenth commandment:

"Q. What does the tenth commandment require of us?

"A. That not even the slightest inclination or thought contrary to any of God's commandments shall ever rise in our hearts, but that at all times we shall hate all sin with our whole heart and delight in all righteousness."

It is not surprising, therefore, that Paul states, "Sin, grasping the opportunity afforded by the commandment, produced in me coveting of every variety." On the other hand, remove that tenth commandment, with its almost endless multitude of suggestions as to how it can be transgressed, and sin lies dormant.

9. Once I was alive apart from law; but when the commandment came, sin sprang to life[192] and I died.

Meaning: There was a time when I felt secure, under no conviction of sin. At that time the full implication of the law had not yet registered in my consciousness, had not yet become an unbearable burden upon my heart. I thought that morally and spiritually I was doing quite well.

But when the commandment came, that is, when it was brought home to me what the law really demanded (nothing less than that which is summarized in Mark 12:29–31), I realized what a great sinner I was. It was then that I died; that is, that was the end of me as a self-satisfied, self-secure person.

10–12. And I found that the very commandment which was intended to bring life, in reality brought death. For sin, grasping the opportunity afforded by the commandment, deceived me, and through the commandment killed me. So then, in itself the law is holy, and the commandment holy and righteous and good.

---

192. When the prefix ἀνά in the verb ἀναζάω retains its full force, as it does in a variant reading of Rom. 14:9, the meaning is *to live again, to return to life*. Here, in Rom. 7:9 the prefix has probably lost some of its force, as happens often in the case of prefixes, so that the meaning of the entire verb is simply *became alive, sprang to life*. See L.N.T. (A. and G., p. 53). With respect to the simple verb ζάω, the basic meaning is *to live*. As to Rev. 20:4 (ἔζησαν) translators are divided in their opinion: some (R.S.V., N.A.S., Phillips, N.I.V.) have adopted the rendering *they came to life* or even "These came to life again" (N.E.B.). Others (A.V., A.R.V., Beck, Williams, Berkeley) translate "They lived." It is a matter if interpretation, the result in some cases probably depending on the theology of the translator. In order to reach the right conclusion the subject of the sentence ("souls") should be taken into account. For the rest, see the author's *More Than Conquerors*, pp. 230, 231; and *The Bible on the Life Hereafter*, pp. 154–156.

The purpose of the commandment had indeed been to bring life; yes, life everlasting. It was true from the beginning and has always remained true that loving God with all of one's heart, soul, mind, and strength, and loving the neighbor as one loves himself brings life, salvation. Cf. Lev. 18:5, "Keep my decrees and laws, for the person who obeys them will live by them." See also Ezek. 20:11. That Paul has in mind the quoted passage seems probable, in view of Rom. 10:5.

And so, the self-righteous Jew, the one with little self-knowledge, imagined that by trying very hard, he would be able to earn everlasting life. There was a time when Paul too was of that opinion, as Phil. 3:6 implies. That was before he discovered that all his righteous deeds (lit. "righteousnesses") amounted to nothing better than filthy rags (Isa. 64:6). So for Paul too that very commandment, whose intention was to bring life, actually brought death.

How was it that while Paul expected life, he found death; and that while he expected happiness, he found gloom? The reason was not that something was wrong with the law. On the contrary, that law was, and always is, holy and righteous and good, since it not only strives to promote these very qualities, as becomes clear from the reading of each commandment, but also reflects the holiness and righteousness and goodness of God.

Is it not a merciful arrangement that, by means of the first and second commandments, God warns against the evil of idolatry, with all the corruption, filth, disappointment, and grief that attends it? That by means of the fourth commandment he sets aside a much needed day of rest and worship for man? That by means of the fifth commandment he places the child under the rule, care, and protection of those who love him most? That by means of the seventh commandment he guards the sacredness of marriage, and by means of the sixth and the eighth, protects human life and property?

So it is made very evident that it was not the law, as such, but it was sin—in the present case Paul's own sinfulness—that made it impossible for the law to make a person holy and happy. The commandment, operating by itself, never kills or even hurts anyone. It is sin that kills. It was sin that even deceived Paul, in his unconverted state, into thinking that he would be able to live in strict obedience to God's law. It deceived him, . . . until one day, in a very dramatic way, it was made clear to him that no matter how hard he tried, he would never, no never, be able *thus* to attain to the status of righteousness before God.

13. Did that which is good then become death to me? Not at all! But sin, in order that it might stand out as sin, produced death in me through that which is good, in order that through the commandment sin might become thoroughly sinful.

Paul had stated that the commandment brought death (verse 10). But how can something that is holy and righteous and good (verse 12) bring death? Paul answers, as it were, "It is not the commandment, operating by itself, that brings death. It is the transgression of the commandment that does this." In the final analysis, therefore, the real cause of death is *sin*. The serious character of sin becomes apparent in this very fact that, in order to expose the sinner, it makes use of something which in itself is perfect, namely, God's holy law. The very *whiteness*—that is, moral-spiritual purity—of God's commandment makes the *blackness* of sin stand out all the more sharply! In the background is the comforting thought, "How majestic, holy, wise, and loving is the God who has provided a way in which sin is removed for those who trust in him!"

As has become clear, Paul has allowed us to take a look into his own diary. He has given us a glimpse into his experience prior to, during, and shortly after his conversion. He has said, "Once I was alive apart from law, but when the commandment came, sin sprang to life and I died."

There are those who link this and similar expressions with Paul's experience when, as a lad of thirteen, he became a *bar mitzvah* (son of the law). It was then that, in accordance with Jewish custom, he assumed responsibility to keep the law.[193] However, such a statement as, "Sin sprang to life and I died" seems to point to a far more radical experience; namely, to that which is recorded in Acts 9:1–22; 22:3–21; 26:1–23; and especially to what Paul tells us in Gal. 1:13–18. While we should certainly leave room for earlier influences upon Paul's mind and heart, not excluding those exerted on his subliminal consciousness, it was in connection with (a) the dramatic experience on the way to Damascus, (b) the events that took place during the days immediately following, and (c) the happenings during the three years spent in Arabia, that "sin sprang to life and Paul—the old, Pharisaic Paul—died." It was then that the former persecutor had time to reflect on: the kind of man he had been, the witness of Stephen and other Christian martyrs, the way of salvation as summarized in such passages as Gen. 15:6; Ps. 32; Isa. 53; Hab. 2; etc., and the words spoken to him by Ananias and by Jesus himself.

Was Paul's conversion experience unique? In certain respects it surely was; in other respects not. There are traits of similarity between the path the apostle had to travel before he surrendered himself wholeheartedly to Christ, and the path others traveled, among them that wonderful child of God, namely, Robert M. McCheyne (1813–1843), as he describes so touchingly in his poem:

JEHOVAH TSIDKENU = JEHOVAH OUR RIGHTEOUSNESS
(Jer. 23:6)

> I once was a stranger to grace and to God,
> I knew not my danger, and felt not my load,
> Though friends spoke in rapture of Christ on the tree,
> Jehovah Tsidkenu was nothing to me.

---

193. For more on this see N.T.C. on Luke, p. 183.

I oft read with pleasure to soothe or engage,
Isaiah's wild measure and John's simple page;
But e'en when they pictured the blood-sprinkled tree,
Jehovah Tsidkenu seemed nothing to me.

Like tears from the daughters of Zion that roll,
I wept when the waters went over his soul,
Yet thought not that my sins had nailed to the tree
Jehovah Tsidkenu— 't was nothing to me.

When free grace awoke me by light from on high,
Then legal fear shook me; I trembled to die;
No refuge, no safety in self could I see,—
Jehovah Tsidkenu my Savior must be.

My terrors all vanished before the sweet name,
My guilty fear banished, with boldness I came
To drink at the Fountain, life-giving and free:
Jehovah Tsidkenu is all things to me.

Jehovah Tsidkenu! my treasure and boast;
Jehovah Tsidkenu! I ne'er can be lost:
In thee shall I conquer by flood and by field,
My cable, my anchor, my breastplate and shield!

Even treading the valley, the shadow of death!
This "watchword" shall rally my faltering breath;
For while from life's fever my God sets me free,
"Jehovah Tsidkenu!" my death-song shall be.

---

14 For we know that the law is spiritual, but I am carnal, sold as a slave to sin. 15 Indeed, that which I am accomplishing I do not approve of. For not what I want (to do), that do I practice, but what I loathe, that I do. 16 But if I do the very thing I do not want to do, I agree that the law is good. 17 But, this being so, then it is not I who accomplish it, but it is sin dwelling in me. 18 For I know that nothing good dwells in me, that is, in my flesh. For I have the desire to do what is good, but I cannot accomplish it.[194] 19 For what I do is not the good I want to do; no, it is the evil I do not want to do, this I practice. 20 But if I am doing the very thing I do not want to do, it is no longer I who am doing it, but it is sin dwelling in me.

21 So I discover this law[195]: When I want to do good, evil lies close at hand. 22 For according to my inner being I delight in God's law; 23 but I see in my (bodily) members a different law, waging war against the law of my mind and making me a prisoner of the law of sin which is in my members. 24 Wretched man that I am! Who will rescue me from this body of death? 25 Thanks be to God through Jesus Christ our Lord! So then, I myself with my mind serve the law of God, but with my flesh the law of sin.

---

194. Or: For to will is present with me, but to do that which is good is not.
195. Or: rule, principle. So also three times in verse 23.

3c. *Paul's own experience and that of others like him*
(continued):
The wretched man's struggle and victory.
"Wretched man that I am! Who will rescue me from this body of death?
Thanks be to God through Jesus Christ our Lord."
7:14-25

In connection with Rom. 7:14-25 the question that must be answered is:
Who is the person described here?
Is he:

a. *An unconverted person,* whether Paul himself before his conversion, or
any other unregenerate individual, perhaps a Jew who has not embraced
Christ?

b. *An immature believer?*

c. *Paul himself, the believer,* and by extension, *the believer generally*

An Unconverted Person?

From the days of the early church, throughout the middle ages, and also
today, there have been and are many who claim that what Paul says in
7:14-25 cannot refer to the believer but must have reference to the unbeliever. The older Greek fathers endorsed this view. For a while even the
great Augustine was of this opinion.

The one who in the twentieth century has perhaps done most to per-
petuate this theory was W. G. Kümmel. See his book, in which there is
much that is valuable, *Römer 7 und die Bekehrung des Paulus,* Leipzig, 1929.
H. R. Ridderbos, whose fine commentary on Romans (*Commentaar Op Het
Nieuwe Testament,* Kampen, 1959) deserves diligent study, also defends the
view that Rom. 7:14-25 portrays a man apart from Christ, a person en-
gaged in a desperate struggle under the law (*op. cit.,* p. 165). Ridderbos
presents a series of arguments in defense of his view, and claims that his
position was not only favored in the early church but is also shared by most
present-day exegetes (p. 162). Those who are able to read Dutch should by
all means make a careful study of pp. 153 f.; 162-170. Not only is such a
study fair to the author but it is also advisable because in my commentary
there is no room to enter into all the details of the Dutch scholar's lengthy
reasonings. In part he argues as follows:

a. In verse 14 Paul says "For (γάρ) we know that the law is spiritual but I
am carnal..." How can the fact that "I am carnal," if that "I" indicates a
person redeemed by Christ and led by the Holy Spirit, prove the superior
power of sin mentioned in verse 13?

b. Between 8:1 and 7:14-25 there is a sharp contrast. The "now" of
Rom. 8:1 ("Therefore, there is *now* no condemnation") does not represent
the deplorable situation pictured in Rom. 7:14-25 but a situation which
arises afterward; that is, the reign of the Spirit cannot be identified with but
follows the reign of sin.

c. The view according to which 7:14–25 pictures the discord that remains in the life of the believer conflicts with the statements of Paul in chapter 6 and elsewhere regarding this new life. Thus, according to 6:2, 6, 7, 11, 12, 13, 17, 18, 22, for the Christian sin is the dethroned lord, the lord who has lost his ruling power. In fact, all of chapter 6 is a continuous refutation of the position according to which the "I" of Rom. 7:14–25 could represent the new man, redeemed by Christ.

Answer

As to a. This argument misinterprets the word *for* (γάρ) as here used. Here, as frequently, this word belongs not merely to a part of verse 13 but to the verse taken as a whole.[196] It has a continuative sense, and by some— e.g., N.I.V.—is not even translated. The apostle is saying that the fact that the law is spiritual but I am carnal is in harmony with the fact that the law is good but I am exceedingly sinful.

As to b. The situation pictured in 7:14–25 is not all dark. The contrast between 7:14–25 and 8:1f. must not be exaggerated. To be sure, the earlier passage dwells on sin, but it also dwells on the struggle against sin. *Victory* over sin is even recorded (verses 24, 25). The words, "Thanks be to God through Jesus Christ our Lord" (7:25) harmonize beautifully with, "So then there is now no condemnation for those who are in Christ Jesus," etc. (8:1).

Similarly, the situation pictured in 8:1f. is not as bright as some represent it to be. Even chapter 8 recognizes the paradox in the Christian's life between good and evil. This conflict is implied in verse 10 and clearly expressed in verse 13.

Elsewhere too Paul teaches that a spiritual struggle continues in the life of the believer until the day he enters glory. See I Cor. 9:27; Gal. 5:17; Phil. 3:12–14. The child of God receives the assurance that the One who has begun a good work in him will carry it on to completion until the day of Christ Jesus (Phil. 1:6).

As to c. Though these statements do indeed picture the Christian as walking in newness of life, having been brought from death to life, and in a sense having died to sin, nevertheless, nowhere does chapter 6 or any other Pauline chapter or passage either state or imply that the believer during his present life here on earth has been completely delivered from his struggle against sin. Do not the exhortations of 6:12, 13, 19 imply that this struggle must be continued?

With respect to the claim that many present-day exegetes favor Kümmel's view, as did also many earlier scholars, this must be granted. As could be expected, the view according to which the unbeliever is able to do whatever is mentioned in 7:14–25, including even the good things, is in favor with Pelagians and to a certain extent with Arminians. However, even some Reformed writers have endorsed the position of Kümmel. But, on the

---

196. So also Cranfield, *op. cit.,* p. 355.

whole, Reformed theologians reject this theory, and so do, and did, many others, as will be shown.

Since the arguments proving that the man pictured in 7:14-25 cannot be an unbeliever are the same as those establishing the fact that this person must be a believer, see below (p. 228) for the defense of the latter theory.

An Immature Believer?

The question can be asked, however, "Though it be granted that the man pictured by Paul in 7:14-25 cannot be an unbeliever, nevertheless, in view of the fact that he makes many unfavorable statements about himself—see 7:14, 15, 18, 19, 21, 23, 24—is it possible that he is a mere 'babe in Christ' (cf. I Cor. 3:1; Heb. 3:13)?"

According to this theory three stages of religious position and development are pictured by Paul: (a) that of a person still under the dominion of sin (7:5, 9a); (b) that of the struggling individual, one who hates sin but has not advanced very far on the road of sanctification (7:14-25); and (c) that of the mature and grateful believer, rejoicing in the fact that for him there is now no condemnation (8:1 f.).

But according to Scripture it is exactly the more advanced Christian, the mature believer, who is most deeply concerned about his sin. The more a person has made progress in sanctification, the more also will he abhor his sinfulness.

Thus, Scripture pictures *Job* as a paradigm of virtue (Job 1:1; Ezek. 14:14; James 5:11). Nevertheless, it was exactly Job who exclaimed, "I abhor myself and repent in dust and ashes" (Job 42:6). All will agree that Daniel, the hero of the book of *Daniel,* was an example of Godfearing life and conduct.[197] But listen to his humble plea, in which he confesses his own and his people's sin: "Alas, O Lord, we have sinned and done wrong ... We are covered with shame because of our sins against thee" (Dan. 9:4, 5, 8). A king among the prophets, a most Godfearing person, was *Isaiah.* Yet, it was precisely Isaiah who cried out, "Woe is me, for I am ruined, because I am a man of unclean lips ..." (Isa. 6:5).

This should indicate that the person whom the apostle has in mind in Rom. 7:14-25 need not be considered, and was not necessarily, an immature believer.

Paul Himself, and by Extension, Believers Generally, Including Even the Most Mature

In line with the humble and self-incriminating language of eminent believers is the fact that Paul too, in referring to himself elsewhere, uses language not far removed from "Wretched man that I am!" Note the following:

---

197. The question whether the "Daniel" mentioned in Ezek. 14:14 was the one of Dan. 1:6 or was someone else need not detain us.

"I am the least of the apostles, not fit to be called an apostle, because I persecuted the church of God!" (I Cor. 15:9).

"To me, the very least of all the saints, was this grace given, to preach to the Gentiles the unsearchable riches of Christ" (Eph. 3:8).

"Christ Jesus came into the world sinners to save, foremost of whom am I!" (I Tim. 1:15).

The person described in Rom. 7:14–25 hates sin (7:15), wishes to do what is good (verses 19, 21), in his inner being delights in God's law (verse 22), deeply regrets his sins (verses 15, 18–24), and thanks God for his deliverance (verse 25). Is it at all probable that such a person has not been regenerated by the Spirit of God? Contrast all this with the description of the unregenerate (7:5, 9a; 8:5a). Clearly, in Rom. 7:14–25 the apostle, in the words of John Calvin, "in his own person describes the weakness of believers and how great it is" (*Romans,* p. 264).

Important also is the change of tense between 7:5, 9a, on the one hand, and 7:14–25, on the other. Surely the most natural explanation is that there has been a radical change; that is, that the "I" of the second passage is no longer the unregenerate of 7:5, 9a but is spiritually reborn.[198]

But this regenerated individual is still experiencing a struggle. He has not yet reached heaven. Those who reject the existence of a kind of dualism within the rescued person Paul and, in general, within believers, find it very difficult to explain 7:24, 25:

"Wretched man that I am! Who will rescue me from this body of death? Thanks be to God through Jesus Christ our Lord! So then, I myself with my mind serve the law of God, but with my flesh the law of sin."

The reasons for believing that in 7:14–25 the regenerated individual, Paul, is describing his own condition and that of believers generally, have been given. It has been shown that *it cannot be the unbeliever who is here being pictured.* Something should now be said about the claim that the opposite view was held by many in the early church and is cherished by most present-day exegetes.

It has already been admitted that there was a time when Augustine, along with many others, supported the view according to which the person described in Rom. 7:14–25 is the unregenerate. Calvin points out what happened next, and, in doing so, also again reveals his own interpretation of the disputed passage:

"Augustine was for a time involved in the common error, but having more thoroughly examined the passage, not only retracted what he had

---

198. The point made by both Mitton and Robinson (for reference see footnote 199) that in verse 14 ("The law is spiritual, but I am carnal") the contrast is not between what I *am* and what I *was*, but between *the law* and *myself*, can be readily granted. But the real argument in favor of viewing verses 14–25 as a description of Paul the believer, is the contrast between, on the one hand, the *past* tense in such passages as 7:5, 9a, and the *present* tense, from *start to finish*, in 7:14–25.

falsely thought, but in his first book to Boniface proves, by many forceful arguments, that what is said cannot be applied to any but the regenerate" (Calvin on *Romans,* p. 264).

It has also been admitted that throughout the centuries many exegetes,[199] especially but by no means exclusively Pelagians, have endorsed the theory according to which Rom. 7:14-25 is a description of the unregenerate, and that today that view is being propagated, at times even by those confessing the Reformed faith.

However, it certainly merits serious reflection that in one way or another, and with varying opinions on details, the belief according to which Paul is here referring to himself and, in general, to believers, is endorsed by the following, among many others:

Batey, R. A., *The Letter of Paul to the Romans,* Austin, 1969, pp. 98-104.

Bavinck, H., *Gereformeerde Dogmatiek,* third edition, Vol. III, p. 65 f.; IV, pp. 282, 283.

Berkhof, L., *Systematic Theology,* Grand Rapids, 1949, p. 540.

Berkouwer, G. C., *Dogmatische Studiën, Geloof En Heiliging,* Kampen, 1949, p. 61, tr. *Faith and Sanctification,* pp. 59, 60.

Bruce, F. F., *The Epistle of Paul to the Romans, (Tyndale Bible Commentaries),* Grand Rapids, 1963, pp. 150-156.

Calvin, J., as has been shown.

Cranfield, C. E. B., *op. cit.,* Vol. I, pp. 344, 355-370.

Fraser, J., *A Treatise on Sanctification,* London, 1898, pp. 254-356.

Greijdanus, S., *op. cit.,* Vol. I, pp. 337-339.

Haldane, R., *The Epistle to the Romans,* London, 1966, p. 299.

Hamilton, F. E., *The Epistle to the Romans,* Grand Rapids, 1958, pp. 111-121.

Hodge, C., *op. cit.,* pp. 357, 386.

Knox, J., *op. cit.,* pp. 498-500.

Kuyper, A., *Het Werk van den Heiligen Geest,* Kampen, 1927, pp. 583, 612. Engl. tr., *The Work of the Holy Spirit,* Grand Rapids, 1941, pp. 636-640.

Lenski, R. C. H., *op. cit.,* pp. 473-492.

Luther, M., *Lectures on Romans,* p. 203.

Murray, J., *op. cit.,* Vol. I, pp. 256-273.

Nygren, A., *Commentary on Romans,* Philadelphia, 1949, pp. 284-296.

Pronk, C., "Who is the man of Romans 7:14-25?," article in *The Outlook*

---

199. For example, J. A. Bengel, R. Bultmann, J. Denney, C. H. Dodd, A. E. Garvie, F. Godet, C. Gore, K. E. Kirk, W. Sanday and A. C. Headlam, J. Weiss, to mention only a few, in addition to W. G. Kümmel and H. R. Ridderbos. For a kind of compromise position—*Rom. 7:14-25 is the description of the experience of any morally earnest man, whether he be a Christian or not*—see the interesting article by C. L. Mitton, "Romans vii Reconsidered," *ET* 65 (1953, 1954), pp. 78-81, 99-103, 132-135. Interesting and instructive, but to me not entirely convincing! For a view somewhat resembling that of Mitton see John A. T. Robinson, *Wrestling with Romans,* Philadelphia, 1979; see especially p. 82 f.

(Journal of Reformed Fellowship, published in Grand Rapids, Mich.), Nov. 1978, pp. 9-13.

Steele, D. N., and Thomas, C. C., *Romans, An Interpretive Outline*, Philadelphia, 1963, pp. 126-130.

Van Andel, J., *Paulus' Brief Aan De Romeinen*, Kampen, 1904, pp. 143-151.

Van Leeuwen and Jacobs, *op. cit.*, Vol. I, pp. 124-137.

Wilson, G. B., *op. cit.*, pp. 117-126.

This is also the stand taken by *Evangelical Creeds:*

The Westminster Confession of Faith, 1647, speaking about the believers' "best works" (Chapter XVI, par. VI), states, "they are defiled and mixed with so much weakness and imperfection that they cannot endure the severity of God's judgment." The annexed scriptural passages include Rom. 7:15, 18. See *Creeds of Christendom*, edited by Philip Schaff, Vol. III, p. 635.

The Belgic Confession, 1561, referring to those who have received Jesus Christ as their only Savior (Article XXIX), states, "But this is not to be understood as if there did not remain in them great infirmities; but they fight against them through the Spirit all the days of their life..." To the French text of the quoted words are appended the following references: Rom. 7:6, 17, etc.; Gal. 5:17. *Creeds of Christendom*, Vol. III, p. 420.

The Heidelberg Catechism, 1563, in Lord's Day XLIV, Q. & A. 114, asks, "But can those who are converted to God keep these commandments perfectly?" and answers, "No, but even the holiest men, while in this life, have only a small beginning of this obedience; yet so that with earnest purpose they begin to live not only according to some but according to all the commandments of God." The appended references include Rom. 7:22. See also Lord's Day LII, Q. & A. 127.

For *Lutheran* creedal support for this interpretation, see Lenski, *op. cit.*, pp. 473, 474.

14. For we know that the law is spiritual, but I am carnal, sold as a slave to sin.

As has been indicated, there is a close connection between verses 13 and 14 (see p. 226). Now here in verse 14, Paul starts out by making it very clear that he is not finding fault with God's holy law when it exposes him, even Paul, as being still a sinner. He says that the law is spiritual. He means, as he has already explained (see verse 12), that the law is holy, and the commandment holy and righteous and good; that it is the work of God, the product of the Holy Spirit. Cf. Mark 12:36; Acts 1:16; 4:24, 25; II Peter 1:20, 21.

The same absolute goodness and purity cannot be ascribed to the confessor, Paul. On the contrary, he is carnal.[200]

---

200. Though it is true that the best reading favors σάϱϰινος, basically meaning "composed of

Care should be exercised in defining this quality. The apostle does not say, "I am in the flesh," or "controlled by the flesh"—see 7:5; 8:8 (cf. 8:5), but " I am carnal," which is something else. To be "in the flesh" means to be basically controlled by one's sinful human nature. A person so described is not a believer. To be fleshly or carnal, on the other hand, means to be the opposite of what the law is. The law of God is spiritual, perfect, divine. In a sense Paul is unspiritual, imperfect. As I Cor. 3:1, 3 indicates, such a carnal person can still be a Christian.

Moreover, in verse 18 of the section now under discussion the apostle makes an important distinction. By saying, "I know that nothing good dwells in me, *that is, in my flesh,*" is he not clearly implying that there is more to him than his flesh, his sinful human nature? Both verse 18 and verse 25—note contrast between "my mind" and "my flesh" in the latter verse— show that Paul is making a distinction between that which he is with respect to his sinful human nature and that which he is in his more basic inner self. Even a Christian can therefore say, "We know that the law is spiritual, but I am carnal."

The question occurs, however, "What about the second characterization, namely, 'sold as a slave to sin' "? On the surface this description would seem to exclude Paul from the company of the saved; or, if not, it might appear to indicate that when the apostle says "I" he is here not thinking of himself but of somebody else, an unbeliever. On closer inspection, and without in any way doing injustice to the deplorable situation here described, we will, however, have to conclude that it is the apostle Paul, the Christian, who is here speaking, and describing his own state, as well as that of all other believers still dwelling on earth.

In the present connection we should first of all take note of the fact that Paul is not saying that he had sold or abandoned himself to sin, as had been true with respect to King Ahab (I Kings 21:20, 25=LXX III Kings 20:20, 25; II Kings 17:17=LXX IV Kings 17:17). Paul has not sold himself. Someone else has sold him. He, Paul, deplores this situation. It is as if we hear him utter a sigh of agony when he complains, "I am . . . sold as a slave to sin!" Can one who so intensely laments his remaining sinfulness be anything but a true believer? When Paul confesses,

"I am carnal, sold as a slave to sin,"

does he not remind us of another contrite child of God, who sighed:

"Surely I have been a sinner from birth,

A sinner from the time my mother conceived me"? (Ps. 51:5).

Does this mean, then, that when David made this confession he was not a believer? See also Luke 18:13, 14.

When Rom. 7:14 is interpreted in light of verses 22–25, it becomes clear that the one who in verse 14 deplores his sinful condition is the same

---

flesh"—in II Cor. 3:3 note contrast between *stone* and *flesh*—, and not the more usual σαρ-κικός; yet, as used here in Rom. 7:14, σάρκινος must mean *carnal*, that is unspiritual, worldly. Proof: (a) "sold as a slave to sin"; (b) in I Cor. 3:1 σάρκινος is contrasted with πνευματικός; hence, *carnal* with *spiritual*.

person who in the chapter's closing verses expresses his delight in the law of God, looks forward with impassioned and irresistible longing to the day of his deliverance from his present momentous inner struggle, and is filled with the blessed assurance that Victory is bound to come; in fact, that "in principle" it is here already!

However, for the present, the Christian is living in an era in which two ages, the old and the new, overlap. There was a time when Paul was *exclusively a sinner*. There will be a time when he will be *exclusively a saint*. Right now, as he is dictating this letter, he is *a sinner-saint*. A "saint," to be sure; but also still a "sinner"; hence the tension, the inner conflict. It is a struggle which every true believer experiences, and about which the apostle continues to speak, as follows:

15. Indeed, that which I am accomplishing I do not approve of. For not what I want (to do), that do I practice, but what I loathe, that I do.[201]

In view of the fact that the speaker ("I") is serving "in newness of the Spirit" (verse 6) and heartily confesses God's law to be holy, and his commandment holy, righteous, and good (verse 12, and cf. verses 22–25, to which reference has just been made), it is again obvious that Paul, the sincere and humble child of God, is continuing to speak.

As a grateful, warm-hearted believer, his ethical standard is nothing short of moral-spiritual perfection. Cf. Phil. 3:12–14. But when—shall we say at the close of day—he reviews what he has accomplished, he is disgusted with himself: God has done so much for him. He (Paul) has done so little in return. Not only that, but the little he has accomplished is tainted with sin. His aim is so much higher than his reach.

It is indeed wonderful to say with Longfellow:

> Not enjoyment and not sorrow
> Is our destined end or way,
> But to live that each tomorrow
> Finds us farther than today.

---

201. κατεργάζομαι. As is clear from other instances of its use, the meaning of this verb is basically *to work out, to accomplish;* hence also: *to bring about, to produce.* The emphasis is generally on effective action. Thus Rom. 1:27 makes mention of persons who *perpetrate* indecent acts; and 2:9 castigates evil-*doers.* According to 4:15 the law *produces* wrath. According to 5:3 suffering *brings about* perseverance. See also 7:8, 13.

γινώσκω. For the use of this verb (basically: *to know*) in the sense of *to recognize, acknowledge* (perhaps Rom. 7:15) see Josephus, *Antiquities* V. 112 ("They acknowledge but one God"). A slight transition in meaning produces: *to approve of, acknowledge as one's own;* see Matt. 7:23; I Cor. 8:3; Gal. 4:9. *To approve of* is probably the meaning here in Rom. 7:15. See the explanation.

πράσσω. Basically this verb means *to do, to practice, to be occupied with.* It is therefore a synonym of ποιέω, in one of the latter's meanings. In the New Testament πράσσω is often used in an unfavorable sense (Luke 22:23; John 3:20; Acts 19:36; 25:11, 25; Rom. 1:32; 2:1–3; 13:4; II Cor. 12:21; Gal. 5:21). In Rom. 7:19 note the contrast: *do good—practice* evil.

However, there are exceptions. In Rom. 9:11 and II Cor. 5:10 the verb πράσσω is used with objects both good and bad; while the objects mentioned in Acts 26:20; Rom. 2:25; and Phil. 4:9 are wholly good.

But what if that ideal is not always realized? The merely *moral* man may be able to deceive himself into thinking that he is, after all, doing quite well. It is precisely *the Christian* who will say with Paul, "Indeed, that which I am accomplishing I do not approve of. For not what I want (to do) do I practice, but what I loathe, that I do."[202]

And is not this the very conflict also mentioned in Gal. 5:17, where the same apostle states, ". . . the flesh sets its desire against the Spirit, and the Spirit against the flesh: for these are opposed to each other, so that these very things y o u may wish to be doing, those y o u are not doing"?

There are those, however, who have objected that Gal. 5:17 and Rom. 7:14-25 cannot be referring to the same inner conflict, because while the former passage mentions the Spirit, the latter does not. But why would it have been necessary for Paul to repeat his mention of the Holy Spirit, as the Author of sanctification? Are not the references to the Spirit in Rom. 2:29; 7:6 sufficient? They are, unless they are interpreted as indicating a "spirit" other than the divine. But in view of such parallel passages as II Cor. 3:6, 17, this position would be difficult to defend.

I repeat, therefore, what I wrote in N.T.C. on Galatians, p. 215: "Paul, writing as a converted man (Rom. 7:14-25) and recording his *present state of grace* experiences . . . complains bitterly about the fact that he practices that in which his soul no longer takes delight; in fact, practices that which his regenerated self *hates*."

16. But if I do the very thing I do not want to do, I agree that the law is good.

But is there not an easy way out of this painful conflict? Why not simply throw out the law? Why not call it bad and reject it?

Though, on the surface, this might seem to be an easy solution, in reality it is not a solution at all. The Holy Spirit is dwelling in Paul's heart (and in the hearts of all true believers). So very close is the relationship between that Spirit and Paul's own spirit that the apostle is able to say, "The law is good. It is excellent! I must not disobey it!" And though Paul does indeed disobey, and is therefore experiencing a bitter struggle, his own voice and that of the Holy Spirit are joined in a marvelous *symphony* when they eulogize the law.

17-20. But, this being so, then it is not I who accomplish it, but it is sin dwelling in me. For I know that nothing good dwells in me, that is, in my flesh. For I have the desire to do what is good, but I cannot accomplish it. For what I do is not the good I want to do; no, it is the evil I do not want to do, this I practice. But if I am doing the very thing I do not want to do, it is no longer I who am doing it, but it is sin dwelling in me.

The logical deduction—note the words "this being so"—derived from the

---

202. It is clear that in this statement the verb γινώσκω is in *apposition* with θέλω, and in *opposition* to μισῶ. Therefore, from among a series of possible meanings for the verb γινώσκω, the meaning *approve* (of) is probably the best.

situation as described in verse 16 is that, since Paul himself does not want to act contrary to God's will, the sins committed should be *basically* ascribed not to him but to sin. It is *sinful nature,* here and elsewhere called *the flesh,* which is the real culprit, the actual offender. It is that wicked squatter, dwelling with Paul in the latter's own house (his soul) who is at the bottom of all this inquity. It is that intruder who so often makes it impossible for Paul to do the good he wants to do.

It may seem as if Paul, by means of this line of reasoning, is disavowing responsibility for his own sins. That, however, is not actually the case. Two facts remain true: (a) even the squatter is not a total stranger but is Paul's own sinful nature; and (b) a wicked intruder, an illegal squatter, must not be allowed to remain!

The latter part of verse 18 and the entire verse 19 are similar in meaning to the thought expressed in verse 15. Verse 20 substantially repeats verses 16a, 17.

21. So I discover this law: When I want to do good, evil lies close at hand.

The word "So" shows that the apostle here summarizes the contents of the preceding verses (14-20). It is immediately clear that when he here uses the word "law," he is not thinking of the Ten Commandments. "Law," as here used, must mean something like *operating rule* or *governing principle.* For more on this see verse 23.

The inflexible "law" to which reference is here made, and which the author of this epistle—as well as every believer—is constantly discovering, is this: "When I want to do good, evil lies close at hand." In view of the fact that, according to verses 17, 20, sinful human nature has established its residence in Paul's own house (his soul), and has done this with a wicked purpose, the statement "evil lies close at hand," is indeed very logical. This "evil," here personified, may be lying down, but is certainly not sleeping. It is pictured as if it were watching the apostle to see whether he is about to carry out a good intention. Whenever such a noble thought or suggestion enters Paul's heart, evil immediately interrupts in order to turn the good deed into its opposite.

In complete harmony with verse 21 the author continues:

22, 23. For according to my inner being I delight in God's law; but I see in my (bodily) members a different law, waging war against the law of my mind and making me a prisoner of the law of sin which is in my members.[203]

---

203. συνήδομαι, not here "rejoice with" but "rejoice in." See M. M., p. 607; cf. Liddell & Scott, *Greek-English Lexicon,* Vol. II, p. 1715. For a different view see A. T. Robertson, *Word Pictures,* Vol. IV, p. 370; also L.N.T. (A. and G.), p. 797.

ἀντιστρατευόμενον, acc. s. masc. pres. participle of ἀντιστρατεύομαι, to wage war against.

αἰχμαλωτίζοντα (same construction as the above), from αἰχμαλωτίζω (from αἰχμή, spear, and ἁλίσκομαι, to capture); hence, originally, to capture with the spear; then, as here, simply:

The word *"For"* shows that what is found in verses 22, 23 explains the contents of verse 21. The conflict between good and evil mentioned in the earlier verse is amplified and clarified in the present passage.

The apostle speaks of two opposing "laws." The first is "God's law." Though there is a wide difference in opinion with respect to the meaning of this expression, yet in view of the fact that Paul has been referring to God's law as being the revelation of his good and perfect will, and has even quoted a specific commandment of the Decalog (see verses 7, 8, 12), how can there be any good reason to doubt that also here in verse 22 the expression "God's law" indicates that very system of moral principles or rules that is summarized in the ten commandments and even more concisely in Matt. 22:37–40 (and parallels)?

It should be borne in mind, however, that for the believer that divine law is not a dead letter, and it certainly is not in any sense a means of salvation. On the contrary, for him it is *the ruling principle* for the expression of his gratitude.

Understood in this sense, it is not at all strange that he "delights" in God's law. Right-minded children delight in discovering a way in which they can show their parents, or other benefactors, how much they love them! For the manner in which God's children express this delight in God's law see above, p. 214.

Now the apostle states that he delights in God's law according to his "inner being." When he uses such phraseology he is not copying Plato or the Stoics. He is not expressing a contrast between man's rational nature and his lower appetites. With Paul the inner man is the one that is hidden from the public gaze. It indicates *the heart.* It is here that a new principle of life has been implanted by the Holy Spirit. By means of this implantation the sinner has become a *new* man, a person who is being daily transformed into the image of Christ. In this connection study such passages as II Cor. 4:16; Eph. 3:16; Col. 3:9, 10.

In his "bodily members" (more about that in a moment) Paul sees a different law, one that is constantly waging war against the law of his mind and is making him a prisoner of the law of sin.

If "God's law" should be interpreted as *a governing principle,* as has just now been shown, logic requires that also this "different law" must be thus explained. Clearly—as the apostle states in so many words—that "different law" is the law of sin. How it operates has been indicated in verse 21. That it

---

to capture, to carry off as a captive or prisoner. The verb also occurs in Luke 21:24; II Cor. 5:10; II Tim. 3:6. See N.T.C. on Luke, p. 947.

It is clear that Paul is here making use of military metaphors. For another possible example see on 6:13, pp. 202, 203. If the word ἀφορμή (7:8, 11) is rendered "base of operations," this would be still another such figure of speech. On military metaphors see also N.T.C. on Ephesians, pp. 271–280.

is making the apostle, and all true believers everywhere, prisoners is probably another way of expressing the thought of verse 14b.

Again and again "the law of sin" causes the author of this letter to do what he does not want to do, and again and again it prevents him from doing what he wants to do, facts about which he bitterly complains, and which he deeply and sincerely deplores.

Emphasis should be focused on the phrase "the law of sin which is *in my members.*" Often this phrase is either passed by in silence or touched on very lightly. Nevertheless, it could be more important than is generally realized. That it must have been rather significant to the mind of the writer is clear from the fact that he makes frequent use of it. See 6:13 (twice); 6:19 (twice); 7:5; 7:23 (twice); all this in addition to the figurative (or at least largely figurative) use of this expression, for which see Rom. 12:5; I Cor. 6:15; 12:12, 27; Eph. 4:16, 25; 5:30.

In addition to the comments made previously with respect to these bodily *parts* or *members* (see on 6:13, 19; 7:5; pp. 202, 206, 207) note, therefore, also the following: Paul was an ardent missionary. His soul was wrapped up in his work. See Rom. 15:17–29; I Cor. 9:22; II Cor. 5:20, 21. To win people for Christ, to the glory of God, meant more to him than even his personal freedom (Phil. 1:12 f.). He desired intensely that others too would share this enthusiasm (Phil. 1:4, 18).

Now he was well aware of the fact that the way to reach his audiences was through his and their bodily organs. Very important were: the swiftness of his *feet,* the utterances of his *lips,* the look in his *eyes,* the movements of his *hands,* the attentiveness of their *ears,* etc., the more so because such communication devices as airplanes, eye-glasses, hearing-aids, etc., had not yet been invented.

Unsurprisingly, therefore, in both the Old Testament and the New, far greater emphasis is placed on bodily parts or members than in present-day literature. In many of the following passages would we today even make mention of the involved bodily members?[204]

mouth

Gen. 24:57; Job 3:1; Ps. 17:10   Matt. 5:2; 13:35; Luke 11:54

lips

Lev. 5:4; Num. 30:6; Deut. 23:23   Matt. 15:8; Heb. 13:15; I Peter 3:10

tongue

II Sam. 23:2; Job 6:30; Ps. 35:28   Acts 2:26; Phil. 2:11; I Peter 3:10

---

204. Those who are unable to read the original are advised to look up these references in the A.V., since in the more recent translations the names of these bodily parts are sometimes omitted.

feet

II Sam. 22:37; I Kings 14:6, 12   Luke 1:79; Acts 5:2; Heb. 2:8

hands

Gen. 3:22; 8:9; Josh. 2:24   Luke 21:12; Acts 7:41; Heb. 10:31

eyes

Deut. 7:16; Job 7:7; Isa. 13:18   Luke 11:34; I Cor. 2:9; Rev. 1:7

ears

Neh. 1:6; Job 4:12; 13:1   Matt. 10:27; Luke 12:3; I Cor. 2:9

A striking instance of this constant reference to bodily parts occurs in this very epistle to the Romans (3:13–18), where tongue, lips, mouth, feet, and eyes, are mentioned in one breath, in quotations from the Old Testament.

In *mentioning* the physical parts and qualities the *possibility* must not be ruled out that the spiritual part of man's being may have been included. So interpreted, what the writer is saying is this: "If I could only serve God in a thoroughly unhampered manner! If only *all* my faculties of body and soul could be made effective for him and his cause!" In any event the continuation is understandable:

24. Wretched man that I am! Who will rescue me from this body of death?

The writer genuinely deplores the fact that due to the law of sin still operating in him, he is unable to serve God as completely and wholeheartedly as he desires.

The poignant grief here expressed is definitely that of a believer. No unbeliever would ever be able to be so filled with sorrow because of his sins! The author of the outcry is Paul, speaking for every child of God.

The cry he utters is one of distress, but not of despair, as verse 25 proves. Paul suffers agony, to be sure, the wretchedness brought about by strenuous exertion; that is, by trying hard, but never satisfactorily succeeding, to live in complete harmony with God's will but failing again and again. He is looking forward eagerly to the time when this struggle will have ended.

With that in mind he yearns to be rescued from "this body of death," that is, from the body in its present condition, subject to the ravages of sin and death.[205] He knows that as long as he lives in this present "body of humilia-

---

205. The correct translation of the phrase τὸ σῶμα (here gen. τοῦ σώματος, after ἐκ) τοῦ θανάτου τούτου is probably not "the body of this death" but "this body of death." Reasons:

a. The immediately preceding verse clearly refers to members or parts of Paul's physical body.

b. Previously there has been a reference to "y o u r mortal body" (6:12).

c. In 8:23 the apostle is still speaking about a physical body.

For the opposite view see Murray, *op. cit.*, p. 268.

tion" (Phil. 3:21) the terrible struggle will be continued. But once the life in that body ceases, the state of sinless glory will commence; first for the soul, then also for the body.

So he answers his own question with a jubilant: **25. Thanks be to God through Jesus Christ our Lord!** He speaks with full assurance. He knows that when a believer dies, this death is gain. To be with Christ is better by far (Phil. 1:21, 23). Sin will have been left behind forever. The conflict will have ended, never to return. In the language of the apostle John, nothing that is impure will enter the Holy City (Rev. 21:27). Moreover, the time is coming when even the body will be redeemed (Rom. 8:23; cf. John 5:28, 29).

In his jubilant thanksgiving the apostle goes back to the Source of every blessing. He exclaims, "Thanks be to *God!*" See John 3:16; Rom. 8:32; II Cor. 9:15. He realizes too that it was through the One whom he mentions by his full name *Jesus* (Savior), *Christ* (Anointed One), *our Lord* (Sovereign Ruler, Owner), that salvation, full and free, was obtained. Obtained, moreover, not only for Paul but for all believers. And so he looks forward to the day of glory for them all (I Cor. 15:56, 57; II Tim. 4:8).

Summing up the entire argument, Paul concludes this chapter by writing, **So then, I myself with my mind serve the law of God, but with my flesh the law of sin.**

Note the sharp contrast:

a. the law of God *versus* the law of sin;

b. my mind *versus* my flesh.

Is the apostle saying, then, that his *mind* (verse 25b) or *inner being* (verse 22) serves *the law of God* (verses 14, 16, 22); but his *flesh* (verses 18, 25b) or *indwelling sin* (sinful human nature, verses 17, 20), serves *the law of sin* (verse 23)?

Here we should be very careful, for the writer does not consider such things as *mind* and *flesh* to be independent beings. On the contrary, as has been pointed out previously, both of these belong to Paul. It is he himself—that is, it is the believer himself—who remains fully responsible, as is clear from a careful reading of verses 15, 16, 19.

On the other hand, it is also clear that these two (mind, flesh; Paul the saint, Paul the sinner) are not strictly co-ordinate. No, it is with his inner being or mind that Paul wants to do the will of God (see verses 15, 16, 18, 20, 21, 22). The flesh is the intruder, who is being driven out and will certainly lose the battle. That is due not to Paul's goodness but to God's grace, as the apostle loudly and cheerfully proclaims by shouting, "Thanks be to God through Jesus Christ our Lord." Compare I Cor. 15:57, also written by the triumphant believer, Paul!

We see, therefore, that the passage (verse 25b), considered in both of its parts—(a) "I myself with my mind serve the law of God"; and (b) "but with my flesh the law of sin"—links beautifully with chapter 8, note verse 10 of that chapter; and also that verse 25a—"Thanks be to God through Jesus

Christ our Lord!"—is a very appropriate introduction to 8:1, "There is therefore now no condemnation for those who are in Christ Jesus."

For more on Rom. 7:14–25; see pp. 245, 246, 249, 250.

Practical Lessons Derived from Romans 7

Verses 4 and 6

"So, my brothers, y o u too were made dead to the law through the body of Christ, so that y o u might belong to another, even to him who was raised from the dead, in order that we might bear fruit for God . . . We have been released from the law, so that we serve in newness of (the) Spirit, not in oldness of (the) letter."

It is clear from this that the genuine Christian life is not that of bondage but that of freedom. It is not motivated by external regulations but by love for the One to whom believers belong, even Christ. It is not guided by selfish interests but by the Spirit. And it is not barren but fruitful.

Verse 7

"What shall we say then? Is the law sin? Not at all! On the contrary, I would not have come to know sin, had it not been through the law."

Often the statement is heard, "We have nothing to do with the law." Or "The law was for the Jews. It is not for us." That is not the language Paul uses. For him God's holy law was of value in more ways than one. See above, p. 184. But it cannot save. It can and does reveal our sinfulness, and because of its very impotency, it points to Another, namely, Christ, as our Savior. See Rom. 7:13; Gal. 3:24.

Verses 15 and 20

"For not what I want (to do), that do I practice, but what I loathe, that I do . . . But if I am doing the very thing I do not want to do, it is no longer I who am doing it, but it is sin dwelling in me."

A very frequent and practical question is, "Am I a child of God?" Would not the answer be, "Do you recognize yourself in the words quoted just now?" If you do, then will you not also be able to say, "Wretched man that I am! Who will rescue me from this body of death? *Thanks be to God through Jesus Christ our Lord!*"? Those who can say that are surely Christians.

A dear child of God told the author of this book, "whenever I read Rom. 7:14–25, I see myself." By sovereign grace this brother had within his heart the blessed assurance, "Jesus is mine."

Summary of Chapter 7

Just as a woman, by means of a death (that of her husband) is released from her marriage bond and allowed to marry another man, so also by a death (the believers' death with Christ) God's children are released from indebtedness to the law, the latter's "bill" having been fully paid by Christ's voluntary and vicarious sacrifice. Believers have, accordingly, obtained *lib-*

erty. This liberty is a freedom *from* and a freedom *for.* It is a freedom *from* the obligation to keep the law in order to be saved, and is therefore also a freedom *from* the curse which the law pronounces upon the disobedient. But it is at the same time a freedom *for* or *with a view to,* a freedom *in order* to render service to God "in newness of the Spirit, not in oldness of the letter" (verses 1–6).

Release from the law, in the sense indicated, does not imply that the law is sinful. On the contrary, the law is good and useful, for it lays bare our sinfulness. It puts to death our sinful pride and vaunted self-sufficiency. "I would not have come to know sin, had it not been through the law. For I would not have known what it meant to covet if the law had not said, 'You shall not covet.'" Therefore, "In itself the law is holy, and the commandment holy and righteous and good."

Paul has stated that the commandment slays us. But how can something that is good bring death? The apostle answers that it is not the commandment, operating by itself, that slays us; it is our transgression of the commandment that does this. Hence, the real cause of death is sin. It remains true, however, that the very whiteness (moral-spiritual purity) of God's commandment causes the blackness of our sin to stand out all the more sharply.

By saying such things as "*Once I was alive* apart from the law, but when the commandment came, sin sprang to life and *I died* . . . the commandment *killed me* . . .," Paul gives us a glimpse into his own experience prior to, during, and shortly after his conversion (verses 7–13).

In verses 14–25, which section follows logically upon verses 7–13, Paul, the believer, reflecting on his own situation and that of others like him, discusses *The Wretched Man's Struggle and Victory.* He does not find fault with God's holy law when it exposes him, even Paul, and others like him, as being still polluted with sin. He clearly and openly confesses, "We know that the law is spiritual, but I am carnal, sold as a slave to sin." He admits, therefore, that although absolute goodness can be ascribed to God's law, it cannot be predicated of himself, Paul. He knows that as long as he is on this sinful earth, he is *carnal,* that is, unspiritual, worldly, far from perfect. Being a true child of God, the apostle genuinely deplores the fact that he had been sold as a slave to sin. He confesses, "Indeed, that which I am accomplishing I do not approve of. For not what I want (to do), that do I practice, but what I loathe, that I do . . . For what I do is not the good I want to do; no, it is the evil I do not want to do, this I practice."

Is not this the very conflict which is also mentioned in Gal. 5:17, where the same apostle states, "The flesh sets its desire against the Spirit, and the Spirit against the flesh: for these are opposed to each other, so that those very things y o u may wish to be doing, those y o u are not doing"? And is not this realization of imperfection similar to that expressed in Phil. 3:12, 13, "Not that I have already gotten hold or have already been made perfect . . . I do not count myself yet to have laid hold"?

However, the very fact that in his inner being Paul does not really want to do what is contrary to God's will but loathes this situation, fills him with courage, so that he is able to exclaim,

"For according to my inner being I delight in God's law; but I see in my (bodily) members a different law, waging war against the law of my mind and making me a prisoner of the law of sin which is in my members. Wretched man that I am! Who will rescue me from this body of death? Thanks be to God through Jesus Christ our Lord!" The fact, frankly admitted by him in a summarizing statement, namely, "So then, I myself with my mind serve the law of God, but with my flesh the law of sin," does not cancel the essence of the assurance of victory expressed in those memorable words, "Thanks be to God through Jesus Christ our Lord!" (verses 14–25).

Outline (continued)

Justification by Faith

4a. *"No condemnation" for those in Christ Jesus. The indwelling Spirit imparts life to them, assures them of the realization of their hope of eagerly awaited glory, helps them in their infirmities, and intercedes for them, so that everything turns out for their welfare. The three groanings.*
"And we know that all things work together for good to those who love
God, that is, to those who are called according to his purpose."
8:1–30

4b. *It produces the fruit of **super-invincibility**; i.e., of being more than conquerors.*
"No, in all these things we are more than conquerors
through him who loved us"
8:31–39

CHAPTER 8

8 1 There is therefore now no condemnation for those who are in Christ Jesus. 2 For through Christ Jesus the law of the Spirit of life has set me[206] free from the law of sin and of death. 3 For what the law could not do, because it was weak through the flesh, God did: by sending his own Son in the likeness of sinful flesh and for sin, he condemned sin in the flesh, 4 in order that the righteous requirement of the law might be fully met in us, who do not walk according to the flesh but according to the Spirit. 5 For those who live according to the flesh set their minds on the things of the flesh, but those who live according to the Spirit set their minds on the things of the Spirit. 6 Now the mind of the flesh is death, but the mind of the Spirit is life and peace; 7 because the mind of the flesh is hostility to God, for it does not submit to the law of God, nor can it do so. 8 And those who are in the flesh cannot please God.

9 Y o u, however, are not in the flesh but in the Spirit, seeing that God's Spirit dwells in y o u. (Anyone who does not possess Christ's Spirit does not belong to Christ.) 10 But if Christ is in y o u, though the body is dead because of sin, yet the Spirit is life because of (y o u r) justification. 11 And if the Spirit of him who raised Jesus from the dead dwells in y o u, he who raised Christ from the dead will also impart life to y o u r mortal bodies through his Spirit, who dwells in y o u.

12 Therefore, brothers, we have an obligation, but it is not to the flesh, to live according to its standard. 13 For if y o u live according to its standard y o u are doomed to die; but if, by the Spirit, y o u put to death the disgraceful deeds of the body, y o u will live. 14 For as many as are being led by the Spirit of God, these are sons of God. 15 For y o u have not received a spirit of slavery, to fill y o u once more with dread, but y o u have received the Spirit of adoption, who moves us to cry, "Abba!," that is, "Father!" 16 This Spirit himself bears witness with our spirit that we are children of God.

17 And if children, then heirs, heirs of God and fellow-heirs with Christ; since the fact that we are now sharing in his sufferings means that (hereafter) we shall share in his glory. 18 For I consider that the sufferings of this present time are not worthy to be compared with the glory that is to be revealed in us.

19 For the creation, with outstretched head, is eagerly looking forward to the revelation of the sons of God. 20 For it was not by its own choice that the creation was subjected to futility, but (it was) because of him who subjected it, in hope, 21 because the creation itself too will be set free from its bondage to decay, so as to share the glorious liberty of the children of God. 22 For we know that the whole creation, with one accord, has been, and still is, groaning as in the pain of childbirth.

23 Not only this, but also we ourselves, who possess the firstfruits of the Spirit, even we ourselves groan within ourselves, as we eagerly await our adoption, that is, the redemption of our bodies. 24 For it was in hope that we were saved; but when once something hoped for is seen it is no longer an object of hope, for who hopes for what he sees? 25 But since we hope for that which we do not see, we wait for it with patient endurance.

---

206. Or you.

26 And in the same way the Spirit too is helping us in our weakness, for we do not know what we ought to pray, but the Spirit himself intercedes for us with unspoken groanings. 27 And he who searches the hearts knows what is the Spirit's intention, that he is interceding for the saints in harmony with God's will.

28 And we know that to those who love God all things work together for good, that is, to those who are called according to (his) purpose. 29 For whom he foreknew, he also foreordained to be conformed to the image of his Son, so that he might be the firstborn among many brothers; 30 and whom he foreordained, these he also called; and whom he called, these he also justified; and whom he justified, these he also glorified.

4a. *"No condemnation" for those in Christ Jesus. The indwelling Spirit imparts life to them, assures them of the realization of their hope of eagerly awaited glory, helps them in their infirmities, and intercedes for them, so that everything turns out for their welfare. The three groanings.*

"And we know that all things work together for good to those who love God, that is, to those who are called according to his purpose."

8:1–30

As was true with respect to chapters 5, 6, and 7, so also chapter 8 points to a result of the believers' justification by faith. The fact that justification is indeed at the center of Paul's thinking is clear from the opening words, "There is now no condemnation," for condemnation is the opposite of justification.

Moreover, as has been stated previously, Paul himself seems to endorse the co-ordination of chapters 5, 6, and 7, causing each to close with the same (or a very similar) phrase. This holds too for chapter 8, ending with "in Christ Jesus our Lord."

The question as to the theme of this chapter is easily answered. It is not expressed immediately, though everything in verses 1–30, and again in verses 31–36, leads up to it; as, for example, verse 28, printed above the present section, indicates. The central thought, which is also the fourth main fruit of justification by faith, is found in the words, "No, in all these things we are more than conquerors through him who loved us" (verse 37). Note: not merely conquerors but *more than conquerors;* not merely invincible but *super-invincible.*

1. There is therefore now no condemnation for those who are in Christ Jesus.[207]

The statement, "There is therefore now no condemnation" is closely connected with the main thrust of Paul's previous reasoning, taken as a unit. See especially verses 1:16, 17; 3:21, 24; 5:1, 2, 6–8, 15–21; 7:6. In these passages the apostle has been setting forth the fact that, through Christ's debt-removing and sanctifying self-sacrifice, believers have been released from the curse of the law. Because of the entrance of sin (cf. 8:3) the law cannot now be regarded as a means of obtaining salvation, nor does

---

207. The continuation (as a whole or in part): "who walk not after the flesh but after the Spirit" lacks sufficient textual support, and is probably an interpolation from verse 4.

it have the power to condemn believers. Rather, the law is the means for the expression of their gratitude. As such it is the object of their delight, even though, as 7:14 f. has shown, in the present life complete obedience is impossible.

This does not mean that there is no connection between 8:1 f. and the immediately preceding context. As has been indicated—see pp. 238, 239—there is a close connection between "Thanks be to God through Christ Jesus our Lord" (7:25a) and "There is therefore now no condemnation, etc." (8:1). But even what Paul says in 7:25b—and more generally in 6:1-7:25—about the enslaving power of sin, is not absent from his mind in 8:1, as the sequel (8:1 f.) indicates. For Paul "no condemnation" means freedom not only from sin's *guilt* but also from its *enslaving power.*

To be sure, a distinction must be drawn between justification and sanctification. But this distinction must never become a separation. Calvin has made this clear by stating, "As Christ cannot be divided, so also these two blessings which we receive together in him are also inseparable" (*Institutes* III, xi, 6).

In line with this twofold reference of the words "no condemnation" is the phrase "in Christ Jesus." What Paul is saying is that for those who not only *forensically* are in Christ Jesus—the guilt of their sins having been removed by his death—but also *spiritually*—the sanctifying influences of his Spirit dominating their lives, there is *now* (=consequently) no condemnation. For them there is justification and therefore salvation full and free (see 8:29, 30). For more on the phrase "in Christ Jesus" see above on 3:24, p. 131, and on 6:3 f., p. 196. See also N.T.C. on Ephesians, pp. 70, 71.

Justification and sanctification always go together. The fact that the expression "no condemnation" implies both pardon and purification is also clear from verse

2. For through Christ Jesus the law of the Spirit of life has set me free from the law of sin and of death.[208]

Paul speaks about "the law of the Spirit of life." That the Holy Spirit is life in his very essence and also imparts life, both physical and spiritual, is

---

208. Technical questions that should be touched upon are the following:

a. What does "through Christ Jesus" modify: "the law of the Spirit of life"? Or "has set me free"? The contents of verses 3 and 4, showing that it was through the sending of God's Son that the law was fulfilled (so that sinners might be set free) favors the latter construction.

b. Does "of life" modify "the law" or does it go with "the Spirit"? I see no reason to depart from the rule that, unless there is cause to do otherwise, a modifier should be construed with the noun that is nearest to it. Besides, in ever so many passages Scripture associates the Holy Spirit with the impartation of life.

c. Should we read "has set *me* free" or "has set *you* free: με or σε? Textual evidence, though somewhat favoring σε (א B G), is not entirely conclusive. Since from 7:7 on the apostle has so very frequently been referring to himself, με seems more natural. On the other hand, a change of style from the more strictly personal to the far more general has already occurred (see 8:1). This may account for the fact that even the reading ἡμᾶς (us) has some support. The matter is not very important. We may rest assured that through Christ Jesus the law of the Spirit of life has set free *all* who place their trust in the Savior: you, me, us.

clear from ever so many passages of Scripture. The basis for this doctrine is probably found already in Gen. 1:1; Ps. 51:11; 104:30. For closer references see John 6:63; II Cor. 3:6; Gal. 6:8; and do not forget Rom. 8:11. *The law of the Spirit of life* is the forceful and effective operation of the Holy Spirit in the hearts and lives of God's children. It is the very opposite of "the law of sin and death," for which see on 7:23, 25. Just as the law of sin produces death, so also the law, or ruling factor, of the Spirit of life brings about life. Cf. Rom. 6:23. It does this "through Christ Jesus," that is, on the basis of the merits of his atonement, and by means of the vitalizing power of union with him.

The question arises, "If in Rom. 7:14–8:2 Paul throughout speaks about himself as a believer, how can he say not only, "I am carnal, sold as a slave to sin . . . a prisoner" (7:14, 23); but also, "Through Christ Jesus the law of the Spirit of life has set me free from the law of sin and death"? How can a slave and prisoner also be a free person? Does not this very contradiction show that we have erroneously interpreted Rom. 7:14, 23?

The answer is, "Not at all." On the contrary, when we read these passages—both 7:14, 23 and 8:1, 2, we say, "How wonderful is the Word of God! What a true picture it draws of the person I really am! On the one hand I am a slave, a prisoner, for sin has such control over me that I cannot lead a sinless life (Jer. 17:9; Matt. 6.12; I John 1:8, 10). Yet, on the other hand, I am a free person, for though Satan tries with all his might and trickery to keep me from doing what is right—such as trusting God for my salvation, invoking him in prayer, rejoicing in him, working for his causes, etc., he cannot throughout stop me from doing so. He cannot completely prevent me from experiencing the peace of God that transcends all understanding. The sense of victory, which I possess in principle even now and will possess in perfection in the future, sustains me in all my struggles. I rejoice in the freedom which Christ has earned for me!" (cf. Gal. 5:1).

When an interpreter of 7:21—8:2 limits Christian experience to what is found in 7:22, 25a, 8:1, 2, leaving out 7:21, 23, 24, 25b, does he not resemble the musician who tries to play an elaborate piece on an organ with a very restricted number of octaves, or on a harp with many broken strings?

3, 4. For what the law could not do, because it was weak through the flesh, God did: by sending his own Son in the likeness of sinful flesh and for sin, he condemned sin in the flesh, in order that the righteous requirement of the law might be fulfilled in us, who do not walk according to the flesh but according to the Spirit.

a. **For what the law could not do, because it was weak through the flesh, God did.**

The word "For" indicates that what, according to verses 3, 4, God accomplished by sending his Son into the world, is the basis of the believer's freedom (verse 2). The law was unable to provide this basis. That, however, was not the law's fault. Sinful human nature ("the flesh," see p. 217) was to blame. It was that which made perfect obedience impossible. Does this mean, then, that sinners are never going to be saved, and that God's plan, made before the founding of the world (Eph. 1:4), is not going to be carried out? It does not, for—O glorious divine love!—what the law was unable to accomplish God accomplished! It was he who, by sending into the world his own Son to die for sinners, satisfied the demands of justice, thereby setting sinners free and flooding their hearts with love for God and a desire to do his will out of gratitude.

b. by sending *his own* Son.

What depth of feeling, what compassion, what pathos is contained in this expression! Involuntarily our mind travels back to Gen. 22:2 (God addressing Abraham), "Take now your son, your only son, whom you love, Isaac . . . and offer him for a burnt offering. . . ." See also John 3:16, "For *so* loved God the world that his Son, the only-begotten he gave. . . ." Cf. Matt. 21:37.

Philosophers may argue that implied in the doctrine of God's immutability is the fact that the Divine Being cannot experience any emotions. The question may be asked whether that inference does full justice to such passages in this epistle as the present one and 8:32 ("God did not spare his own Son but gave him up"). In order to save us, God did not spare *his own*—yes, his very own, his dear and only—Son. He caused him to descend to hell for us, the hell climaxed at Calvary.[209]

c. in the likeness of sinful flesh.

In his incarnation the divine Son assumed the human nature, so that from that moment on he has two natures, the divine and the human, indissolubly united, yet each retaining its own properties. But he took on that human nature not as it came originally from the hand of the Creator ("and behold it was very good," Gen. 1:31), but *weakened by sin,* though remaining itself without any sin. Note: *not* "in sinful flesh" but "*in the likeness* of sinful flesh." He "emptied himself, assuming the form of a servant" (Phil. 2:7). "Though he was rich, yet for our sake he became poor" (II Cor. 8:9). See also N.T.C. on Philippians, pp. 102–113.

d. and for sin.

Probable meaning: and in order to deal with sin.[210]

e. He condemned sin in the flesh, in order that the righteous requirement[211] of the law might be fulfilled in us.

---

209. For more on this subject of divine emotion see pp. 251, 276, 277, 287.

210. Though it must be granted that περὶ ἁμαρτίας can mean "For a sin-offering" (cf. Lev. 9:2), that sense would seem to be somewhat foreign to the present context.

211. Though the basic notion of justice or rightness is never absent, the various shades of meaning the word δικαίωμα has in the New Testament can be summarized as follows:
   a. righteous demand, requirement (Luke 1:6; Rom. 2:26; 8:4)
   b. righteous deed or act (Rom. 5:18; Rev. 15:4; 19:8)
   c. judicial ordinance, decree, sentence (Rom. 1:32)
   d. justifying sentence, justification (Rom. 5:16)
   e. regulation (Heb. 9:1, 10).

That righteous requirement is clearly indicated in such passages as Lev. 19:18b; Deut. 6:5; Mic. 6:8; Matt. 22:35-40 (cf. Mark 12:28-34; Luke 10:25-28). See also Matt. 23:23; Luke 11:42; Rom. 13:9.

It was in Christ's "flesh," his human nature, that God condemned and punished[212] the sins of his people. It was in his people's place that Jesus bore God's wrath. See Isa. 53:4-6, 8, 11b; Matt. 20:28; Mark 10:45; John 1:29; 10:11, 15; Rom. 5:6-9, 18, 19; II Cor. 5:21; Gal. 3:13. The purpose and result of Christ's work of redemption was that his people, by means of the operation of the Holy Spirit in their hearts and lives, should strive, are striving, to fulfil the law's righteous requirement. Out of gratitude for, and in response to, the outpouring of God's love, they now love God and their neighbor.

f. who do not walk according to the flesh but according to the Spirit.

Such devout conduct, being the result of the Holy Spirit's active indwelling, reveals "the fruit of the Spirit." The opposite way of life, that which is "according to the flesh" stems from men's sinful nature and is characterized by the acts associated with that nature. For both see Gal. 5:16-25. Does not the present passage give a hint with respect to the *obligation* voiced in verses 12, 13?

5-8. For those who live according to the flesh set their minds on the things of the flesh, but those who live according to the Spirit set their minds on the things of the Spirit. Now the mind of the flesh is death, but the mind of the Spirit is life and peace; because the mind of the flesh is hostility to God, for it does not submit to the law of God, nor can it do so. And those who are in the flesh cannot please God.

As the word "For" indicates, verse 5 (in a sense verses 5-8 considered as a unit) gives a further description of the two classes of people to whom reference was made in verse 4b: (a) those who walk according to the flesh (their existence *implied* in verse 4b), and (b) those who walk according to the Spirit (their existence *mentioned* in verse 4b).

Those who live according to the flesh allow their lives to be basically determined by their sinful human nature. They set their minds on—are most deeply interested in, constantly talk about, engage and glory in—the things pertaining to the flesh, that is, to sinful human nature.

Those who live according to the Spirit, and therefore submit to the Spirit's direction, concentrate their attention on, and specialize in, whatever is dear to the Spirit. In the conflict between God and sinful human nature the first group *sides with*[213] human nature; the second sides with God.

Paul is reminding the members of the church in Rome that it is impossible to be on both sides at once; that is, the *basic*—this adjective should be

---

212. Here the verb κατακρίνω clearly has the double meaning: to condemn and to punish; to sentence and to carry out that sentence. So also in I Cor. 11:32; II Peter 2:6.

213. φρονοῦσιν, 3rd per. pl. indicat. of φρονέω, to be minded; cf. φρήν, mind. To the Greeks τὰ Ῥωμαίων φρονεῖν meant: to join the party of the Romans, to be on their side.

stressed!—disposition or direction of our lives is either on God's side or on the side of sinful human nature. If a person persists in being worldly, he is on the side of the world and must expect the world's *doom*. On the other hand, if the things concerning God and his kingdom are his *chief* concern, he can expect *life:* sweet communion with God, God's love shed abroad in the heart, joy unspeakable and full of glory, all this and far more forever and ever. See on 2:7, pp. 92, 93.

He can expect *peace:* the inner assurance that past sins are forgiven, that present events, no matter how painful, are being overruled for good, and that nothing that might occur in the future will be able to separate him from the love of God in Christ. Such peace means basic freedom from fear and from restlessness. It implies contentment, sense of security, inner tranquility.

Among the many passages of Scripture where peace is mentioned are Ps. 4:8; 37:37; 119:165; Isa. 26:3; 48:22 (cf. 57:21); Luke 1:79; 2:14; John 14:27; Rom. 5:1; 14:17; 15:13, 33; Phil 4:7, 12. See also the Pauline and Petrine opening salutations. Often, especially in the Old Testament, the line of demarcation between *peace* and *prosperity* or *well-being* is almost imperceptible; cf. Ps. 122:7.

When Paul says, ". . . but the mind of the Spirit is life and peace," does he mean that the believer is *never* disturbed? Does he intend to say that the Christian's heart and mind are *always* filled with *perfect* peace, and therefore, that the exclamation, "Wretched man that I am!" (7:24) could not have been uttered by the child of God?

The answer must be, "Not at all." Though the *basic* disposition of the person whose life is controlled by the Holy Spirit is indeed life and peace, this does not mean that such an individual is no longer deeply sorry for his sin and ardently wishing to be rid of it. *In fact, the more thoroughly he is under the Spirit's control, the knowledge of which gives him life and peace, the more also he will regret and fight against his still remaining sinfulness!*

The idea that the believer is a person who is always staying on an even keel should be given up. A believer's life is not that simple. It is tremendously complex. Are we willing to say that Simon Peter, the man who made the great confession (Matt. 16:16), was not a believer? Read what Jesus said about him (16:17). Nevertheless, it was Peter who afterward denied his Lord, and this not once but thrice!

And the writer of Ps. 77, was he not a believer? Yet, what a struggle he endured!

> The thought of God brought me no peace,
> But rather made my fears increase;
> With sleepless eyes and speechless pain
> My fainting spirit grieved in vain.
> The blessedness of long ago
> Made deeper still my present woe.

> Recalling days when faith was bright,
> When songs of gladness filled my night,
> I pondered o'er my grievous woes
> And searching questioning arose:
> Will God cast off and nevermore
> His favor to my soul restore?

The Lord answers his plea, so that his response is:

> These doubts and fears that troubled me
> Were born of my infirmity.
> Though I am weak, God is most high,
> And on his goodness I rely;
> Of all his wonders I will tell,
> And on his deeds my thoughts shall dwell.

Does this mean, then, that the believer is "a split personality"? When this term is used to indicate a personality structure composed of two or more behavior patterns, each apparently operating independently of the other(s), it would, of course, be improper to use it in connection with the present subject. And since we cannot always know in what sense this term is used, might it not be best to avoid it altogether in the present context?

However, according to the plain language of Scripture, and the testimony of ever so many Christians, even the believer may experience a tremendous struggle between "the old man" and "the new man," between doubt and trust, unrest and peace. In addition to Ps. 77 see also Ps. 73; Gal. 5:17; Eph. 4:22f.; 6:10f.; Heb. 12:4. To be sure, the Christian is comforted by Isa. 26:3, "Thou wilt keep him in perfect peace whose mind is stayed on thee," but during his earthly life the believer's mind is not always stayed on God. It is not always steadfast.

As long as Peter's faith was fixed on Jesus he was able to walk on water, "But when he saw the wind he was afraid and . . . cried out, 'Lord, save me!'" (Matt. 14:29, 30).

It is clear, therefore, that the interpretation of Rom. 7:14–25 which this interpreter, in common with many others and with the Evangelical Confessions, holds, must stand.

Nevertheless, when one compares the mind of unbelievers with that of believers, as Paul does in 8:5–8, the contrast is striking, for *basically* the mind of believers, that is, the mind of the Spirit, is life and peace. The very opposite is true with respect to the mind of unbelievers, a mind that is hostile to God. And since this is true, it stands to reason that the fruit of this mind or disposition is death (verse 6).

Such a mind is self-centered, which explains the fact that it does not submit itself to God's law. In fact, as long as it continues to concentrate its attention upon itself, it is, of course, not even able to submit to God. Those people who are "in the flesh," that is, who in their affections, purposes, thoughts, words, and deeds, are basically controlled by their sinful nature, are unable to please God.

It is interesting and instructive to note how often Scripture, especially Paul, describes the purpose of human life to be that of *pleasing God* (Rom. 12:1, 2; 14:18; I Cor. 7:32; II Cor. 5:9; Eph. 5:10; Phil. 4:18; Col. 3:20; I Thess. 4:1). Paul even exhorts *children* to obey their parents in everything "for this pleases the Lord" (Col. 3:20); as if to say, "It fills God's heart with delight." God's heart is not an iceberg! In this connection see what was said previously (p. 247), with reference to God sending "his own Son."

Paul, either explicitly or by implication, expresses his disapproval upon those who please not God but themselves. Cf. Rom. 15:3; I Thess. 2:15.

Like Paul, the apostle John also regards doing what is pleasing to God as being the true goal of the believers' life. He points out how God regards this kind of life (I John 3:22). And the author of Hebrews directs the attention of the readers to the fact that without faith it is impossible to please God (11:6).

From those who are "in the flesh" and therefore "cannot please God" (verse 8) Paul's attention now turns more directly to the members of the church to which he is writing. With the warmth of heart that is characteristic of a true pastor he addresses them as follows:

9–11. Y o u, however, are not in the flesh but in the Spirit, seeing that God's Spirit dwells in y o u. (Anyone who does not possess Christ's Spirit does not belong to Christ.) But if Christ is in y o u, though the body is dead because of sin, yet the Spirit is life because of (y o u r) justification. And if the Spirit of him who raised Jesus from the dead dwells in y o u, he who raised Christ from the dead will also impart life to y o u r mortal bodies through the Spirit, who dwells in y o u.

The meaning of the entire passage, viewed in light of the immediately preceding context, can be summarized as follows:

Y o u, by contrast, are not basically under the control of sinful human nature but of the Spirit. Y o u are therefore not unable to please God, since God's Spirit is dwelling in y o u. (Now if there should be anyone who shows by his life and actions that he does not possess the Spirit of Christ, such a person does not belong to Christ. He is not a Christian at all.) But if Christ is living in y o u, then, though because of sin the body must die, nevertheless, because y o u have been justified, the Spirit, himself Life, is alive within y o u. And if that Spirit, namely, the Spirit of him who raised Jesus from the dead, is dwelling in y o u, then he who raised Christ from the dead will, on the day of the resurrection, impart life also to y o u r mortal bodies. He will do it through the agency of the Spirit who is dwelling within y o u.

Brief comment on words and phrases:

a. "Y o u, however, are not in the flesh but in the Spirit ..."

Lovingly Paul assures the addressees that, as far as the basic direction of their life is concerned, they are under the control not of sinful human nature but of the Spirit. This implies that, speaking collectively, they do not belong to the category of those concerning whom the apostle just now (verse 8) has stated that they cannot please God.

b. "seeing that God's Spirit dwells in y o u."

The rendering "if the Spirit of God dwells in y o u," as if Paul was not sure about the collective indwelling of the Holy Spirit in the hearts of these people, is incorrect. In view of what the apostle says about them in 1:6, 8; 15:14, such a low estimate on his part must be rejected.[214]

c. "(Anyone who does not possess Christ's Spirit does not belong to Christ.)" More literally: "(If anyone does not have the Spirit of Christ, he is not of his)."

Though, speaking collectively, the apostle has assured the Roman congregation that he regards it as being under the control of, and indwelt by, the Spirit, this does not mean that a church member can take his salvation for granted, in the sense that self-examination would no longer be necessary. Besides, in the church of Rome by no means everything was perfect. See 11:17–25; 14:10–15, 19; 15:1f.

Paul states that if anyone's life marks him as lacking Christ's Spirit, he has no right to consider himself a Christian.

Note in this verse the interchange of the designations "God's Spirit" and "Christ's Spirit." This certainly indicates that in Paul's thinking Christ was fully divine.

d. "But if Christ is in y o u, though the body is dead because of sin, yet the Spirit is life because of y o u r justification."

Meaning: not only is it true that because of sin the body of each of y o u is bound to die, but it is also true that because y o u are justified y o u can be assured of the fact that the Spirit, who is Life and life's Author, is dwelling within y o u.

The word *Spirit*, occurring in verse 10, should not be spelled with a small "s," as if the reference were to any person's invisible entity, but with a capital "S," for the apostle is definitely thinking of the Holy Spirit. Proof:

(1) In all the preceding eight instances of its use (verses 1–9) the word *pneuma* (Greek word for the divine *S*pirit as well as for the human *s*pirit) refers to the Holy Spirit. In verse 11 the apostle refers twice to this Spirit ("the Spirit of him who raised Jesus from the dead," "his Spirit who dwells in y o u"). It would be rather strange, then, if the intervening *pneuma* (here in verse 10) would have a different meaning.

(2) The *pneuma* of verse 10 is taken up again in verse 11. Note resem-

---

214. Besides, the word εἴπερ (=Latin si quidem) refers to a fulfilled condition. It can be rendered "seeing that," or "since," or "since indeed," or "if . . . as is certainly true." See the use of the same word in Rom. 3:30; 8:17; I Cor. 15:15; and see N.T.C. on II Thess. 1:6, p. 157.

blance: verse 11 refers to the life-imparting Spirit, naturally the Holy Spirit. This corresponds to "the *pneuma* of life" of verse 10.

(3) Also in verse 2 of the present chapter the Holy Spirit is called "the Spirit of life." Similarly in John 14:6 Jesus calls himself "the life."

e. "And if the Spirit of him who raised Jesus from the dead dwells in y o u, he who raised Christ from the dead will also impart life to y o u r mortal bodies through his Spirit, who dwells in y o u."

It is clear from verses 9–11 that the designations "Spirit," "*God's* Spirit," "*Christ's* Spirit," "the Spirit of him who raised Jesus from the dead," and "his Spirit who dwells in y o u," all refer to the same Holy Spirit. The variety of titles is by no means meaningless. It indicates the glorious unity existing between *Father, Son,* and *Holy Spirit,* a unity not only of *essence* (ontological oneness) but also of *operation* in the interest of our salvation.

Similarly John 14:26 informs us that *the Father* was going to send *the Holy Spirit;* John 16:7, that *the Son* would send him. There is no contradiction but glorious harmony. Note John 14:16, "I will ask the Father, and he will give y o u . . . the Spirit of truth." Also 14:26, "the Holy Spirit, whom the Father will send in my name."

In verse 11 the subject "He who raised Jesus—or Christ—from the dead," refers, of course, to the Father. Does it not also follow from such passages as Rom. 6:4; Gal. 1:1; and Eph. 1:20 that in the activity of raising the Savior from the dead it was the Father who, as it were, took the lead?

But note how very closely the two other persons of the Holy Trinity are related to the Father, hence also to each other. That the Father acts through the Spirit is plainly stated in verse 11. That even Jesus himself did not remain entirely passive in his resurrection is implied in John 10:17, 18. It is he who claims the power not only to lay down his life but also to take it up again. Moreover, the very One who in Rom. 8:11 is described as the Spirit *of the Father* is in verse 9 called *Christ's* Spirit. In fact, as it were in the same breath, *God's* Spirit is in verse 9 called *Christ's* Spirit. The relationship between Father, Son, and Holy Spirit is so close, the union so intimate and indissoluble, that it is impossible to dishonor the Son without also dishonoring the Father and the Holy Spirit. Cf. John 5:23.

This truth is filled with practical significance. We are living in an age in which in some evangelistic circles a disproportionate interest is shown in Jesus, as if honor and glory should be ascribed to *the Son* alone. Others, again, filled with the wrong kind of ecumenical fervor, the kind that aims at uniting all religious bodies into one huge world-church, minimize the work of the Savior and emphasize that all men are brothers, God being *the Father* of them all. And a third party, of late becoming more vocal, magnifies charismatic gifts, and cannot stop talking about *the Spirit.*

As Rom. 8:9–11 shows, and as Scripture throughout proves, it is God Triune, that is, Father, Son, and Holy Spirit, the one and only true God, who should be the central object of our love and worship.

12, 13. Therefore, brothers, we have an obligation, but it is not to the flesh, to live according to its standard. For if y o u live according to its standard y o u are doomed to die; but if, by the Spirit, y o u put to death the disgraceful deeds of the body, y o u will live.

At this point there is a transition from exposition to exhortation; from concentration on blessings bestowed by the Giver, to focusing on the obligation incurred by the recipients, including Paul himself.

However, the recipients are by no means represented as being able to act independently. Salvation is not a 50-50 affair. It is God's gift from start to finish. It is *by the Spirit* that God's children must put to death the disgraceful deeds of the body (verse 13), that they are being led (verse 14), and are being moved to cry, "Abba!" (verse 15). It is *from the Spirit* that they receive the assurance that they are indeed children of God (verse 16). But all this does not take away the fact that the recipients of these favors must go into action. They have an obligation to perform; nevertheless, they cannot do this in their own power. How then? As already indicated, "by the Spirit," and see also Phil. 2:12, 13.

The apostle calls attention to this obligation by saying, "Therefore," that is, in view of all the blessings *we* have received, are receiving, and are going to receive, stretching from one eternity to another (see verses 29, 30), *we*—note how he includes himself, a hint for pastors, etc.—have an obligation.

We do not owe this obligation to the flesh (corrupt human nature), however, to live according to its standard. That we owe the flesh no favors is clear from the fact that it was because of that very flesh that the law was unable to save us (8:3). In fact, having the mind or disposition of the flesh spells death (verse 6), a thought which Paul, in somewhat different phraseology, repeats in verse 13, by saying, "If y o u live according to its standard y o u are doomed to die."[215] So, instead of catering to the flesh, this enemy should be put to death. Has not the apostle already clearly stated this in 6:1, 6, 11, 12-14?

A rich reward is promised to those who "by the Spirit"—for they have no power of their own—put to death the disgraceful deeds[216] of the body: they *will live,* and this, of course, in the most glorious sense; see above, pp. 92, 93 on 2:7.

With Paul all this is not a piece of abstract theology, dry as dust. On the contrary, his heart is in his epistle. He loves these Romans, and desires most intensely to keep them from going astray. In fact, he also wants them to keep others from making the wrong choice. That his soul is, indeed, deeply

---

215. Note μέλλετε ἀποθνῄσκειν. The periphrastic future stresses the inevitability of their doom.
216. πράξεις, acc. pl. of πρᾶξις, here used in an unfavorable sense (cf. Luke 23:51; Acts 19:18), as is often the case with respect to the cognate verb πράσσω, see p. 232 on 7:15.

moved is clear from the fact that here again he makes use of the affectionate term of address "brothers" (verse 12). See what has been said about this word previously (pp. 214, 215).

Note the sharp contrast: those who are living according to the standard of the flesh are doomed to die. Those who by the Spirit are putting to death the disgraceful deeds of the body will live.

Scripture is full of illustrations of

The
Inescapable Alternative
Behold, I am setting before y o u today

a blessing	a curse (Deut. 11:26 f.)
life and prosperity	death and destruction (Deut. 30:15 f.)
building one's house on rock	building it on sand (Matt. 7:24–27)

Many other examples could easily be added. Among them would be those to which reference is made in such passages as Ps. 1; Matt. 25: 31–46; II Cor. 2:16; Gal. 5:19–22; I John 4:2, 3; Rev. 22:14, 15.

The fact to be emphasized is that the right choice must be made, for where a person will spend eternity is at stake. Even more important: whether a person's life will reach what should be its goal depends, in a sense, upon his decision (I Cor. 10:31; cf. I Cor. 7:32; Phil. 1:20, 21; I Thess. 4:1). "Choose for yourselves this day whom y o u will serve, whether the gods y o u r forefathers served beyond the River . . . but as for me and my household, we will serve the Lord" (Josh. 24:15).

Those, and those alone, who by the Spirit, put to death the disgraceful deeds of the body, are able to rejoice in the fact that they are being led by the Spirit, and therefore will truly live.

14. For as many as are being led by the Spirit of God, these are sons of God.

The connection between verse 13b and verse 14 is clear; note the word "For." In other words, the people who are putting to death the disgraceful deeds of the body are able to do so because they, being sons of God, are being constantly led by the Spirit of God.

Being Led by the Spirit

1. *Its Beneficiaries*
An illustration may be helpful. Whether the incident about to be related actually happened is not the point. One may have his own opinion about that. Suffice it to say that those who told the story were convinced of its historicity:

It was the year 1834 or shortly afterward. Religious persecution raged in The Netherlands. On one of these days, in the late afternoon, the faithful

255

minister of village X was informed that a certain member of his congregation, a devout widow, was seriously ill and would welcome a pastoral call.

The minister decided not to wait until the next morning but to start out at once on foot. The path from the parsonage to the widow's home, a distance of about two miles, led through heavily wooded territory, where men intending to commit murder could easily conceal themselves. But the minister arrived safely at the widow's home. His call was deeply appreciated and greatly strengthened the sick lady.

On the way back to the parsonage ... nothing happened. Apparently there had been no ambush.

A few years passed by. Then one day two men, who through the faithful efforts of this very minister, had recently been brought from darkness to light, spoke to him as follows:

"Do you recall that a few years ago—it was on a Friday afternoon—you went to visit the widow living in the house on the other side of these woods?" When the minister answered affirmatively, they continued, "Who were those two men, in shining armor, walking on either side of you, guarding you?" The astonished minister replied, "I was alone, my friends; I was all by myself; either going or returning no one accompanied me." The two continued, "This is very strange, for we distinctly saw them. It made us afraid. So we hurried away. And now, having been brought to the knowledge of Christ through your ministry, how happy we are that we were prevented from carrying out our sinister plot."

Those who told the story were sure that this minister must have been one of the few very special "saints" of God who, being led by the Spirit, were the objects of exceptional divine protection.

However, this view, which in certain religious circles used to be rather popular—whether this is still the case I do not know—is certainly not what Paul had in mind when he wrote Rom. 8:14. The spiritual leading of which he speaks is definitely not the Spirit's gift to the select few. It concerns every Christian. Every child of God is being led by the Spirit. Everyone who is being led by the Spirit is a child of God.[217]

Those who are being led by the Spirit are the people who are described as being in Christ Jesus (8:1), walking according to the Spirit (verse 4), being Spirit-indwelt (verses 9, 11), and putting to death the disgraceful deeds of the body (verse 13).

2. *Its Nature*

What, then, does *the leading of the Spirit*—to change from the passive to the active voice—actually mean? It means sanctification. It is the constant, effective, and beneficent influence which the Holy Spirit exercises within

217. An excellent chapter on "The Holy Spirit and Guidance," written in a very interesting style, is found in E. H. Palmer's book *The Holy Spirit,* Grand Rapids, 1958, pp. 101–117.

the hearts and lives of God's children, enabling them more and more to crush the power of indwelling sin and to walk in the way of God's commandments freely and cheerfully.

The influence which the Holy Spirit exercises is:

a. Not sporadic but constant.

It is not being injected into the lives of God's children now and then, in moments of great need or danger. On the contrary, it is steady, constant, as even the tense here in Rom. 8:14 implies. Believers *are being led*[218] by the Spirit.

b. It is not (at least not primarily) protective but corrective.

In the entire context nothing is said about guarding God's children from receiving physical harm, nothing about keeping them out of danger when traveling. On the other hand, the immediately preceding context refers to putting to death the disgraceful deeds of the body, doing this "by the Spirit."[219]

c. It not merely directs but controls.

To be *led* by the Spirit means more than to be *guided* by him, though, to be sure, the Spirit is also our Guide (John 16:13). Cf. Matt. 15:14; Luke 6:39; Acts 8:31. But the leadership provided by the Spirit amounts to more than merely pointing out the right way. It reminds us not so much of the Indian guide who pointed out to the white explorers the pass through the Rockies, as of the people who led the blind man (of Jericho) to Jesus (Luke 18:40). Merely pointing out the way to him would not have helped him. When the Holy Spirit leads believers he becomes the controlling influence in their lives, bringing them at last to glory.

d. On the other hand, it does not stifle or repress but helps and encourages.

When the Holy Spirit leads God's child, the latter's responsibility and activity are not canceled or repressed. The blind man of Jericho *was not carried* to Jesus. He did his own walking. It is exactly as Warfield has pointed out: "Though it is indeed the Holy Spirit who keeps us in the path and brings us at last to the goal, it is we who tread every step of the way; our limbs that grow weary with the labor; our hearts that faint . . . our faith that revives our sinking strength, our hope that instills new courage into our souls, as we toil over the steep ascent."[220]

3. *Its Fruits*

These are so numerous that it would be impossible to mention them all. Accordingly, no attempt will be made to list them all, for this would be just as impossible as to

---

218. ἄγονται, third per. pres. (continuative) indicat. of ἄγω, here, as often, to lead.

219. By all means ask God to give you traveling mercy and guidance. But that is not the theme here in Rom. 8:14. *However, see on 15:30-33.*

220. *op. cit.,* p. 555.

Count your many blessings
Name them one by one.

It is for this very reason that in Gal. 5:22, 23 Paul, after stating, "Now the fruit of the Spirit is love, joy, peace, long-suffering, kindness, goodness, faithfulness, meekness, self-control," continues, "against *such* there is no law." He means, "The list I have given is incomplete; therefore I say, 'against *such*,' meaning: against *these and other* fruits." Another *summarizing* description of these fruits is certainly this one, "He who sows to ... the Spirit will from the Spirit reap *life everlasting*" (Gal. 6:8), for who has ever been able to give a definition of life everlasting from which nothing is lacking? An orchard may contain a rich variety of fruit trees: orange, mango, tangelo, lemon, grapefruit, etc. However, each tree bears only one kind of fruit. The tree of grace, watered by the Spirit of life, bears *every* variety of spiritual fruit, and apart from that Spirit no spiritual fruit has ever been produced.

The fruit on which Paul's epistle to the Romans now rivets our attention is that of assurance of salvation, more precisely, that of *assurance of adoption as children of God:*

15, 16. For y o u have not received a spirit of slavery, to fill y o u once more with dread, but y o u have received the Spirit of adoption, who moves us to cry, "Abba!" that is "Father!" This Spirit himself bears witness with our spirit that we are children of God.

Blessed Assurance

One might summarize the meaning of this passage as follows: Y o u who are being led by the Spirit are not slaves but children. Having been adopted as *children,* y o u, of course, are no longer filled with the spirit of slaves, that of dread. No longer are y o u oppressed with fear as y o u were when y o u were still living in paganism or in Judaism, with their emphasis on all the rules one has to keep in order to be saved. On the contrary, y o u have received the Holy Spirit, who transforms slaves into children. That Spirit would not even think of filling y o u once more with dread. No, that Spirit fills us with the sense of freedom and confidence, so that, in approaching God, we utter the cry of joyful recognition, sweet response, overwhelming gratitude, and filial trust, "Abba!" (Father). In fact, that Spirit confirms that to which our own regenerated souls already bear witness, namely, that we, believers, are God's own children, having been adopted by him.

Among the various matters with respect to which opinions differ there are especially these three:

1. When the apostle mentions *adoption* did he have, in the background of his mind, (a) Greek-Roman or (b) Jewish adoption practices?

Those who favor the first alternative point out that "adoption," as a legal institution, did not even exist among the Hebrews, and that in the entire Old Testament the word never occurs. In the Roman world, on the other hand, the custom was rather common. Thus in his will Julius Caesar named Octavian (later called Emperor Augustus) his "son and heir." See N.T.C. on Luke, p. 137. On inscriptions the word "adopted son" occurs with great frequency.

It should be borne in mind, however, that (a) the *purpose* of this adoption practice was generally not philanthropic but egocentric: the perpetuation of property ownership and political and/or social privilege in the line of one's descendants, (b) its *beneficiaries* were males—legal adoption did not extend to females.

How completely different is the nature of adoption as pictured in the Old Testament. Instances of *essential,* though *not formal* or *technical, adoption* are indeed recorded in that sacred document. Did not Pharoah's daughter "adopt" Moses (Exod. 2:10), even though he was only a "humanly speaking" helpless child? Did not Mordecai bring up his cousin, *a girl* named Esther (Esther 2:7)? A *New Testament* passage which in a summarizing manner reproduces the teaching of the *Old Testament* regarding adoption—that is, *divine* adoption—is certainly II Cor. 6:17, 18:

> Come out from among them
> and be separate, says the Lord,
> And touch no unclean thing;
>   And I will receive y o u,
> And I will be to y o u a Father,
>   And y o u will be to me sons and daughters.

Note how beautifully this New Testament passage reflects the sense of the following passages: II Sam. 7:8, 14; Ps. 27:10; Isa. 43:6; and Hos. 1:10. Note especially that Isa. 43:6 as well as II Cor. 6:17, 18 mention both "sons *and daughters*" as the objects of God's adopting love.

It is clear, therefore, that when in Rom. 8:15 and Gal. 4:5 Paul uses the term "adoption" the *word* and the *legal standing* were borrowed from Roman practice, but the *essence* from the divine revelation in the Old Testament.

2. Is the outcry "Abba!" to be interpreted as the exclamation of the individual believer in addressing his God, or as the collective (perhaps congregational or liturgical) utterance of the church, gathered for worship?

A form of the word *Abba*, meaning "father," was originally used by small children. Later on its use became far more general. It was the very word uttered also by Jesus when, in deep agony, he, in the garden of Gethsemane, unburdened his soul to his Father in heaven (Mark 14:36). In this word filial tenderness, trust, and love find their combined expression.

It was, of course, a very personal word, that is, a word by means of which the intimate spiritual relationship between the believer and his God expresses itself. As such it reminds one of a line in a popular hymn,

> And the joy we share as we tarry there
> none other has ever known.
>
> From *In the Garden*
> by C. A. Miles

There are those who have criticized this hymn, and particularly this line. I believe, however, that this criticism is unfair. Is it not true that between each individual Christian and his God there exists a very personal relationship; or, expressing it differently, that God, in addition to loving and caring for his redeemed collectively, also enters into a uniquely personal fellowship with each of them, so that, prompted by the Holy Spirit (Gal. 4:6) the individual, in pouring out his heart, cries, "Father"?

Of course, the very personal use of this word in individual prayer, including *The Lord's Prayer* (in the original the first word; see Matt. 6:9), by no means excludes the possibility that it was also uttered collectively by the congregation, gathered for worship; just as even today we use The Lord's Prayer both collectively and individually.

Being a Hebrew of Hebrews (Phil. 3:5) Paul must have been fond of the language spoken by the Jews as they returned from the lands of their captivity, namely Aramaic, akin to Hebrew (cf. Acts 21:40). Aramaic, in fact, was a very important language in those days, spoken not only by the Jews, but by others besides, even by many people living far away from the borders of Palestine. Jesus too spoke Aramaic, and it is probable that in his frequent teaching about the Father he had often used the term *Abba.* His disciples therefore relished the use of this word. Thus it entered into the vocabulary of the primitive church. Naturally in writing to a church or to churches consisting of people who for the greater part were non-Jews, the word *Abba* had to be translated into the Greek word ὁ πατήρ (Father). Understandably Mark, addressing a Greek-speaking audience, wrote "Abba!" and quickly added the Greek word for "Father"; and so, probably for a similar reason did Paul.[221]

3. Does Rom. 8:16 mention one witness or two witnesses?

There are those who say that in reality Paul mentions only one witness or testifier, and that accordingly the correct rendering of verse 16 is, "The Spirit himself assures our spirit that we are children of God." Thus, or along this line, the Vulgate, Beck, Cranfield. The reasoning that lies at the root of this interpretation is that the verb used in the original, and generally rendered *to bear witness with,*[222] or *to testify in support of* (someone), can also mean *to assure,* and that our spirit in and by itself has no right to testify

---

221. Here (Rom. 8:15; cf. Mark 14:36; John 20:28) the articular nominat. form indicates the vocative. See Gram.N.T., p. 261.

222. συμμαρτυρεῖ, third per. s. pres. indicat. of συμμαρτυρέω.

to our being sons of God. However, in fairness to those who so argue, one should read what Cranfield himself says on pp. 402, 403 of his excellent commentary.

Fact is, however, that in each of the other instances in which Paul uses this verb there are two that bear witness: one testifies along with the other. Thus in Rom. 2:15 what is written on a man's heart is one witness; the other is the voice of his conscience. Similarly, in Rom. 9:1 Paul himself testifies that Israel's unbelief is for him a heavy burden. His conscience confirms this, and in so doing proves to be the second witness. I see no good reason, therefore, to depart from the rendering of Rom. 8:16 that has been adopted, with slight variations, by most translators, namely, "This Spirit himself bears witness with our spirit that we are children of God."

Just how the Spirit does this, Paul does not indicate. According to some, the Spirit testifies along with our regenerated consciousness by exerting a *direct* influence on heart and mind. See Gal. 4:6. Others insist that he works *by applying the Word* to the heart and mind of individual believers and also of the church viewed as a unit. See John 8:47; 16:13. Could not both positions be true?

In the midst of these debates and differences of opinion we are in danger of forgetting "the wonder of it all." Just think of it:

a. At the cost of the death—and what a death!—of his own Son, God decided to save *us*. (Did y o u notice how in 8:15 Paul makes the change, as he does often, from *y o u* to *we?*). See p. 217.

b. As if this were not enough, God even adopts us, so that we become his sons and daughters, his dear children (8:15).

c. His infinite and tender love extends even beyond this, for not only does he save us and make us his children but he also wants us to know that these great blessings have been bestowed upon us. By means of two witnesses he imparts to us this "blessed assurance" (8:16). *He saves, adopts, assures!*

"Behold what love the Father has lavished on us, that we should be called children of God! And that is what we are!" (I John 3:1).

And the glory of *sonship* expands very logically into that of *heirship*, as Paul now continues:

17. And if children, then heirs, heirs of God and fellow-heirs with Christ; since the fact that we are now sharing in his sufferings means that (hereafter) we shall share in his glory.

If Children, Then Heirs

The state of being a child implies that of being an heir, which, in turn, implies that there is an inheritance in store for us. That this inheritance is reserved for the future, Paul makes clear when he states, ". . . we shall share in his glory." In verses 11 and 13 the apostle had already kindled the hope of those whom he addresses. He had pointed to glories to come for both body and soul. He now enlarges on that theme. He tells us something about the Testator, the Inheritance, and the Heirs.

A. *The Testator*

If there is to be an inheritance there must be someone who bequeaths it. Our passage does not leave us in doubt with respect to the identity of this Testator. It reads "heirs of God," meaning, of course, that God is that Testator. Also, Christ is clearly the main Heir, and "we," says Paul, are fellow-heirs with Christ, destined, accordingly, to share in his glory.[223]

In looking forward to receive an inheritance, very much depends on the character of the testator. So we commonly ask, "What kind of person was the testator? When did he die? Was he rich or poor? Just or unjust?"

In the present case the answers are most encouraging. Earthly testators die. This means that a purely earthly inheritance is limited. When it is used up, no goods can be added. But the Testator whom Paul has in mind is "from everlasting to everlasting." Therefore our inheritance will not give out; in fact, will never even diminish.

Moreover, this Testator is rich. Not only is it true that all the silver and gold is his (Hag. 2:8), and that he owns every animal of the forest, and the cattle on a thousand hills (Ps. 50:10), but it is also a fact that his riches cannot even be measured. Also, so generous is he that whatever he demands of us he is eager to give us. For example, he demands that we repose our trust in him (John 3:16). This very trust or faith is also his gift to us. See N.T.C. on Ephesians, pp. 120–123 (on Eph. 2:8).

A very common item of human experience is dissatisfaction over the stipulations of a will. However, so just and fair is the Testator whom Paul has in mind that on that future day when God's children will take possession of their inheritance, they will be saying, "The boundary lines have fallen in pleasant places for me; indeed, a delightful inheritance is mine" (Ps. 16:6).

B. *The Inheritance*

Two facts with respect to this inheritance have already been made clear: (a) that it pertains to the future, and (b) that it consists of riches which we shall posssess "in connection with Christ."

That in full measure "the inheritance of the saints in the light" (Col. 1:12) is indeed a blessing that pertains to the future follows also from the fact that Rom. 8:18 speaks of a glory that "is to be revealed in us." It will, moreover, be a glory to which the whole creation looks forward (verse 19).

According to the book of Revelation *together with Christ* we shall inherit a new name (3:12) and a crown of gold (4:4; cf. 14:14). With him we shall reign (20:4). In fact, we shall even sit beside Christ on his throne (3:21). To be sure, all this is symbolic language. But do not these passages indicate that

---

223. Confusion arises when, since God is, in a sense, the believers' possession (Ps. 73:25, 26; Lam. 3:24), the idea that the apostle is viewing God as the believers' inheritance is injected into the interpretation of Rom. 8:17. As I indicate, *the context* points in a different direction. The inheritance here described pertains not to something or Someone we possess even now, but distinctly to the future.

the blessing of communion with Christ, which is our portion even now in principle, will be ours in a far higher degree then?

Moreover, this future bliss will not be confined to the soul. It definitely will pertain also to the body. We shall bear the image of the heavenly (I Cor. 15:49). For more on this see below, on verse 23.

Along with this transformation of soul and body we can look forward to the transformation of the universe. Creation itself will be set free from the bondage of corruption. See on verses 19–22.

What will make all this even more wonderful is the fact that, in close fellowship with the Savior, each of the redeemed will inherit these riches *together with all the others* (Eph. 3:18; II Tim. 4:8), and with the purpose of glorifying God Triune forever and ever.

Moreover, it should be emphasized that this future glory for soul and body, though indeed a gift of God's sovereign grace, is also *more than a gift.* It is *an inheritance,* which, in the present connection can imply no less than (a) that it will be the possession of God's children *by right,* that right having been established by Christ's self-sacrifice; and (b) that it is inalienable (I Peter 1:4; cf. I Kings 21:3, 4).

C. *The Heirs*

Paul says, "If *children,* then heirs."

If children, *not "if enemies."* Even among those who wish to be regarded as believers there are those who actually are "enemies of the cross of Christ" (Phil. 3:18). As long as they remain enemies the inheritance is not for them.

If children, *not "if slaves."* There are those who serve Christ outwardly, not inwardly, not motivated by love and trust, not wholeheartedly. Think of the Galatians (Gal. 3:1 f.), of Ananias and Sapphira (Acts 5:1), of Demas (II Tim. 4:10), and of Diotrephes (III John 9).

If *"children"* then heirs; otherwise not. This is also entirely in line with Christ's teaching (Luke 18:17).

But how do I know that I am a child? In light of the present passage the answer is, "I know that I am a child if I am willing, when necessity demands, to endure suffering for the sake of Christ." (See Matt. 5:11, 12; 10:22, 39; 24:9; Mark 8:35, 13:13; I Peter 4:16).

When we suffer *as Christians,* then Christ's afflictions overflow toward us, as the following passages clearly indicate: Matt. 10:25; John 15:18–21; Acts 9:4, 5; II Cor. 1:5, 10; Gal. 6:17; Phil. 3:10; I Peter 4:13. We can add nothing to Christ's redemptive suffering for us, but by means of our willingness to suffer for his sake we are drawn closer to the Savior's heart.

Paul assumes that *the church* he is addressing is indeed willing to suffer for Christ, just as the apostle himself is also constantly enduring such affliction. That is why he states, ". . . since the fact that we are now sharing in his suffering means that hereafter we shall share in his glory."[224] But let every *individual member* answer for himself the question, "Am I willing to suffer *as a Christian?*" Could it be that the reason why some boldly affirm, "I have

---

224. Note here again εἴπερ, as in verse 9. See footnote 214 on p. 252.

never suffered for Christ," is that they are such poor Christians . . . if Christians at all?

Suffering as a Christian takes many forms. It does not mean that our experience has to be that of a Polycarp or a John Huss. Today a believer may lose his job because he refuses to perform unnecessary work on the Lord's Day. Or because he says No when he is being tempted to participate in a crooked business deal, or makes up his mind not to marry an unbeliever, or insists on honoring the Word of God in the classroom. How many have not been expelled from positions in school, church, or government because of their stand for the truth?

It is comforting to know that all who share in Christ's suffering will at last hear from his lips the welcoming words, "Well done, good and faithful servants. Enter into my rest."

18. For I consider that the sufferings of this present time are not worthy to be compared with the glory that is to be revealed in us.

SUFFERING AND GLORY
A COMPARISON

The conjunction "For" indicates that what follows is a further explication and amplification of the *glory* to which reference was made in the preceding verse.

A. *The Two Elements Compared*

"I consider (or reckon)," says Paul, making use of an understatement,[225] for what he actually means is, "I am firmly convinced."

Of what is he firmly convinced? Of the fact that the sufferings of this present time are not worthy to be compared with the glory that is to be revealed in us. It is clear that the apostle is, as it were, holding in his hand a scale or balance. As always, it has two scalepans. In the one pan he places "the sufferings of this present time"; in the other "the glory that is to be revealed in us."

The first (sufferings) is a result of sin. Had there been no sin, human beings would not have had to suffer (Gen. 3:16–19). The second (glory) is the result of grace. As far as God's children are concerned, the first is temporal, the second never-ending.

What kind of sufferings does Paul have in mind? Those experienced as a result of our relation to Christ? Such sufferings are certainly included. Otherwise there would be no connection between verses 17 and 18. Nevertheless, it is not advisable to limit the word "sufferings" as here employed,

---

225. The verb is λογίζομαι, cf. λόγος in the sense of *account;* hence, to take into account (Love does not take into account a suffered wrong, I Cor. 13:5); and so: to reckon, consider, regard, etc. Sometimes even: to impute a quality to a person which in and by himself he does not possess; see above, p. 147, on Rom. 4:3.

to such afflictions. As verses 19–23, 28, 38, 39 clearly indicate, other afflictions are also included. The apostle is thinking of sufferings in general; therefore also including pain (physical as well as mental), sickness, disappointment, unemployment, poverty, frustration, etc. This follows too from the fact that he uses the very broad expression "the sufferings of this present time," that is, "of this present age," the "time" or "age" which extends to, and ends with, Christ's second coming.[226]

And what about the glory of which Paul speaks? Is he referring to the blessings of the intermediate state; that is, the beatific joys which the souls of the redeemed begin to experience the very moment they breathe their last? That this intermediate state is real, and that at this very moment the departed dear ones who died "in the Lord" are participating in its activities I have tried to prove in my book *The Bible on the Life Hereafter,* Grand Rapids, 1959. See especially pp. 53–57. However, that cannot be what Paul has in mind here in Rom. 8:18. Verses 19 and 23 make very clear that he is referring to what will transpire at the time of "the revelation of the sons of God," and of "the redemption (glorious resurrection) of our bodies"; in other words, at the time of Christ's Return.

Significant is also the fact that the apostle, in dictating this letter, did not say "the glory that is to be revealed *to* us," but "the glory that is to be revealed *in* us." In other words, this glory will, as it were, come to us, enter us, and then, having filled us and enveloped us, will be revealed in us. We ourselves will be part of that glory: the redeemed will see it in each other. The angels will behold it in us, and will be filled with thanksgiving and praise to God.

B. *The Result of This Comparison*

"I consider that the sufferings of the present time are not worthy to be compared with the glory that will be revealed in us," says Paul; that is, the pan in which the glory has been deposited outweighs the other one by so much that the heavier pan drops to the bottom immediately. Our present sufferings, be they ever so many and severe, fade into insignificance when compared with our future glory.

C. *The Reason for This Comparison*

The very strategically situated church of Rome, surrounded by dangers and enemies (16:3, 4, 17–20), was in need of encouragement. The present passage richly supplies it.

In reflecting on the glory to be revealed *in* us, as well, of course, as *to* us,

---

226. Mark 10:30 makes clear that the terms *time* (καιρός) and *age* (αἰών) are synonyms: the *now* or *present* time = the *now* or *present* age; and the *coming* time = the *coming* age. One might call these expressions "technical terms." See also Matt. 12:32; Luke 16:8; 20:34, 35; Rom. 12:2; Gal. 1:4; Eph. 1:21.

we realize that the reality will by far surpass our *fondest* expectations. Mrs. Elizabeth Mills was surely correct when she wrote:

> We speak of the land of the blest,
> A country so bright and so fair,
> And oft are its glories confest,
> But what must it be to be there?

Especially to be there, in redeemed soul and body, at Christ's glorious Second Coming and forever afterward!

19-22. For the creation, with outstretched head, is eagerly looking forward to the revelation of the sons of God. For it was not by its own choice that the creation was subjected to futility, but (it was) because of him who subjected it, in hope, because the creation itself too will be set free from its bondage to decay, so as to share the glorious liberty of the children of God. For we know that the whole creation, with one accord, has been, and still is, groaning as in the pain of childbirth.

THE THREE GROANINGS

The word "For" is understandable: the glory to be revealed (verse 18) is so marvelous that the (whole) creation is eagerly looking forward to it (verses 19-22), we ourselves are ardently awaiting it (verses 23-25), the Spirit too joining us (verses 26, 27). All three (creation, we, the Spirit) groan as in childbirth, hopefully looking forward to the birth of the promised glory. We might say, therefore, that "For" introduces *The Three Groanings.* It continues the discussion of the subject (future glory) that had already been mentioned, a very common use of "For."

A. *Creation's Groaning*

What is here three times called "the creation" is finally (in verse 22) called "the whole creation." How much does it include? It cannot include the good angels, since they were never subjected to futility (verse 20) and never succumbed to corruption or decay (verse 21). Satan and his demons are also ruled out, for they will never be set free (II Peter 2:4; Jude 6). This holds also for all those people who will never be saved, the non-elect (II Thess. 1:8, 9). And the elect are not included *here,* for they are here treated as a separate group. We are told that the creation is looking forward to the revelation of the sons of God, implying that creation's deliverance from the bondage of corruption will take place at the time when the revelation of God's children will occur. Besides, what the elect are doing and what is going to happen to them is described in verses 23-25.

With the exclusion of all these four groups, what is left is the animate and inanimate irrational creation. One might call it the sub-human creation or simply Nature.

We are told, therefore, that this remaining "whole creation" is, with outstretched head,[227] eagerly looking and watching for the revelation of the sons of God. It is, as it were, craning its neck to see this.

When the question is asked, "But how is it possible for birds and plants to show such intense interest in what will happen to God's children, the answer might well be, "If, according to Scripture, trees can rejoice (Ps. 96:12), floods can clap their hands (Ps. 98:8), the wilderness can be glad (Isa. 35:1), and mountains and hills can burst into song (Isa. 55:12), why should not birds and plants be able to look forward with longing? As is clearly evident, we are dealing here with *personification*.

However, that answer is incomplete. More must be added: (a) that the restoration of the animate and inanimate irrational creation is intimately related to "the revelation of the sons of God." The two are linked together, so that restoration and glory for "the sons of God" implies the same for "the whole creation." And (b) that it will most certainly take place.

Beautiful and very meaningful is the phrase "the revelation of the sons of God.[228] It indicates that not until the day of Christ's Return will it become a matter of public knowledge how much God loves them and how richly he rewards them. "Then, in the kingdom of their Father, the righteous will shine as the sun" (Matt. 13:43), "as the brightness of the firmament and as the stars forever and ever" (Dan. 12:3). They will be on exhibition, so that all will be able to see what God has wrought for and *in* them.

The whole creation is looking forward eagerly for the revelation of the sons of God because that event will also mean glory for the whole creation. We must bear in mind that "it was not by its own choice"—hence, was not its own fault—that the creation was made subject to futility. It was not the irrational creation that sinned. It was man. And the One who subjected the creation to futility was God. It was he who, because of man's sin, pronounced a curse on . . . what or on whom? Well, in a sense on creation, but in an even deeper sense upon man:

> Cursed is the ground because of you;
> In toil you will eat of it
> All the days of your life.
> Thorns and thistles it will produce for you,
> And you will eat the plants of the field.
> By the sweat of your brow
> you will eat your food

---

227. Note ἀποκαραδοκία = ἀπό, away from κάρα, head; δοκία, cf. δοκέω, meaning (in Ionian) *to watch.r*

228. That in all such cases the word υἱός, son, has nothing to do with sex (male or female), and amounts to τέκνον, child, is clear from a comparison of passages: those who, in one passage, are called *sons* are, in another passage, called *children*. Cf. our present passage with verse 16. *If there is any shade of difference at all in such cases, it would be that sons emphasizes legal standing; children, (spiritual) offspring.*

> until you return to the ground,
> because from it you were taken;
> For dust you are,
> and to dust you will return.

Gen. 3:17–19

So, since creation's humiliation was not its fault, as the passage specifically states, it will certainly participate in man's restoration. Nature's destiny is intimately linked up with that of "the sons of God." That is why the whole creation is represented as craning its neck to behold the revelation of the sons of God.

Note the expression, "The creation was subjected to futility." A.V. reads "to vanity." However, when this word is interpreted as meaning *inflated pride,* it has nothing to do with the present passage. The word used in the original does not refer to ambitious display. It indicates that since man's fall Nature's potentialities are cribbed, cabined, and confined. The creation is subject to arrested development and constant decay. Though it aspires, it is not able fully to achieve. Though it blossoms, it does not reach the point of adequately bearing fruit. It may be compared to a very powerful world-champion boxer or wrestler, who is chained in such a manner that he cannot make use of his tremendous physical prowess. The curse of plant disease decimates the crops. The loss is estimated at many millions of dollars for each separate disease. Plant pathologists direct their efforts toward developing methods of disease *prevention* or at least *reduction* or *control.* And, in a modified sense, what is true with respect to the world of plants holds too for the animal sphere.

What a glorious day that will be when all the restraints due to man's sin will have been removed, and we shall see this wonderful creation reaching self-realization, finally coming into its own, sharing in "the glorious liberty of the children of God!"

That this hope is not unrealistic is shown by the words, "in hope, because[229] the creation itself too will be set free . . ."

Paul compares the earnest yearning and eager forward looking of creation to the groaning of a woman who is in the process of giving birth to a child.[230] To be sure, such groaning indicates suffering, but it also implies hope. As Calvin reminds us, these groans are birth-pangs, not death-pangs. The addition "with one accord" or "together" indicates that every division of this "whole creation" participate in these birth-pangs.

---

229. Is the true text ὅτι (A B C etc.) or διότι (D* F G)? If the latter, the meaning is probably *because,* though even διότι can mean *that.* If the true reading is ὅτι, the choice between *because* and *that* is about even. In the present case making the right decision is not important since either reading introduces a clause that is true to fact and harmonizes with the context.

230. The two third per. s. pres. indicatives he uses are συστενάζει and συνωδίνει. They rhyme, as do groaning and moaning. Meaning: "is groaning and travailing"; but the two form a unit: hence, "has been, and still is (note ἄχρι τοῦ νῦν) groaning as in the pain of childbirth."

Does the rest of Scripture furnish any further information about the meaning of Nature's future deliverance from bondage and participation in the glorious liberty of God's children?

Indeed, it does! It informs us that the universe is going to be purged by *a great conflagration* (II Peter 3:7, 11, 12).

Closely linked with this conflagration there is going to be a *rejuvenation*. The fire will not destroy the universe. It will still be the same heavens and earth, but gloriously renewed, and in that sense *a new heaven and earth* (II Peter 3:13; Rev. 21:1-5). Accordingly, not only will we be going to heaven, but heaven will, as it were, come down to us; that is, the conditions of perfection obtaining in heaven will be found throughout God's gloriously rejuvenated universe.

We can also view this wonderful transformation as a *self-realization,* as has been explained. See above, p. 268.

Finally, this transformation will include *harmonization*. At present Nature can be described as being "raw in tooth and claw." Peace and harmony are lacking. Various organisms seem to be working at cross purposes: they choke each other to death. But then there will be concord and harmony everywhere. There will be variation, to be sure, but a most delightful blending of sight and sound, of life and purpose, so that the total effect will be unity and harmony. The prophecy of Isa. 11:6-9 will reach ultimate fulfilment:

> The wolf will dwell with the lamb,
> And the leopard will lie down with the goat,
> And the calf and the young lion and the yearling together,
> And a little child will lead them.
> The cow and the bear will graze,
> The young will lie down together,
> And the lion will eat straw like the ox.
> And the nursing child will play near the hole of the cobra,
> And the weaned child will put his hand into the viper's nest.
> They will not hurt or destroy in all my holy mountain,
> For the earth will be full of the knowledge of the Lord
> As the waters cover the sea.

23-25. Not only this, but also we ourselves, who possess the firstfruits of the Spirit, even we ourselves groan within ourselves, as we eagerly await our adoption, that is, the redemption of our bodies. For it was in hope that we were saved; but when once something hoped for is seen it is no longer an object of hope, for who hopes for what he sees? But since we hope for that which we do not see, we wait for it with patient endurance.

B. *Our Own Groaning*

Not only does the whole subhuman creation groan, but so do also "we ourselves," says Paul, thus including himself, as well as those whom he

269

addresses, in the sphere of those who groan. When he adds "who possess the first fruits of the Spirit" does he mean, "We groan *even though* we possess," etc. or "*because* we possess," etc.? Either would make excellent sense. He may have meant, "Even though we are already so rich, we are reaching out for riches even more precious." Or he may have intended to convey the thought, "Since we already have the Spirit, we are convinced that more, much more, is still in store for us. We are therefore eagerly yearning to receive it." In view of the fact that we are not sure which of these alternatives was uppermost in the apostle's mind, it may well be best, *in our translation,* to leave the participle exactly as it is, namely, *having* or *possessing.* Personally I, along with many other commentators, rather favor the concessive interpretation, since it seems to harmonize best with the idea of *great surprise* implied in the emphatic introduction, "also we ourselves . . . even we ourselves,"[231] as if to say, "Though we have already received so much, we are still groaning within ourselves for more."

Paul says, "we ourselves, who possess the firstfruits of the Spirit." What does he mean?

From Exod. 23:19; Deut. 18:4, and other passages, we learn that the Israelites were told to offer to God the firstfruits of the soil (grain, wine, oil), and even of the wool from the shearing of the sheep. But the reverse is also a fact. God too gives firstfruits. He gives the firstfruits of the Spirit, so that Paul could state that he himself and those whom he addresses are now in possession of this blessing.[232]

Was the apostle referring to a certain supply of the Spirit that had been poured out so far, with more of the Spirit to follow later? See L.N.T. (A. and G.), p. 81, an opinion that is rather popular, especially among people who frequently refer to "the second blessing." It is, however, erroneous.

There is no reason to doubt that the apostle, here in Rom. 8:23, is referring to *the Holy Spirit himself.* That Spirit is himself the firstfruits or pledge of subsequent salvation in all its fulness, in store for God's children at Christ's Return. There is no reason to believe that Paul refers to one thing in Eph. 1:13, 14, and to something else here in Rom. 8:23.[233]

"Also we ourselves . . . even we ourselves groan within ourselves, as we eagerly await our adoption, that is, the redemption of our bodies." How is it to be understood that even Christians groan? Is it not reasonable to assume that the groaning of God's children resembles that of Nature (verse 22)? If then the groaning of the whole creation consisted of two elements, namely,

---

231. This surprise element is lost in the rendering, favored by some, which, rather arbitrarily, it would seem to me, abbreviates the original into the mere "Not only so, but we ourselves."

232. In addition to "the firstfruits of the Spirit" (Rom. 8:23) the New Testament mentions: the firstfruits of dough (Rom. 11:16); firstfruits = first convert (Rom. 16:5; I Cor. 16:15); Christ as firstfruits of those who fell asleep (I Cor. 15:20, 23); firstfruits of creatures (James 1:18); and the 144,000, offered as firstfruits to God (Rev. 14:4). See also N.T.C. on I and II Thessalonians, pp. 187, 188, on II Thess. 2:13.

233. So also Ridderbos, *op. cit.,* p. 188; and J. Behm (on ἀρραβών, Th.D.N.T., Vol. I, p. 475).

(a) experiencing pain and (b) looking forward in hope, we may conclude that the same holds also for those who possess the firstfruits of the Spirit, God's dear children.

Is Paul thinking of the fact that Christians realize that they are still very imperfect? So sinful that at times they cry out, "Wretched man that I am, Who will rescue me from this body of death?" (Rom. 7:24)? That they are indeed imperfect is clear from Scripture throughout. Nevertheless, the present context—think especially of the combination *pain* and *hope*—points also in a different direction. The very fact that God's children even now possess—that is, are indwelt by—the Holy Spirit, arouses within them a painful sense of lack. What they already have makes them hungry for more; that is, for salvation in all its fulness. It is in this sense that pain and hope are here combined.

Even now believers have been adopted as God's sons (8:15, 16). But, in another sense, they are still waiting for their adoption. They are waiting for the public display of their standing as children of God. As of right now their bodies are still subject to death. But one day their souls will have been completely delivered from sin, and their bodies will have become transformed, so that they will resemble the glorious body of the Lord Jesus Christ himself. To that great day they now look forward *in hope* (Rom. 8:11; I Cor. 15:50-55; II Cor. 5:2, 3; Phil. 3:21; I John 3:2).

Verse 24 takes up this subject of the Christian's hope. The translation of this verse in the A.V. is, however, not the best (to put it mildly). It is as follows:

"For we are saved by hope; but hope that is seen is not hope: for what a man seeth, why doth he yet hope for?"

We naturally ask, "Has Paul changed his theology? Did he not always tell us that we were saved *by faith* (Rom. 1:16, 17; 3:22, 26, 28, 31; 4:5, 11, 12, 16, 20, 24; 5:1, 2), and is he not going to confirm this same truth later on (Eph. 2:8)? Yet here I read that we are saved *by hope!* Besides, what does the apostle mean when he mentions "hope that is seen"? How can a person see hope?

In order to understand Rom. 8:24 we should start out by affirming that the rendering "We are saved by hope" is wrong. Paul wrote "in hope." What he meant was that when, sometime in the past (probably at different dates for each person) we *were* saved, that salvation was not delivered to us complete in one package. It did not arrive "cut and dried." On the contrary, it came to us "with a promise of more to follow." Such elements included in salvation, as election, calling, regeneration, basic conversion, faith, justification, and even, in part, sanctification, had already occurred. Still to come were further progress in sanctification, and finally, at death, and even more fully at Christ's Return, glorification. It is clear, therefore, that Paul could write, "We were saved *in hope.*"

Christian hope, however, must be distinguished from the "hope" we speak about in daily life. Such hope often amounts to no more than a desire

271

that something nice may happen to us, plus a belief that it might just take place. In fact, such hope can frequently be defined as "that which precedes disappointment." Its picture is at times that of a drowning man grasping at a straw. But Christian hope is "an anchor for the soul, safe and sure, entering into the inner sanctuary, behind the curtain, where Jesus has gone as a forerunner on our behalf." (Heb. 6:19, 20).

As to the rest of the verse (24), everything becomes clear when we realize that the word *hope* can have three different meanings. It can indicate (a) *a feeling* or even *a conviction* that what is desired will take place; (b) *the person* who is considered able to make it take place, as in "Our Hope for years to come," and (c) *the thing* hoped for. It would seem that in Greek this last meaning is more common than in English. So we translate the remainder of verse 24 as follows:

"But when once something hoped for is seen, it is no longer an object of hope, for who hopes for what he sees?"[234]

The truth here expressed is obvious: when that for which a person was hoping has arrived, and is now standing or lying in front of him, so that he sees it (implying: and can take hold of it), it ceases to be an object of hope.

Paul is emphasizing the necessity of making use of the anchor of hope. He is, as it were, saying, "Just as *faith* is necessary to appropriate the salvation which Christ merited for y o u in the past, so *hope* is necessary to take to yourselves future blessings. Those bounties are reserved for all who humbly confess their shortcomings and rely wholly on God, the Merciful Giver. Remember, y o u were saved 'in hope.'"

The present-day practical application is clear. There are those who seem to think that they have already arrived. They believe that the petition "Forgive us our debts, as we also have forgiven our debtors" (Matt. 6:12) was not meant for them. Perhaps they also believe that they have received "the second blessing" and are therefore superior Christians. There are even those who make propaganda for the error that also the body is already perfect, sickness being a figment of the imagination. Any future "redemption of the body" (8:23) has little significance for them. To them all Paul is, as it were, saying, "Y o u have done away with the biblical doctrine of salvation *in hope,* for how can one hope for what he already has . . . or thinks he has?"

The objection might be raised, "But the apostle was not living in our day. Was there any reason why he felt it to be necessary *in this epistle* to stress the importance of hope, in the life of the believer? Are we able to prove that there were people in the Roman church who considered themselves *strong,* and able, accordingly, to dispense, at least to some extent, with *hope,* since they had already arrived?"

The answer is in the affirmative. By and large the Roman church ranked

---

234. The reading of $P^{46}B^*$ is followed here, being the shorter.

high in Paul's estimation. See 1:8; 15:14. But there were exceptions, as the following passages indicate:

"Do not think too highly of yourself" (12:3).

"You, then, why do you judge your brother?" (14:10).

"Therefore let us stop passing judgment on one another" (14:13).

"We who are strong ought to bear with the failings of the weak, and not to please ourselves" (15:1).

The conclusion is truly beautiful: "But since we hope for that which we do not see, we wait for it with patient endurance."[235]

This reminds us of a similar Pauline passage, namely, "We fix our eyes not on the things that are seen, but on the things that are not seen; for the things that are seen are temporal, but the things that are not seen are eternal" (II Cor. 4:18). In the meantime:

> Ye fearful saints, fresh courage take;
> The clouds ye so much dread
> Are big with mercy and shall break
> In blessings on your head.
>
> His purposes will ripen fast,
> Unfolding every hour,
> The bud may have a bitter taste,
> But sweet will be the flower.
>
> William Cowper, 1772

26, 27. And in the same way the Spirit too is helping us in our weakness, for we do not know what we ought to pray, but the Spirit himself intercedes for us with unspoken groanings. And he who searches the hearts knows what is the Spirit's intention, that he is interceding for the saints in harmony with God's will.

C. *The Spirit's Groanings*

Having discussed the groaning of the creation (verses 19–22) and of God's children (verses 23–25), Paul now introduces the groanings of the Spirit (verses 26, 27). He tells us something about their (a) necessity, (b) Author and character, and (c) effectiveness.

1. *Their Necessity*

The apostle points to "our weakness," human limitation due to sinfulness. That weakness consists, at least in part, in this, that "we do not know

---

235. δι' ὑπομονῆς (gen. of attendant circumstance). For the noun see also 2:7; 5:3, 4; 15:4, 5; cf. footnote 142 on p. 170. In view of the context (see especially verse 23), "patient endurance" is probably the best translation. The apostle was thinking of *the power to bear up persistently under stress.* This patient endurance is accompanied by *ardent longing;* for note also ἀπεκδεχόμεθα, first per. pl. pres. indicat. of ἀπεκδέχομαι, which, by means of its double prefix, emphasizes the ardent character of the believers' waiting. This recalls to our minds a form of the same verb in verse 19, but there with the addition of "with outstretched head."

273

what we ought to pray." We are not sure about the prayer content that is in harmony with God's will (see verse 27). By saying "we" the apostle is including himself.

It may seem strange for a man of Paul's stature to make this admission. How was it possible for this marvelous missionary, ardent lover of souls, divinely inspired author, to make such a statement? With the exception of the prayers of Jesus Christ, is there anything in the line of prayer more thought-filled, fervent, and sublime than the apostle's prayer recorded in Eph. 3:14–19?

The solution is probably along this line: Paul certainly knew what the general content of prayer should be. He knew that one should pray for the forgiving spirit, for peace among the members of the church, increase in knowledge of spiritual things, readiness to bear witness for Christ, courage amid affliction and persecution, helpfulness toward all who are in need, gratitude toward God; in fact, all the fruits of the Spirit (see Gal. 5:22, 23). But what to pray for *in any particular difficulty* or *situation* was not always clear.

A good illustration is the incident recorded in II Cor. 12:7, with reference to "the thorn in the flesh." Exactly what that thorn may have been no one knows. What we do know is that the apostle found it to be very bothersome. So he prayed, "Lord, please remove that thorn." Three times he uttered this prayer. He seems to have been of the opinion that the removal of the thorn would make him *a more powerful* witness for Christ. But God's answer was, "My grace is sufficient for you, for *my power* is perfected *in weakness.*" And see also Phil. 1:22–24.

Another illustration taken from life runs as follows: A pastor, loved by his people, became grievously ill. The congregation prayed, "Lord, please restore him to health." But he died. At the funeral a minister who had been a lifelong friend of the departed made this remark to the assembled mourners, "Perhaps some of you are in danger of arriving at the conclusion that the heavenly Father does not hear prayer. He does indeed hear prayer, however. But in this particular case two prayers were probably opposing each other. *Y o u* were praying, 'O God, spare his life, for we need him so badly.' *The Spirit's* unspoken prayer was , 'Take him away, for the congregation is leaning altogether too heavily upon *him,* not upon *thee.*' And the Father heard that prayer."

If the objection should be raised, "Then why not permit the Holy Spirit to do all the praying? Why should *we* pray at all?," the answer would be: (a) a child of God needs to, and wants to, pour out his heart to God in prayer and thanksgiving; (b) the Holy Spirit prays only in the hearts of those who pray; (c) God has commanded his people to pray and has promised to grant all such requests as are in harmony with his will; and (d) there must be many prayers which do not need to be counteracted by the Holy Spirit.

The words, "the Spirit is helping us in our weakness" must not be interpreted too narrowly, as if the meaning would be that the Spirit only helps us *to pray*. He helps us "in our weakness," of whatever nature that weakness may be, including our weakness in prayer.

2. *Their Author and Character*[236]

How does the Spirit help us? The answer is, "The Spirit himself intercedes for us with unspoken groanings." What do these words mean?

The most obvious interpretation, the one which the person unacquainted with doctrinal presuppositions would be most likely to adopt is certainly this, that *these unspoken words are those of the Spirit.*

Not all interpreters agree with this conclusion, however. In order to prove their contention that these groanings are those of the saints, not those of the Holy Spirit, an appeal is made to Gal. 4:6, where the same apostle states, "And because y o u are sons, God sent forth the Spirit of his Son into our hearts, crying, 'Abba! Father!'" The further reasoning is as follows, "Even though Paul seems to be saying that *the Spirit* is crying 'Abba! Father!' he cannot mean this, for God cannot be the Father of the Holy Spirit. Therefore, it must be true that the cry is uttered not by the Spirit but *by God's children,* although through the Spirit. The same must be true here in Rom. 8:26b: the groanings, though ascribed to the Spirit, who may well be their Author, are actually those of God's children. It is they who groan."

With due respect for those who so reason, I must, nevertheless, disagree. The appeal to Gal. 4:6 is not conclusive. Note the following meaningful differences, which at the same time are reasons for believing that the groanings are those of the Spirit:

1. Here in Rom. 8:26b Paul does *not* say, "the Spirit intercedes for us." He says, "The Spirit *himself*[237] intercedes for us with groanings," etc. There is therefore a real difference between Gal. 4:6 and Rom. 8:26b.

2. In order to make his meaning even more unambiguous, the apostle continues in verse 27 by saying, "And he who searches the hearts knows

---

236. The following Greek words are in need of some comment: ὡσαύτως, in the same way; similarly (Matt. 20:5; 21:30, 36; 25:17; Mark 12:21; 14:31; Luke 13:5; 20:31; 22:20). Paul uses it also in I Cor. 11:25, and 6 times in the Pastorals, beginning with I Tim. 2:9

συναντιλαμβάνεται, third per. s. pres. middle indicat. of συναντιλαμβάνομαι, to take hold of along with someone, to help. See N.T.C. on Luke 10:40, p. 603.

προσευξώμεθα, first per. pl. aor. middle deliberative subjunctive (after an indirect question) of προσεύχομαι, to pray.

ὑπερεντυγχάνει, third per. s. pres. indicat. of ὑπερεντυγχάνω basically: *to come upon* (or meet) and speak or act *in behalf or* (ὑπέρ); to intercede.

στεναγμοῖς, dat. pl. of στεναγμός, groaning, sighing. Cf. German *stönen;* Dutch *steunen* (also *stenen*).

ἀλαλήτοις, masc. dat. pl. of ἀλάλητος. Some interpret this to mean unutterable, inexpressible, (groans and sighs) "too deep for words" (Ridderbos, Lenski, etc.); others translate unuttered, unspoken, wordless. We cannot be sure, although verse 27 seems to favor the latter interpretation. The Spirit's groanings do not need to be translated into actual words because the Father is able to discern the Spirit's meaning even though no words were spoken. But interpreted either way, the main thought of verses 26, 27 remains about the same.

237. αὐτὸ τὸ πνεῦμα.

what is *the Spirit's* intention." Not: the intention of believers, but that of *the Spirit*. Exegetically, therefore, I am forced to agree with those who say that the groanings to which reference is made here in verse 26 are those of the Spirit.

Is not the real reason why certain eminent interpreters refuse to ascribe these groanings to the Spirit *theological* rather than exegetical? They do not wish to ascribe to any of the three persons of the Holy Trinity qualities that would seem to be unworthy of him. At times this reason is stated in so many words.[238] And even though I cannot agree with their exegesis of Rom. 8:26, particularly with their unwillingness to ascribe *to the Spirit* these groanings, I honor them for their desire to remain doctrinally sound, especially in a day and age when by many such soundness is ridiculed. But exegetical accuracy is as important as doctrinal purity. Both are needed.

To the reasons given for believing that the groanings of verse 26 are those of the Spirit, the following should be added:

3. Since in verse 23 Paul has already discussed the groanings of the saints, it is hard to believe that he would return to this subject in verse 26. Moreover, the words introducing verse 26, namely, "And in the same way" imply a comparison; most likely between, on the one hand, the groanings of the creation and of believers (respectively verses 19–22; verses 23, 24); and, on the other, the groanings of the Spirit (verses 26, 27).

4. In verse 26 these groanings are linked inseparably with the Spirit's intercession. This intercession is mentioned again in verse 27. In verse 34 the verb which in verse 27 describes *the Spirit's* intercession, is used in connection with *the Son's* intercession. If, then, verse 34 refers to *Christ's own* intercessory prayer, why should not verse 27 describe *the Spirit's own* intercession, accompanied by groanings?[239]

Exactly what this groaning of the Holy Spirit implies would be difficult to define. Are we in error when we state that it means at least the following: the Spirit loves the saints so exceedingly that he yearns for that great day when, delivered from every speck of sin, they will glorify God forever and ever in the perfection of holiness and joy? Although it would be difficult to prove that the words, "That Spirit which he made to dwell in us yearns for us even unto jealous envy" (James 4:5) are the best translation of the original, yet, they may shed light on the meaning of the Spirit's groaning. And do we not meet with similar highly emotional expressions by means of which we are given a glimpse into the very heart of God? See, for example, the following:

> How can I give you up, O Ephraim?
> How can I cast you off, O Israel?
> How can I treat you like Admah?

---

238. See, for example, Lenski, *op. cit.*, p. 547.

239. It must have become clear that my interpretation of verse 26 (and also of verse 27) agrees with that of A. Kuyper, *Het Werk van den Heiligen Geest,* pp. 787, 788; Engl. tr., p. 636.

How can I make you like Zeboiim?
My heart is turned over within me,
All my compassions are kindled.

Hos. 11:8

If one wishes he may call the statement, "The Spirit himself intercedes for us with unspoken groanings," "highly anthropomorphic." Still, it expresses a truth we can ill afford to neglect. If human knowledge points back to divine omniscience; and human power, to divine omnipotence, it is hard to believe that human emotion reflects nothing at all in God. According to Scripture God is not Buddha, and heaven is not Nirvana!

Romans 8 teaches that believers have two intercessors: the Holy Spirit and Christ. Christ performs his intercessory task in heaven (Rom. 8:34; Heb. 7:25; I John 2:1); the Holy Spirit, on earth. Christ's intercession takes place outside of us, the Holy Spirit's within us; that is, in our very hearts (John 14:16, 17). Christ prays that the merits of his redemptive work may be fully applied to those who trust in him. The Holy Spirit prays that the deeply hidden needs of our hearts, needs which we ourselves sometimes do not even recognize, may be met. Christ's intercession may be compared with that of a father, the head of the family, for all the family members. The Holy Spirit's intercession reminds us rather of a mother kneeling at the bedside of her ailing child, and in her prayer presenting that child's needs to the heavenly Father.[240]

3. *Their Effectiveness*

The Spirit's intercession, accompanied by groanings, is not fruitless. Would not he who is constantly searching human hearts be able to read the intention of his own Spirit, who dwells in these hearts? Would he not know the meaning of that Spirit's unspoken groanings?

Again and again Scripture bears testimony to the truth of God's omniscience. See, for example, the following passages:

"Man looks at the outward appearance, but the Lord looks at the heart" (I Sam. 16:7).

"Thou alone knowest the hearts of all the sons of men" (I Kings 8:39).

"The Lord searches every heart and understands every motive" (I Chron. 28:9).

"O Lord, thou hast searched me and known me. Thou knowest when I sit down and when I rise up . . ." (Ps. 139:1, 2). The entire Psalm bears testimony to God's omnipresence and omniscience.

"Sheol and Abaddon lie open before the Lord" (Prov. 15:11).

"The heart is deceitful above all things. It is exceedingly corrupt: who can know it? I, the Lord, search the mind. I try the heart" (Jer. 17:9, 10).

---

240. For a similar representation see A. Kuyper (for reference see above, footnote 238, p. 276); and R. C. Harder, in *De Heilige Geest,* edited by J. H. Bavinck, P. Prins, and G. Brillenburg Wurth, Kampen, 1949, p. 396.

"Lord, thou knowest everyone's heart" (Acts 1:24).

"The Lord will bring to light what is hidden in darkness and will expose the motives of men's hearts" (I Cor. 4:5).

"There is no creature hidden from God's sight. All things are open and laid bare before the eyes of him to whom we must give account" (Heb. 4:13).

But not only does God *know* everything. What is emphasized is that he knows that the Spirit is interceding *in harmony with his (God's) own will.* Are not Father, Son, and Holy Spirit the *One* true God? Any clash between them is therefore impossible.

Note too that the Holy Spirit is described as constantly interceding "for the saints," that is, for those people who have been set apart in order to live lives to the glory of the Triune God as revealed in Christ Jesus. See on 1:7.

And since there is perfect harmony between the persons of the Holy Trinity, so that the Spirit's intercession, accompanied by groanings, coincides completely with the Father's will, the result must be that this intercession is always effective. It never fails. None of the saints is ever lost. All reach heaven at last. Better still: see verse 28.[241]

28. And we know that to those who love God all things work together for good; that is, to those who are called according to (his) purpose.

The present passage is a kind of summary of 8:1–27. It prepares for, and to some extent is similar to, the grand climax found in verses 37–39. It cannot be fully understood except in the light of verses 1–27. It draws a conclusion; in fact, a very comforting conclusion.

Paul has shown that for those who are in Christ Jesus there is now no condemnation (verses 1–8). They are indwelt by that Spirit who will even raise their bodies gloriously (verses 9–11). They receive the assurance that they are God's children, and as such, his heirs (verses 14–16). Their present suffering for Christ and for his cause means that one day they will share his glory, a glory so marvelous that in comparison with it hardships fade away into nothingness (verse 18). They will dwell in that new heaven and earth to which all creation with groaning is looking forward (verses 19–22). They themselves also groan as they eagerly await their adoption (verses 23–25). In all their weaknesses the Holy Spirit helps them. That Spirit always intercedes for them in harmony with God's will, so that this intercession, accompanied by wordless groanings, will certainly be effective (verses 26, 27).

So Paul says, "*And we know*—see also 3:19; 7:14; 8:22; I Cor. 8:1, 4; 13:9; II Cor. 5:1; I Tim. 1:8—that to those who love God all things work together for good . . ." On what else does he base this knowledge? Probably on two

---

241. In verse 27 note ἐραυνῶν, pres. participle of ἐραυνάω, to search; in the New Testament occurring only here and in John 5:39; 7:52; I Cor. 2:10; I Peter 1:11; and Rev. 2:23: "I am he who searches hearts and minds."

Because of the context ὅτι in verse 27 should be rendered *that*, not "because."

additional grounds: (a) *Experience;* that is, the effect on him of knowing how God had dealt with him and with others in the past. See such passages as Gen. 46:30; 48:3, 4; Deut. 5; Josh. 24:1–15; I Sam. 7:1–12; II Sam. 23:1–5; I Kings 8:22–24; Isa. 63:9; Acts 26:1–23; Gal. 2:19, 20. And (b) Acquaintance with *specific biblical passages* which teach that in God's providence all things result in blessing for God's children, evil being over-ruled for good (Gen. 45:5, 7, 8; 50:20).

Some find it difficult to accept the statement, "All things work together for good." They seem to think that such an expression ascribes to mere "things" qualities—such as wisdom and intelligence—which these things do not possess. In order to overcome this difficulty these interpreters suggest that the statement should read, "In all things [or: in everything] *God* works for good," or "*God* causes all things to work for good." Somehow the word *God* must be included in this clause. Otherwise, as some see it, it would result in heresy: a materialistic, perhaps evolutionistic, philosophy of life and history. Even if we must disagree, should we not love and honor these people for their motive? And if we answer them by stating "Y o u have no right to insert the word *God* where the original does not have it," they quickly answer that they have found a reading that supports their view.[242]

The answer to this is as follows:

Though no one knows how this variant originated, its acceptance results in a sentence that would make Paul a rather clumsy stylist.[243] Besides, if Paul really dictated, and Tertius really wrote, "In all things *God* works for good," or "*God* causes all things to work for good," it is very hard, indeed, to believe that this second mention of the word *God*—the first was in the clause "who love God"—would ever have been dropped from the text.

Others, rightly dissatisfied with making the word *God* the subject of the clause, borrow a subject from the preceding context. They go back to "*The Spirit* is helping us in our weakness … intercedes for us," etc., and then continue the sentence as follows: "and in everything, as we know, he [that is, the Spirit] co-operates for good with those who love God."[244]

But this rendering, if adhered to all the way, runs into difficulty when it reaches verse 29, for that verse would then read as follows, "For whom he [the Spirit, *if* N.E.B.'s translation of verse 28 is correct] foreknew, he also foreordained to be conformed to the image of his [the Spirit's] Son." This,

---

242. P⁴⁶ A B Origen, by Grk. N.T. (A-B-M-W) included in the apparatus, while the adopted text (without ὁ θεός) is given a C rating.

243. Note the doubling of the word θεός in what Paul then supposedly wrote: τοῖς ἀγαπῶσιν τὸν θεὸν πάντα συνεργεῖ ὁ θεὸς εἰς ἀγαθόν. Is it not reasonable to assume that it was a very early burdened soul who inserted the second θεός? Besides, unless there are sound reasons to do otherwise, should not the shorter reading—in this case the one without the second θεός—prevail? Also "causes to work" is not a faithful rendering of συνεργεῖ.

244. See N.E.B.'s translation in its *text*. To the credit of N.E.B. it should be stated that in a footnote it recognizes what I would call the correct reading and translation, the one that makes "all things" the subject of the clause.

of course, is impossible, for nowhere in Scripture is Jesus Christ called the Son of the Holy Spirit! So at this point N.E.B. inserts the word *God:* "For God knew his own . . ." But here the word *God* is not in the original Greek text.

As I see it, every attempt to avoid making "all things" the subject of the clause has failed.[245] The old—yes, *very old!*—rendering, namely, ". . . all things work together for good"[246] should stand. It is only fair to add that whether one translates one way or the other—that is, whether one (a) erroneously accepts the word "God" or "he" [the Spirit] as the subject of the clause; or (b) correctly views "all things" as being the real subject—hence, "all things work together for good"—the result remains about the same, namely, that in God's all-embracing providence all things work together for good to those who love God.

What is more important and necessary is that we accept the following three facts:

a. *"All things,"—no less!—cooperate for good.*

Not only prosperity is included but so also is adversity; not only joy and happiness but also suffering and sadness (Rom. 8:18, 35–37). Evil designs are by God overruled for good (Gen. 50:20; Neh. 4:15). Not only what the saints themselves experience is included but also whatever lies outside the sphere of their personal experience. Specifically, the following entities are among those that are divinely ordered and directed so that they work together for good to those who love God: the good angels (Heb. 1:14) and Satan together with his hosts (Rom. 16:20; Eph. 6:10–16); the nations of the world and their rulers (Ps. 2:2–9; 48:4–8; 149:9; Acts 9:15); rain and thunder (I Sam. 12:18–20); streams, mountains, and clouds (Ps. 46:4; 72:3; Matt. 24:30; Rev. 1:7); and even the stars in their courses (Judg. 5:20).

b. *It is only to those who love God that all things work together for good.*

In the original—as also in A.R.V. and in my rendering—the words "And we know that to those who love God all things work together for good" stand *at the very beginning* of the sentence. The meaning is this: they, and they alone, have a right to be comforted by this fact. Only in the case of those who love God is it true that all things work together for good. This is clear from such passages as the following: Exod. 20:6; Deut. 7:9; Neh. 1:5; Ps. 37:17, 20, 37–40; 97:10, 116:1 f.; Isa. 56:6, 7; I Cor. 2:9; 8:3; James 1:12; 2:5. All these references emphasize the importance of loving God and/or delighting in him.

c. *They love God because he first loved them.*

That surely is the meaning of the words, ". . . to those who love God all

---

245. For a more complete list of these attempts see the excellent summary and discussion by Cranfield, *op. cit.,* pp. 425–428.

246. Some prefer "co-operate for good"; others "prove advantageous for (their true) good." But these variations do not touch the main issue and, I believe, require no further discussion.

things work together for good; that is, to those who are called according to
(his) purpose." Though it is true that the word "his"—that is, God's—does
not occur in the original, nevertheless, the only other passage in the entire
book of Romans where this word *purpose* is found, namely 9:11 ("in order
that God's purpose in election might stand"), proves that Paul was thinking
about *God's* purpose, not man's.

The people who were called according to God's purpose are, therefore,
those who were effectively called. They are those whose hearts and minds
were so thoroughly influenced by the Holy Spirit that they became aware of
their sinfulness, began to understand their need of Christ, and embraced
him as their Lord and Savior. See above, on Rom. 1:7, p. 47. See also Rom.
8:30; 9:24; I Cor. 1:2, 24; 7:17f.

Paul felt that it was necessary to add the words, "to those who are called
according to his [God's] purpose," in order that the Romans and all who
would read this letter or hear it read to them would realize that no one can
ever truly love God unless first of all he is effectively called. In other words,
the apostle to the Gentiles is here expressing substantially the same thought
as did the apostle John when he wrote, "We love God because he first loved
us" (I John 4:19).

What Paul is really saying then, here in Rom. 8:28, is this, "We know that
to those who love God and do so because of God's work in them, as determined by his sovereign, elective purpose, all things work together for
good." In this manner human responsibility is fully maintained, but God
Triune receives all the honor. Cf. Phil. 2:12, 13; II Thess. 2:13.

**29, 30. For whom he foreknew, he also foreordained to be conformed
to the image of his Son, so that he might be the firstborn among many
brothers; and whom he foreordained, these he also called; and whom he
called, these he also justified; and whom he justified, these he also
glorified.**

THE SALVATION CHAIN

When Paul states that to those who love God and are called according to
his purpose all things work together for good, he is not thinking only of
those things that can be seen round about us *now,* or those events that are
taking place *now;* no, he includes even time and eternity. The chain of
salvation he is discussing reaches back to that which, considered from a
human standpoint, could be called the dim past, "the quiet recess of eternity," and forward into the boundless future.

One very important fact must be mentioned: every link in this chain of
salvation represents a divine action. To be sure, human responsibility and
action is not thereby ruled out, but here (Rom. 8:29, 30) it is never specifically mentioned.

There are five links in this chain. Note that the predicate of the first clause becomes the subject of the next one, a construction called *sorities*.[247]

A. *Foreknowledge*

". . . whom he foreknew."

Is it possible to interpret Paul's words in this sense: Before the world was created God foresaw who were going to believe in him and who would not. So, on the basis of that foreseen faith, he decided to elect to salvation those good people who were going to exercise it?

Answer: such a construction is entirely impossible, for according to Scripture even faith is God's gift. See N.T.C. on Ephesians, pp. 120–123 (on Eph. 2:8). See also John 6:44, 65; I Cor. 4:7; Phil. 1:29. In fact, even the good works performed by believers are prepared beforehand by God! (Eph. 2:10).

On the contrary, the foreknowledge mentioned in Rom. 8:29 refers to *divine active delight*. It indicates that, in his own sovereign good pleasure, God set his love on certain individuals, many still to be born, gladly acknowledging them as his own, electing them to everlasting life and glory. Note the following:

"For I have known him [Abraham] so that he may direct his children and his household after him" (Gen. 18:19).

"Before I formed you in the womb I knew you, Before you were born I set you apart" (Jer. 1:5).

"I am the good shepherd, and I know my own" (John 10:14). Cf. 10:28.

"The Lord knows who are his" (II Tim. 2:19).

Add the following: Ps. 1:6; Amos 3:2; Hos. 13:5; Matt. 7:23; I Cor. 8:3; Gal. 4:9; I John 3:1; and see also on Rom. 11:2.

"The term *prognosis* [foreknowledge] reveals the fact that in his purpose according to election the persons are not the objects of God's 'bare foreknowledge' but of his 'active delight.'"[248]

B. *Foreordination with a View to Conformation*

". . . he also foreordained to be conformed to the image of his Son, so that he might be the firstborn among many brothers."

In reality "foreknowledge" already imples "foreordination." Nevertheless, there is a difference of emphasis. Whereas the first term directs our attention to the persons whom God elected and only in a general way to their final destiny (everlasting life, glory), the term *foreordination* fixes our thought more definitely on the purpose for which they were elected and on

---

247. F. F. Bruce, *op. cit.*, p. 176.
248. H. Bavinck, *The Doctrine of God*, Grand Rapids, 1951, Vol. II, p. 343; my published translation of Bavinck's *Gereformeerde Dogmatiek;* see above, footnote 16.

the means of attaining it. That goal is not just "to enter heaven at last" but "to be conformed to the image of God's Son."

Man was created *as*—this is probably better than *in*[249]—God's image. That image was distorted by sin, but was restored in Christ, who was and is the image of God (II Cor. 4:4; Col. 1:15).

The question has been asked, "When Paul describes the purpose of foreordination to be that those whom God foreknew should be conformed to the image of his Son, does he have in mind (a) *only* the *final* conformation; that is, only that part of transformation into Christ's image that will take place at his Return; or is he referring to (b) the entire process of transformation, beginning already when the sinner is brought out of the darkness into the light?" On this point there is a difference of opinion among commentators.

Position (a) *Only Final*	Position (b) *Also Present*
Greijdanus, Vol. I, p. 390	Calvin, p. 318
Lenski, p. 561	Cranfield, Vol. I, p. 432
Murray, Vol. I, p. 319	Lekkerkerker, Vol. I, p. 354
Ridderbos, p. 196	Robertson, W. P., IV, p. 377
	Van Leeuwen-Jacobs, p. 160
	Zahn, p. 417[250]

Those who accept Position (a) point out that the context favors this position: verses 11 and 23 refer to the glorious resurrection of the body, and verse 21 to a gloriously renewed universe. These renewals will not take place until the day of Christ's Return. From this they draw the conclusion that also the conformation to the image of Christ must be interpreted as a great eschatological event that will occur on the day of The Great Consummation.

Now if the conformation to the image of God's Son is limited to the refashioning of our lowly body so that it will have a form like Christ's glorious body (Phil. 3:21, to which reference is often made in this connection), then the question is immediately settled in favor of Position (a), for that conformation will certainly not take place until then.

However, in a context which deals with such matters as calling, justification, and glorification not many interpreters would accept this narrow interpretation of the words "to be conformed to the image of his Son." It is the *spiritual* conformation or transformation Paul has in mind here.

Once this is granted, the weight of the evidence, I believe, turns sharply in the direction of Position (b), and this for the following reasons:

1. In arriving at the meaning of "He also foreordained to be conformed

---

249. So also G. Ch. Aalders, *Het Boek Genesis (Korte Verklaring)*, Kampen, 1949, Vol. I, p. 96.
250. The references are to the *Commentaries*—not to any other works—written by these authors.

to the image of his Son" the chief determining factor is not 8:11, 21, 23, but the much closer "For whom he foreknew" of verse 29a. That word carries us back to the "eternity" which, humanly speaking, preceded the foundation of the earth (Eph. 1:4). Is it not logical, therefore, to view the conformation "to the image of his Son" to pertain not only to what will happen on the day of Christ's Return but also to what happens in the lengthy period before that Return? If we do not do this, are we not then creating a gap of very lengthy duration about which nothing is said?

2. Other passages—such as Rom. 12:1; Eph. 4:32—5:2; Phil. 3:10; Col. 3:10—regarding spiritual renewal cannot be interpreted as being connected with the day of Christ's Return.

3. *Basically* the required transformation is not man's work but God's. Is not that also the thought expressed in II Cor. 3:18—which even contains the words "we are being transformed into the same image"? Here, again, the renewal described is happening *now*, not solely at Christ's Return.

4. If gradual renewal into the image of Christ is not what Paul had in mind, are we not forced to conclude that one very important link in the chain of salvation, namely the link of *sanctification*, is missing? The answer given by some that justification includes sanctification does not satisfy. There is indeed a very close relation between these two but never are they identified.

On the basis of the given reasons I believe that the conformation to the image of his Son, of which the apostle speaks here in 8:29, refers to sanctification. This, too, is basically *God's* work (II Thess. 2:13).

Very significant are the words "*so that he might be the firstborn among many brothers.*"

Two ideas are emphasized here. They form a contrast, yet also harmony. The *first* is that of *Christ's pre-eminence*. Decorating a wall of a certain home in Florida—and no doubt many other walls elsewhere—is a plaque that reads:

> THAT in All Things
> HE Might Have
> THE PRE-EMINENCE
>
> Col. 1:18

This makes sense; for, if the duty as well as the destiny of believers is to be conformed to the image of God's Son, then *he* must indeed be preeminent. Besides, what a worthwhile reminder this plaque is in the interest of day-to-day Christian life and practice!

The *second* idea conveyed by this passage is that of *Christ's humility and marvelous love* for those whom he, by means of his redemptive sacrifice, has made his own. Note "that he might be the firstborn *among many brothers!*" In other words, the Exalted Savior does not consider himself complete apart from those whom he came to save! See Heb. 2:11, noting also its reference to *sanctification*.

For the idea of Christ as firstborn see also Col. 1:15; Heb. 1:6; and Rev. 1:5.

C. *Calling*

"... and whom he foreordained, these he also called."

From that which pertains to *eternity,* namely, foreknowing and foreordaining—though their effects are being historically realized, Paul now, by a very logical transition, enters into the realm of *time.* The apostle refers, of course, to the effective call. What this call means has been explained in connection with Rom. 1:7 (see p. 46) and 8:28 (see p. 281). By means of Spirit-wrought conversion and faith man responds to this call.

D. *Justification*

"... and whom he called, these he also justified."

As has been explained earlier, in a sense "Justification by Faith" is the theme of Romans. Its meaning has been set forth on pp. 61–66, 128–131.

E. *Glorification*

"... and whom he justified, these he also glorified."

Believers will share in Christ's glory (Rom. 8:17). Nothing can be greater glory than that which is bestowed upon Christ's followers because of their intimate union with Christ (Col. 1:27).[251]

Not only will God's children receive gloriously transformed bodies (Rom. 8:11, 23; I Cor. 15:43–53; Phil. 3:21; I John 3:2), but on and after the day of the resurrection they will shine forth in all their glory in both soul and body, these having now become reunited.

So certain is the believers' future glory that, even though it can be considered an object of hope (Rom. 5:2), and therefore a matter pertaining to the future, here in Rom. 8:30 it is described as if it had already become a reality: "he also glorified."[252] And is it not true that in a sense believers "were raised with Christ" (Col. 3:1), and were in his train when he ascended to heaven (Eph. 4:8)? Are they not even now being transformed from glory to glory (II Cor. 3:18)?

This past tense (cf. Jude 14; also most of Isa. 53) indicates the certainty that a future event will take place and, perhaps, in the present connection, also the fact that the glory promised for the future has already begun to be realized.

All this reminds us of a stanza from Wordsworth's *See the Conqueror Mounts in Triumph:*

---

251. For the meaning of δόξα (glory) see footnote 38 on p. 74.
252. ἐδόξασε, third per. s. aor. indicat. of δοξάζω, to glorify.

Thou hast raised our human nature
On the clouds to God's right hand;
There we sit in heavenly places,
There with thee in glory stand.
Jesus reigns, adored by angels,
Man with God is on the throne,
Mighty Lord in thine ascension
We by faith behold our own.

---

31 What, then, shall we say in response to these things? If God is for us, who is against us?
32 He who did not spare even his own Son, but gave him up for us all, how will he not also with
him graciously give us all things? 33 Who will bring any charge against God's elect? It is God
who justifies. 34 Who is he that condemns? (It is) Christ Jesus who died, what is more, who
was raised from the dead, who is at the right hand of God, who is also interceding for us.
35 Who will separate us from the love of Christ? Affliction or distress or persecution or
famine or nakedness or peril or sword? 36 As it is written:
"For thy sake we are being put to death all the day long;
We are considered as sheep to be slaughtered."
37 No, in all these things we are more than conquerors through him who loved us. 38 For I
am convinced that neither death nor life nor angels nor principalities nor things present nor
things to come nor powers 39 nor height nor depth nor any other created thing will be able
to separate us from the love of God which is in Christ Jesus our Lord.

4b. *It produces the fruit of* **super-invincibility;** *i.e., of being more than conquerors.*
"No, in all these things we are more than conquerors
through him who loved us."
8:31–39

**31. What, then, shall we say in response to these things? If God is for
us, who is against us?**

What Paul means is, "To what conclusion do these things lead us?" The
expression "these things" probably refers not only to the matters mentioned in verses 28–30, or even 18–30, but to everything the apostle has so
far written in this epistle. What, then, is the summary of that which Paul has
been saying in this letter?

He has pointed out that the one thing a sinner needs above all else is
right standing with God, and that this right standing is not obtainable by
human exertion or merit. That inestimable blessing is God's free gift, and
there is only one way to obtain it, namely, by faith. See 1:17; 3:24, 28, 30;
4:1, 2, 7, 8; 5:1, 8, 9; 7:24, 25; 8:1. The blessing of salvation has been
earned for everyone, whether Jew or Gentile, who will, by God's power and
grace, repose his trust in the Savior. It was *he* who earned salvation for his
people by the shedding of *his* blood. They are saved by *his* substitutionary
death, *his* resurrection, and *his* intercession (1:4, 5; 3:21–26; 4:25; 5:1, 2,
8–21; 6:23; 7:24; 8:1–4; and see also 8:34).

If, then, God is on our side, as he clearly proved by what he did and does
for us, who is against us? Not as if all the enemies have already been swept
away, but what is any enemy able to achieve *against* us, God being *for* us?

When Paul says, "*If* God is for us," he is not calling in doubt God's protecting care, love, and promises. On the contrary, *this* "if" means, "If . . . as he certainly is!"

In light of all this the opening question, "What, then, shall we say in response to these things?" will have to be answered with a very strong, "We have nothing to fear. Victory is certainly on our side."

But the apostle himself gives a far more complete answer in verses 32–39. The beginning of this answer is found in the next verse:

32. He who did not spare even his own Son, but gave him up for us all, how will he not also with him graciously give us all things?

"He . . . did not spare even his own Son, but gave him up." The depth of feeling implied in the words of verse 3—"sending his own Son"—is expressed even more vividly here in verse 32.[253] If this does not mean that, in a sense, giving up his only-begotten and fathomlessly beloved Son was for the Father a genuine sacrifice, words no longer have meaning.

It is possible to think of a judge who does not spare a vicious criminal but pronounces on him the severe sentence he deserves. It is not inconceivable that such a judge might afterward enjoy a good night's sleep.

But what we have here in Rom. 8:32 is something else. The following facts should be kept in mind:

God, the Judge, has a Son, an only Son, very precious to him. That Son never committed any sin. In all he did he was ever pleasing his Father (John 8:29).

On the other hand:

> *We* all like sheep have gone astray,
> Each of *us* has turned to his own way.
>
> Isa. 53:6.

Yet, on this precious and beloved Son God now pronounces the sentence *we* deserved. It is a sentence immeasurable in its severity, and is carried out in every detail. *God did not spare* his Son, did not mitigate the severity of the sentence in any way whatever, the Son himself agreeing with the Father and the Spirit in all this. He, the Son, fully bore that horrendous curse. He drank the cup of unspeakable agony to the very last drop. "That bitter cup, Love drank it up. It's empty now for me." See Isa. 53; Rom. 5:6–8; 8; 3, 4; II Cor. 5:21; Gal. 3:13. It would have been unthinkable for God to reject the demands of his justice. "Will not the Judge of all the earth do right?" (Gen. 18:25).

We ask, "But why was the curse lifted from our shoulders and transferred to the Son of God?" The answer is: So deeply, intensely, and marvelously did God love the world that his Son, the only-begotten, he gave, in order that everyone who believes in him should not perish but have life everlasting. Is not that the meaning of John 3:16?

---

253. Note presence of γε in the clause ὅς γε τοῦ ἰδίου υἱοῦ οὐκ ἐφείσατο.

There is, of course, a resemblance between:

"You [Abraham] have not withheld your son, your only son" (Gen. 22:12, 16)

and

"He [God] did not spare even his own Son . . ." (Rom. 8:32).

Yet, it is not the similarity which arrests our attention most of all. It is the contrast. Abraham was rescued in the nick of time, and so was his son Isaac. But Christ bore the wrath fully, willingly.

" . . . for us all." In accordance with the immediately preceding context, the apostle must have been thinking of all those who love God (verse 28), who were foreknown and foreordained (verse 29), were (or were going to be) called, justified, and glorified (verse 30). To this can be added the similar expressions contained in the statements which follow; namely, the elect (verse 33), those for whom Christ makes intercession (verse 34), those who are "more than conquerors" (verse 37). It was to these people, to them all, to them alone, that the merits of Christ's death had been, were being, or were going to be savingly applied.

Here again, as in connection with 5:18—see above, pp. 182, 183, it is not at all improbable that when Paul says, "He [God] gave him [his own Son] up for *us all*," he included in his thought this idea: "God gave up his Son *for Jew and Gentile alike*," for all his dear children regardless of race, sex, nationality, social standing, etc. See also Rom. 3:22, 23, 29; 10:11–13.

"How will he not also with him graciously give us all things?"

The argument is from the greater to the lesser, as in 5:9, 10, 15, 17; 11:12, 24. Nothing could ever be a greater gift than the gift of Christ to the church. That gift is clearly implied in the statement, "God did not spare his own Son but gave him up for us all." Moreover, even though giving this Son was an unfathomable sacrifice as plainly implied in "God did not spare," nevertheless, it is never a solitary gift: how will he not also *together with him* graciously—that is ungrudgingly, freely, gladly, generously—give us *all things*?

I can see no good reason to limit the expression "all things" to spiritual blessings, as some do. Paul was a very practical man. He knew that the people he was addressing were men of flesh and blood, who were vexed at times with worries over matters mundane. The expression "all things" should therefore be interpreted in an unqualified sense: material as well as spiritual things; cf. 8:28, where it has the same broad meaning.[254]

It is not only about matters in general, both physical and spiritual, that anxieties arise. Underneath everything else, there is that basic worry, "What is my standing with God?" Paul answers as follows:

33, 34. Who will bring any charge against God's elect? It is God who justifies. Who is he that condemns? (It is) Christ Jesus who died, what is

---

254. F. F. Bruce, *op. cit.*, p. 179, correctly refers to Matt. 6:33. Note context: "What are we going to eat, drink, wear?" See also Denney, *op. cit.*, p. 653.

**more, who was raised from the dead, who is at the right hand of God, who
is also interceding for us.**

Verse 33 is probably an intentional echo of words found in Isa. 50:8, 9a:
"He is near who justifies [or vindicates] me. Who is my accuser?...
Behold, the Lord Jehovah will help me. Who is he that will condemn me?"[255]

The rhetorical questions—"Who will bring any charge...?" "Who is he
that condemns?"—amount to a vigorous denial of the suggestion that there
could be any valid charge or condemnation.

Are these people not God's elect? Is that not what is implied in 8:29:
"foreknown... foreordained"? Surely, when, in the dispute between
Joshua the highpriest and Satan, God defended Joshua and rebuked Satan,
the latter was immediately silenced (Zech. 3:1–5). When God justifies a
person, all accusations at once lose their validity.

The logical nature of this answer is brought out even more clearly by the
words that follow, namely, "It is Christ Jesus who died... was raised from
the dead.. is at the right hand of God... is also interceding for us."

Here note especially the phrase "what is more" inserted between the
reference to Christ's death and his resurrection. It probably expresses the
climactic relationship not only between the first two items but between all
the items in the series. To be sure, by means of Christ's death the sins of his
people were blotted out. But this fact was established beyond possibility of
successful contradiction by the resurrection from the dead. See on Rom.
4:25, p. 161. And the exaltation of God's Son to the right hand of God—
Matt. 26:64; Mark 14:62; Luke 22:69; Acts 2:33; 3:13; 5:31; 7:55, 56; Eph.
1:20; Col. 3:1; Heb. 1:3; 2:9; 8:1; 10:12; 12:2; I Peter 1:21; 3:22; Rev.
5:12, symbolizing the honor, power, and authority given to him as a
reward for his fully accomplished mediatorial work, strengthens this conclusion even more.

The *climax* of assurance is reached in the clause, "who is also interceding
for us"—Isa. 53:12;[256] Luke 23:34; John 14:16; I John 2:1; Heb. 7:25,
for how would it even be conceivable that the Father should deny the
intercessory prayers of the Son, who so fully, marvelously, and gloriously
accomplished the task assigned to him (John 17:4)? Did not the Son himself
say to the Father, "I knew that thou dost always hear me"? (John 11:42a).

**35. Who will separate us from the love of Christ? Affliction or distress
or persecution or famine or nakedness or peril or sword?**

Another rhetorical question, meaning, "No one will ever be able to separate us from the love Christ has for us." Not our love for Christ is meant but
Christ's love for us, as verse 37 clearly indicates: "through him who loved
us."

To give an adequate description or definition of that love of Christ is

---

255. When this close relation between Rom. 8:33, 34 and Isa. 50:8, 9a is accepted, this will
solve the problem of the punctuation of the Pauline passage.
256. See what was said in footnote 139, p. 162, about Isa. 53:12 in Hebrew.

impossible. Cf. Eph. 3:19. All we can do is stammer. We might say, for example, that it is the outgoing disposition of Christ's compassionate heart which revealed itself in the most marvelous and self-sacrificing action that was ever taken. See John 15:13; Rom. 5:8; I John 4:10. God is Love (I John 4:8), and since Christ is God, Christ too is Love.

Charles Wesley, in his hymn *Love Divine,* probably came about as close to describing Christ's love as anyone can get apart from quoting the words of Scripture:

> Jesus, thou art all compassion,
> Pure, unbounded love thou art.

Paul enumerates seven circumstances that might be brought up for consideration in answering the question whether anything can separate us from Christ's love:

a. b. *affliction, distress.* Not only is "affliction" a good translation of the first of the seven Greek words but it is even etymologically related to it. While this word occurs more than forty times in the New Testament, the apostle uses it only four times (besides here in Rom. 8:35, also in Rom. 2:9; II Cor. 6:4; 12:10). In the first three instances both words *affliction* and *distress* occur. The fact that Paul uses both words indicates that in his mind there was a distinction between them. The suggestion of several commentators that the two words used in the original[257] refer respectively to *outward affliction* and *inward distress* is probably correct. In the New Testament Paul is the only writer who uses the word *distress,* and even in his epistles it is found only four times (in addition to Rom. 8:35 also in 2:9; II Cor. 6:4; 12:10).

c. *persecution.* In the New Testament this word occurs for the first time in Matt. 13:21, "When affliction or persecution arises on account of the message he immediately falls away." Paul uses the word *persecution* five times (here and also in II Cor. 12:10; II Thess. 1:4; twice in II Tim. 3:11).

d. *famine.* The word used in the original means hunger, famine. Its first occurrence is in Matt. 24:7, "There shall be famines and earthquakes in various places." See also Luke 15:14, "When he had spent everything a severe famine arose. . . ." Though the word is used a dozen times in the New Testament, Paul has it only here and in II Cor. 11:27 (hunger).

e. *nakedness.* In the New Testament this noun is found only three times: here, in II Cor. 11:27; and in Rev. 3:18, but the related adjective (naked) occurs several times; for example, in Matt. 25:36, "I was naked, and y o u clothed me." Often the meaning is somewhat more general than *naked* might suggest; hence, *in need of clothes* is at times a better rendering.

f. *peril.* This noun occurs here and eight times (!) in II Cor. 11:26.

g. *sword,* a word of frequent occurrence in the New Testament, begin-

---

257. θλῖψις and στενοχωρία (basically *narrow place*).

ning with Matt. 10:34, "I did not come to bring peace but a sword." Paul uses it only here and in Rom. 13:4; Eph. 6:17.

We should not forget that when Paul spoke about these adverse circumstances which Satan and the other enemies of the cross used in order to bring about separation between believers and their Lord, he was not speaking as an armchair theologian or philosopher. On the contrary, as II Cor. 11:23–29 indicates, he had already suffered the first six of these seven hardships before writing this epistle to the Romans. Moreover, by means of the seventh, i.e., the sword, he was going to be put to death. The apostle was speaking not only by inspiration but also from experience, therefore, when he stated that none of these things can bring about separation between believers and their Lord. He knew what he was saying!

Moreover, by implying, "Nothing will separate us from Christ's love" was he not also saying, "On the contrary, suffering for Christ's sake will bring us closer to him and to his love"? Cf. Phil. 1:29, "For to y o u it has been granted in behalf of Christ not only to believe in him but also to suffer in his behalf." On the theme *Suffering for Christ a Blessing* see N.T.C. on Philippians, pp. 90, 91.

36. As it is written:
"For thy sake we are being put to death all the day long;
We are considered as sheep to be slaughtered."

By quoting Ps. 44:22 (Heb. 44:23; LXX 43:23) Paul shows that there is nothing strange or unexpected about present-day suffering for the Lord's sake. The Psalmist trusted in God. Otherwise how could he have exclaimed, "Thou art my King, O God." And how could he have said, "In God do we boast all the day long"?

Yet, *he* did not derive the comfort from this suffering that *Paul* derived from his painful experiences. Otherwise he would not have said, "Awake, O Lord! Why sleepest thou? Rouse thyself! Do not reject us forever."

The apostle, on the other hand, understood that suffering for the sake of Christ meant entering into closer communion with him. Such suffering was gain, not loss.

Where did Paul learn this lesson? Is it possible that he had learned it not only from experience and by direct inspiration but also from tradition, early believers having transmitted to him the words of Jesus? It was Jesus who had said:

"Blessed those persecuted for righteousness sake, for theirs is the kingdom of heaven. Blessed are y o u whenever people heap insults upon y o u and persecute y o u, and, while telling falsehoods, say all kinds of evil against y o u for my sake. Rejoice, yes, be filled with unrestrained gladness, for y o u r reward is great in heaven, for in the same way did they persecute the prophets who lived before y o u r time" (Matt. 5:10–12).

37–39. No, in all these things we are more than conquerors through him who loved us. For I am convinced that neither death nor life nor angels nor principalities nor things present nor things to come nor pow-

ers nor height nor depth nor any other created thing will be able to separate us from the love of God which is in Christ Jesus our Lord.

Paul has been speaking about affliction, distress, persecution, famine, nakedness, peril, and sword. For the moment it almost seemed as if he was unable to think of anything but suffering and hardship. Nevertheless, his real intention was the very opposite: he wanted to emphasize that in the midst of all these unpleasant experiences, in fact even by means of them and with their help, we are more than conquerors. Not just: we shall conquer in the end; no, even now we *are* super-conquerors. And this *not*—let it be added immediately—by reason of our marvelous character and unflinching courage.

Mrs. Merrill E. Gates, 1886, was surely right when she wrote:

> Thy love to me, O Christ,
>   Thy love to me,
> Not mine to thee, I plead,
>   Not mine to thee.
> This is my comfort strong,
> This is my joyful song,
>   Thy love to me,
>   Thy love to me.

Just what does the apostle mean when he calls believers "super-conquerors"? Did he mean, "We are winning a sweeping, overwhelming victory"? To be sure, that is what he meant. But is that all he wanted to say? Words, after all, should be interpreted in light of their context. The apostle says, "in all these things." The reference is, of course, to the things enumerated in verse 35. Other "things" and "beings" will be added in a moment, those mentioned in verses 38, 39: death, life, angels, etc. The structure of the sentence (note the conjunction *for*) indicates that these too should be added. Finally, note the very close connection between verse 28 and verse 31 f. ("for" verse 29; "what then" verse 31); and also the parallel "all things" (verse 28) and "in all these things" (verse 37).[258]

The similarity will become apparent when the two lines are placed under each other:

Verse 28
"And we know that to *those who love God all things* work together for good."

Verse 37
"No, in *all these things* we are more than conquerors through *him who loved us.*"

Since our love for God results from his love for us, a sequence that never fails, for by nature we do not love God, the two statements resemble each other also in that respect. They are not the same, but they are certainly similar.

---

258. In the original: πάντα. . . . ἐν τούτοις πᾶσιν.

Once this close connection is grasped, we begin to understand that what Paul is saying is that not only do these various hardships and forces which he mentions not hurt us, but they help us: they all work together for *good*. It is for this reason that he states that in connection with them we are *more than conquerors*. A conqueror is a person who defeats the enemy. One who is more than a conqueror causes the enemy to become a helper.

If anyone knew the meaning of "more than conquerors" it must have been Paul. Was it not exactly this apostle who had been "more than conquered" by God? From a bitter persecutor he had been changed into an enthusiastic supporter! No wonder he could say, "I am convinced." *He* would be!

A few words should be added with reference to the "things" and "beings" enumerated in verses 38, 39. There are four pairs of objects plus two separately mentioned ones.

THE PAIRS

1. neither death nor life (can separate us from God's love in Christ Jesus our Lord).

Having just now made mention of *death* (verse 36), it is not surprising that Paul makes this word the first of the series. The questions of psalmists regarding the possibility of fellowship between God and man even after death—see Ps. 6:5; 30:9; 88:10–12—are answered here (Rom. 8:38, 39) with a definite "Yes," a confession already anticipated in the Old Testament (Ps. 49:5; 73:24, 25; Job 19:26, 27). The fact that even death would bring about no separation between God and the believer was firmly entrenched in the heart and mind of Paul (II Cor. 5:8; Phil. 1:21–23). For further confirmation see Luke 23:43; John 14:2; 17:24; Heb. 12:18–24.

As to *life,* in spite of all its distractions, especially for the unbeliever (Luke 8:14), the believer's life is one in communion with God. That is the teaching of both Testaments (Ps. 23:42; 63:1–8; 73:23; 116:1, 2; Rom. 14:8, 9; Col. 3:1–3).

2. nor angels nor principalities.

Angels are mentioned with great frequency in both Testaments (Gen. 24:7, 40; 31:11; Ps. 68:17; Matt. 1:20, 24; 2:13, 19; 28:2, 5; Luke 1:11; Col. 2:18; II Thess. 1:7; etc.) For a Chart summarizing Scriptural doctrine regarding the angels see N.T.C. on Matthew, p. 694.

In Jewish literature *principalities* are angels. In Eph. 3:10 the reference may well be to a category of good angels. See N.T.C. on Ephesians, pp. 158, 159. See also I Cor. 15:24; Eph. 1:21; 6:12; Col. 1:16; 2:10, 15. The Dead Sea Scrolls too contain many references to angels, especially *evil* angels. Other references are found in the pseudepigraphic Book of Enoch. The names of angels, the various categories into which they were to be classified, the worship due to them, were some of the topics on which especially heretics would concentrate their attention.

What Paul is saying in the present context (Rom. 8:38) is simply this, that even angels, whether *good or bad,* real or unreal (the latter referring to classes of supermundane spirits that exist only in people's imagination) can do nothing to separate us from the love of God in Christ.

3. nor things present nor things to come.

This grouping is along a horizontal time line.

Time, whether *present* or *future*—the present with its problems, the future with its forebodings—can do nothing to separate us from the great and deep love with which God in Christ smiles down upon us, and which from moment to moment he bestows on us, forgiving, helping, and encouraging us on our way through life.

4. nor height nor depth.

This classification is along a vertical line.

Does danger coming from above seem to threaten? Does hell seem to open its jaws? God's child is safe. If time cannot separate him from God's love, neither can space: nor *height* nor *depth.*

THE SINGLE ITEMS:

1. nor powers.

In the New Testament *powers* are included in the angel groupings. See Eph. 1:21; 3:10; 6:12; Col. 1:16; 2:15; I Peter 3:22). That is where they belong.[259]

Just why it was that Paul placed "nor powers" between "nor things present nor things to come" and "nor height nor depth" is unknown.

2. nor any other created thing.

The apostle adds this comprehensively inclusive item in order to emphasize that *nothing whatever* will be able to separate believers from "the love of God which is in Christ Jesus our Lord."

And so this lengthy subdivision of Paul's epistle to the Romans, namely chapters 5–8 (see pp. 30, 167) ends as it began: note in both cases (5:1 and 8:39) the reference to "our Lord Jesus Christ" (or "Christ Jesus our Lord"). Everything mentioned must serve to strengthen the saints' experience of the love of God which is in his Son. To God be all the glory!

Romans 8 In Poetry

Verses
1-4   For those who in Jesus their refuge have found
There's no condemnation. Their blessings abound.
For through what Christ Jesus has done within me
The Spirit from sin and from death set me free.

---

259. I can see no merit in the suggestion that δυνάμεις, as used *here* might refer to "mighty works" or "miracles." Tbe context (angels . . . principalities) does not favor this interpretation.

For that which the law, by our nature laid low,
Could never achieve and much less could bestow,
God wrought, when, in order to save us from sin,
He sent his own Son our salvation to win.

God did this in order that Law's just demand
In us might be met, and we righteous might stand,
And show by our conduct from day unto day,
That, shunning the flesh, we his Spirit obey.

5–8   For those who have chosen the flesh as their Guide,
In things of the flesh, not the Spirit, take pride.
But those who have chosen the Spirit as Guide
In things of the Spirit, not flesh, do take pride.

Now those who take pride in the flesh sure should know
That flesh and its fruit, death, together will go.
So, too, those who honor the Spirit will see
That life and deep peace their requital will be.

For fav'ring the flesh will mean hating the Lord,
Since keeping God's statutes it cannot afford.
And it should be obvious to those in the flesh
That pleasing both God and one's sin do not mesh.

9–11   But not in the flesh, my dear brothers, are y o u.
The Spirit who's in y o u proves this to be true.
If one lacks the Spirit, it sure would be wrong
To say that *this* man could to Jesus belong.

But if Christ is in y o u, then though, due to sin,
The body may die, yet the Spirit within
Is life and brings life, so that y o u before God
Stand sinless and pure through the ransom Christ brought.

And if y o u're indwelt by the Spirit of God
Who raised Christ from death, then that Father who brought
To life the dead Jesus will also restore
Y o u r bodies from death. They'll be living once more.

12–16   Therefore, my dear brothers, our duty is clear:
To live by the standard of flesh while y o u're here
Will lead but to death. It's y o u r duty to give
The deathblow to sin's shameful ways. Then y o u'll live.

It is by the strength of the Spirit alone
That this is successful and this can be done.
For all God's true children, with him as their Head,
Are by the blest Spirit of God being led.

Y o u're children indeed, for y o u've not received
The spirit of slavery when y o u believed.
No longer does sickening dread *y o u* oppress,
With joy y o u y o u r God as y o u r *Father* address.

The Spirit bears witness, and not from afar,
But from close within us, that children we are,
Confirming the voice of our own heart and mind,
And leaving uncertainty far, far behind.

17, 18   And if we are children, then, too, we are heirs
Of God and with Christ, for the person who shares
With Christ in his sufferings must certainly know
That on him indeed God will glory bestow.

For this I consider; of this I am sure!
That sufferings and hardships which now we endure
Are nothing compared with the glory which then
Will shine from within us, ne'er leave us again.

19–22   And this is established that Nature entire
For the revelation of saints does aspire,
For not by its own choice did Nature grow dim.
'tWas man who transgressed, and the Lord punished him

By rendering Nature unable to cope
With enemies many; yet not without hope
That Nature itself, though now bound to despair
One day will the freedom of God's children share.

Now *all of creation,* all Nature, 'tis known,
In anguish of childbirth does *suffer and groan.*
23–25   Not only is this true but we must confess:
We also do groan, who the Spirit possess.

Yes, we also groan, even though we are free,
Enriched by the Spirit, as firm guarantee
That also our bodies the Lord will display
As dear to himself on that glorious day.

In hope we were saved, for its object, though near,
Is hidden from view and does not yet appear.
But when we no longer of it are deprived,
It stops to be object of hope; 't has arrived!

But since for the present we hope for still more,
For fulness of bliss which for us is in store,
We long for these blessings, so rich and so great,
And therefore with patient endurance we wait.

26, 27   The Spirit, too, knows that we sinners are weak,
And often unable to find what we seek,
Not knowing at certain times just how to pray:
The words will not come; we don't know what to say.

The Spirit then helps us, for he knows our need.
With unspoken groanings he does intercede.
The Searcher of hearts knows the Spirit's intent;
He'll ever agree, and the Spirit's plea grant.

28–30 Therefore we conclude that to those who love God
All things, in a sense not restricted but broad,
Co-operate fully, in line with God's plan
Established and ordered before time began.

In line with this program or purpose of old
The lovers of God were effectively called.
For whom he foreknew he did also elect
The image of Jesus, his Son, to reflect.

In this way it was that God did foreordain
That Christ should become and forever remain
Close linked to his people, *firstborn* among all,
Yet humble, and willing them *brothers* to call.

Resulting is therefore salvation's firm chain:
Those whom God foreknew he did, too, foreordain,
And those foreordained he did afterward call,
And justify later and glorify all.

31–34 How then shall we answer? How shall we reply?
If he who is for us is God from on high?
Who, now, of all creatures against us can be
When he who is for us is certainly he?

His love is so matchless, so tender his care
That even his own Son he never did spare.
For us, wretched sinners, he gave him to die.
How will he not with him our own needs supply?

Who dares to bring charges against God's elect?
Whom God declares pure, and will ever protect?
Who's really so bold that he dares to condemn
The children of God when he justifies them?

It's Jesus who died, and what's more, who was raised
From death to God's right hand. Let heaven be praised!
Christ Jesus this place of trust occupies thus.
It's he who is now interceding for us.

35, 36 Who then can he be who will tear us apart
From Christ and his love, which was ours from the start?
Distress, persecution, pain due to the Word?
Or famine or nakedness, peril or sword?

It is as the Psalmist declared long ago:
"Each day we face death and are being brought low.
As sheep that are led to the slaughter are we,
For doing thy will and for honoring thee."

37–39 And yet it's a fact that by these very things
Which might seem to harm us God victory brings
To us whom he loves, so that conquerors we,
No, rather far better than this, we should be.

For this I know well, and on this I can count
That nothing at all can forever be found
That causes the Savior his own to forsake,
Twixt him and his dear ones division can make.

Not death and not life and not angels above
Can ever exclude us from God's lasting love.
Nor present nor future can ever avail
To cause that great love for his dear ones to fail.

Not demons or powers, not depth and not height
Can weaken its glow or diminish its might
No creature can part us, whatever the sort,
From God's love that is in Christ Jesus our Lord.

Practical Lessons Derived from Romans 8

A most comforting chapter is Romans 8. It answers some of the most soul-stirring questions often asked by believers and/or by serious enquirers.

1. It is a fact of common knowledge that during the last few decades the science and art of healing has made great progress. Smallpox has been wiped out, if the reports are true. Antibiotics have saved many lives which, humanly speaking, otherwise would have been lost. Cancer research is having many favorable results, and so one could continue. *Is there, however, also a remedy for those who are standing at death's portal; worried, perhaps, about entrance into the halls of glory?* For God's children there is this comforting answer:

Verse 1 "There is therefore now no condemnation for those who are in Christ Jesus." Add also verses 33, 34 and 38, 39.

2. *How can I know whether I am a Christian?* Answer:
Verse 5 "For those who live according to the flesh set their minds on the things of the flesh, but those who live according to the Spirit set their minds on the things of the Spirit." In other words, "What is your—my—*one absorbing interest?* Is it the world or is it God's kingdom?" If the latter, then I am indeed a child of God.

3. *I know that I love God. But how do I know that he loves me?* Answer:
Verse 28 "And we know that to those who love God all things work together for good; that is, to those who are called according to his purpose." Cf. I John 4:19, "We love God because he first loved us."

4. *I know that God loves me, but will he continue to do so?* Answer:
Verses 38, 39 "I am convinced that neither death nor life nor angels nor principalities nor things present nor things to come . . . nor any other created thing will be able to separate us from the love of God which is in Christ Jesus our Lord."

5. *How do we know that prayer is effective?* Answer:
Verses 26, 27 "And in the same way the Spirit too is helping us in our weakness, for we do not know what we ought to pray, but the Spirit himself intercedes for us

with unspoken groanings. And he who searches the hearts knows what is the Spirit's intention, that he is interceding for the saints in harmony with God's will."

6. *How rich are we going to be in the life hereafter?* Answer:
Verses 17, 18 "And if children, then heirs, heirs of God and fellow-heirs with Christ; since the fact that we are now sharing in his sufferings means that (hereafter) we shall share in his glory. For I consider that the sufferings of this present time are not worthy to be compared with the glory that is to be revealed in us."

7. *What, according to Romans 8, etc., is the Christian's chief duty?* Answer:
To conduct oneself according to the Spirit's direction.
Verse 14 "For as many as are being led by the Spirit of God, these are sons of God." They walk (verse 4) "not according to the flesh but according to the Spirit." They exhibit in their lives "the fruits of the Spirit," for which see Gal. 5:22, 23.

8. *Has the Christian the right to be an optimist?* Answer:
The Christian alone, of all people, has that right. See verses 15–18, beginning with, "For y o u have not received a spirit of slavery, to fill y o u once more with dread, but y o u have received the spirit of adoption . . ." Also verses 35–39, beginning with "Who will separate us from the love of Christ?"

Summary of Chapter 8

A. *For God's children all things work together for good* (verses 1–30).

In close connection with the immediately preceding paragraph—note "Thanks be to God through Jesus Christ our Lord" (7:25)—, as well as with the entire preceding contents of this epistle, this chapter opens with the triumphant exclamation, "There is therefore now no condemnation for those who are in Christ Jesus." Christ's substitutionary atonement has removed the guilt of their sins. As to sin's polluting power, the effective operation of the Holy Spirit, who dwells within their hearts and is the controlling influence in their lives, has "set them free from the law of sin and death."

God did for them what the law, operating by itself, could never have accomplished. Because of sin the law was unable to save. But God, by means of his Son's vicarious death, brought about salvation. He did this without in any way sacrificing the demand of divine righteousness according to which sin must not be allowed to go unpunished. Only those people whose aim is to live in accordance with the demands of the Spirit can derive comfort from this great truth. On the other hand, those who are "in the flesh," that is, who allow their lives to be basically governed by their sinful human nature, do not have this comfort. They "cannot please God" (verses 1–8).

Directly addressing his Roman audience, Paul continues, "Y o u, by con-

299

trast, are not basically under the control of sinful human nature; on the contrary, y o u are being governed by the Spirit," implying, "Therefore y o u are, indeed, able to please God, and y o u do, in fact, please him. (Of course, not necessarily every one of y o u: if any individual reveals by his words, actions, and attitudes that he does not wish to be controlled by the Spirit, that person does not belong to Christ)."

It should be our aim, therefore, to live in harmony with the Spirit's direction for our lives. Those who do so will truly live. Those who do not are doomed to die. All those, and only those, whose lives prove that they are being led by the Spirit are truly sons of God.

Those people are not slaves but *children*. The Spirit adds his own testimony to the voice of their regenerated consciousness, thus providing them with a double assurance that they are God's children. And if they are *children*, they are also *heirs*. Their Testator is God. It is he who will bestow on them a glorious inheritance, an inheritance which they will share with Christ, who, being God's Son by nature, is Chief Heir. They are co-heirs, that is, heirs along with him. Those who here and now share Christ's suffering will afterward share his glory (verses 9–18).

To the day of this future glory for God's children the entire sub-human creation is eagerly looking forward. As the groaning of a woman who is in labor indicates both pain and hope, so does also Nature's groaning. The entire sub-human creation is, as it were, craning its neck in order to behold "the revelation of the sons of God," because that event will also mean glory for the entire creation.

But this is not the only groaning that is taking place. "Not only this, but we ourselves, who possess the firstfruits of the Spirit, even we ourselves groan within ourselves, as we eagerly await our adoption, that is, the redemption of our bodies."

Not only does Nature groan and do we groan, but "the Spirit too is helping us in our weakness, for we do not know what we ought to pray, but the Spirit himself intercedes for us with unspoken groanings."

Such groaning is not ineffective. God discerns and grants the ardent desire of the Spirit, so that full salvation for both soul and body will come to us (verses 19–27).

This is true not because of the saints' love for God, but because of his love for them, as is shown by the words, " . . . to those who love God all things work together for good; *that is, to those who are called according to his purpose.*"

Moreover, this cooperation of all things for good is happening not only now but *has always been the case*—"For whom he foreknew, he also foreordained to be conformed to the image of his Son, so that he might be the firstborn among many brothers; and whom he foreordained, these he also called; and whom he called, these he also justified"—*and will continue thus:* "and whom he justified, these he also glorified," that is, "these he will most certainly also glorify." So certain is this fact that the past tense is used, as if it had already happened! (verses 28–30).

B. *Therefore More Than Conquerors Are They* (verses 31–39).

"If God is for us, who is against us?"

It is God who gives. In fact, he did not spare even his own Son, but gave him up for us all. "How will he not also with him graciously give us all things?"

It is God who forgives. He blots out our sins so completely that no sustainable charge can be brought against God's elect. "It is God who justifies. Who is he that condemns?" The assurance that our sins have been blotted out is, however, not based solely on the fact that Christ died for us, but also on the fact that in addition the Father raised him from the dead, thereby proving that this death had been accepted as a fully adequate atonement for our sins. To make assurance even more sure we are comforted by the Savior's session at God's right hand. Here he is interceding for us, without ceasing taking care that the merits of his sacrifice are fully applied to us (verses 31–34).

It is clear therefore that Christ loves us with a love from which no one and nothing can ever separate us. And for this very reason we are "more than conquerors." Not merely conquerors, so that the forces that oppose us are neutralized, rendered ineffective, but *more than* conquerors, so that death, life, angels, principalities, things present, things to come, heights and depths, yes every created thing that has anything to do with us, works in our favor, for in all of them, and in the manner in which they affect us, there is revealed to us the love of God which is in Christ, a love from which no one and nothing will ever be able to separate us (verses 35–39).

Select Bibliography On Romans 1—8

Calvin, J., *Commentaries on The Epistle of Paul The Apostle, To The Romans,* translated and edited by J. Owen, Grand Rapids, 1947.

Cranfield, C. E. B., *A Critical and Exegetical Commentary on The Epistle To The Romans (The International Critical Commentary),* Volume I (on Romans 1–8), Edinburgh, 1975.

Murray, J., *The Epistle To The Romans (The New International Commentary on The New Testament),* Volume I (on Romans 1–8), Grand Rapids, 1959.

A *General Bibliography* is planned for Vol. II; also a *Select Bibliography* for chapters 9–16.